# A PROSPECT

# OF MALDON

## 1500 -1689

### BY W.J. PETCHEY

ESSEX RECORD OFFICE · PUBLICATIONS ·

### 1991

*Pl.1. The outlines of Maldon's market place preserved by late-Georgian reconstruction*

# A PROSPECT OF MALDON

## 1500 – 1689

THE ESSEX RECORD OFFICE
County Hall, Chelmsford, Essex CM1 1LX

© ESSEX COUNTY COUNCIL 1991

ISBN 0 900360 81 X

*A catalogue record for this book is available*
*from the British Library*

Essex Record Office Publication No. 113

*Designed by Keith Mirams MCSD*
*Printed in England for Essex County Council Supplies Department*

# CONTENTS

|                                                          | *Page* |
|----------------------------------------------------------|--------|
| Preface                                                  | ix     |
| Explanatory notes to the reader                          | xiii   |
| 1 A Distant Prospect of Maldon                           | 1      |
| 2 Freemen and Decenners: the Community of Maldon         | 22     |
| 3 The Immigrants                                         | 51     |
| 4 Housing a Transient Population                         | 77     |
| 5 Commerce                                               | 105    |
| 6 The Company: a Treatise on Magistracy                  | 150    |
| 7 Religious Changes and Dissension                       | 187    |
| 8 Maldon in Retrospect                                   | 246    |
| Appendix I    High Officers of the Borough of Maldon     | 256    |
| Appendix II   Burgesses in Parliament for Maldon, 1504-1688 | 263 |
| Appendix III  Sources                                    | 269    |
| Index                                                    | 280    |

# PLATES

Pl.1 The outlines of Maldon's market place preserved
by late-Georgian reconstruction          Frontispiece

Pl.2 Thomas Cammock and all his family          73

Pl.3 Title page of textbook by John Danes for his
pupils in Maldon Grammar School          75

Pl.4 Late 15th-century stairway of Darcy's Tower          91

Pl.5 Crosse's Great Tenement, extended in 1539 as
the Blue Boar          139

Pl.6 Queen Mary I and Philip II of Spain in the
heading to Maldon's 'Magna Carta' of 1555          153

Pl.7 The Bailiffs' seal as Admirals of the Port of
Maldon          160

Pl.8 Muniment chest remaining in the Moot Hall          166

Pl.9 Crown of the Borough's mace made in 1687          182

Pl.10 The accumulation of medieval piety at All Saints
Church          192

Pl.11 Dr John Whitgift, Archbishop of Canterbury,
1583-1604          204

Pl.12 St Mary's Church Tower, rebuilt after 1628
following its collapse in 1596          232

Pl.13 Thomas Plume's Library          239

Pl.14 James II, King of Great Britain 1685-1688          253

# MAPS AND DIAGRAMS

| Fig.1 | Maldon: the town | p.4 |
| Fig.2 | Maldon: the parishes | 8 |
| Fig.3 | Burials at Maldon, 1601-1636 | 17 |
| Fig.4 | Baptisms at Maldon, 1601-1636 | 17 |
| Fig.5 | Twenty Decenners and Freemen: patterns of residence | 29 |
| Fig.6 | Annual totals of Freemen and Decenners, 1569-1582 | 34 |
| Fig.7 | Decenners and Freemen: decrease, 1569-1582 | 37 |
| Fig.8 | Decenners and Freemen: increase, 1569-1582 | 37 |
| Fig.9 | The composition of the male population of Maldon, 1569-1582: units of residence | 38 |
| Fig.10 | Long-distance migration, 1500-1688 | 59 |
| Fig.11 | Short-distance migration: freemen and apprentices 1500-1688 | 65 |
| Fig.12 | Non-resident litigants in the Maldon Court of Record, 1499-1614 | 66 |
| Fig.13 | Non-resident property holders in Maldon, 1530-1688 | 66 |
| Fig.14 | Landcheap − house prices | 79 |
| Fig.15 | Housing and fields | 86 |
| Fig.16 | The Market Place, 1500-1688 | 135 |
| Fig.17 | Water Bailiffs' receipts, 1550-1690 | 147 |

# TABLES

Table 1    Origins of Maldon Freemen, 1515-1641    p.15

Table 2    Freemen's methods of enfranchisement,
           1471-1641                                   15

Table 3    Occupations at Maldon, 1560-83 and
           1601-43                                    108

Table 4    Occupations at Leicester, Northampton
           and Maldon                                 114

Table 5    Essex inns in 1686: capacity for guests
           and horses                                 138

Table 6    Variations in the sources of the Borough
           revenue, 1550-1690                         175

Table 7    Corporation fees                           181

Table 8    Voting measured in years of membership
           of the Corporation, 5 September 1592       227

# PREFACE

When the Hervey Benham Charitable Trust proposed that they might support the publication of a dissertation which (long before) I had written about the Borough of Maldon in the sixteenth and seventeenth centuries, they even more generously acceded to my proposal that a new text should be published which would be substantially derived from that thesis but re-written with a wider readership in mind than the academic audience to which such dissertations for higher degrees are necessarily directed. In fact the book they have thus made possible is the latest stage in some thirty years of occasional exploration of Maldon's archives which commenced in 1952 when I was encouraged to begin an exploration of the borough records so as to enter the prize essay competition for fifth- and sixth-form pupils established by the Essex County Archivist, Dr F. G. Emmison, whilst about the same time a lecture by Miss Grieve to the Essex Branch of the Historical Association about her use of John Walker's Survey of Chelmsford led me to attempt a similar topographical exercise for Maldon. Subsequently the formal undergraduate study of history and, later, a professionally supervised research project made their mark on my continuing concern with the sixteenth and seventeenth century town and its inhabitants, and so has that impressive development of English urban history which has taken place since the 1950s. My original attempt at a topographical reconstruction of late-medieval Maldon has proved to be as yet unattainable and in these latter stages of writing it has been necessary to cut back some topics for which there is not really adequate material (such as the borough's militia, military impressment, bridge construction, details of corporate lawsuits), and to avoid a discussion of how Dissent established itself after 1660 because that will at some time be better considered in a study of the eighteenth and nineteenth century town. Nor do I consider this to be my final statement on Tudor or Stuart Maldon, although I have been and remain quite sure that the interpretation of its history which I reached between 1968 and 1972 is valid and will continue to be so.

Before the 1960s little had been written about any of the smaller market towns of England: Alderman E. A. Fitch's *Maldon and the River Blackwater*, the Reverend Leonard Hughes' historical essay on All Saints' Church — both published between 1895 and 1910 — some articles in the *Essex Review* or the Essex Archaeological Society's *Transactions* (again, mostly written before 1914), Philip Morant's eighteenth century *History of Essex* were my only available 'secondary sources' on the town itself when I was a schoolboy and only occasionally did surveys of social history appear to offer more than very general information about towns of the later Middle Ages or of the seventeenth century. By 1966 that had begun to change, to a great extent through the writing and teaching of Professor W. G. Hoskins and the influence of his Department of English Local History at Leicester University. It was my good fortune to be able to pursue a serious study of Maldon's history under him and his eventual successor, Professor C. V. Phythian-Adams, by which time a number of scholars, some working full-time, others part-time, were active across a wide range of studies in urban history, on which such a spate of books, articles and dissertations began to appear soon after my thesis went before its examiners that it would have been a presumption to leave the text of 1972 unreviewed in the light of the more substantial and richly varied literature that was soon afterwards available. Editorial policy (that there were to be none of the footnotes which are a substantial and integral feature of most theses) has also made necessary the extensive re-writing of the dissertation which the Hervey Benham Charitable Trust's Trustees originally thought might be published.

Every town has its own History, not only from circumstance but also because so much depends on the nature − and the quantity − of available materials. Many of England's smaller market towns have lost the bulk of their earliest manuscripts and so the remarkable quantity which has survived from the late fifteenth to the mid-eighteenth centuries for this Essex borough means that, although the millenary year of the battle of Maldon may seem a strange moment to publish a study of this town as it was no more than three to four hundred years ago, a prudent historian can go little further back in time than 1500 before speculation begins to replace information. And for any town the type and quality of its record material must greatly influence the kind of history which can be written. In Maldon's case it became clear that almost all the subjects adequately represented in its registers and rolls or in the diocesan and county records − religious change, housing, occupational structure, the government of the borough, family histories, for example − were going to be best understood in the light of the evidence I was accumulating about the impressive mobility of the town's population. There has been no reason to modify my original conclusions. Instead I have derived either confirmation or a clearer understanding of Tudor and Stuart Maldon, of its government and commerce, its demographic characteristics and the changing beliefs of its successive inhabitants from those studies of other communities and all those books and articles on particular aspects of English institutional, social and economic history which are listed in this book's bibliography. I hope their inclusion will be taken as an acknowledgement of the stimulus they have provided: frequently I have gone back to my sources, provoked by what I have read, to reconsider an assessment or to see how a topic might perhaps be more substantially treated.

A vigorous discussion has been underway for some twenty years about the extent of a late-medieval urban crisis, throughout which I have continued to maintain that here was one town, at least, which managed prudently to avoid the economic collapse or the irreversible decline in population which certainly affected some others. This is one of the many aspects of the subject where the discussion in general has been invaluable even though I have still considered that my conclusion in the case of this particular town remains the most probable.

There are at least two distinct readerships for essays in local history and I have tried to write for both. Some will be looking principally for information about places or particular families, or be especially concerned with the historical features of the town's topography, scenery and facilities or institutions: these antiquarian, archaeological and genealogical concerns have a long and honourable place in the literature of provincial England but they are now overshadowed by developments in social and economic history which would make a simple up-date of Alderman Fitch's *Maldon and the River Blackwater* inadequate, a classic of its kind though it is. The far greater availability of records has ensured that there is now a wide interest in the organisation of communities, family structures and demography, religious change, economic history, and I hope that I have gone some way towards showing that the requirements of both readerships are but two sides of the same coin.

The invaluable assistance for which I gave thanks in the 1972 dissertation must again be gratefully acknowledged. Since then Mr John R. Smith of the County Record Office has kept me in close touch with his own reasearch on eighteenth and early nineteenth century Maldon. I have also been able to discuss many aspects of Maldon's history with groups of adults from many walks of life at talks to the Maldon Society and to members of the Oakwood Arts Centre in Maldon and also during lectures at, and field excursions from, the Essex Education Committee's Wansfell College, whilst the Maldon Archaeological Group has involved me in discussion of its activities since its formation in 1979. These occasions have made me many friends who will not, I hope, be offended by my acknowledgement of their incidental help in envisaging the interests of the potential readers of this study. Several whose opinion I would have valued are, sadly, no longer in this life to read the book about whose progress they sometimes enquired. There are others who will, I hope, find it of some interest, especially my oldest friend − and mentor for hundreds of Essex people interested in history over many years − Mr A. C. Edwards, and, of course, my mother who has for so many years provided a base camp for my work and been wonderfully patient of her son's preoccupation with the past.

I must also record my thanks to the Trustees and Friends of Thomas Plume's Library, to Mrs G. Shacklock (Thomas Plume's Librarian at Maldon) and to Canon Arthur Dunlop for much local help; to Dr Alfred Knightbridge for his advice on the materials available in the Public Record Office; to Dr Emlyn Thomas who originally set me to work on the chamberlains' accounts; and to Dr David Jackson and Mr Michael Wallace who shepherded me into the basics of Information

Technology with much more success than they can have imagined to be possible. But for the past fifty years every student of the county's history has had cause especially to record vast indebtedness to the successive Essex County Archivists, as I do; to Dr F. G. Emmison and his successor the late Mr K. C. Newton, and to Mr Victor Gray, the present County Archivist, for the personal interest taken in my research; and to the ever-helpful staff of the Essex Record Office. My debt to Mr Victor Gray, is great, for he has somehow borne with my Fabian strategy during the final composition of this book and, as Editor he has organised its publication. The illustrations have been his responsibility, except for the diagrams which, of course, had to be drafted by myself. Several years ago I was gently warned that the chances of getting a book such as this published were going to get ever more slim; how fortunate I have been then, in this enterprise, to have received the support of the Hervey Benham Charity Trust. To its Trustees I offer hearty and grateful thanks and in particular to Maura Benham, without whose interest in and enthusiasm for the history of the area this work would not have appeared.

W.  J.  PETCHEY

# *Explanatory notes to the reader*

## NAMES AND STYLES OF ADDRESS

For most surnames the form preferred in the Indexes of Essex Wills has been used but in some cases the spelling most frequently adopted in the borough records has been adopted. One family which lasted in Maldon over the period 1550 to 1650, certainly preferred the spelling *Harris* for their surname in their grander days and this has been used throughout, even though the hares depicted on the coat of arms of Vincent *Harrys* in 1577 suggests that originally Essex people pronounced it and spelt it *Herris* or *Herries*.

The abbreviated style *Mr* has been extended to its original form of *Master*. Not all men were thus addressed (nor were all women called *Mistress*) so the use of these styles now may help to indicate the social respect in which contemporaries held their bearers. And 'Master Bailiff' is clearly preferable to 'Mr Bailiff'.

## QUOTATIONS

Almost all quotations from manuscripts and from early printed books have been rendered into modern spelling with any necessary extensions of the original text inserted within square brackets. Where the original spelling of a word or portion of text has been kept it is printed in italics and within quotation marks.

## MONEY AND DECIMAL EQUIVALENTS

Until February 1971 a pound sterling (£1) was composed of twenty shillings (20s); and one shilling (1s) was worth twelve pennies (12d). So . . .

| | | | | |
|---|---|---|---|---|
| 20s = | 100p | | 240d = | 100p |
| 10s = | 50p | | 120d = | 50p |
| 5s = | 25p | | 24d = | 10p |
| 1s = | 5p | | 12d = | 5p |

A Mark was a unit of account representing two thirds of £1, which was 13s 4d (£0.66) and half a mark (£0.33) was 6s 8d. An Angel was a coin worth 10s (£0.50); the Crown was worth half that (5s or £0.25). A Groat was a coin worth one third of a Tudor penny (4d). Halfpennies were occasionally issued and pennies (which were of silver, as was most coinage of the denominations ½d to 1s) could each be split into four farthings.

## MAPS

The maps of the town are derived from comparisons of the plans accompanying the three parishes' Tithe Awards of 1838–1859 and the Ordnance Survey's 1/500 Plans of 1875 (that is, on the scale of 10.56 feet to 1 statute mile). Field and messuage or tenement names have been added, where possible, from information in deeds but, in Maldon's case, there are few opportunities to produce many firm site locations from manuscript information. Those indicated on the maps in this book are ones for which there is sufficiently clear evidence but the result should be considered diagrammatic, not definitive.

## DATES

All dates are in the New Style adopted in 1752.

## SOURCE MATERIALS

In the absence of footnotes, readers who wish to consult any of the documentary evidence on which the text is based can refer to a marked-up and annotated copy of this book in the Essex Record Office, where most of the manuscript material which readers may wish to consult for themselves is to be found, whilst it is intended that the notes on source materials at the end of this book will show which items are to be found in other record repositories.

## CHAPTER 1

# A DISTANT PROSPECT
# OF MALDON

U NTIL THE EARLY twentieth century nearly all the town of Maldon lay along the spine of the whale-backed hill that juts eastward out of moderately high ground into the waterlogged lands of the Essex coast. At some time in the Dark Ages an East Saxon settlement had taken its name from this dry, airy site; it was called Mael-dun, 'the hill marked by a cross'. Below its north-facing slope two rivers, the Chelmer and the Blackwater, converge and flow out to the sea, some fifteen miles to the east, in a broad, shallow estuary flanked by great stretches of saltmarsh. Just to the east of the town this estuary's gleaming surface is broken by two wooded islands created from silt washed down from inland by the rivers, washed back from the sea by the tides.

To the west and to the north, however, ridges of boulder clay, gravel-capped like Maldon's site, rise steadily to about a hundred feet, here and there to as much as 200 - 270 feet above sea level. (Danbury, five miles west of Maldon and one of the highest places in the county, rises to 346 feet.) Some of these ridges of land are still covered by woods and undergrowth, a remainder from the ancient forest that once covered much of Essex. A similar line of low hills closes off the southern horizon; the long edge of a plateau closes off the northern view.

Coastal and inland scenery meet around the slopes of the town hill. Until comparatively recently the town has been very much isolated from the rest of the county; its inhabitants have looked out from their hilltop home across almost a hundred square miles of woodland, water and marsh, which has been one of the more sparsely populated areas of South Eastern England. When John Constable travelled across it in July 1814 he wrote to his sister 'I saw much more of the county of Essex than I ever saw before, and the most beautiful part, as I was at Maldon, Rochford, South End, Hadleigh, Danbury ...' At his visit to Woodham Mortimer Hall, two miles west of the borough, he would have appreciated its panorama of wooded inland hills, broad sloping grassland and eastward the great, shining sweep of the estuary at high tide.

Maldon's eastern landscape is wide, flat, composed of tidal water, mud banks, salt marshes, grassland. Nineteenth century watercolours record blustery, lonely scenes of sky and grassland with occasional, isolated cottages, one or two far distant towers, a landscape which may have been to the East Saxons who colonised this land reminiscent of the bare heaths and gentle fiords of eastern Jutland and Schleswig from which they had come. The Blackwater estuary has been the haunt

1

of myriads of wild fowl of many species, so that, as sportsmen even recently have recalled, the sky was sometimes darkened by vast flocks of wild geese circling above the river channels and over the saltings, and it resounded with their cries. Here human activities were either solitary pursuits such as the herding of cattle and sheep along the verges of the marshland, or they involved only small groups engaged in oyster-dredging, wild-fowling, inshore fishing, coastal shipping, salt evaporation. These are reflected in the place-names with which the map of this area is studded, especially the element 'wick', meaning a dairy farm for the herding of sheep on the 'inned' land and along the edge of the marshes, or the name 'Saltcote' which refers to the ancient technique for the evaporation of salt from tidal water at the Red Hills which lie along the river banks. The lateness of much of the settlement in this area is suggested by the number of place-names which first occur as Middle English words ('la Mayland', 'Goldhanger', 'Newlands') of soon after the thirteenth century.

Westward of the town, and curving round to north and south of this estuarine scene, the heaths and woods which clothed the ridges of higher ground, the swampy valleys of the Chelmer and Blackwater, formed a barrier between Maldon and the central plain of the county. Its place-names ending in *leigh* and the three parishes called *Woodham* record the forested character of this countryside. By the sixteenth century a large part of it had been emparked for hunting. Until the eighteenth century the royal falcon mews were at Woodham Walter Hall whose park lay along the borough's western boundary. Over all this inland area the place-name evidence is of scattered, often late, settlement and the roads out of Maldon all passed through this wooded land, winding their way in the manner of forest tracks, narrow, rutted and with frequent inclines up and down the gravel ridges. The main routes across the county, to and from London and East Anglia, lay beyond the woodland barrier so that until the late eighteenth century Maldon was a place to which travellers had to make a deliberate journey − and with some difficulty.

## A FIRST PROSPECT OF MALDON

Whilst the southern side of the town hill slopes away very gradually, its north side is abrupt, sweeping up from the rivers and marsh at a steep gradient. Among the gentle inclines of the east Essex countryside it comes as a a surprise; the position of Maldon is visually most striking. A traveller coming across the marshland between the two rivers must look up to the roofs and towers which stand against the sky a hundred feet above him. The view appears to be broadly unchanged from the picture drawn for a county history of 1831: unmistakeably ancient houses behind more recent facades lead from the bridge and frame the scene; the steep, tree-lined hillside provides the backdrop, crowned by the tall tower of St Peter's church, the turretted Moot Hall and the pagoda-like wooden spire of All Saints' church.

Yet on closer inspection the town has little of substance remaining from the sixteenth or seventeenth centuries or earlier. The hill-top tower of St Peter's is largely a rebuilding of 1699, a piece of Queen Anne Gothick (and that now altered by necessary renovations in the 1980s); the medieval nave and chancel behind it were entirely replaced about 1699 with a sash-windowed brick library and school room. A hundred yards along the hilltop is a massive late-fifteenth century tower of brick. It was remodelled in 1576 as the Moot Hall of the free burgesses and corporation of Maldon but its external walling, fenestration and parapets and, especially, its grand Classical porch are an early nineteenth century renovation and re-modelling in late-Georgian style. Internally the renovation of this medieval tower in 1810 made even fewer concessions to the past: a fine court room (indeed, a well preserved example of a 'Dickensian' nineteenth-century court house), a Council Chamber and a ground floor room with a prisoners' exercise yard behind it, the station of the borough's own police constabulary, have retained only the splendid brick spiral staircase of the original tower.

Of earlier buildings there are few visible traces. Nothing survives of Maldon's Carmelite Friary, or the Elizabethan mansion made out of that, which was entirely destroyed about 1810 and replaced with two immense, dignified brick mansions. Very little is left of Beeleigh Abbey in the fields west of the town: so little that it is almost impossible to reconstruct the lay-out of the extensive buildings referred to in the inventory made at its dissolution in 1536. A few shattered walls remain of St Giles, a thirteenth century hospital building. The fabric of the surviving two parish churches have been much altered and restored since 1600. There was a great Anglo-Saxon burgh, created in 916 A.D. on the summit of the town's hill: now, no more than a few eroded traces of the earth ramparts remain. Even the old street names have been replaced: Fullbridge Street and St Peter's Lane are now combined as Market Hill; St Helen's Lane is now Cromwell Hill; Rankstile Lane has become Wantz Road; Sligges Lane and Keton's Lane are respectively changed to Gate Street and Mill Road. Other place-names have been completely lost — Maydenpond, Roebuck Street, The Friars' Gate, St Helen's Cross and Jacob's Cross — and so have most of the houses' names.

An article in the *Encyclopaedia Londiniensis* of 1816 remarked that Maldon 'is greatly improved within these thirty years, as the old houses are beautified, new ones built and a handsome new bath erected which brings much genteel company'. That is, the surviving older parts of the town wear the same late-Georgian face as does the Moot Hall; extensive reconstruction around 1790-1820 has masked earlier structures, so that what remains behind the wood and plaster or painted

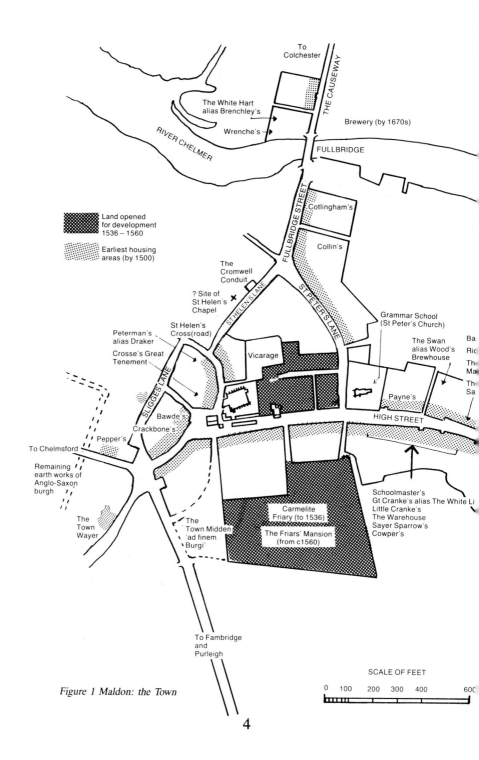

Figure 1 Maldon: the Town

4

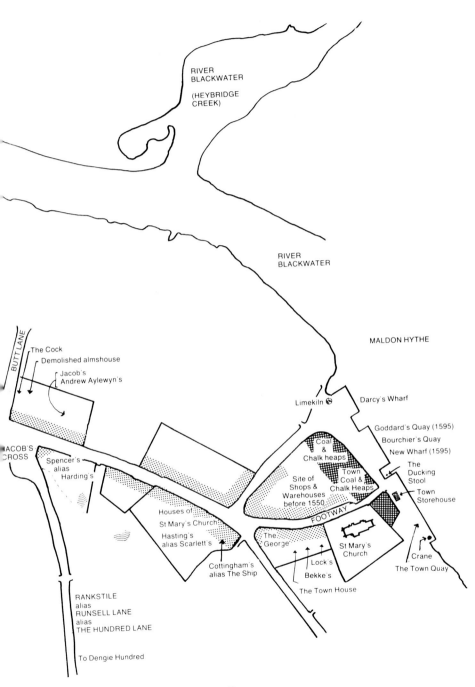

RIVER
BLACKWATER

(HEYBRIDGE
CREEK)

RIVER
BLACKWATER

MALDON HYTHE

BUTT LANE

The Cock
Demolished almshouse
Jacob's
Andrew Aylewyn's

Limekiln ⊗
Darcy's Wharf

Goddard's Quay (1595)
Bourchier's Quay
New Wharf (1595)

JACOB'S
CROSS

Spencer's
alias
Harding's

Coal
&
Chalk heaps

Town
Coal &
Chalk Heaps

The
Ducking
Stool

Town
Storehouse

Site of
Shops &
Warehouses
before 1550

Houses of
St Mary's Church

FOOTWAY

Hasting's
alias Scarlett's

The
George

St Mary's
Church

Crane
The Town Quay

Cottingham's
alias The Ship

Lock's

Bekke's

The Town House

RANKSTILE
alias
RUNSELL LANE
alias
THE HUNDRED LANE

To Dengie Hundred

5

brick frontages are fragments of earlier buildings which are further masked by many internal additions or alterations. From the mid-nineteenth century many of the domestic buildings of the High Street began to be replaced, beginning with a Corn Exchange of 1859, then with a range of High Street buildings replacing ones burned down in a great fire, 1892. The period between the two World Wars saw the replacement of more domestic buildings with shops appropriate to the approach roads of suburban railway stations. After the Second World War building activity (from 1946 to 1957 and even later) was set on the same destructive course and only the advent of an adequately empowered planning authority and the creation of a civic society could successfully attempt to thwart that insensitive, penny-pinching redevelopment which has been so detrimental to so much of England's urban landscape.

Furthermore, the earliest existing plan covering the entire town is a very small-scale representation in Chapman and André's Map of Essex, published in 1777. No surveys of any sections of the borough are known earlier than 1721 and 1759, except a copy made in 1818, for a lawyer's brief, of a vanished sketch map of Maldon Hythe made c1598. A plan and prospect 'very curiously finished' for the map publisher John Ogilby, which had been compiled in 1672 or 1673 by Gregory King and an Essex surveyor called Felgate, appears to have reached the stage of production where it was sent out 'on approval' but no copies are known to survive. Apart from the evidence to be gained from the descriptions and abuttals of buildings or land in title deeds, there are no contemporary descriptions of the sixteenth or seventeenth century topography of Maldon.

## THE TOPOGRAPHY OF MALDON

Almost everything in Maldon has been re-used, adapted, moved around. Yet the old town's bones remain, fossilised in the outlines of the modern street plan, only a little eroded by subsequent encroachments or improvements. They can be traced in the shape of the housing area and by the course of the parish boundaries. Fragments (or sometimes the greater part) of early timber framing, brickwork or masonry are embedded amongst the later deposits of building materials all along this skeletal matrix of the medieval and early modern town and to those material remnants there must be applied the documentary evidence which has survived. Fortunately a great quantity of the borough's archives have been preserved which, with public and probate records and private collections of manuscripts, can be used to reconstruct the features of this lost town.

This study of the borough of Maldon and its inhabitants has thus involved a reconstruction of the topography which has this advantage, that those who know the place well and those who have never set foot in it are equally strangers to what was there in the sixteenth and seventeenth centuries. For the town is a palimpsest, where the traces of its past are visible only in its re-used materials. So, as much for the sake of those who are familiar with the place as for the complete stranger, it is essential to begin with an outline prospect of the town — but still a distant and faint prospect — as it stood by 1500.

This was never a compact or a walled town. Its buildings were strung along the hillside, grouped in four distinct areas : one group had the market place as its centre; the other three may originally have looked like separate hamlets. This appears to have been the result of the town's origin as a single Anglo-Saxon estate in which a town had been planted, perhaps at or soon after the establishment at *Mael-dun* of a burgh in 916 by King Edward the Elder. The origins of towns (and Maldon certainly was a town before the Norman Conquest) are controversial matters in most cases and it is not intended here to consider any possible relationship between the words 'burgh' and 'borough'. However, the proposition that an urban settlement was planted here matches well with an explanation of the evolution of the medieval town's plan.

At some time around 1060 part of the original estate was granted to the London church of St Martin (later, St Martin-le-Grand), whose clergy subsequently became the corporate Rector of St Mary's Church beside Maldon's Hythe or quayside. The Domesday Survey of 1089 describes the existence of burgages, burgesses and a mint. So by the Conquest the original estate at *Maeldun* had been divided into at least three portions, of which one was the township beside or within the ramparts of the burgh, another was the land and church granted as an endowment to St Martin's clergy at London, the rest was the manor later known as Little Maldon.

This situation is still reflected in the shape retained by the parishes, as may be seen in Figure 2: the original estate is the total area of them all (which amounts to almost 3,000 acres); St Mary's parish is the estate granted to St Martin-le-Grand (and it is still in the patronage of the Dean and Chapter of Westminster Abbey who are direct inheritors of the college of St Martin's endowments); St Peter's parish, originally some 1,667 acres, represents the remaining territory from the original estate; whilst the parish of All Saints' Church is an 'island' of 57 acres within -and plainly carved out from — St Peter's parish.

The boundaries of All Saints' parish follow closely the line of the burgh ramparts, except on the eastern side where the housing area and the market were located, and so this parish would be the best candidate for consideration as the site of a 'planted' town. It was one of the four distinct areas of settlement which had emerged by the middle of the twelfth century. Here, just below the summit of the hill, was the market place. Coins were minted for distribution in it between 958 and 1100

7

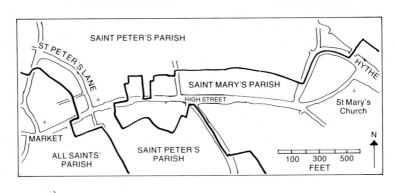

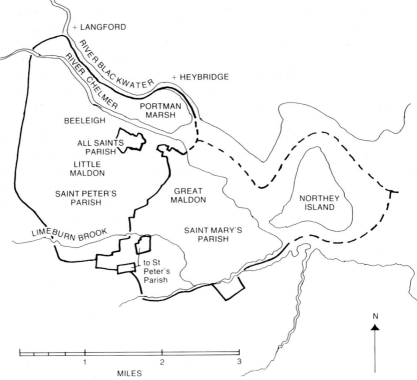

*Figure 2 Maldon: the Parishes*

and although it had probably belonged to St Peter's parish at first, this distinctly urban area had acquired its own church before 1189. This, the church of All Saints, is clearly one of those which were founded beside many market places, its walls on one side abutting the street, having only a constricted churchyard and superseding the two more ancient parish churches of Maldon to become the largest and most lavishly appointed of the town's places of worship by the mid-fourteenth century.

The second settlement was a straggle of dwellings along the street that ran down the spine of the hill from the market to the waterside. The course taken by the boundary between St Peter's and St Mary's parishes is the most revealing feature, for it crosses and re-crosses the street (as may be seen in Figure 2) in such a way as to enclose small groups of house plots alternately in either parish. At one point St Mary's parish boundary comes to within a stone's throw of the other parish's church. Since this boundary marks the disposition of titheable property to the Rectors of the parishes (the Canons of St Martin-le-Grand and the Canons of Beeleigh Abbey) and since the area forming St Peter's parish was established by 1244, this boundary indicates that these blocks of housing existed by at least that date. Excavations (1971-1972) have shown that in the late ninth century there was at least one very substantial house in this area and facing it on the other side of the street was St Peter's Church, which seems to have been even older.

At the Hythe the same boundary reflects the original division of the single estate of *Maeldun*, for most of this area lies in St Peter's parish, including the street right down to the waterside. St Mary's Church overlooks the Hythe from its perch on the final steep bluff in which the long ridge of the town hill ends; it is placed in a corner of the long urban edge of its parish, so that the shadow of its tower could touch St Peter's parish boundary, it was reached only by a footway and most of the houses belonging to its parish were a third to half a mile away. Purchasers of the estate called Maldon Hall in 1691 found themselves possessed of a rent payable from one of the quays at the Hythe because the Hall was once the demesne land of the manor of Little Maldon, the surviving portion of the original single estate. So the settlement at the Hythe, with its attachment to the distant church of St Peter, had perhaps developed from specialised maritime activity by tenants of the pre-Conquest estate.

Like the Hythe, the fourth housing area was quite separate from the market place. It had grown up on the lower slope of the steep northern side of the hill, beside the River Chelmer, whose channel there flows directly alongside the hill. Trackways leading from the market place and from St Peter's Church crossed the river by a great wooden bridge called the Fullbridge or 'muddy bridge' and house plots were there by 1185, when there was a man named Stephen of Fullbridge. A colony from this settlement was created on the further side of the bridge after some of the marshland between the Chelmer and the Blackwater had been embanked. This was the Portman or Townsman's Marsh (later called Potman Marsh), across which a causeway was built carrying the roadway from the Fullbridge over the Chelmer River to the High Bridge over the channel of the Blackwater. (It was this second bridge which caused the replacement of the Old English village name *Tidwalditun* with the Middle English *Heybridge* in the twelfth or thirteenth century.)

## CHANGE AND DECAY IN ALL AROUND . . .

About 1500 Maldon would seem to have been a place of some consequence and esteem. Along with Colchester it returned members to parliaments; no other towns in Essex did so then. There were indeed only three towns in the whole of the county which ranked as boroughs: Colchester, Thaxted and Maldon. Of all the places which were referred to as towns in Essex, Maldon ranked third for purposes of taxation, as is evident in the first payment of the lay subsidy, levied and collected in the period Martinmas 1523 to February 1524.

Esteem was not necessarily merited, for when sheriffs sent out the writs ordering the election of burgesses for a new parliament they used long-standing and usually un-revised lists. The term 'borough' did not necessarily refer to the urban features of a community but to its long-standing local organisation, sealed against replacement by charters: Witham was a town but not a borough; Chelmsford was certainly a town of as much, if not more consequence and social esteem as Maldon, but it was not a borough. So the levy of the tax known as a lay subsidy is of great value as a present-day guide to English society and its economy in the early sixteenth century (despite the limitations inherent in the use of such records, outside the study of taxation). It recommends itself as a reliable source because the Act granting the Crown this subsidy in 1523 reorganised the assessment and collection on new principles, so that each layman would be personally assessed and personally rated on whichever of the categories Land, Goods, Wages provided the highest valuation. The subsidy was so novel a system that evasion may have been very limited for at least the first year or two and now it recommends itself for comparing communities by numbers of taxpayers and by the valuations of their taxable inhabitants. It is likely to be a fair reflection of the standing of towns in the 1520s and, using the tax returns for the first payment, 1523-24, to provide a league table of the county's towns.

Colchester and Saffron Walden certainly each had more taxpayers and higher aggregate valuations than any others; their incomplete tax lists are still far larger than any others in Essex in numbers of payers and in aggregate valuations. Maldon appears to have ranked third, with 194 taxpayers and an aggregate valuation of £1,791. For Thaxted equal third place might be claimed: it had the same number

10

of taxpayers but its aggregate valuation (£1,097) was only 60 per cent of Maldon's total. After Thaxted came Bocking, Great Goggeshall, Braintree and, in eighth place, Chelmsford with Moulsham. As Braintree and Bocking were contiguous, joined by Bradford Street, they could be regarded as a unit and if so they might contest Maldon's third place in this league table of the 1520s, with 239 taxpayers but a gross valuation of £1,130. They were, however, separate communities. Only the record of their inhabitants' second payment of the subsidy has survived (of January 1525) and Maldon's tax return at that time had 157 taxpayers against Braintree's 100, Bocking's 139, whilst its aggregate valuation of £1,199 in this payment must be set against theirs' of £546 and £583 respectively.

Going beyond the confines of Essex, Maldon can be compared with Sudbury, which paid a little less in tax (£60 - 14s - 4d to Maldon's £71 - 9s - 4d) but had slightly more taxpayers (219). If the lay subsidy is indeed a guide to the relative size and wealth of towns in the 1520s, then Maldon may also have held a rank comparable with Aylesbury, High Wycombe or, perhaps, Nottingham and appears to have been among those towns which formed a third layer in the hierarchy of English urban communities. Above it came, first, London and the great cities of the realm; then, in second place, the large provincial centres, of which Colchester, Ipswich and Cambridge were geographically the nearest to Maldon, with populations generally running to three or four thousand inhabitants. The third grade was composed of market towns whose populations have been estimated to have ranged between one and two thousand people, not large enough to be confused with the provincial centres but often much greater than the mass of country towns whose size was often far below a thousand inhabitants.

Lavenham, Stamford, Abingdon, Bideford, Faversham, Stafford, would appear to have been in this third level, the urban peers of Maldon and Sudbury, Nottingham, Aylesbury and High Wycombe. That assembly of names introduces the snags in attempting to position this (or any other) late-medieval community in a hierarchy. Gross size is not a sufficient measure, for some of Maldon's peers by numbers of inhabitants were county towns, or were formerly far greater towns which were in economic decline (like Stamford, which it seems absurd to rank with Maldon).

Graded on calculations of per capita wealth − or rather by an average sum − Maldon was decidedly prosperous: its average in 1524 was £9.2 as against Chelmsford's £8.3, Aylesbury's £5, Coggeshall's £5.9 but the gross valuation of a community was sometimes vastly increased by the great wealth of one or two of its inhabitants. One may be grading these towns by their reliance on the wealth of these men, of Coggeshall on the Paycockes, Lavenham on the Spring family. At Maldon almost one third of the total valuation in January 1524 was provided

11

by the assessments on goods of three taxpayers: Thomas Wyborough, a lawyer, John Dawes, a merchant, and Joan Wersoppe, widow. Comparisons of towns on this basis are thus not very convincing.

The most important caveat which has to accompany this league table of towns is that great change appears to have been occurring in English urban life, so that one cannot be certain that like is being compared with like. It is certain that from the late fourteenth century towns had tended to suffer from poor economic conditions. Those who have argued the case of a crisis in English urban communities have suggested that it was the mid- to late-sixteenth century before recovery and new development began, and 1500-1525 lies roughly at mid-point in the period of urban decay, decline or, for some communities, collapse. In surveying the Maldon of 1500 or 1525, one might perhaps be seeing nothing more than the shell of a once-prosperous but now decaying town. And perhaps there was no real recovery to come. A comparison of the rank of Maldon c1524 with its position according to the Hearth Tax returns of the early 1670s, in which the tax was levied at a standard rate per hearth, suggests a distinct decline over the intervening hundred and fifty years. Third (or third equal) among Essex towns c1524 it was down to the fourteenth place, measured by the number of occupied households listed in 1671.

Colchester still came a clear first with 2,096 households, then Coggeshall (455) shooting forward to overtake Saffron Walden (435), followed by Chelmsford, West Ham, Great Dunmow, Bocking, Thaxted, Braintree, Witham, Halstead, Dedham, and Harwich.

There seems to be no reason to discount this order. The returns of 1671 are among the fullest of the Hearth Tax assessments. They list both occupied and unoccupied households; they also list all those which were exempted from payment. The positions of Colchester, Saffron Walden and Chelmsford (1, 3 and 4) cannot be doubted. All the places which had overtaken Maldon (except West Ham) were in that northern half of the county which was the location of its clothing trades and this suggests that the rank order is a correct reflection on economic trends from the early sixteenth century. 'A brief declaration concerning the state of the manufacture of wools in the County of Essex' compiled in 1629 reported that

> 'there are within this county about 12 or 14 towns wherein is exercised the manufactures upon wools ... the principal of the clothing is Colchester, Coggeshall, Witham, Bocking, Braintree, Dedham ...'

all of which had overtaken Maldon by 1671. There had been -and there was- textile manufacture in Maldon, of course, but its operators never formed a prominent

12

occupational group and of all the freemen whose occupations are known between 1561 and 1670 (597 persons), those engaged in textile production formed only 7 per cent. Numerically the associated crafts of this occupation were insignificant by comparison with the northern Essex townships. Witham in 1629 was said to have 2,000 persons who were 'maintained and have dependence by the manufacture of wools into bays and says'. At that time only four baymakers are known to have lived at Maldon and it would have required ten times that number, each with five dependent operatives or working wives and children to match Witham's total in the early seventeenth century. If the inhabitants of Maldon were concerned about these changes in fortune, they might have enjoyed the little rhyme about these growing, populous clothing towns of humbler origin, included by John Ray in his book of proverbial sayings:

> Bocking for the poor and Braintree for the pure,
> Coggeshall the jeering town, Kelvedon for the whore.

How Harwich came to overtake Maldon must also be noted. Its great and enduring fillip from the passenger trade to Holland and North Germany came a little later, with England's Dutch and Hanoverian connections after 1688. Throughout the seventeenth century it had benefitted from its deep water anchorage as the draught of ships increased. By 1700 Maldon had no foreign-going ships at all but only coasters which mostly plied between the Thames and London and these were small vessels which Dr Burley, in his study of the economic development of Essex, estimated would require only half the crews needed for the ships of Colchester and Harwich. As with textile workers, the mariners formed only a tiny fraction of the freeman body in Maldon and the number of known mariners (excluding as far as possible wage-earning crew) remained steady for over 150 years at approximately 34 in the 1570s, at least 20 in 1664 and 31 in 1702. Harwich had 78 seamen in 1702, Colchester had 344.

It begins to look as if the inhabitants of this little town were refusing to compete. To the absence of any occupational innovations, the failure to share in the textile manufacturing developments just to its north, there must be added the misfortunes which came its way from the 1590s when there was serious dissension between the Corporation and the townsmen. That was succeeded by schism within the Corporation and meanwhile the tower of St Mary's Church collapsed (1596) and it was only rebuilt some thirty two years later with the aid of a charitable collection throughout the Eastern Counties. In 1603 and 1604 the plague struck, followed by two more outbreaks of the sickness in 1625-26 and 1638-39. The Bailiffs of Maldon excused defects in their militia armaments as being 'occasioned and grown by the great decay of the wealth and former estate of the Town within few years past, and much impaired'. When ordered by the Privy Council to increase the town's

13

militia from fifty to sixty trained men in 1636 the Bailiffs pleaded poverty and decay in that, first, they had been promised a respite in the Council's demands after it had billeted a company of Irish soldiers on the town; that secondly, on top of paying twelve separate subsidies to the Crown they were being charged Ship Money for two warships; and thirdly, that

> 'the state of our township being much decayed, some of our principal houses inhabited by men of mean estates (in comparison of former times) and some houses standing empty, void of dwellers, and the townsmen for the general decayed in their estates' forced them 'to be suitors to your Lordships that the township may stand charged with fifty arms ... (which in regard of the present abilities of the township we do assure your Lordships it is a great charge by much than threescore in former times were)'.

Struck down by successive epidemics, suffering a declining trade, crippled by social divisions and broken corporate authority, there was also the spectre of 'the decay of the haven' to haunt the town. That phrase first occurs in a petition organised by a group of shoemakers in 1585 who attempted to persuade the Corporation to exclude others of their trade from selling in the town market: otherwise, they suggested, they would be 'less able to contribute unto the charges of the decayed haven and bridges in the time of scot and lot'. £120 was bequeathed by Alderman Breeder in 1609 'towards the repairing, making and amending of the haven and Channel and the Bridges called Fullbridge and Heybridge', which suggests that there must have been some real problem by then and the brief for the rebuilding of St Mary's tower issued in 1628 also referred potential contributors to the decayed state of the harbour as a reason for the townspeople's inability to meet the rebuilding costs themselves. There had been a beacon for the harbour on that tower, so the collapse of the building may have seemed symptomatic of a decline in Maldon's maritime trade. The collapse of another tower about 1665, and it was the tower of a church in the middle of the town (St Peter's) which had been redundant and closed for worship since at least 1577, added a final touch of physical decay and the imposition − four times − of new charters by James II in 1687-88 a final humiliation.

## STABILITY AND CONTINUITY

More detail could be added to this tale of urban woe but it is possible to present a more optimistic picture of Maldon's fortunes between 1500 and 1700, beginning with the recorded admissions of new freemen to its liberties which stretch right across the period. There are some years for which the memoranda of these enfranchisements are now missing, and the earliest series (of the fifteenth century and up to 1515) do not provide as much information on each new freeman as do the later ones but the entire sequence from 1471 to the 1640s provides a profile

14

of the size and the composition of the most significant sector of the community in this town in those times. It is not a profile of decline and decay.

Table 1 sets out the enfranchisements in four periods of continuous records, stopping at 1641 because thereafter political considerations began to influence the reasons for men wishing to become freemen: many were thereafter non-residents who obtained a vote in the parliamentary elections at Maldon by being freemen. Before the Civil Wars, however, the majority were resident at, or soon after, their enfranchisement and the totals indicate a continuous and slightly increasing flow of applicants.

| Birth Places | (1)<br>1515-51 | (2)<br>1556-81 | (3)<br>1606-23 | (4)<br>1624-41 |
|---|---|---|---|---|
| Maldon | 58 | 38 | 43 | 52 |
| Essex | 88 | 80 | 48 | 68 |
| Beyond Essex | 34 | 46 | 18 | 19 |
| All | 180 | 164 | 109 | 139 |

Table 1. Origins of Maldon Freemen, 1515-1641

Table 2, which covers a longer period by using only the information common to all the memoranda, shows that the average number of freemen admitted per year doubled, with the most noticeable increase occurring towards the end of the fifteenth century, when one would have expected to find a decrease reflecting a late-medieval urban decline. The years when Acts of Parliament declared Maldon to be a greatly decayed borough, 1515-1556, were when the largest number of freemen were seeking enfranchisement. Three quarters of them paid fees (20 shillings was the standard amount) and were therefore in-comers having no previous family connection with Maldon. Whilst they may well have been replacing emigrants and taking up vacancies created by a high mortality rate in the town, they did more than replace the older body of freemen.

| Method | 1471-1514 | 1515-51 | 1556-81 | 1606-23 | 1624-41 |
|---|---|---|---|---|---|
| Purchase | 86 | 136 | 116 | 40 | 49 |
| Inheritance | 24 | 29 | 25 | 38 | 53 |
| Marriage | 16 | 15 | 11 | 10 | 22 |
| Apprenticeship | - | - | 12 | 21 | 15 |
| All (718) | 126 | 180 | 164 | 109 | 139 |
| Number of years: | 37 | 36 | 26 | 17 | 17 |
| Average number<br>per annum: | 3 | 5 | 6 | 6 | 8 |

Table 2. Freemen's Methods of Enfranchisement, 1471-1641

15

Townsmen at the time may have been more impressed by the numbers leaving Maldon, which would be obvious to them, and have sensed some kind of decay, whereas the change which is apparent now in these two sets of figures is seen to be accompanied by Stability. Both Tables show that there was a gradual settling down of the population, at least among its freemen families. More and more young men began to claim their freedom by right of inheritance (without payment of any fee) and by marriage to freemen's daughters. The proportion of fee-payers and of men born outside the borough decreased from the latter years of the sixteenth century, although it must be noted that the years 1618 to 1629 were the only time when sons of Maldon freemen formed the majority of new admissions: 44 of them, excluding others who had become clergy in the locality. By replenishment from without and by replacement from within, the community at this level in its society maintained its stability in its numerical size.

What mattered most was immigration. That is demonstrated for the whole population by the parish registers from 1601 to 1640, at the time when these 'natives' appear to have become almost the majority in the freeman body. (The earlier register entries for all three parishes are transcripts with many deficiencies. From about 1641 until the 1680s they are again incomplete.) There were more burials than baptisms in most years: against the total of 1,861 baptisms for these forty years there are to be set the 2,197 burials, with an average annual excess of 8.4 burials. If these had been the records of a closed community, reliant on a sufficient number of live births to replace itself and requiring also the survival of a sufficient number of children beyond infancy, then on the evidence of these registers Maldon would have disappeared within the century, just as the freemen as a body would have become extinct in both centuries if there had not been a continuous recruitment of men born outside the borough.

The five-year moving average of baptisms (as in Figure 4), which smooths out the sharp fluctuations of the yearly totals to show up the general trend, shows that the birth rate was fairly steady. That indicates a fairly constant replacement of families whose husbands and wives were in the twenty to thirty-five year age range. Moreover, the mortality among their children was high. At least one fifth of all burials were of children aged between less than one month and just under five years; when any family is reconstituted from these registrations, one frequently finds a string of children baptised with one especially favourite name, each time replacing an infant who had died soon after being baptised. And the continuing steadiness of the birth rate suggests a population of young immigrant parents. If so the excess of burials also needs explanation and that is to be found in the three peaks of burials shown in Figure 3. Each peak marks a time when plague struck the town: 1603-04, 1625-26 and 1638-39. Each was part of a wide-spread epidemic and, compared to the experience of many other towns, Maldon's inhabitants were

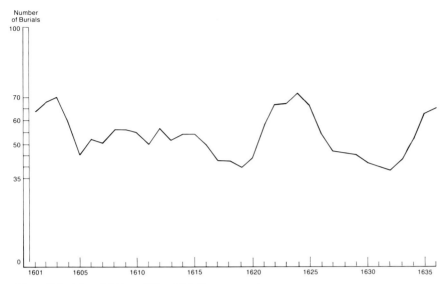

*Figure 3 Burials at Maldon, 1601 – 1636: five-year moving averages*

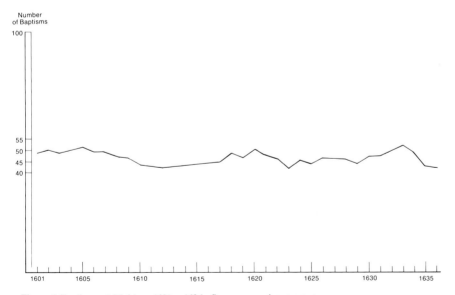

*Figure 4 Baptisms at Maldon, 1601 – 1636: five-year moving averages*

not very badly affected. None of the three outbreaks was so severe that the population was decimated and the Corporation learned enough from the first about the preventive measures that could be taken to be able to contain the next ones quite successfully. Even so, three comparatively mild epidemics were enough to create a mortality rate which was not compensated with a sufficiency of live births in healthier years. Thus the governing factors in the formation and maintenance of the population of this town must have been social and economic, not biological; immigration rather than natural increase, emigration as much as mortality formed and supplied the community.

The calculations made from the 1523-24 lay subsidy contained both the concept of urban size — ranking towns by their taxable population — and the concept of wealth. In purely numerical terms, and looking on to the 1670s, what can be seen is a town whose size neither grew nor declined significantly over two centuries: it held steady at between about 900 and just over 1,000 inhabitants. Nor was it alone in this respect. Although there were some towns which increased in size over these two centuries, and new ones which established themselves, and although the population of the country as a whole was growing fast, in many of England's smaller towns, those of the 'third level' in the hierarchy of urban communities, population growth was barely noticeable until the last third of the seventeenth century. Since migration from rural to urban areas was also a distinctive demographic feature, either some controls were exercised by towns such as Maldon, so as to prevent over-population, or the mortality rate must have been as appallingly high as it was in the larger towns and cities.

And on looking at the assessments made for the first payment of the lay subsidy one is struck by the number of fairly well-off people in each parish. What the lay subsidy returns and the hearth tax lists provide most clearly are statements about relative wealth: either in terms of household size (measured by the number of hearths) in 1671; or in terms of poor relief as shown by the exemptions in 1671 from taxation; or as an expression of *per capita* valuation in the lay subsidies. In 1523-24 Maldon was outstanding among its peers as having very few of its inhabitants taxed at less than £3 — but not so exceptional as to be incredible, for Chelmsford offers a similar case. Towns with larger populations had a higher proportion of poor inhabitants, so that where 25 per cent at Maldon were assessed at less than £3 in goods or wages, the clothing towns of Coggeshall, Hadleigh and Lavenham had over 50 per cent in that category. (At Chelmsford 32 per cent were assessed on goods or wages less than £3.) Just over half of the Maldon taxpayers were assessed on their goods — only three men had lands estimated to be worth more than their goods — and over a third of the total valuation was on goods worth between £10 and £99. In the second payment (1525) just under half of the valuation came from goods assessed between £10 and £99. And in another

18

lay subsidy levied in 1543-44, the valuation of this category amounted to 69 per cent of the aggregate. So not only was Maldon the third wealthiest town in Essex in the 1520s, it was substantially well-off, its £9.2 per capita valuation was based on higher-than-usual assessments made on the goods of a substantial proportion of its inhabitants, not merely on the great fortunes of a very few.

Wealth is reflected in the Hearth Tax returns of 1671 by the number of hearths per household. The assumption is that the greater the number of hearths, the larger a house was and that this is more likely than not to indicate the wealth of the householder, and although one must allow for anomalies such as persons who preferred to live in a less well-heated home so as to save money, or whose standard of living was falling, it can give a broadly truthful indication of the inhabitants' wealth. Over much of England the majority of people lived in houses equipped with less than four hearths (over half the housing in the three vast Ridings of Yorkshire had only one hearth or 'fire-house'). At Maldon, the average number was 3.2 per household (which, quite incidentally was the case at York), whereas Colchester averaged 2.33 hearths per household. And as in 1523-24, the borough comes third among Essex towns when they are ranked according to the percentage of all occupied domestic dwellings having six or more hearths. West Ham comes first and far ahead of all others (22 per cent of its dwellings had six or more hearths); Chelmsford, as the county town with houses for the gentry who needed to reside there frequently on public business and with merchants, tradesmen and innkeepers prospering in the consequent services and retail business, comes second (14.8 per cent) but followed closely by Maldon with 14.2 per cent. The fourth and fifth were Dedham and Harwich, with 11 and 10.75 per cent respectively, then Colchester, Saffron Walden, Billericay, Braintree and Bocking.

In considering deprivation instead of wealthiness, Maldon also came third in the county when ranked by the proportion of its householders who were exempted from payment of the Hearth Tax. 32 per cent of its households were exempt (20.6 at Harwich, 25.6 per cent at West Ham). In fourth to sixth place with percentages of 44.7, 46.9 and 49.1 came Dedham, Chelmsford and Saffron Walden. In the earlier returns this group of exempted people were not written into the collectors' lists but in the 1670s they were included at the foot of each parish return as 'discharged by a legal Certificate'. Because those who were exempted were either in receipt of poor relief or eligible for it, this calculation should indicate the position of Maldon over against the larger but more artisan populations of the North Essex townships. Those which had overtaken Maldon in sheer size by 1672 had a larger proportion of their inhabitants in receipt of (or eligible for) charitable relief, with no less than 81.3 per cent exempt at Bocking, 52.5 per cent at Colchester.

As with the lay subsidies, these hearth tax figures indicate that in both 1500 and

19

1700 Maldon did not have a large wage-earning artisan group. It would be among such people that subsidy assessments on wages or goods valued at less than £3 per annum would occur; the hearth tax assessments for them would most probably be on houses with only one or two hearths and − along with the infirm or elderly- it would be out-of-work artisans and labourers who would be represented by the exemptions from taxation in 1671. It may therefore be significant that poor relief does not appear to have been a special feature of communal activity at Maldon during the period under review. There had been almshouses in the fifteenth century, when the borough appointed freemen each year to collect rents secured to their maintenance but by the first of the sixteenth-century chamberlains' accounts the office of Warden and the administration of the rents had been absorbed by the chamberlains and after that there is no reference to almshouses. By 1630 the site of the buildings was a vacant plot of land. Many other towns could show new almshouses in 1630. Nor did Maldon have a House of Correction until 1676.

Since all the parishes' account books and minutes have been lost or destroyed there is no means of knowing how much poor relief they provided, for although the Overseers of the Poor were appointed by the Corporation their funds were always collected and administered by the vestries. However, the churchwardens of All Saints were occasionally asked to make loans to the borough chamberlains and were on each occasion able to provide substantial sums; and money bequeathed for poor relief was also handed over in long-term loans (bearing interest) to the borough. The poor do not seem to have been much of a burden in the late-sixteenth and early seventeenth centuries when these loans were made. This does not necessarily mean that they did not exist − 'the poor are always with you' − and there is a hint in two wills that the Overseers' judgement of individual needs was stingy: ten poor folk of St Mary's parish in 1621 were given 3 shillings which was to be distributed by the curate and a parishioner, at their discretion and with no mention of the Overseers; whilst John Soan in 1636 bequeathed £10 for distribution to the poor of all three parishes at the two incumbent ministers' discretion with an injunction that the money

> 'shall not come to the hands of the Overseers by reason that they use not to distribute the same to the present poor, which my interest is the present poor should have it as their need requireth'.

But Master Soan's bequest implied the distinction his contemporaries often made between the 'honest' and 'undeserving' poor. The two clergymen were requested 'to the more honest poor to be more liberal' and the stipulation 'as their need requireth' suggests that the money was to be disbursed over a period of time to meet special needs, rather than as relief to an existing body of paupers.

20

The bequests made by many Maldon people of money, firewood or funeral doles to the poor of the three parishes were no more than the generalised charitable actions expected of Christian persons in the final disposition of their worldly goods. In some seventeenth century wills there is evidence of houses being maintained to the use of widows who were particular friends of the legatees (such as a house which Ezekiel Finch and Michael Cooper had bought 'for the Widow Pettit's life' before 1688) but not of tenements being bequeathed to the use of the poor generally. Charitable trusts for the permanent relief of the poor are not to be found, except for three legacies whose conditions may be indicative of the kind of poverty to be found at Maldon in the early seventeenth century. One was a charity founded in 1594 by John Hunwicke, a Colchester alderman, not a resident of Maldon, who bequeathed £300 to the poor of Colchester or − in default of that borough's Corporation to employ the fund − to the poor of Ipswich, Sudbury and Maldon. The second and third legacies were specifically for the relief of impoverished Maldon freemen but each provided no more than short-term loans: a gift of £40 by Samuel Bedell in 1651 was to be lent to poor freemen in sums of no more than £10, repayable within one year without interest charges but on security; and similarly a non-resident freeman, Nicholas Catton of Hornchurch,

> 'did many years before his death, and of his pious disposition give twenty pounds in perpetuity to be always lent out by the Bailiffs ... freely, without use or interest for the forbearance thereof, upon sufficient security by them always to be given for the repayment thereof at the end of one year next after every such lending'.

Poverty does not, from the tenor of these bequests, seem to have been pressing or of serious proportions in seventeenth-century Maldon. The special problem to which they addressed themselves was securing the livelihood of temporarily embarrassed tradesmen or craftsmen who were clearly expected quite quickly to achieve self-sufficiency. It will be shown later on that many of the truly poor, the unemployed, the unemployable but able-bodied, and the vagrants who swarmed across England in both centuries, were kept out of Maldon as a matter of policy. Indeed, there was an element of deliberate population control at Maldon which was aimed at preventing any influx of unemployed people from other areas.

Urban societies have always been fragile and apart from the obvious cases of failure or collapse -by 1500 the country was littered with still-born market ventures- much depends on the criteria by which growth or stability or decline is measured now, and also on the criteria contemporaries applied. It is partly to such assessments that the following chapters of this study are addressed and here it must be enough to propose that whilst urban greatness does not seem ever to have come Maldon's way it never plunged into that state of decline which has by some been seen as its sixteenth and seventeenth century fate.

21

## CHAPTER 2

# FREEMEN AND DECENNERS:
# THE COMMUNITY AT MALDON

WHEN POPULATION STUDIES are concerned with the centuries before any kind of Census existed they are, of all topics in urban history, the most apt to encounter almost insuperable difficulties. Even the total number of people in one administrative area at a given time cannot be easily determined, for Tudor and Stuart Englishmen did not usually see any need for statistical information of a personal nature (although their sovereigns' councillors often did try to obtain it) and only tentative steps were taken in the latter part of the seventeenth century to develop the science which they called 'political arithmetic' for the consideration of current social and economic conditions. The immense difficulty in collecting appropriate information, compounded by suspicions that the collectors had ulterior motives and a determination to safeguard individual liberties, ensured that little exists by way of direct demographic information. Yet questions about the size and structure of a Tudor or Stuart community do, now, need to be asked and, if possible, need to be answered with some degree of precision. For Maldon most of the sources which have become the principal guides for the student of population history − the parish registers, the tax returns, the militia muster rolls, ecclesiastical 'censuses' − are no less opaque than they are for so many other places. Yet some knowledge of a town's population − how it was structured, how stable, continuous or mobile it was − is an essential key to understanding the nature of the community.

By good fortune there are, buried within the town clerks' registers of the borough courts, two immensely useful local sources: the Catalogues of the Freemen and the Catalogues of the Decenners. There should be one for each year in the case of the freemen, there ought to be two yearly lists or catalogues of the decenners (and who the 'decenners' were is explained below); but, as is bound to be the case with working lists of almost every institution, such comprehensive documentation has not survived. A great number of freemen's lists exist, especially from 1611; only a few of the Catalogues of the Decenners for the period 1569 to 1583 have survived, bound into one register kept by Master John Barnardiston who was the Town Clerk at that time. Some manuscript parish lists of decenners also survive for 1622 and 1623 but for a study of the population one needs a series like those of 1569-83. which, combined with the Catalogues of Freemen of those years, have proved to be far more illuminating, far more fruitful of interesting answers to the questions that ought to be answered about the population of Maldon, than the standard sources could possibly be. They provide an informative basis for a study of the male sector of the borough's population, despite the brevity of

22

the period which, in combination, they cover. And some features of the population structure of Maldon which these sources describe for the years 1569-1582 can be found to have applied in the preceding and following seventy year periods 1500-1569 and 1583-1650.

One elementary piece of information which can reasonably be demanded at the outset and which cannot be supplied by these registers alone is the estimated total number of inhabitants of Maldon in, say, 1500, 1600 and 1700, and of the changes in the total size of the community over the two centuries. For this two of the standard sources have to be used and they supply an unusual answer for a period in which the English population, especially in the south-east of the country, at least doubled in size. In the mid-1520s, basing the estimate on the Lay Subsidy returns of 1524-5, there may have been about 900 inhabitants of Maldon and apparently this number barely rose during the next 150 years, for an estimate based on the Hearth Tax of 1672 indicates a population of about − and perhaps rather less than − one thousand. At any time between 1500 and 1700 there was some fluctuation in numbers of people, sometimes rising a little above 1,000, then falling back towards 900, 800, then temporarily rising again. Until about 1550 the numbers may have been the last part of a long, steady downward trend that reached back into the late fourteenth century; by the time of the first Census, 1801, there were about 2,150 persons in the town (2,358 including the rural parts of the borough), so that a doubling in size may have occurred during the eighteenth century and the stagnation of Maldon's average population size between 1500 and 1672 can be seen as a period of stabilisation between a decline in the fifteenth century and the rapid increase of the eighteenth century.

Total size is not very helpful except as an initial guide to the study of the population of those times, whereas the size of the adult male working population is significant, for that was the principal productive sector of the urban economy. For most purposes only these inhabitants were expected to hold any responsibilities, despite the influence or the initiative of action which many women, both good and bad, exercised in practice; women and children for the most part accompanied these males, providing supportive activity at both a domestic and an occupational level but without a voice in the community. That is why the registration of freemen and of decenners is of special interest: the most detailed information, accurate and comprehensive, about the population structure of Maldon exists in the form of lists of the freemen and other adult, working males.

## THE REGISTRATION OF FREEMEN

There was an assembly of all freemen at Maldon every year, near the beginning of January, from at least the end of the fourteenth century until the dissolution

23

of the corporation in 1768. It was in effect their Annual General Meeting, when their officials and common councillors were appointed for the ensuing year, and all versions of the borough's Custumal include a regulation making obligatory the attendance of all freeburgesses at this, the Court of Election, as in the version written in 1468:

> '...all the free menne of the towne shall assemble in the commone halle the Fryday next after thapyphanye of oure Lorde for to here there accompte befor the baillies and them alle/ And the xviij wardemenne that day shall chese there newe baillies and other officeres of the most worthy menne of the tounne...'

and the Oath of the Burgesses in a collection made c1530 includes this undertaking by each freeman at his admission to the liberty of the borough:

> "...I shall be here at the court every year on the Friday next after the Epiphany of our Lord God if I be within 7 miles ...'

Although the elections were made by only eighteen councillors (the wardemenne referred to in the 1468 Custumal) all the freeburgesses were expected to attend, give their assent by their presence and − because the elections were to offices in which men were sometimes unwilling to serve − to be witnesses to the validity of the proceedings at the court. Fines or ultimately deprivation of privileges were prescribed for defaulters even if they were living outside the town, unless they had reasons good enough to excuse their absences. The seven mile limitation in the Oath of c1530 was at a later date abandoned. All had to attend unless they had acceptable reasons for being absent from this Court of Election. So a nominal roll was needed for each court, listing every one of the freemen. The purpose of each list, described in Latin or English as a Catalogue, required it to be comprehensive and many have annotations referring to accepted excuses for absence such as illness, death, residence at some distance away from the borough, or note the cases of default in the required suit of court. Thus − and it is an important point − these annual lists of Maldon's freemen, each stating clearly which of them was and who was not resident within the borough, are the most reliable guides which could be wished for.


DECENNERS AND VIEWS OF FRANKPLEDGE

These freemen were always a minority among all the male inhabitants. The rest of the adult, male laymen of the town, the unenfranchised men and the boys aged twelve years and over, were referred to as 'decenners'. Sometimes the English spelling of that word in the borough records is 'diziner' or (confusingly) "doziner' but in the Latin texts it is desinerius or, most accurately, decennarius, meaning

24

a member of a tithing. Originally the decenner was one in a group of ten men who were collectively under oath to maintain the laws of the realm and with responsibility for each others' observance of the law. Decenners took their oaths, witnessed other tithings' 'pledges' (oath-takings) and were mustered for periodic review in courts called the Frankpledge.

It was a medieval method of binding men over to be of good behaviour, with the additional value to the authorities of putting each man on oath to be of good behaviour before he had committed any offence. It may seem unusual to find the system still operating in Elizabethan Maldon and so to suspect that it had become an insubstantial formality but it appears to have been maintained in full force in many parts of Essex (at least), probably because the exercise of a jurisdiction over tithings in the later Middle Ages was seen by the lords of manors as a way to safeguard from encroachment by the Crown their rights to retain the fines levied in the leet courts of their manors and to claim the chattels forfeited by felons. And in Essex the leet jurisdiction of manor courts was maintained with surprising vigour into the seventeenth century.

The change which had occurred in the system long before the sixteenth century was from groups of ten to groups of fewer or more men based on areas within each manor, such as the tithings of 9, 13, 14 men and two more of 16 men each at the Baynard manor in the parish of Messing in the 1290s. At Maldon there were no separate tithings but all males over 12 years of age and of at least one year's residence within the town were under oath as decenners. In many places the manors which exercised their rights to hold Views of Frankpledge had only partial jurisdiction in the townships across which their manorial tenements were scattered. Their tithing lists cannot be supposed to have included all the males resident in those townships or parishes but at Maldon the borough was itself a manor and was declared to be so by the charters of 1554 and 1555 which created its Corporation. Other manors had properties and tenements in the town, such as Beeleigh Fee, Great and Little Maldon, Earl's Maldon, the manors of Langford and Purleigh, but the authority of the borough itself as a Manor was declared to include all the inhabitants, and specifically so by the 1555 charter which required the Corporation of Maldon to exercise a frankpledge jurisdiction twice a year over 'all tenants, inhabitants and residents within the borough aforesaid and the suburbs of the same'. Clergy, wealthy freeholders and single women had never been required to belong to tithings and these were excluded from the Maldon Frankpledge in the 1570s despite the charter's apparent instruction to include 'all residents'. Women and children never had been understood to be within the system − their husbands or parents were responsible for their actions − and the clergy were under the jurisdiction of their own canon law but in the 1570s the borough did summon the wealthiest freeholders to appear before its Views of Frankpledge if they were also resident within the town.

25

The status of freeman to which the membership of a tithing had always been restricted must not be confused with the status of a freeburgess or 'freeman of the borough'. The freemen of the tithings were those men who were not villeins or of other servile condition within that manor to whose frankpledge they belonged. (And there were none at Maldon who were of servile condition by at least the mid-fifteenth century.) Lest there be any confusion over this, the freeburgesses of the borough are here called freemen and those who were not freeburgesses are referred to as decenners.

Every man in Maldon who was not a freeman and every boy who came of age – at his twelfth birthday – and had been resident for the greater part of the preceding twelve months was required to take the Oath of the Decenners. He swore loyalty to the Crown, to maintain the Peace and to obey the borough magistrates 'in all things they lawfully command' as in this text of the oath, written c1530, in which *thevis fere* means 'an accomplice of a thief':

> *I shall trewe liege man be and trewe feithe and trouthe bere to our sovereigne Lorde the kynge, Kynge N now kynge of Ynglond, and to his heires kynges. I shall be no thefe nor thevis fere, nor no theft or treson know nor kepe but I shall shortly enforme the Kynges officers that hathe the law in governance.*
>
> *I shall be obedient to the Bailiffes and other officers of this towne for the tyme beynge in all thynges they bid me do liefull, and well and truly use me lyke a trewe liege man.*
> *So help me God.*

Twice a year the Bailiffs and Justices of the Peace of Maldon were required by their charters and by custom to satisfy themselves that all males aged twelve and over who were not freemen had sworn this oath. Freemen, of course, were similarly bound by the oath they took at their admission to the liberties of the borough. As with the Courts of Election, the town clerks had to prepare nominal rolls of the decenners for each View of Frankpledge and the comprehensive nature of these documents is announced by the title of each surviving example: 'A Catalogue containing all the names of the decenners'.

If a complete series of both sorts of list, of freemen and of decenners, had survived for the whole or a greater part of the sixteenth and seventeenth centuries they would have provided a detailed register of the adult, lay, male population of Maldon which would have been without parallel in English urban history. The reason for giving so extensive an introduction to them has been to show how reliable they are: they were meant to be reliable. Only three or four beneficed or stipendiary clergy, a few very elderly laymen and, perhaps, the severely handicapped, were not included

26

in these catalogues but these surely would not have amounted to more than a score, sometimes barely a dozen and the clergy can mostly be traced from other sources. Many of the lists, especially the catalogues of decenners, were kept as separate sheets of paper which were filed away after use by the town clerk and either destroyed when they were no longer needed for reference or lost subsequently along with a large part of the borough records in the eighteenth and early nineteenth centuries. The few complete catalogues of decenners which have survived cover only the years 1569 to 1582; for all but one of those years there are records of only one of the two annual Views; there are none for 1575; and in this period only some of the freemen's catalogues have survived.

Issued with writs by the town clerk the constables made diligent perambulations of their parishes' houses a day or so before each View. They listed all whom they warned to be present at court and their returns provided the town clerk with up-to-date information which he amalgamated to form a single catalogue of the decenners who should come before him at the View. The clerk, or his scrivener, did not merely copy the lists handed to him by the parish constables; he rearranged the names in groups based on the decenners' forenames, with all the Williams in one block on the sheet of paper, all the Johns in another column, the Edwards and Edmunds together in another block and so on, with the miscellaneous, uncommon names such as Oliver, Christopher, Mardochaeus, together at the bottom of the page. This speeded up the proceedings in the court as it was a quick way of locating each man as he came forward 'to make his royal suit and service'. Where there were two or more identically named persons they were differentiated by notes such as 'Junior' and 'Senior' or by their distinctive occupations.

The clerk's lists were also lavishly annotated during and immediately after the Views of Frankpledge, for all manner of events might reasonably prevent dutiful decenners from attending. A dot was placed beside the name of each man who did appear but some had left the town during the (short) interval between the constables' perambulations and the day of the View, to live elsewhere and against their names the clerk wrote *ex'* meaning *extra burgum* ('outside the borough'). There are 241 certain cases of that in the catalogues of 1569-1582 and it is worth noting that the View was held at Easter and at Michaelmas, the two times in the year when hired servants and seasonal labourers would be on the move. It was possible to be 'essoined', that is, to be excused attendance without payment of a fine, and against some names the annotation *esson'* is accompanied by the name of a friend, master or neighbour who presented the excuse. Thus: *Will's Johnes al's Rog's esson' p' Petr' Kyrk* appears on the catalogue for 18 April 1571, meaning 'William Johns alias Rogers is essoined by Peter Kirk'. Those who failed to attend without reason or permission were marked *def'* (*deforciator*) and sometimes the clerk preferred to place a cross against the names of absentees instead of dotting those who were present. Some were at sea or were excused because there was an acceptable reason for their absence such as sudden illness, and against such

27

persons the clerk wrote *super mare* or *pard'* or *egrot'* (*egrotatus*, ill). If a man had just become a freeman and was exercising his right not to be summoned to the View, *liber* for 'freeman' was placed against his name so that the jury would not pursue him with summonses for non-attendance. *Mort'* (for *mortuus*) was written against some names but it is not always clear if the death had occurred between the constables' perambulation and the View, or if the clerk had added a note of the man's death after the View had been held.

These were all necessary annotations. When the View was finished the clerk had to abstract a list of all who were to be prosecuted for their unexcused or unacceptable absence. He also had by the end of the View a record of recent newcomers and of boys who had just passed their twelfth birthdays, against whose names in the catalogue he wrote *novus juratus* or 'newly sworn' if they had taken the decenners' oath during the court session.

## USING THE EVIDENCE OF THE VIEWS OF FRANKPLEDGE, 1569-82

There is a world of difference between establishing the comprehensiveness and accuracy of the catalogues at the time each was compiled and using them four hundred years later as roll calls of the adult male population of Maldon. Nor is there space to describe here how these manuscript lists have been checked against all other available references to Maldon's inhabitants over the same period of time which can be found in other records of the corporation, in the parish registers and in records compiled outside the borough such as the wills proved in the probate courts, archdeaconry visitation and cause papers and in the prosecutions at the Essex Assizes. Care has been taken to avoid confusion over similar (and dissimilar) names − the problem of nominal linkage − and the result is a late-twentieth century edition in index form of a collection of working lists made long ago. It is a descriptive list of no less than 1,106 persons contrived from documents which were intended to be accurate on the days they were used.

Of the rules observed in using it the most important is that where any estimate of migration or of population replacement is to be made, it is preferable to lean towards an understatement whenever there is any cause for doubt as to the completeness of the available information. A small descriptive selection from these 1106 names will demonstrate the decisions that have been made. It will also serve as an introduction to the kind of people who form the crowds and the 'extras' of the *dramatis personae* in the Tudor and Stuart scene at Maldon and whose residential histories are displayed in the twenty examples assembled as Figure 5.

Some men's record was very simple: one, two or three years' residence continuously as a decenner, normally making suit of court at the Views of Frankpledge but

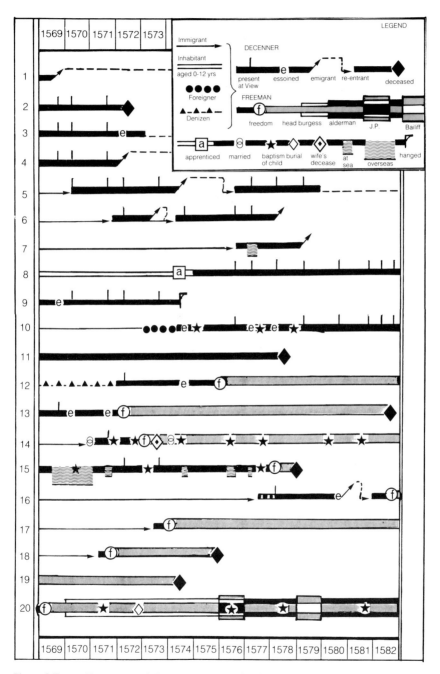

*Figure 5 Twenty Decenners and Freemen: patterns of residence*

29

sometimes being essoined; theirs' were modestly conducted subservient lives as wage-earners until their departure for employment in similar conditions elsewhere, or until death in Maldon. An enquiry about a right of way, a matter in which the length of the witnesses' memories was relevant, shows that (2) and (3) − Cuthbert Roo and Stephen Roo − were about sixty years old in 1570. They must have been decenners in Maldon for many years to have been summoned as witnesses and the absence of Stephen Roo's name from the catalogues after 1570 may be an example of the exemption from attendance at the View granted to the elderly, for his burial is not recorded. Most decenners seem to have spent much less time living in Maldon than these two old men.

14 per cent of the 1106 persons listed in the catalogues (that is, 155 men) spent two or more distinct and brief periods in the town within these thirteen years. Some were clearly present for two separate periods, others for three and a few for four distinct periods, as with numbers (5), (6) and (16) in Figure 5. For the purposes of this study a style has to be coined for such persons: here they are classified as occasional residents.

In some cases there must be the possibility that the entries in the catalogues refer to different men with identical names so, to diminish the distortion such a situation might have on an estimate of population replacement, it is sometimes more useful to deal in de-personalised Units of Residence rather than to count individuals. The name of an 'occasional resident' with its contingent assumption that the name refers to one and only one person thus comes to be counted as two, three or four 'units of residence', of which there are 1,291 (instead of 1,106 persons).

Some who were not named in particular catalogues may nevertheless have been living in the borough. Thus the sons of Maldon residents would be classified as immigrants if it were not known from incidental sources that they had been born in Maldon and had just passed their twelfth birthday (after 1569). When that is known to have been the case, their residential history has been assumed to have been continuous. William Wiseman, number (8) in Figure 5, was one of three identically named males but he is identifiable as having been an apprentice of Brice Smith, shoemaker, according to an indenture of 2 August 1574. He was sworn as a decenner in April 1576 (and thus aged between 10 and 11 when he became an apprentice) and, being the orphan son of a former Maldon husbandman according to the indenture, it has been assumed that he lived continuously in the town from his birth in about 1564. There are at most twenty such cases.

Some apprentices were born outside the borough but came into it before their twelfth birthdays. Some may have been living with their masters for up to a year before the enrolling of their indentures in the borough Court of Record and it was customary for decenners to be sworn in only after they had been living in the manor or borough for one year. If their indentures state that they were born outside Maldon it has been assumed that they had been resident for most of the year preceding their formal indentured service began. Those born within the borough have been assumed to have lived in it continuously.

Another allowance has to be made for the men who were styled 'Foreigners' such as (10). They were defined as being *commorantes*, persons tarrying in Maldon for purposes of trade but not permanent residents. Not being freemen they paid a yearly fine for the right to keep shops (*officinae*) whose windows had to be covered with lattice-work, and the borough chamberlains kept lists of these men to record their payment of these fines. Just how 'commorant' or occasional they were as members of the town community is uncertain. Some were living in Maldon permanently but had not yet been able to afford to become freemen; others were more probably *commorantes* only during fairs and around market days, with shops or stalls in other markets as well as at Maldon. The residential unit for each of these men has been counted as beginning just before their first appearance in the lists of the Foreigners and the treatment of their entries leans towards an over-estimate of continuous residence.

Some men had by 1569 grown so old that they were not expected to attend the Views any more, as probably happened after 1570 to Cuthbert and Stephen Roo. Doubtless their number was always small and (because freemen seem rarely to have been excused from their Courts of Election) these aged persons were predominantly decenners. They are represented in Figure 5 by (11), a fletcher named John Spuddell, who was 82 in 1570 when he gave evidence in the right of way enquiry with the two Roo's. His is certainly the only name to be found in both the 1570's and in the Lay Subsidy returns of 1524 but the only other reference to him between those dates is in the 1540's and 1550's when he was the Sergeant-at-Mace of the Bailiffs and Common Council. Such aged persons would rarely figure in public business, unless the benefit of their long memories was needed, and their personal occupations would not, at their age, be significant. Perhaps some of the burial entries in the parish registers which cannot be linked with any named freemen or decenners refer to such elderly inhabitants as John Spuddell. No allowance, however, has been made for them in estimates of the community's size.

Freemen are the most fully documented inhabitants because so much service was likely to be expected of them by their borough, as with (20) in Figure 5, because their purchase or assumption of the freeburgess status was mostly recorded in very informative memoranda, because they were more frequent litigants in the borough courts than were the decenners, and because they took apprentices. One notable feature of the 1570's was that most of them were imigrants who purchased their freedoms rather than inheriting the right from their fathers or from their wives' fathers. The case of John Clay — (17) in Figure 5 — illustrates this group. He was a shipwright, born at Shotley in Suffolk, who became a freeman in January 1574 by purchase. Barely two months before he had been the defendant in two pleas of debt laid against him in the borough court by a Maldon merchant for timber costing altogether £17 - 18s - 4d which included 'pieces of ship timber, crooked' and 1,000 sawn planks. As he was not listed in any of the preceding catalogues of decenners he must have arrived in Maldon after October 1573, purchasing on credit and immediately the necessary materials to set up his shipyard and also arranging to pay by installments the entry fine of thirty shillings for his freedom of the borough. Many of the freemen present by 1583 had similarly bought their freedoms by installments and did so soon after arriving in the town since they, like Clay, are not listed in the catalogues of decenners, nor (in many cases) are they listed as Foreigners in the year before they became freemen. An exception is the Cockney seaman John Peacock (number 14), who married into the most influential family of Maldon shipowners and seafarers, the Poulters, in November 1570. Whilst married to Margaret Poulter he remained a decenner, although in right of his wife he could have claimed the freedom of the borough without payment of any fee. Instead he preferred to purchase his freedom in January 1573.

The sons of freemen were, of course, decenners from their twelfth year until they took up their freedom (if they were entitled to do so, which only applied if they had been born after their father had become enfranchised) but it should not be assumed that the few young men who can be found in this category were necessarily long-term or continuous residents. Matthew Abraham — (16) in Figure 5 — was baptised in All Saints' church at Maldon 24 September 1559. As his father had become a freeman before Matthew's birth he was eligible for admission without fee and he appears on the tail of the freemen's catalogue of January 1583, aged 23. During the previous twenty three years it may be assumed his infancy and early childhood were spent with his parents but, as he was not listed as a decenner from his twelfth year (1571) until his nineteenth year (1578), it must also be assumed that he spent at least seven years out of the town. Probably he was apprenticed in another market town, perhaps in his subsequent occupation as a linendraper, perhaps at Sudbury (his father's birthplace) or one of the nearby market towns such as Hadleigh, Haverhill or Lavenham. But that is mere speculation. What is clear is that this was not the end of his travelling for, as Figure 5 shows, after he had been sworn a decenner of Maldon he was out-of-town for another two years before taking up his freedom as a resident freeburgess.

Thus the facts which can be collected around the names in the Catalogues reveal a wide range of personalities and social types. Some stayed only for a few months.

Some found prosperity of a kind and stayed the rest of their lives in Maldon. One finds a sailor who was overseas at the time of one View, because *extra mare* was written against his name instead of the usual *super mare*. There is an alien, a Fleming or German, waiting for his naturalisation before purchasing his freedom of the borough because the fee would then be 33s 4d instead of £3 - 3s - 4d. There are in the lists men who were eventually hanged; some who escaped execution by 'pleading clergy' at the Assizes; there is one crazed man, presumably in his late thirties, who was eventually hung, drawn and quartered at Brentwood because he proclaimed that he was really King Edward VI. There are apprentices listed beside minor county gentry, artisans next to graduates of Cambridge University, servants and masters, a very varied assembly, continuously changing in membership, which twice yearly passed in review before the Town Clerk in his capacity as Steward of the Leet Court of the Manor of the Borough.

## MEASURING POPULATION MOBILITY AT MALDON, 1569-1582

Within this period the decenners and freemen fall into one of three categories: continuously, occasionally or temporarily resident. The outstanding feature of the entire body of registrations is that out of 1,106 identifiable males only 265 lived continuously in the borough in this period. That is, only 24 per cent of all these males were resident throughout thirteen years.

To discover just how mobile the population was the list of 1,106 names must first be pruned of seventy seven items, each being a name that occurs only once in the parish registers' entries and not at all in any of the catalogues, each being the name of a man or boy of whom nothing more is discoverable than that he was either baptised, married or buried in the town. That leaves a working total of 1,029 persons who were certainly present for all or some of the time between April 1569 and January 1583.

The annual totals of decenners and freemen which are depicted in Figure 6 show that this male part of the population ranged in number from just under 300 in some years to just over 350 in others, except for 1582 when the town experienced a level of immigration which was unprecedented in the 1570's. On average Maldon had a population of 333 males aged 12 to about 60 (at least in this decade). No more than ninety of these 1,029 are recorded as having lived continuously in Maldon throughout the thirteen years. Twenty names, at most, must be added: of boys who probably lived in Maldon from at least 1569 until their twelfth birthdays and who were thenceforth continuously resident until the end of 1582. That means the number of males continuously resident was 110: a tiny group forming only 10.6 per cent of all the men and youths recorded as inhabitants.

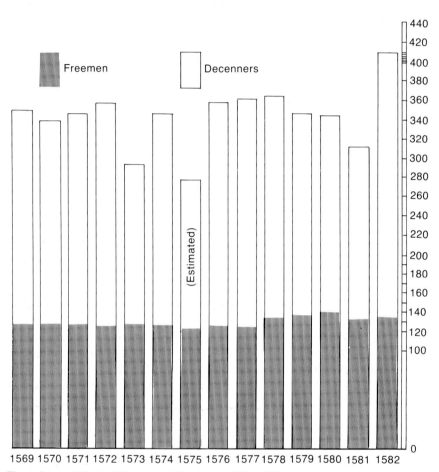

Figure 6 Annual Totals of Freemen and Decenners, 1569 – 1582

That does not mean that the remaining 89.4 per cent of the residents both entered and left the borough within this period. Some who arrived after 1569 remained as residents until after 1582; some disappear from the catalogues because of old age but were still residents; others died in the town and must not be counted in with the migrants. Some came and went at brief, irregular intervals. There are two methods of expressing movement at any community for which at least two lists of its members exist (provided, as here, that the data within them are similar). These 110 continuous residents can be compared with the total number of males

34

listed as present year by year. The percentage which they form provides a Persistence Rate:

31 per cent of the males listed in 1569 (100% is 350)

37 per cent of the males listed in 1573 (100% is 294)

31 per cent of the males listed in 1576 (100% is 356)

32 per cent of the males listed in 1579 (100% is 346)

35 per cent of the males listed in 1581 (100% is 311)

27 per cent of the males listed in 1582 (100% is 408).

So Maldon was at this time clearly dependent on a high rate of immigration to maintain an average population of 333 males and, obviously, was certainly experiencing a considerable and continuous emigrant flow.

The second method of expressing movement within a community is to calculate the percentage of leavers − the Exits Rate − and similarly an Entrants Rate. Since the processing of the material has included information on deaths and children under the age of twelve, the strict procedure of counting the number of exits per year and expressing that as a percentage of the number present the year before (and calculating the Entries Rate as a percentage of the later population) has had to be modified for this study.

Figure 7 shows how the numbers of males present in 1569, 1570, 1571 and 1572 decreased over the next ten years. It depicts the males who were (i) continuously resident plus (ii) the entrants of 1569-72 and indicates the general Exits Rate for them over the period 1569-82. Figure 8 shows how numbers of another set of residents gradually accumulated between 1569 and 1582 to reach the totals of 1579 - 1582. In each diagram the maximum number of males is expressed as 100 per cent and all the succeeding or (in the case of Figure 8) preceding year totals are scaled proportionately. This generalisation indicates that in the period 1569-1582 the rate of immigration which produced the accumulations shown in Figure 8 tended to be balanced by a simultaneous rate of out-migration such as is depicted in Figure 7.

Thus at any time during the 1570's a majority of the town's population had been living there for less than ten years and was not likely to be living there for a further ten years. Provided there was no marked change in the natural factors affecting

35

population size — the onset of a prolonged excess of births over deaths or a series of epidemics momentarily creating much higher death rates — this apparent balance of Exits and Entries, of in- and out-migration would hold steady the population size of this town.

One feature of Figures 7 and 8 which is to be expected of a Tudor or Stuart town is that the freemen were its most stable component. The twenty males — no more — who lived there as decenners continuously for thirteen years, and the nine freemen who lived there only temporarily were exceptions to the rule. In the limited period with which we are presently dealing the residential pattern is conformable to the simplest model of a small urban community. Its principal employers and producers, the freemen, were the most stable element. Its workforce was much more transient and was likely to have been by habit and by occupational necessity mobile. A very large section of the male population thus consisted of serving men, apprentices, journeymen artisans, alien craftsmen, mariners (other than ships' masters) and hired labourers whose numbers fluctuated as masters paid off some men at the end of a season or recruited more when local enterprises suddenly created a demand for additional workmen. One would expect the replacement rate in the male population to have been very high and it seems that Maldon, a market town and both a river and sea port, functioned with an establishment of one long-staying inhabitant to two transients.

A conversation between a blacksmith, John Jenkins, and a servant of a woollendraper, a youth named John Price, which was reported to the magistrates in June 1570, illustrates in some detail an extreme case of the frequency with which some of these servitors changed jobs and flitted about the countryside. In the course of describing to Jenkins his current financial difficulty, John Price said that not long before 'he did work at Billericay,' where he still owed fifteen shillings. He had left there because he could not repay the debt, borrowing a dagger which he had then 'laid to gage at Baddow with a certain cloth.' He had been living at Chelmsford, too, where "I made a widow believe I would marry her," he said, "and I spent her twenty nobles and then I gave her the slip." He owed another twenty shillings at London: the creditor would soon be coming to Maldon but Price could not pay that debt either and he had further arranged to go to the Midsummer Fair at Colchester with two 'maidens,' for which he needed more money 'to make a hand' because he had a reputation to maintain as 'a great company keeper.' Five places, stretching from London to Colchester, are reported in this brief conversation. Whilst the listener, Jenkins, was only an inhabitant of Maldon for two years, Price was never listed as a decenner and had fled the town before Midsummer 1574, perhaps taking with him, as he proposed, either £16 of his master's money or "so much cloth from my master" that he could "make a piece of money and he [The master] shall never miss it ... then I can take my leave of him and depart honestly."

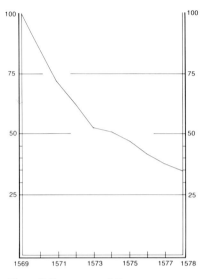

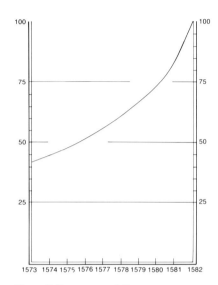

*Figure 7 Decenners and Freemen:*
*decrease 1569 – 1582*

*Figure 8 Decenners and Freemen:*
*increase 1569 – 1582*

An alternative method of surveying population movement at Maldon is to eliminate all obvious alternatives to out-migration. That can be done by working in Units of Residence instead of counting individuals, each unit representing one period of continuous inhabitation so that those Occasional Residents described earlier in this chapter, whose repeated departures and returns confuse the general pattern of migration, become several units according to the number of times they were residents. This is best represented diagrammatically, as in Figure 9 whose principal feature is that 57 per cent of the residential places were occupied by males who both entered and departed from Maldon within these thirteen years.

Each approach to the evidence of the catalogue entries indicates Maldon's great dependence on immigration to maintain its population. But there is a difficulty in arriving at an estimate of the replacement rate, for the material represents a slice taken out of a sequence of overlapping events, each of perhaps long duration and it is impossible to determine how representative these thirteen years may be of a long-term trend. At one extreme it can be noted that ...

   (i) since only 10.6 (say 11) per cent of the adult, male population was continuously resident (where 1,029 is 100 per cent), the remaining 89 per cent were immigrants between late 1569 and the summer of 1582.

37

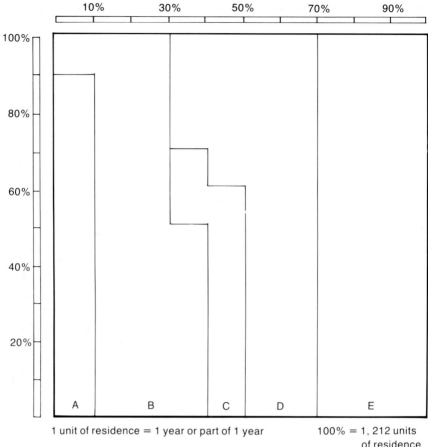

1 unit of residence = 1 year or part of 1 year          100% = 1, 212 units
of residence

A Continuously resident 1569-1583
B Continuously resident from after 1569
C Continuously resident 1569 until decease (before 1583)
D Resident only for 2-4 years
E Resident only for 1 year

*Figure 9 The Composition of the Male Population of Maldon 1569 – 1582: units of residence*

That ignores the possibility that many established a reasonably lengthy settlement in the town or became permanently settled there, so alternatively the replacement can be better represented by an average year in which ...

(ii) the adult male population was only maintained at its average size of 333 by the immigration (over the preceding one to six years) of 222 males.

38

Alternatively, and supposing that the population of 1569 - 1582 can be taken as a truly representative slice out of a repeat-pattern of human settlement in the town, either ...

(iii) 49 per cent of the identifiable males (where 1,029 is 100 per cent) or ...

(iv) 52 per cent of all recorded males aged over 11 years (where 1,106 is 100 per cent) ...

were both immigrant and emigrant in this period, or ...

(v) as much as 57 per cent was settled in Maldon for less than thirteen years.

But each estimate establishes clearly enough the presence of a very massive tide of human migration during the 1570s, sufficient to show that over thirteen years there was a replacement of at least 50 per cent of the male inhabitants of the borough. What these Catalogues and the allied sources show tallies with the nearly contemporary comment of a parson in the City of London that a majority of his parishioners were replaced by newcomers every twelve years or so. Many studies of the English population made from other types of source material, especially studies made in the 1970s and 1980s, have shown that a replacement rate as high as 50 per cent per 10 - 13 years in this, one of the less populous market towns, would be neither unlikely nor unique. Nor does it seem unreasonable to press here a claim for an even higher rate and to suggest that as much as 57 per cent of the adult male population of Maldon was impermanently settled there during the 1570s.

If there were no more information about Maldon's population over the two centuries than this for 1569-83, then two or perhaps three theoretical views would have to remain in constant debate in the discussion of the long-term population history of the town. One of those views might propose that the high replacement rate of the 1570s was unique, that these were years when unusual circumstances, especially a series of catastrophes − plague, influenza epidemics, fires − created seasons of exceptional out-migration and high mortality, alternating with compensatory seasons of better conditions in which the inflow of people was greater than the outflow of the disaster years. There are, however, no reports of any exceptional catastrophes in the 1570s. Instead there is evidence of corporate ambitions flowering in that decade and a prevailing optimism which sudden visitations of adverse circumstances and an unusually transient population would not have encouraged.

It is more reasonable to assume that the 1570s formed an indistinguishable part of a far longer sequence of demographic events, one of which might have been a steady, long-term accumulation of permanent settlers with permanently settled descendants throughout the sixteenth and early seventeenth centuries, with immigration gradually exceeding the rate of out-migration until, by the 1640s the residential pattern would be far more stable than it had been in the 1520s. Conversely, an ever-increasing replacement rate as a relatively stable late-medieval community broke down, the permanently settled families decreasing, might have been the sequence of events, with the town's dependence on immigration steadily increasing, until the imposition of curbs on resettlement by the Poor Laws of 1594 and 1601 and further settlement laws in the seventeenth century finally halted this trend.

If the first of these contrasting 'models' were the most nearly representative of the borough, with decreasing migration rates, then a very serious upset in the population structure would have to be proposed as having occurred somewhere between 1500 and 1560, because by the 1570s the replacement rate was still running at some 57 per cent of all inhabitants every ten to thirteen years and a greater stability could not be looked for until perhaps the first quarter of the seventeenth century. The second 'model' would seem to propose a population of extremely transient short-term inhabitants by 1600-30, with replacements at much more than 60 per cent per thirteen year period, and to imply the creation of some very deliberate policy (and a successful one) or of an exceptional change of circumstances such as would reverse this trend and pave the way for the doubling of the population which occurred in the eighteenth century.

But there is another 'model' and one which has the preliminary support of the estimates of population size offered at the beginning of this chapter, a 'model' of an almost static population so far as average total size is concerned, increasing by perhaps no more than one hundred in a hundred and fifty years but with the same annual fluctuations occurring from 1524 to 1568 and 1583 to 1672 as have been detected from the Catalogues of the 1570s. This fourth 'model' does not preclude the existence of tendencies toward a general decline or toward overall growth but presumes that there were some brakes on either tendency. So long as the issues of decline and renewal remain contentious in the study of late-medieval and early-modern towns a consideration of these alternative scenarios must be central to any discussion of Maldon's place in the urban scene of Tudor and Stuart England. So it is desirable to determine as satisfactorily as possible how far the structure of the population and its level of migration in the 1570s was like or unlike that of the preceding seventy years and of the succeeding seventy years up to the Civil Wars of 1642-49. Despite the lack of any sequences of decenners' catalogues there are sources which indicate the importance of migration in the composition of three distinct groups in the town's population.

# POPULATION MOBILITY OUTSIDE THE 1570s: THE FREEMEN

A descending degree of permanence might be expected among the classes which composed Maldon's community: a highly mobile work force including migratory seasonal labourers would form the base of the social pyramid; just above them in rank and settled condition would be the smaller workforce of covenanted servants; then a smaller number of apprentices living with their masters for up to seven or eight years or, as journeymen, for perhaps much longer; and at the top of the town's social pyramid, the freemen who ought to have formed the most permanent element in this community.

Yet all the records associated with the freemen are instinct with evidence that membership of their body was constantly changing. Certainly they were less prone to migration within any ten-year period than were the lower orders of their community, but freemen do not seem often to have established long-lasting family settlements. A rough preliminary indication of this can be observed in the surnames of the Bailiffs of Maldon (as listed in Appendix 1) who, by convention and necessity were men with the longest experience of the government of the borough. Only three of those families which had provided Bailiffs between 1500 and 1550 are to be found in the list for c1565 to 1600 and none of the later-sixteenth century Bailiffs' surnames are to be found in the lists after 1615, other than Vernon. Nor by intermarriage did any of these families indirectly maintain a perpetual succession to aldermanic office. Moreover, their emigration is frequently recorded, as with Thomas Young (a Bailiff in 1589) who had 'removed himself and his dwelling out of the borough for the space of this whole year' (ie. 1591) 'and intendeth not to return again'. A gravestone of 1596 in Roxwell parish church, which commemorates this Thomas Young and his father as country gentlemen of a great estate called Newlands, is a monument representative of the continuous resettlement of men who were, but only for a part of their lives, the resident governors of the borough.

The Catalogues of the freemen form a continuous series from 1613 to 1735, each preserving a distinction between the residents and the 'forinsec' or non-resident freemen and these show us a steady annual drifting of freemen and their households out of the borough at a rate which seems remarkably high.

The annual Catalogues also indicate how much the freeman group in Maldon relied on regular recruitment of immigrants to maintain its numbers. That is confirmed by the memoranda of the admission of freemen, which show that this steady inflow of new freemen replacing emigrants was continuous for at least two thirds of the sixteenth century and for almost the whole of the seventeenth. Possibly as many as two thirds, certainly one half, were born outside the borough. Of course that does not mean all such men had lived outside Maldon until the moment of their admission to the freedom of the borough but only one fifth of them were able to claim their freedom by inheritance or by marriage (such men paid no admission fee) and the fee-paying entries show over 60 per cent as having had no connection by birth, kinship or marriage with existing freemen. The composition of this body of the best-circumstanced inhabitants of the borough is thus a mirror of the population at large in those two centuries: a fairly static level of resident membership was maintained largely by immigration, and emigration was a more notable factor than mortality in creating the vacancies which the newcomers filled.

The necessity of maintaining a comprehensive dossier on all freemen's admissions, whether fee-paying or not, has provided a near-complete record for long periods, and especially from c1520-1551, 1556-95 and from 1606. There can be no doubt that the predominance of immigrants, even though they had to pay fees of 20 shillings before 1555 and 30 shillings thereafter, is no illusion. Without them the annual assemblies of some ninety men at the Court of Election would soon have dwindled to a score or so and indeed would eventually have ceased to exist. As the researches of Mr J.R. Smith have shown, this reliance on immigration continued to be the dominant characteristic of population replacement right through the late seventeenth century and the first half of the eighteenth.

One further view of the residential experience of Maldon freemen can be offered from reconstructed family histories compiled out of the wills, parish registers and borough records. The five best detailed cases are of families derived from (1) a Devon man (the Moores) and from four other men born outside Maldon but within fifteen miles, who were (2) the Maldons, (3) the Welles, (4) the Hutts and (5) the Robinsons and whose principal occupations as shoemakers, haberdashers, glovers, shearmen and apothecaries placed them among the more affluent of the freemen between the 1550s and the 1660s. What all five families have in common is that the length of their continuous family presence in the borough, which averaged eighty six years between the arrival of the founder member of each family in Maldon and the departure or death of the last to be resident, depended greatly on the longevity of the founder. Thus John Maldon (I), originator of the Maldons of Maldon, came from Chelmsford in (approximately) his twenty eighth year and stayed as a haberdasher and linendraper until his fifty ninth year. When he retired to his native Chelmsford he had six sons and eleven grandsons, of whom only three maintained his trade in silks, linens and made-up clothing in Maldon. Thirty years after his retirement to Chelmsford, all his descendants had vanished from the borough's occupational records and from its parish registers, although another group of Maldons appeared in the later seventeenth century as minor urban gentry.

Just as the Maldons lasted 73 years in the borough (1584-1657), of which the founder was resident for 34 years, the Welles family (or rather, the largest and longest standing of many 'Welles' families) lasted 78 years (1565-1643), of which the founder, Thomas Welles of Little Totham, was a Maldon resident for at least 40 years (1565-1605). The Moores lasted 86 years (1560-1646) and their founder, Nicholas Moore (I) who had been born at Plympton, Devonshire, was resident 34 years. The Hutt family originated with Thomas, a shearman born at Bocking who had no children when he became a freeman in 1576. His eventual family and its descendants lasted 117 years in Maldon, of which this Thomas Hutt (I) was resident for 49 years. And the Robinson family, who were descended from a clergyman (Elias Robinson, vicar first of Fairstead, then of Terling) who apprenticed his three sons in pharmacy at Maldon, dwelt prosperously in the borough for 78 years, of which the youngest of the three brothers (Reuben Robinson) lasted as 'Professor of Physic' for 58 years, 1607-65. In these families the originators were present for between 40 per cent and 79 per cent of the time they lived in Maldon.

Altogether, ninety members of these five families have been traced (including three in-laws). Forty nine were males, of whom only 29 per cent were permanently resident in the borough, 22 per cent spent part of their adult lives as residents, 22 per cent were born there but left the town during childhood or adolescence. The remainder, 27 per cent, died in infancy or childhood. And in all five families no more than two successive generations maintained these periods of continuous residence. Infant mortality was high and nearly half the male survivors left Maldon during childhood or early in their adult lives. Professor Hoskins observed that in the early sixteenth century 'successful urban families came and went in a matter of three generations at most'. These five were all 'successful' in the context of Maldon society (indeed, more will be heard of them in the course of this study) and his general observation for the 1520s accurately describes their settlement in Maldon. For many freemen's families, perhaps for the majority, continuous inhabitation of the borough lasted less than three generations, in some cases for less than one generation's span. Of them all the career of the Maldons is an apt epitome.

## POPULATION MOBILITY OUTSIDE THE 1570s: TAXPAYERS, DECENNERS AND SERVANTS

Apart from the bi-annual catalogues of decenners — almost all of those now lost- no systematic records were required for any but the freemen; only incidental information exists of the remaining two thirds of the town's population and although it is for some years and for some purposes copious, it can provide only two indications of the probable trends in the settlement pattern below the level of the freemen which are worth consideration.

One of those indicators is to be found in the comparison of surnames in the lay subsidy returns of 1524 and 1544, offering at least some illumination on the state of the community in a period which has little else by way of relevant information on the general movement of Maldon's population. The two returns have altogether 246 different surnames, some occurring in both subsidy returns but 187 occur only once (some in the 1524 list, the others only in the 1544 return), which suggests that in the 1530s upwards of one half to three quarters of the taxable population was migrant. The numbers taxed in each of these subsidies were, however, sufficiently different (194, 165) for this observation to be of questionable value, especially as it does not allow for deaths. It can be refined by inspecting the proportion of the 1524 taxpayers whose surnames did not reappear in the 1544 subsidy. That is, 108 persons, 55 per cent of the 1524 subsidy payers, were almost certainly replaced by unrelated persons in the intervening years. If they were lost to the town by natural causes, they were still replaced by unrelated men and since the untaxed inhabitants were likely to have been the most transient people, the total replacement in the 1520s and 1530s may well have been considerably higher than 55 per cent and thus comparable with the 1570s.

The second indicator is offered by the records of Maldon apprentices. They were almost all decenners (some may have been apprenticed when ten or eleven years old) and they formed a distinctive group in this two thirds, non-freeman part of the community. They ought to have been a privileged group, the youths to whom a skill was to be imparted and a future occupation in the borough offered. The Custumal of Maldon, at its revision in 1555, went out of its way to favour them: the freedom of the borough was to be theirs after completion of their indentured terms of service at a special, reduced fee of 6s 8d (one third of £1 compared to the standard £1.50) to be paid not by them but by their former masters. The great register of their enrolled indentures begun in 1566 supplies information on 521 apprentices up to 1660, of whom only seventy six became freemen: 13 per cent. That is a curiously tiny proportion, considering the incentives and privileges accorded to them. If the revisers of the Custumal had intended to stimulate the settlement of a special group of skilled craftsmen and tradesmen from 1555, they signally failed to do so.

It is worthwhile returning to the decenners' lists of 1569-82 and the freemen's records to trace the residence of the seventy two boys or youths apprenticed between 1566 and 1576. Only one sixth became freemen. There was no high mortality rate among them, only one died in these thirteen years, but just one half of them were emigrant within six years of being apprenticed. Indeed, ten (almost as many as those who did become freemen) appear to have shaken the dust of Maldon off their feet whilst the ink was still drying on their indentures.

44

What cannot be demonstrated is that the same pattern was repeated in subsequent decades. There were none called apprentices earlier than 1566 – the word first appears in Maldon in the 1555 Custumal but the first use of the term to describe an actual person is in the first enrolled indenture – and it was more often than not an artificial term for youths who were really servants, although with a more privileged status than the rest of that class of decenner. The Statute of Artificers of 1563 included apprentices in its regulations because the legislators wanted to impose some form of social stability on the population and tried to do that by ordering, for example, that only the sons of freeholders whose lands were worth more than 40s per annum could be apprenticed in certain trades, that boys should be placed in the same general occupational category as their fathers or that they should be the sons of artificers in cities, market towns and 'towns corporate'. The act should have created a select group of young decenners in Maldon who would have been distinguished from the rest by an exemption from being drafted into haymaking and harvesting at the times when the local Justices might find that necessary for the act's principal purpose of 'the better advancement of tillage and husbandry'. No enforced agricultural labouring for these young men. The borough courted them, as has been shown, with offers of enfranchisement *gratis* to themselves and at a cut-rate price which might not deter craftsmen from taking on apprentices.

Such a privileged Estate among the decenners never existed in practice. The low percentage of all the recorded apprentices who did become freemen between 1566 and 1660 indicates that the same state of affairs existed throughout that period as in the 1570s. On inspection, the indentures show that most of the provisions made for these youths in the Statute of Artificers were ignored from the start at Maldon. It took the borough over two years to begin the enrolment of indentures and even to recognise the existence of such an institution as apprenticeship. Sons of husbandmen, tanners, mariners, fletchers, many being orphans, were apprenticed to haberdashers, drapers, clothiers, despite the statutory limitation of such occupations to the sons of similarly employed men or to the sons of merchants, goldsmiths, ironmongers, embroiderers and occupiers of freehold land worth at least 40s per annum. It is true that entry to the Professions was limited to the sons of professionals but that would have normally applied without any statutory regulations. In every other level of occupation practised at Maldon the selective regulation of entry by the act was disregarded. Indeed a hard-headed attitude towards boys' abilities and careers can sometimes be seen. One Town Clerk, Master John Nash, sent one son, William, to Cambridge University in 1610 and had apprenticed another son, John, to a Maldon tailor in 1609. The town's great preacher, George Gifford, put his sons William and George into leather trades and the more famous preacher of Dedham, John Rogers, apprenticed his son John to the Maldon haberdasher John Maldon.

## POPULATION CONTROL

The regulations in the borough's Custumal and the range of events or activities for which men and women were prosecuted in its courts reflect another important characteristic of the population. It was so well-regulated that there is a case for considering it an oppressively regulated borough, organised more elaborately than its size warranted. There were two annual Views of Frankpledge, four Quarter Sessions, the Petty Sessions, the courts of the borough's Clerk of the Market, the Bailiffs' Admiralty Court, the weekly Courts of Record for bargains, covenants and deeds, all staffed by members of the Corporation. And there were the Common Informers and the spies.

This was no pretence. The borough archive, which is only a fragment of the collection as it was in 1768 (when the corporation was dissolved and the Town Clerk seized the documents) are still immense for a town of barely a thousand souls. There are twenty one bound court registers for the years up to 1688, most of which are of more than 100 folios and full of meticulously compiled court business; there are more than a hundred bundles of papers, fragments of the files from which the Town Clerks of the 1620s and 1630s supported the depositions in their formal records — hundreds of lists, notes, bills, letters and drafts of letters which were the product of the Corporation's constant watch on the inhabitants.

After it had been revised and extended in 1555 the Custumal of Maldon ran to no less than ninety separate regulations; it covered almost every aspect of an inhabitant's life; and the great mass of Tudor social and economic legislation which fell in cartloads on the Justices' shoulders further pinched and hemmed in the Maldon man and his children, his wife, his servants, his lodgers.

All this paper, all those notes, applied to a tiny community no larger than the secondary comprehensive school of many a modern English town of middling size. Since the male inhabitants took responsibility for their households' behaviour, it is not unreasonable to say that at any one time all this administrative and judicial activity bore down on about three hundred men, a number more easily controlled than 1,000. And to maintain good order some forty officials were appointed each year. (In fact there were more than forty but some men doubled minor offices, such as Bell Ringer, which are irrelevant here.) That is, Maldon's staffing ratio was one official to every eight responsible adult males. Even if the officers are restricted to those who were involved in the greatest part of the supervision of the community, there was still a formidable ratio of one to every nine decenners and freemen.

Among its efforts to maintain good order the Corporation attempted to control the character of immigration. The constables of each parish were instructed 'to bring in or present at every Quarter Court, to the Bailiffs, all newcomers into every parish, to the intent that they may be communed withal'. It was thus possible to administer the decenners' oath to them and to mark them down for suit of court at the next View of Frankpledge. The Court Leet also provided an occasion for flushing out vagrants and unemployed persons, so there are two distinct types of incomer represented in the presentments made by these parish constables.

There were the vagrants and unwanted paupers. A variety of pretexts, if not good reasons, could be given to justify such persons' speedy ejection. For beggars there were the statutes prescribing their punishment, varied from one act of parliament to another, and ordering them to be sent back to their 'country' or to the place in which each had last dwelled for three consecutive years. The chamberlains' accounts thus record the purchase of whipcord, hiring carts and horses to which convicted vagrants were tied, and the fees paid to the men who flogged each 'till his or her back be bloody'. In 1573 among sundry items is a note of 4d paid 'for the iron of the compass of one inch for the burning of rogues in the gristle of the right ear, according to the statute'. Some were thus punished, flogged, branded, mutilated, but the magistrates were often more restrained and the statutory orders were kinder than popular legend admits, preferring to create jobs, establish systems of poor relief and arrange resettlement rather than merely to drive wandering paupers from one place to another with lacerated backs and mutilated faces. Some of the borough magistrates supervised the work of moving on the vagrants with discrimination and perhaps with compassion. They once paid someone to carry 'a message for a maid that lay in prison, to her friends dwelling beyond Colchester' (1574); they bought food and bedding straw in 1616 for prisoners such as 'the woman that stole from Goodman Harvey and Joseph Walker' and 'the boy that walked about the streets'. Townswomen were appointed when necessary to examine any female vagrants who were suspected to be pregnant and near the time of their delivery, but not for charitable purposes: the women were promptly loaded on to a hired cart and taken away to the isolated hamlet of Runsell Green (some three miles beyond the borough boundary) lest their babies should become a charge on any of the town's parishes. Any unmarried, pregnant woman was liable to be deported and ordered to stay away, even if she was a resident, as a decision of 1592 made clear:

> 'It is ordered by the Court that Agnes Wall, who is found with child by Moses Manners, shall presently [ie. immediately] depart out of this town and not to return again to bring any charge upon the town by the child that she goeth withal, or by any other means, upon pain to have such punishment as shall be thought meet by the Bailiffs and Justices if she shall do the contrary'.

Just as bluntly the Justices gave poverty or a surplus of labour as sufficient reason for requiring an employable man to depart. John Parham, a tailor and formerly the servant of a freeman, was in 1593 reported to be 'now masterless and keepeth a shop at his own house, being a foreigner and having a wife and family in Suffolk (by his own confession) and hath continued here from them almost three years' so he was ordered 'to depart out of this town and not dwell in any place or with any person within the same ... after the Feast of St John Baptist next, upon pain of imprisonment and there to continue until he be bound with good sureties to perform this order'. A freeman was prosecuted in June 1623 'for that he hath taken into his house ... a labourer lately come into the borough, to the great damage of the poor labourers of the town there having dwelt long ...' At the same court another was fined for harbouring a weaver 'late come from Chelmsford,' a man liable to receive poor relief, but the fine was withdrawn and replaced by the threat of double the amount if the weaver had not left within the next two months. Four paupers were expelled in 1618 because they were 'like to be a charge to the parish' and one of them was prosecuted at the Quarter Sessions because he was a peddler or petty chapman,

> 'lately come into the borough and hath settled himself in the parish of St Mary's, who is a foreigner and useth to sell small wares to the damage of the freemen of this borough and is like to be a charge to the parish; therefore we desire he may have good fines imposed upon him and [be] speedily removed'.

Year by year, at each of the Quarter Sessions, the jurors presented many such demands and whilst some expulsions may have been prompted by trade recessions (and were especially numerous during the clothing trades' slump in the early 1620s), they were also part of a system which maintained a sensitive control on the employed sector of the town's population. The Corporation was able to operate the system judiciously for the maintenance of the best or most appropriate level and quality of immigration. Thus a glover, an immigrant to one of the better-quality trades in this town, was ordered either to depart within one calendar month or else to produce a testimonial to his good behaviour where he had last dwelt for three or more years; and he was also required to bring before the Bailiffs freemen who would be his pledges for his good behaviour whilst he remained in Maldon.

The magistrates' activities were not entirely negative. From time to time efforts were made to attract suitable recruits to the population, as the following letter, returned to the Town Clerk either by the unimpressed recipient, his agent or his executors indicates:

> 'After our hearty commendations.

> 'Sir, at your removal out of the Hundred of Rochford we and our neighbours (for many respects) were very desirous you would have seated yourself in

Maldon. And now, for as much as it hath pleased God this last Monday to take out of this life Master Seaman of this town, we do by these few lines signify and manifest our earnest desires again in this behalf, being well persuaded the place [Maldon] will afford much employment and with good profit and gain in your calling. And if it might please the Lord so to dispose it, we should be very glad and yourself be right welcome unto us.

'Thus leaving this motion and the sequel thereof to your wise consideration and our hearty wishes, we take our leave. Maldon, this 9th of September 1623. Your very loving friends'.

Master George Seaman had been a physician; he was buried 10 September 1623; for some time before his demise the Corporation had been fishing for this highly respected doctor and indeed this letter was written to offer Master Seaman's medical practice to that person before the funeral bake-meats had even been put in the oven.

Whether the Bailiffs succeeded in attracting their correspondent to their town is unknown. Others would have been prudent if they had negotiated their prospective settlement in the borough, for the requirement that its chief officers were to 'commune' with all newcomers, that is, to give them licence to settle there, was more than a superficial courtesy. Some of the freemen's admission memoranda are for men living elsewhere who subsequently became resident in Maldon, as with William King, a sailor born at Paglesham who was living at Heybridge in January 1581, when he became a freeman, but living in Maldon from later in that year; and as with Elias Backhouse of Chelmsford who purchased his freedom in January 1578 but only entered Maldon with his wife and three children in 1580; and William Norris of Billericay, free in 1614, resident from late 1616; and Edward Lee of Harwich, Richard Ford of Grantham, William Watson of Blackmore, who similarly came to live in Maldon two years after becoming freemen.

These, but also poorer men, were likely to come within the scope of one more borough regulation. It was the bye-law that 'no man shall take any inmate into his house without licence of the Bailiffs ..'. which included this strict definition:

'an inmate is to be taken [to mean] where a householder taketh and receiveth some other [person/persons] to dwell in the same house with him and so there be two or more families in one house and dwelling under one roof, and though their going out and in be at several doors to and from the street'.

In addition to lodgers sharing a man's house the custom therefore included the tenants of subdivisions of houses, even if the part they occupied was entirely self-contained. Breaches of the regulation were to be notified to the Justices at the Quarter Sessions and the frequency with which examples occur in the jurors' presentments indicates (apart from manifesting a certain ineffectiveness of the regulation itself) that the Corporation kept a continuous watch on people who were often regarded by contemporaries in other places as a dangerous, potentially sinful section of the population. Many newcomers must have needed cheap accomodation, at least until they had settled themselves in and their trade or craft was established, others such as labourers needed only short-term accomodation, so that the enforcement of the regulation on inmates was a means of excluding undesirable persons from the borough. Dr Hull found that in the south of Essex an influx of artisans and labourers (from the clothing district of northern Essex, he thought) created an acute problem with many old buildings being subdivided into sub-standard housing, and new cottages being built for these migrant workers. It was such a situation which the Corporation of Maldon sought to control, partly by its exercise of the laws on vagrancy, partly by excluding those whom they considered to be in excess of the locally optimum number in each occupation, partly by having all newcomers brought before an 'ad hoc' selection panel, by requiring notification of inmates by the householders and by punishing the landlords of unacceptable newcomers.

CHAPTER 3

# THE IMMIGRANTS

A LTHOUGH THE BELIEF remains deep-rooted that the pre-industrial population of England was largely immobile there was continuous movement and resettlement in Medieval, Tudor and Stuart England, with vital and continuous change consequently occurring in the social structure of the English nation. Not only seafarers, merchants and professional men travelled; entire families resettled themselves, and sometimes did so several times; the mobility applied to individuals and to groups right across the social scale but at different rates and for varying motives. The broadest description of such population movement requires simply the differentiation of two types: those who came into Maldon from other counties in the extensive and perpetual drifting of people across England, which is *long-distance migration*, and the less dramatic but often more influential process of localised resettlement which constitutes *short-distance migration*. In Maldon's case the distinction between the two groups turns out to be for most purposes quite straightforward because those known to have been born within the county of Essex mostly came from within twenty miles of the town. There was a distinctive non-contributory region beyond that, bordering the county boundary, which distinguishes these from the long-distance immigrants. That is, people coming from places more than a day's journey from Maldon, who thereby cut themselves off from regular, informal contact with many of their kinsfolk, were involved in long-distance migration. Those born locally could be in frequent and often unarranged contact with kinsfolk and long-standing acquaintances, they would be known in the area for any special skills they possessed and they grew up familiar with the difficulties and the opportunities of the area. But those who came from beyond the county were in effect interlopers, breaking into the local community — the 'country' as Elizabethans called their own part of the land — and disadvantaged until they had learned the language of its economy and its social peculiarities.

The surnames of the town's residents illustrate these migratory processes. Long-distance immigration accounts for Northern names in the decenners' lists — Plater, Williamson, Whitaker, Pearson, Capstack — and for Northern locative surnames — Cleveland, Pickering, Sedgwick, Ullathorne, Topliffe (*Topcliffe*), Adamthwaite — in the court registers. They cannot however provide any measure of the contribution each region of England made to the local population; they are not evidence of direct migration; they do not indicate its occurrence precisely. They can only faintly suggest the resettlement trend of earlier generations, and they can do that only misleadingly — as with William *Cornish* who was actually born in northern Lancashire- so here all cases of immigration are based on documentary statements of origin, birthplace or previous place of residence. Many origins are

51

derived from the memoranda of admissions of freemen, which usually state that at this or that session of the borough court 'X', born at 'Y' in the county of 'Z', requested admission to the liberties of the borough. Thus:

> 'John Ketyll, born at Rochford in the county of Essex, came into the same court held on Monday 1 February in the sixth year of the reign of King Henry VIII and gave twenty shillings as a fine to have his freedom within this borough ...'

Apprentices' indentures are another major source of information, each usually stating where the boy's father was living when the contract was made (or when he was alive), as between ...

> Richard Bromley of Maldon, glover, and Matthew Sturry, son of Alexander Sturry of *Stoake Clare* in Suffolk, husbandman (1598)

or as between ...

> Thomas Albert of Maldon, chandler and grocer, and Geoffrey Garnige, son of Jeffery Garnige of *Salforne Waldone* in Essex, joiner (1598).

Such statements must be used with reserve because Matthew Sturry was not necessarily born 'at' or 'in' Stoke-by-Clare — his father was at that time 'of' Stoke-by-Clare — and the freeman John Kettle had not just arrived from Rochford when he came into the Moot Hall on 1 February 1515, and conceivably Geoffrey Garnige junior may have been left in Maldon as an apprentice if his father had recently moved out of Maldon to work in Saffron Walden. Used with caution these statements can provide a broadly accurate picture of the trends in migration but that is all. They do not offer any explanation for it.

A traditional explanation is that some kind of misfortune impelled each migrant along the kingdom's roads. Enshrined in the story of Dick Whittington, this is part of an interesting genre of tales in which younger sons or disinherited young men — victims of wicked guardians or evicting landlords — seek new lives, self-determination and (of course) their fortunes either in The Greenwood, where there are only natural constraints, where men are as free as the animals are wild, or in The City whose pavements direct all incomers to golden opportunities. Such stories were expressions of wishful thinking, reversing the real-life situation in which Fortune patently favours the privileged and to those who have much is given, but its broadest outline was true enough: the migrants tended to be young people and mostly they were going to the towns. A true element in the legend is that migration from the country into the towns was a distinctive feature of the resettlement process. Sometimes it was for *betterment* in standards of living and status. Often it was *subsistence migration*, picking up menial work, labouring in construction jobs, getting a hiring as manservant or maidservant and often urban occupation was alternated with spells of agricultural labouring.

The rural-urban stream of migrants at Maldon can thus be sorted into four groups covering long- and short-distance subsistence and betterment migration, although in practice *betterment* has been found principally associated with short-distance movement by men who had some form of patronage helping them towards secure, permanent lives in towns, whereas *subsistence* is particularly associated with long-distance migration by poor or destitute people whose stay in any urban community was normally brief. Most were young people because only they had the stamina to survive the travelling, only they had time on their side for the building of a career. Probably the ages twelve to thirty covered the resettlement of most people because older men would be constrained by the commitments of family life.

'At seventeen years many their fortunes seek
But at fourscore it is too late a week'

says Old Adam in *As You Like It* when he prepares to follow Sir Rowland de Bois' younger, disinherited son into The Greenwood.

The improbable part of the legend is the supposition that unskilled, patronless country boys might achieve self-sufficiency and security, let alone wealth and fame, in this way. Then (as now) London attracted swarms of young men and women but there, and in the towns along the routes by which they made their way from western woodlands and northern moorlands, apprenticeships were often available only by payments of premiums (often heavy ones), the most lucrative trades might be restricted to certain classes, places were reserved for kinsfolk and the sons of particular clients. The letter to a physician (cited above, in Chapter 2) written at the death of Master Seaman the doctor is a reminder that settlement in Maldon was under regular surveillance and sometimes invited.

Only the trap of sweated labour was open for many of any town's newcomers and before concentrating on the more fortunate or better documented members of Maldon's transient population a word must be spared for the rarely recorded majority whose routine, menial, tedious labour was essential to maintain the orderly life of the community in an labour-intensive economy. Their lives were spent in *subsistence migration*. Their employment was often seasonal and led them into a lifetime of wandering over great distances. The yearly flow of labourers, domestic servants and artisans which can be seen in the decenners' catalogues of the 1570s can also be faintly detected in the lay subsidy returns of 1524 and 1525. There were seventy eight men named on the 1524 return for the borough but missing from its 1525 return; and in their places forty new names are listed at the same assessments; and whilst it is difficult to substantiate any identifications it is possible that the movement of at least six can be traced: from Maldon in 1524-5 Robert Annable moved to Langford (two miles), Robert Baker to the household of Lord Marney at Layer Marney (ten miles); to the borough in 1525 came Hugh Brakett (from Langford), Richard Hertzz from Purleigh (three miles), Andrew Purfoote from Heybridge and perhaps John Sylvester from Mayland (five miles).

Here and there information can be found about their movements and in particular a schedule of men enlisted for an army sent to fight for the Protestant cause in the Palatinate of Germany, December 1624, gives the birthplaces and, in some cases, the intermediate places where men had stayed and worked on their way to Maldon. The locations are distributed in the areas from which most of the freemen and apprentices came (see Figure 10) and the lists show that craftsmen such as shoemakers and general handymen mingled with the migrant labour force of landworkers. Enquiries by the town clerks into the movements of people suspected to be vagrants add further illustration of seasonal subsistence migration. A workman had spent part of 1624 wandering from Suffolk into central Essex, working at Witham, moving on through Chelmsford, Billericay, Rawreth and Maldon; sometimes he had found relatives who gave him shelter briefly, some nights he spent in alehouses, once he slept on a haycock; he was uncertain of the names of many places where he had stopped. Another itinerant farm workman of 1624 had made his way southward along much the same general route, threshing corn here, weeding fields there, lodging in a barn in one place, 'finding' for himself at North Fambridge and lodging there at the Ferry House, finally sleeping rough on Southminster Marsh. For most of this workforce there were better conditions, 'living-in' with their employers or occupying − as will be seen − cottages and subdivisions of houses with their young families as inmates.

## 'DUTCHMEN'

Until about 1570 the labour force was partly recruited from a distinctive group of long-distance travellers, the aliens whom the townsmen tended to call 'Dutchmen', even if they were really Flemings, Walloons or Germans, because the name applied to all who spoke a Germanic-sounding language. Thirty one taxpayers in the lay subsidies of 1524, 1525 and 1544 are identifiable as aliens in Maldon, including a Scot and a Frenchman. Neither their numbers nor their presence is exceptional for a coastal town. The lay subsidy returns show 'Dutchmen' in the East Coast towns, Bretons and Normans in towns along the south west coast. Some towns also had Irishmen, Italians and Germans among their alien settlers and Maldon cannot show any as exotic as *Johannes da Salvo a Janua* (a Genoese, no doubt) who appears on the 1524 subsidy return for Witham. As with some English wayfarers it is most probable that Maldon was but a stage in a wandering life for these aliens and by the time they reached the coastal marshlands of Essex many of them may have become virtually stateless persons. In the subsidy returns several have English or else Anglicised names and can only be identified as alien by the descriptions attached to their names or their payment of the poll tax of 8 pence specified for aliens who were below the taxable levels on goods and wages. They can rarely have had documentary proof of their origin and that had been the misfortune of a freeman tailor named Giles Morville in the mid-fifteenth century. He had claimed to be a native of Guernsey until 1457, when a rumour spread that he was really an alien (the Channel Islands counted as part of the realm of England): 'some said he was a Spaniard, some said he was a Breton' and he was unable to satisfy the Bailiffs as to his origin even though he offered to go to Guernsey and bring back proof of his nationality. He lost his freedom and had to surrender his house to the borough in satisfaction for his offence of purchasing his freedom as an Englishman. After a long absence he returned to the borough and settled for being classified as a Fleming. An annual customary rent of assize was due to the borough from his house and its appearance in the chamberlains' accounts throughout the next two centuries as paid from 'the house sometimes Giles Morville's' suggests that his offence and punishment were long remembered.

Many aliens were servants, especially in the shoemaking trade. Beer brewing (which is considered below, in Chapter 5) was another activity to which they contributed specialist skills but although the textile trades are most commonly associated with these Flemings and Dutchmen, none of them appear to have been weavers or engaged in any of the cloth finishing trades at Maldon. One ordinance of the borough entitled 'Good Orders for Aliens and all other Servants' required them to be in their masters' houses by ten o'clock in summertime, eight o'clock in the winter. Half the aliens were described as servants in the lay subsidies; all but six of them were assessed at 40 shillings or less in goods or wages, or were liable to pay the poll tax.

The borough custumal gives the impression that it discriminated against them and possibly suspected them of being liable to violent and disorderly behaviour. No Dutchman, it was ordered in 1464, 'or other alien shall bear no manner of weapon defendable ... but only a knife to cut withal his meat'. Another of the same date required each alien to swear obedience to the Bailiffs 'in all things touching the office of the said Bailiffs' and added that they were forbidden 'to complain to any other persons superior for anything touching the same office'. However, these local regulations only reflect a considerable body of statutes enacted between the thirteenth and the seventeenth centuries to protect the interests of English merchants from the competition of merchant-strangers and against the impression of hostility must be set the favourable circumstances in which some aliens lived at Maldon.

Not all of them came in as serving men and if they had the ability they were as capable of betterment as any English immigrant. Although Acts of Parliament of 1404, 1425 and 1439 ordered them to live within the households of English 'host' merchants who would oversee their bargains and were empowered to set time limits for selling their goods in the country, these laws were not well-observed. Some towns revived the laws when the foreigners seemed to be threatening their freemen's trades and a traditional dislike of Lombards, Flemings, Easterlings and the like generated occasional outbursts of violence against aliens in cities. But so far as Maldon was concerned aliens might enjoy as much freedom as any native immigrant: they could become freemen; they did not have to live with 'hosts' as the law required; they could even purchase or build houses for themselves, as did John Dutchman, whose house on Fullbridge Street (constructed between 1508 and 1536) was large enough to be capable of division into two dwellings c1550 - 1573. Fresh anti-alien legislation in the 1520s sought to restrict the number of servants and apprentices maintained by foreigners but at Maldon, within twenty five years, Richard Frank alias Dyrek was admitted a freeman of the borough (in 1543 as 'born in *Senley* in Guelderland within the dominion of the Emperor') and took three apprentices -all natives of Maldon- into his shoemaking trade in 1549.

There were, then, some aliens who were independent craftsmen and they could be men of some substance. That is implied by the ordinance requiring them to swear obedience to the Bailiffs, for it also stipulates that each shall take the oath 'for him[self] and all his servants'. John Dutchman and Richard Frank were obviously in that category and another was Adrian Johnson whose removal from Witham to Maldon in 1525 can be detected from the lay subsidy returns. In each place he is stated to have had a servant named John King (but also a 'Dutchman') and along with him from Witham came Henry Johnson alias Peter − probably a kinsman and also Dutch − and both of them were shoemakers like Richard Frank and possessed sufficient estate to make wills. Henry Johnson bequeathed 16 pence to the Guild of St Katherine in All Saints' parish, one of the town's three religious brotherhoods, so he was probably a member of the guild and may therefore be classed as an established member of the wealthier part of the local community.

At the top of the social scale there occur a Scots gentleman, Henry Twedy [Tweedie] 'who came out of the House of Dromelzane' in the 1550s according to a herald's visitation pedigree, the son of George Tweedie of Drumelzier near Peebles, and a lawyer, John Boswell, who was in the town by 1536 (when he was an executor to another lawyer's, Richard Benham's, will) and so well established by 1544 that in the lay subsidy he was assessed as an Englishman on goods valued at £30, he was a freeman and one of the two Bailiffs of the borough in 1559. Master Twedy purchased the great pastures of the Friars' Fields but he established a notable Essex family at Stock, towards the centre of the county, not in Maldon. By the death of John Boswell in 1570 (at which point his Scots nationality was rediscovered and the Crown confiscated the lands he had bought in Maldon) aliens had ceased to figure in Maldon's community. No efforts were made to accomodate them so comfortably as at Colchester, Norwich or Canterbury in Elizabeth I's reign and the choice of a Colchester shoemaker, Winken Grenerise, as principal executor by Richard Frank alias Dyrek in 1558 suggests that by then the Colchester Flemings and Dutch were leaders in the alien community of Essex. (Grenerise had, like Frank, been born in Guelderland).

The subsequent exceptions were a decenner named Mardochaeus Depeis (a Frenchman?) listed in 1578 but noted as *extra* in 1579, a physician named Doctor William Vyves, Vinas or 'Vince' who practised in the town in 1625, and Antonio Gratiano 'a Grecian' but also known as 'Master Graham' who was related to the Vernon family of Beeleigh and whose will of 1675 might be that of any contemporary English Protestant gentleman. And 'Master Doresley' must not be omitted. Really he was Dr Isaac Dorislaus of Leyden, a Doctor of Civil Law who had come to England by invitation in 1627 to lecture in Cambridge University on Roman History. He had been forced into a retirement because persons at Court suspected his lectures to be advocating Republican theories on sovereignty and because he had defended his countrymen's rebellion against the Spanish Crown. William Holman, writing about 1720, said that Dorislaus had married a Maldon woman but the event is not recorded in the parish registers. However, he did come to live in the town, a memorial stone 'by the north door of the belfry' of All Saints to his infant son John (1627-31) was recorded by Holman in his notes, and the parish clerk recorded the baptism and burial as of Master Doresley's son. In his time in Maldon Dr Dorislaus acted as clerk for the Admiralty Court of the borough, its proceedings being in Civil Law on which he was the greatest authority the Bailiffs can ever have had living with them. In 1648 he was appointed by the Parliament to be a judge in the High Court of Admiralty and also to act for the prosecution in the trial of Charles I. That led to his assassination in The Hague during 1649 by a royalist exile.

## LONG-DISTANCE MIGRATION

Familiarity with the fact that long-distance migration was not abnormal never stales the discovery of men coming to Maldon from the furthest parts of the kingdom. The sheer scale of their intervening journeys and the comparative isolation of this little borough − it was not on anyone's direct route − point up the question of motive. It is not enough to bundle them into one or other of the four groups suggested above, such as long-distance subsistence migration, because they describe modes of existence and are not explanations of the arrival in Maldon.

In November 1590 two quite different long-distance immigrants were present in the Moot Hall: one was a woman who believed herself to be Joan Anderson, the wife of a shoemaker called William Anderson, and she said that she had originally dwelt at Totnes in Devonshire; the other was one of the Aldermen of the Corporation, Thomas Walker, who had recently won a lawsuit at York Assizes concerning the possession of land in Holden near Bolton-by-Bowland, lately in his father's possession. Joan gave her account of how she came to be living in Maldon, of how she had married an itinerant shoemaker when he was in Totnes, who had 'tarried little with her after they were married but came and went from time to time without long stay', and how she had heard that he had died in Somerset, whereupon another travelling shoemaker, William Anderson, had 'fallen into familiarity with her', taken her after three years to Truro and there married her. They had two children there, both of whom had died; then they had come from Truro to Maldon and William Anderson and herself regularly travelled to Chelmsford market where her first, supposedly deceased husband appeared and confronted them.

Bigamous intention may often have been suspected by the Bailiffs and their clerks whenever they pondered the circumstances bringing newcomers to their borough. In 1622 they sent letters to the Justices of the Peace at Framlingham in Suffolk 'for certain [definite] information and enquiry of the truth concerning an accusation against Henry Marshall, glover, upon his apprehension for suspicion of felony, the said Henry having then a wife in Maldon and charged ... to have another wife then living about the said town of *Franningham*'. The evidence offered by William Anderson about his marriage with Joan Carpenter, in which he alleged that their bigamy had been unintentional, indicates how wide an area many itinerant workmen covered and that they could be reasonably familiar with the country in Somerset, Cornwall, Devon, London and Essex. He and Joan had come thus far from the West Country on discovering that the errant George Carpenter was not dead: whilst at Truro they had heard that he was alive somewhere in Somerset. William Anderson had thereupon sent Joan 'directly' to Essex ('to come into this country to dwell') whilst he tried to locate her first husband in Somerset and in London. At Chelmsford 'a stranger (unknown unto him) came unto the standing of the said William in the market ... and said he was cousin unto the said Joan, whom after [wards] the said Joan affirmed to be the said George Carpenter'. The Justices at Maldon were not too impressed by this tale, so Anderson was ordered to produce a certificate that he and Joan had been lawfully married at Truro fourteen years before. What may be of more interest now is that such people might be expected to travel some three hundred miles for a marriage certificate.

A second examination in the Moot Hall in November 1590 reveals to us another occupational migrant, a servant who had bought a dun gelding from a stranger

Figure 10 Long-distance migration, 1500 – 1688

(and was therefore a well paid servant who expected to have some personal travelling to do) and whose statement to the magistrates was that as he was returning to his master's shop one afternoon he was told that a stranger had been asking for him. He found the stranger in the New Inn, a man on whom he had never set eye before, who 'told this examinate that he dwelt at Maidstone in Kent, where this examinate had lately dwelt and had there his wife abiding ...'

Alderman Thomas Walker, one of the Justices of the Peace who heard the statements of Joan and William Anderson and of this servant (William Luck), was probably descended from a family which had been living since the early fourteenth century at Bolton-by-Bowland on the border of Yorkshire and Lancashire; he had arrived in Maldon between April 1579 and September 1580, according to the decenners' lists; he was farmer of an estate called Maldon Hall, the demesne land of the Manor of Little Maldon; he was styled Gentleman and he had been a J.P. and a Bailiff of the borough before 1590; he lived at Maldon for fourteen years and in 1594 went to live outside the borough. But was his a case of betterment migration? The motive remains hidden, just as for his senior colleague Alderman William Vernon whose career is well documented in outline but without any clue as to why he came to Maldon. Master Vernon's coat of arms displayed him as a close kinsman of the Vernons of Haddon Hall in Derbyshire, the heralds' visitation of Essex rather sketchily indicated his descent from 'Peverel of the Peak' and his enfranchisement in 1563 stated that he was a gentleman and had been born at Nottingham. But why acquire lands in Maldon, live in Maldon for forty seven years with never a sign of any connection with any Nottinghamshire or Derbyshire family or enterprise?

Mystery with a suspicion of sharp practice surrounds the arrival of Thomas Furnes in or just before 1572. Much of his story comes from information concerning alleged wool smuggling which was passed to Sir Francis Walsingham c1582: a dubious source to supplement the local information that this Thomas Furnes was born at Mirfield (*Morefeild in comitatu Eboracensis*) which is near Huddersfield. Before settling at Maldon he had been a merchant in London, according to the informer, where he had been acquainted with merchant-strangers who, it is implied, used him as their agent for smuggling wool to the Low Countries. That would have been in the 1560s. He moved directly from London to Maldon, which must have been between April 1571 and April 1572 (since he is not listed as a decenner at the first date) and he became a freeman immediately − and by outright purchase − with his entry fine recorded in the chamberlains' account roll for 1572 as paid by the 'Innkeeper at the Blue Boar'. From 1576 to 1585 he was a head burgess; he then became an alderman; he was three times a Bailiff of the borough. One of his brother aldermen and a Bailiff, Thomas Clark − a 'native' Maldon clothier − was accused with him of running the smuggling racket.

If the informer had his facts right Furnes' arrival in Maldon may have been subsidised by a group of foreign merchants who had formed a smuggling ring. At London he had been particularly associated with a merchant-stranger named by the informer as Oliver Maenere (or Maynere) and that person also appears in the Maldon Court of Record of 1564 in transactions of £40, £80 and £100 with three London clothiers. When Furnes came to Maldon seven years later he was most probably only the tenant of the Blue Boar because the landcheap accounts which constitute a record of all purchases of land and houses in the borough (and which are described below, in Chapter 4) do not include any receipt from him for its purchase. It was, however, the principal inn of the market place whither 'from London resorted and yet resorteth many merchant-strangers' and Furnes appears to have prospered immediately. He was styled Merchant in the indentures of his two apprentices of 1576 and 1577; he put a manager into the inn and set himself up 'in a great house in the town'; he traded as a wool factor in Lincolnshire and Northamptonshire; he was also a vintner 'trading to a great part of Essex'. It was claimed that he also introduced the New Drapery, the weaving of bays and says, to Maldon, although the informer considered that to be merely a front operation ('a colour to convey wool out of the realm') but there is no local reference to this manufacture in the town earlier than 1604, so that part of Furnes' dossier in Sir Francis Walsingham's files may be ignored.

It is not being suggested here that bigamy, disinheritance or smuggling were the chief causes of long-distance migration to the borough. A much more reasonable explanation is that many people moved south-eastwards through the difficulties of life in their native areas, as from wild Redesdale in the Cheviots, from Mirfield, Bolton-by-Bowland and nearby Colne, from Askrigg and Dent in the Pennine dales, which were the birth places of seven Maldon freemen during the sixteenth century. *Contest mobility*, the search for betterment by men born in areas of difficult farming or where there was stiff competition for occupation of the land, might be the best classification of the eventual resettlement at Maldon of Thomas Furnes from Calderdale, of Henry Capstack (free 1553) and John Burton (free 1592) from Dentdale, of John Donne from Redesdale (free 1541). Dr Joan Thirsk has shown that Dentdale was subject to a system of partible inheritance and, in the sixteenth century, to a steadily increasing population, so that either smallholdings had to be subdivided into steadily decreasing acreages or the surplus population had to emigrate. Apprentices from Dent have been noted in Norwich and Great Yarmouth by Dr J.H.C. Patten. Calderdale in the gritstone moorlands of south-western Yorkshire, deep in the Pennine chain, Wensleydale with its scattered farmsteads and, like its neighbour Dentdale, subject mostly to the custom of partible inheritance, were also areas where conditions might well be supposed to have encouraged emigration. Population pressure in Dentdale also tended to encourage a diversification of occupations rather than simply to precipitate large-scale resettlement. In particular stocking-knitting and other clothing manufacture developed among the inhabitants of Dent and its neighbouring hamlets, as it did in Wensleydale where stocking-knitting became a standard secondary occupation. 'Young and old, male and female ...shepherds attending their flocks, men driving cattle, women going to market, are all thus industriously and doubly employed' commented George Walker in his *Costumes of Yorkshire* of 1814, describing an economy that was some three hundred years old. What remains in question, then, is the extent to which such diversification was a brake on the rate of emigration in such areas of difficulty, or to what extent those who came to Maldon from such areas were on the edge of a south-eastward moving tide of disadvantaged men, boys, women, all seeking betterment in the fatter lands nearer to London.

Henry Capstack and John Burton, both from Dent, and John Adamthwaite whose Wensleydale name and origin is confirmed by his being uncle of an apprentice from Askrigg, were tailors and drapers, as also originally was Thomas Furnes. Had they indeed chosen to abandon their shares in the family landholdings (which Alderman Walker clearly had not!), preferring to develop their secondary skills elsewhere? If so, what guided them so far from their native 'countries'? A number of Sedbergh and Dent men found their way to East Anglian towns, into the clothing trade there. Possibly they originally intended to take their skills back to their homelands but there is no means of tracing them back to Dentdale, nor were the worsted manufacturing processes like those of the northern weavers.

It may seem that explanations for long-distance immigration must usually remain no more than generalisations and highly speculative: without more informative biographical sources little better can be offered than classification by broad types of migration and references to background conditions. But *patronage* has to be considered, the nerve system of sixteenth and seventeenth century society which permeated every level and activity either as 'good lordship' or sponsorship, or by way of exhibitions for scholars and preferments for clergy. It will not be forgotten that settlement in Maldon depended on the goodwill of its Bailiffs, who might even canvass for appropriate settlers. The men considered here as coming from areas of special difficulty became freemen of Maldon, so they were at the outset of their settlement in the borough sufficiently wealthy to set up in trade on their own and to pay either in one lump sum or in a few installments the sizeable sum of thirty shillings for their freedom; they had become men of some substance, trained and self-supporting, by the time they reached Maldon. Either they had become 'known men' in the area, whose skills the leading townsmen wished to secure for their borough, or they were acquainted with others from their native areas who had already settled in Maldon and could act as their pledges when they applied to the Bailiffs for permission to settle. Thus in 1571, eleven years after the enfranchisement of William Cornish, born at Garstang in the Fylde near

Lancaster, his brother James — also born at Garstang — became a freeman; and on the same occasion so did a cooper who was born at Lancaster.

Most of the long-distance settlers in Maldon must have been vouched for and there are tantalizing juxtapositions of localities and trades which suggest that a humble form of patronage maintained the flow of acceptable settlers from distant parts of the kingdom. A clothier of Barking became a resident freeman in 1576 and four years later a weaver of Barking was also admitted to the freedom of this borough. In 1595 a glover took two apprentices (of different families) from Haverhill and another from Great Wratting, which is close to Haverhill on the Essex-Suffolk border; and although there is no explicit relationship stated either between the boys or between them and their master, who was a native of Maldon, their birthplaces near the high chalk ridges of north Essex, south western Suffolk, appear to have had a traditional association with Maldon and it is likely that these boys' apprenticeships was the result of negotiation and acquaintance rather than accidental. The son of a Northallerton yeoman was apprenticed to John Morris in 1597, and Morris was himself a native of that North Riding town. It is also likely that he was involved in the apprenticing of an orphaned Northallerton boy to a Maldon blacksmith in 1593, for John Morris' will shows that he had maintained sufficient connection with his birthplace to bequeath money to the children of an acquaintance there. Another Yorkshire boy (from *Kirby* — the town clerk failed to give a more precise location) was apprenticed in 1592 with the consent of Edward Pyke of Maldon, whom the indenture termed *amicus certissimus* of the boy.

The possibility that inhabitants of an isolated Essex town can have continued to be in touch with distant friends and relations is hinted at by legacies such as forty shillings bequeathed by Agnes Ryeners in 1542 to her sister Joan Angel 'dwelling in St Albans, so that she will come for it herself or else I will she shall not have it' but most strikingly by a travel certificate issued 27 June 1636 by the Bailiffs of Maldon to George Hunt and his wife Sarah, inhabitants of the City of York, who

> 'came to the said town of Maldon upon the 11th of this instant June unto the house of Joseph Hills one of the Aldermen of this borough and brother to the said Sarah and George, with whom they have since their coming hither continued ... neither have they since their coming been near the City of London nor any other infected places ... and now being desirous to return to the said City of York have for their more safety in their travel thither desired testimonial [that Maldon and the County of Essex was not infected]'.

Evidently inland travel by road was well developed by the 1630s, as its recent historians have been emphasising. One could take a month's holiday and visit relatives two hundred miles away as a matter of course.

63

# MIGRATION IN THE LOCAL COMMUNITY

What is writ large by long-distance migration about population movement is repeated in detail for the great majority of its in-comers and emigrants whose lives were chiefly spent within the county and within twenty miles of this town. 49 per cent of its freemen (in the periods 1515-51, 1556-81, 1606-41) were born in Essex; 80 per cent of the known apprentices there from 1566 to 1660 were born either in the borough or within twenty miles and for 74 per cent their birthplaces were within ten miles of the market cross. (100 per cent is 510 apprentices.) There were variations in the frequency with which various classes of people moved from one place to another, and variations in the distances travelled: gentry moved infrequently compared to other classes, although they visited with greater frequency; labouring men and servants moved far more regularly and tended to travel greater distances than craftsmen in search of congenial employment. Apart from the common sense reasons for these differences the resettlement patterns of short-distance mobility for each class were the result of different motives − the search for better opportunities, the acquisition of a skill or trade, the inheritance of land or a house, for example − so it is necessary to investigate the characteristics of the area within which the town's population was predominantly recruited and into which its emigrants departed.

In addition to the data provided by freemen's admissions and apprentices' indentures, pleas in the borough's Court of Record concerning debts and often involving outsiders (both as plaintiffs and defendants) indicate the area within which Maldon had its strongest influence. These pleas (whose principal implications are discussed in Chapter 5) were mostly collusive actions which were withdrawn by the creditor (the plaintiff) on payment of a small fee to the court as soon as the debt was settled. Most were in effect the means by which creditors could ensure deferred payments: any plea could be transferred from one court session to the next until the debt was paid; or if a customer defaulted he could be prosecuted. Non-residents could enter pleas in the borough court by finding freemen to act as sureties, so the thousands of cases recorded between 1400 and 1630 (in patches depending on the survival of the records) include the names of many outsiders who used the borough commercially and were sufficiently well known to be able to find local sureties. For present purposes a distribution map of the outsiders who were litigants is useful as a moderator of the impression of the 'Maldon area' given by the location of the apprentices' and freemen's birthplaces. To these three sources − freemen's and apprentices' origins and the locations of non-resident litigants at Maldon − one can add the known places in which Maldon residents possessed freehold or leasehold property.

The maps drawn from these sources (see Figures 11, 12 and 13) show considerable similarity in the scatter of places at different times. So it is tempting to draw a general boundary and declare it to have been the limits of a 'Maldon area' for at least the period 1550 - 1630; but it must remain ill-defined beyond indicating that it reached only some six to ten miles northward, some ten miles westward to Chelmsford, some twenty miles south east toward the maze of islands along the mouth of the Thames; that it covered two Hundreds of the County entirely (Dengie and Thurstable) and much of three others (Witham, Chelmsford and Rochford); and that it overlapped partly with the market areas of Chelmsford, Braintree and Colchester, and contained entirely within its bounds the market areas of Burnham and Rayleigh.

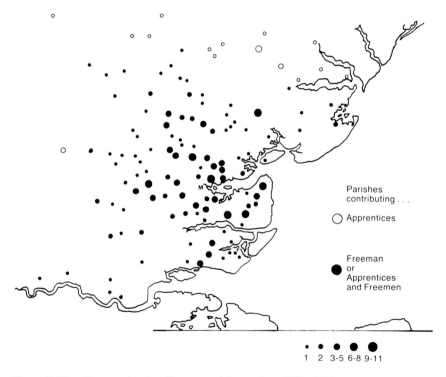

Parishes
contributing . . .

○ Apprentices

● Freeman
or
Apprentices
and Freemen

• • ● ● ●
1  2  3-5 6-8 9-11

*Figure 11 Short-distance migration: Freemen and Apprentices, 1500 – 1688*

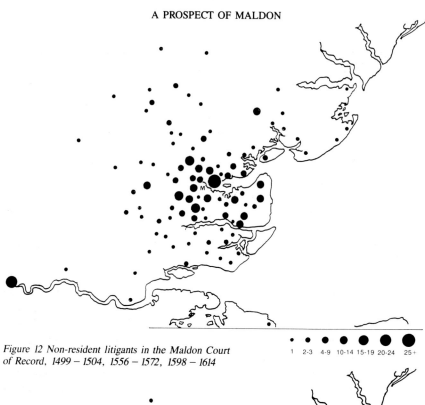

Figure 12 Non-resident litigants in the Maldon Court
of Record, 1499 – 1504, 1556 – 1572, 1598 – 1614

1    2-3   4-9   10-14  15-19  20-24  25+

Figure 13 Non-resident property holders in Maldon, 1530 – 1688

1-2  3-5  6-8  9-11  12+

66

One may note how the catchment areas for freemen and apprentices compare with the locations of non-residents who are known to have held property in Maldon. Their correlation goes along with the clientage and the kinships which brought new men and new families into the town; and it was into this area that many of the inhabitants moved when they left the town. Here is a reminder that towns and their countryside were inter-dependent.

The market area was part of a wood-pasture region, a landscape of marsh and low clayland rising to heathy and wooded hills. It had a lower density of population than the rest of Essex − probably no more than fifty persons per square mile in the late seventeenth century, rarely so many as sixty, sometimes less than forty − and much of it was inhospitable, dictating regular resettlement for its inhabitants. The shallow tidal waterways which crept into it were bordered with wide tracts of saltmarsh behind which stretched a heavy clay which was practically uncultivable until the twentieth century, 'a tough, numb, dumb and impervious soil' declared an agricultural commissioner in 1898, which then necessitated three horses to drag one of the ploughs specifically designed to cope with it, which lay waterlogged and stiff in wet weather, which baked into hard clods 'that would yield to no known instrument of husbandry' in the summer heat. On such land the water supplies were so meagre that the inhabitants had to drink surface water and as a result goitre and ague were common afflictions. Settlements on such land were predominantly dispersed as hamlets or scattered farmsteads. Its sheer unhealthiness provoked resettlement. Maldon, perched on its windswept hill amid this wilderness of reed beds, woodlands, heaths and marshes, offered springs of clean abundant water, a social life instead of isolation, and physicians. Inland the clay is capped with gravel yet although water supplies were easily obtained there and arable farming was possible in clearings on the light gravelly soil, the greater part remained empty, a vast common of woods and bracken for the use of all the townships and scattered hamlets between the Thames and the Colne. And somewhere along those heaths ran the indeterminate boundary of this Maldon area.

The saying 'Essex stiles, Kentish miles, Norfolk wiles many men beguiles' was included by John Ray, the great naturalist of seventeenth century England and an Essex man, in his collection of proverbs. He commented that 'for stiles Essex may well vie with any county in England, it being wholly divided into small closes and not one common field that I know of in the whole county'. There was some open field cultivation in north western and parts of south western Essex, and there was much common heathland but he was right to stress the predominantly 'several', enclosed cultivation and husbandry of the countryside. Around his home at Black Notley and throughout the Maldon area, on whose edge he lived for much of his life, peasant homesteads were scattered along the verge of the woodlands, dotted singly around the marshes, not tightly clustered amid sprawling common fields

67

and common pastures as they were in 'champion' country. This was wood pasture land with freehold enclosures individually worked, often smallholdings or leasehold farms and dairies which had been won from the oak, beech and bracken of the old Forest of Essex. There were manors and they were surprisingly energetic in their maintenance of their leet courts but communal regulations did not restrain the economy of the region: it was a region of independent action and self-help. If the dalesmen who made their way to Maldon were perceptive they would have noticed not only the complete difference between their new surroundings and their native fells but also the great similarity in the occupational structure imposed by the Essex land on its inhabitants. Whilst they were often described conventionally as yeomen or husbandmen the inhabitants of the Maldon area were simultaneously metalworkers and leatherworkers, weavers and fullers, butchers, joiners, wheelwrights, limeburners and salt refiners, sea wallers and brickmakers.

The extensive commons and nominal manorial jurisdictions of similarly sparsely populated areas, in other parts of England, sometimes experienced considerable influxes of settlers but not here, for the land could barely support the population it had and much of that which was suitable for settlement was already parcelled out as grazing land for cattle, as 'wicks' or dairies for sheep. The conditions may have stimulated or even dictated much of the short-distance migration which was so substantial a feature of the population of Maldon, first because of the unhealthiness which drove those who could afford to do so out of the countryside to the prophylactics of the town, secondly because agriculture and fishery could not absorb all the available labour force but the local towns could provide training and experience in the crafts which formed the secondary or alternative occupations of countrymen. As with the long-distance migration of the dalesmen, much of this short-distance movement may have been short-term in intention. Indeed, there were some who might almost be described as transhumant in their way of life. In the pleas before the borough court between 1597 and 1630 there appear men who are stated to have had dual residences, one in Maldon the other in a nearby rural parish or in a neighbouring town, such as Richard Skarlett, a yeoman of Maldon and of Little Totham (1615), Edward Dowsett a husbandman of Maldon and of Great Totham (1624) and John Motte, tanner, of Witham and Tolleshunt Darcy (1597).

Two of the definitions of a Maldon area in the period 1500 - 1700 are thus (1) that it comprised those parishes which shared all the commercial facilities of the markets at Maldon, Chelmsford, Witham, Burnham and Rayleigh; and (2) that it was a thinly populated wood-pasture district where the diversification of occupations and the attractiveness of an alternative urban life promoted considerable population mobility.

The third possible definition springs from the importance of river and coastal transportation: that the Maldon area comprised all those markets and parishes whose commerce and transport lay within the jurisdiction or surveillance of the Port of Maldon. This is easier to accept when the extent of the Port is known. The borough gave its name to an entire *Creek* (division) of the Staple of Ipswich for the collection of customs and it covered a vast area. It reached from Tollesbury on the north bank of the Blackwater Estuary southward to Thurrock on the Thames. Between those limits it wound up and down a maze of waterways, sands and tidal rivers in which the Hythe of Maldon was but one of many lading places. In eastern Essex these rivers and coastal waters provided the usual and preferred means of transport. Road haulage was hampered by the clay land which was as poor a road base as it was unsuitable for farming, waterlogged and hard rutted by turns, and the gravel mantle of the low hills was too loose and shelving a surface for heavily laden waggons to cross easily. In Dengie Hundred the road system remained very primitive until the early twentieth century, with roads impassable in ordinary wet weather. But the tidal creeks into which the south eastern shore of Essex has crumbled and subsided reach deep inland to provide access from the sea to many parishes well behind the coastline.

Instead of being concentrated on the borough of Maldon the economic activity of the area was dispersed for convenience of transport and the ever-increasing demand for supplies by the city of London combined with this dispersal to affect local migration. A farm or a single crop, a dairy, a stand of timber, or a ship: any of these was a sound investment which required little labour from the investor. A single shepherd, the contracted labour of a sawyer, a sailor and his boy competent to handle a hoy would serve the practical side of the business for a townsman who intended to cash in on the provisioning of the capital. Thus Alderman William Brett held a lease of Shopland Parsonage near the Thames (and close to wharves at Barling and Leigh) in 1588. Alderman Breeder had dairy farms and cattle pastures and woodland along the south bank of the Blackwater in 1609, with access to the river at Maldon, Lawling Creek, Stansgate and Bradwell. In 1563 Alderman William Poulter had investments in the shipping of Leigh (his birthplace) on the Thames − £6 stock in the trade of William Fowle, master of *The Dragon*; £10 in the hands of William Smith and a two-part share in *The Mary Grace* − and there was his own ship under construction 'begun and lying in frame at Maldon Hythe according to the covenants devised and made between Robert Guy, shipwright, and me'. This man was an executor in 1545 (when he was 'William Poulter of Leigh, mariner') of the will of William Raven, late a yeoman of Maldon, who had a *monger* and a *crayer* at the Hythe called respectively *The Dorothy* and *The William*, and two other ships at Leigh. Within two or three generations resettlements within the Maldon area could occur when either the inheritors of a townsman's investments in land moved out of the borough to become farmers in earnest, or when the owners of ships chose to move their anchorage to suit the needs of their trade. Between 1545 and 1554 William Poulter moved his base of operations from Leigh to Maldon, where he purchased land and houses and where, in 1554 he became one of the founding members of the Corporation. But he retained his property and commercial interests at Leigh and although his three sons continued his association with the borough they eventually returned to his birthplace. Richard Poulter of Leigh, the second son, became 'one of the principal masters of her Majesty's Navy Royal' according to the indenture made between him and the son of Alderman Thomas Furnes at Maldon in 1596.

Betterment appears to have been the governing motive for many of this area's inhabitants. To come to live in Maldon meant learning a craft or a trade; or it meant a chance of sharing in the commerce of its market place and its Hythe; or, for those growing old, it promised a more comfortable retirement. Did people 'retire' in those centuries? Beeleigh Abbey had been the last home for at least one 'corrodian' just before its dissolution. In 1557 John Burgess desired burial in All Saints' churchyard: he had stock pastured on the grasslands of Abbess Hall (Great Wigborough parish, on the north shore of the Blackwater) and arable on the gravel slopes of Great Braxted, which he shared with his brother according to his will; and late in life he had come to live in Maldon with another brother to whom he bequeathed 'my great cauldron that I brought with me'. In 1574 a Heybridge husbandman sued a gentleman (William Hayes) for not paying for meals (to the value of £7 - 10s - 0d) provided for him, his wife and another man at the husbandman's house, where they appear to have had lodgings. And thereafter Maldon received elderly people such as widows living off annuities, and husbandmen or gentry who retired from active farming to enjoy the comforts and godliness of urban life in their last years. Such a person was William Rochell, described as a yeoman and a native of Mountnessing, who became a freeman of Maldon in 1594 and immediately a member of the Corporation. His income was derived, it seems, from his copyhold lands in Wickham Bishops and the leases of Asheldham Hall, Barn Wick and 'the lease and farm of Shrill' in the Dengie Hundred. Inheritance, investment of the profits of trade in Maldon, and marriage also promoted emigration from the town. Many of the townsmen's wills refer to estates which they had purchased or on which they held unexpired leases and to which their children or nephews departed. Christopher Welles, the son of a prosperous Maldon glover, acquired for himself lands at Messing and went to live there whilst keeping on his grazing lands in the borough. Others moved in order to further their trade in more advantageous places, as did the Poulter family for their merchant shipping interests.

70

# GENTRY

So far it has been the settlement of people who worked for a living which has been considered. To end the catalogue we ought to consider the gentry who could 'live idly and without manual labour' so long as they were prepared to 'bear the port, charge and countenance of a Gentleman' according to the definition given by Sir John Dodderidge early in the seventeenth century. Their residence involved little paperwork for the town clerks and so their numbers as residents of the borough are obscure. By the late sixteenth century 'he is a gentleman who is so commonly taken and reputed' and it is difficult to identify true gentry among the town's inhabitants since Maldon craftsmen could — and did — attain that title by becoming aldermen of the Corporation and incomers of private means but not necessarily members of the county gentry could be accorded the rank by general consent in the town. At least thirty can be identified by chance references (without counting aldermen): for example, Thomas Ball appears only as a name (with 'Gent.' attached) on the decenners' lists of 1569 to 1578; a grant of arms in 1603 is the sole evidence that one George Harvey was a gentleman and 'of the town of Maldon'; an otherwise locally obscure county Justice, Sir Edward Butcher, barely mentioned in the Quarter Sessions rolls, was said to be 'inhabiting next to the parish church of All Saints' in 1624; William Twedy was listed as a decenner in 1577 (with 'Esquire' attached), as *extra* in 1579 and as a foreigner in December 1580. Wills provide evidence that others, such as John Tanner, gentleman, a lawyer with chambers in London, and John Wright, esquire, lived in the town.

By the later seventeenth century, it has been said, a class of 'pseudo-gentry' had become prominent in towns but Professor Everitt's classifications of these gentlefolk also correspond well with those who appear at Maldon from the later sixteenth century. There were younger sons of armigerous and substantially landed country gentlemen, such as Alderman William Wiseman who was brother of Sir Robert Wiseman of Rivenhall, brother-in-law of Sir Robert Brett, son-in-law to Edmund Huddleston of Cambridgeshire. Others were clergy — Masters of Arts and thus gentry by the definition of the heralds — and there were lawyers and perhaps army officers like George Harvey, 'captain in the armies now raising ... for Ireland'. Country landowners — undoubtedly of gentle birth even though some had barely cleared the lower rank of the yeomanry — also made themselves homes in Maldon and of them Master Thomas Cammock still stares out in effigy across All Saints' church from the monument erected to his memory by his children. It shows him with his two successive wives, their twenty two children, his achievement of arms and escutcheons on which his arms are 'impaled' with those of his two distinguished fathers-in-law John Wyrley of Dodford, Northamptonshire, and Sir Robert Rich, Lord Rich of Leez Priory and Rochford Hall. It is these marriages and the fame of Thomas Cammock which occupy almost all his proud father's epitaph in the parish church at Layer Marney.

71

Thomas Cammock was a member of Lord Rich's household and his marriage with Frances, Lord Rich's only daughter, became a story that lasted in Essex memory for over a hundred years until William Holman the antiquary heard it from a man of Rayne near Braintree: that as the Rich household was moving (as it often did) across country to Rochford from Leez, on the south side of the River Crouch at Fambridge Thomas Cammock galloped off with Frances, they swam the river with their horses as the tide flowed in and made off for his home at Maldon and married immediately whilst Frances' brother and guardian, baulked of pursuing them across the river and unable to use the ferry, declared that if she was prepared to risk her life with him, he could have her. Nobody who was attached to the greatest household in a county, as he was to the Rich family, could hope to escape the indignant vengeance which would have been visited on an elopement and it was probably an elaborate, high-spirited charade which he never lived to regret. He was all that the inhabitants of Maldon could have asked for in a resident gentleman. He kept a good household, he was a benefactor of the borough by his gift of land and a piped water supply from the Crom Well on his pastureland to a conduit on St Helen's Lane, pious and with a touch of swagger and romance about him.

When Sir John Bramston of Skreens Park, Roxwell, wrote his autobiograhy in the late seventeenth century he began by mentioning how his father was born in Maldon: Roger Bramston of Boreham and his wife visited the town in 1577 where her sister was married to John Sherman 'and living there at the time'. Mrs Bramston was delivered of a baby during the visit and the child was baptised John in St Mary's church with Gabriel Croft, esquire, Henry Mildmay, esquire, and Mistress Mary Harris of the Friars Mansion as godparents. Casually, because to him it was unexceptional, Sir John Bramston thus referred to two families of gentlefolk being in the town 'at the time' on extended visits and to the ease with which a distinguished christening party could be assembled without delay: a former M.P. for the borough, the brother of the Chancellor of the Exchequer and the widow of another former M.P. for the borough. The baby grew up to become, in 1635, Lord Chief Justice of England.

The autobiography also refers with equal casualness to the boy's education: 'so soon as he was capable he was put to school in the free school at Maldon, from whence he removed to Jesus College in Cambridge ...' Sir John saw nothing exceptional in the education of a gentleman's son in the grammar school of Maldon and indeed the boy's cousin, John Sherman, was also taught in Maldon (1563-67) before going on to Gonville and Caius College. Also in 1567 another boy taught in the town grammar school (Robert Sharpe) was entered at Christ's College and the matriculation and college registers at Cambridge provide names of at least twenty six pupils between 1567 and 1639 who were mostly the sons of gentlemen or aldermen. In the 1630s other boys were taught privately in Maldon by

72

*Pl.2. Thomas Cammock and all his family (this monument was erected in 1602)*

Benjamin Leech, a freeman and the vicar of St Lawrence Steeple — especially members of the Harris family of Creeksea — but as in occupations so in education there was a migratory tendency. There were in the early seventeenth century fourteen grammar schools dispersed about the Maldon market area and nearby, especially those of Colchester, Chelmsford and Brentwood. John Hastler, born in Maldon, was sent to Romford School; Alderman Thomas Plume had his son Thomas educated at Chelmsford Grammar School; William Blunt was taught first in Maldon and then at Brentwood; Christopher Harris of Margaretting and Maldon sent his son to school in Colchester, as did Aaron Maldon of Ramsden Belhouse (a descendant of the Maldons of Bradwell-on-Sea). In all of these places Maldon men or these country gentry were likely to have kinsfolk or acquaintances to whom they could entrust oversight of their sons' upbringing. Conversely the school at Maldon, when it was in the mastership of John Danes, 1612-39, had pupils sent to it from Chelmsford, Prittlewell and Hawkwell in Essex and another from Hampshire. The scholastic life of John Crackenthorpe illustrates the existence within the area of wandering scholars besides migrant families and people with occupations in two places at once. The son of Dr Crackenthorpe, rector of Black Notley near Braintree, he was educated first in his father's rectory, then at Maldon under John Danes, then at Cressing (a parish neighbouring Black Notley) and finally at Braintree before going to Christ's College when he was eighteen.

One of Maldon's services to the gentry was thus the provision of a humanist and Protestant education suitable for the scions of a class proud, even arrogant in its English gentility. Henry and William Dawes, sons of a Maldon freeman, were both exceptionally well educated in the years 1500-1520 — Henry was appointed tutor to Gregory Cromwell, son of Henry VIII's great minister, and was himself possessed of a good humanist education. Where they were taught is not known but by the 1560s it is clear that the town grammar school (of which very little is certain before 1609) was capable of providing the type of education gentlemen wished their sons to have.

One explanation for the choice of Maldon as a residence by gentlefolk in these two centuries can be set aside immediately. They did not come in order to participate in the corporate government established in 1554. A few were offered and did accept aldermen's places, one or two of the borough's Recorders and Counsellors-at-Law happened to be occasionally resident, but most gentlemen neglected even to become freemen — this observation includes the Harris family of The Friars' Mansion in the town, although they were enrolled as freeburgesses at their elections to parliament — and so they did not even seek voting rights for parliamentary elections until after 1660.

More fitting, if less specific, is the explanation that Maldon was a social centre

*Pl.3. Exercises and rules for Latin verse and prose composition, a textbook by John Danes for his pupils in Maldon Grammar School. This copy was presented by him to his friend Alderman Plume.*

almost in the sense of an early spa. It offered dry, warm housing, congenial company and a dignified, well-regulated environment for gentlefolk. It also provided them with professional and skilled services from dress-making to medicine and spiritual comforts. In the latter part of the sixteenth century and in the 1600s the borough counted among its occupations cooks, musicians, seamstresses and merchant tailors, vintners, gunsmiths. There were painters who specialised in oil colour work and stained or painted glass. In 1598 Abraham Johnson was making clocks in the town. Numerous medical practitioners − pharmacists, physicians, barber-surgeons − appear in the borough records as haphazardly as their patrons, the gentry. When Moundeford Bramston's health deteriorated c1678 (he was the Chancellor of the diocese of Winchester) he 'would take no advice of any physician ...' other than '... a surgeon of Maldon'.

There were, moreover, attractions for the young and active men of means. The Earls of Sussex maintained a hunting park at Woodham Walter, the Mildmays had another at Danbury, the Harrises at Creeksea; there was fox-hunting and rabbit catching over the heathlands and along the marshes. Freshwater and sea fishing were amply provided and the marshlands provided the splendid, wet, muddy, exhilarating sport of wild fowling on which Daniel Defoe commented in his *Tour of Essex* that it was 'so well known by our London Men of Pleasure for the infinite number of wild fowl ... and they go from London on purpose for the pleasure of shooting'. Fletchers continued their trade in Maldon throughout the sixteenth century, because bows and arrows remained hunting weapons after they had ceased to be used in warfare.

CHAPTER 4

# HOUSING A TRANSIENT POPULATION

IT IS TIME to put a roof over these immigrants' heads. This is no mere curiosity of local history: plainly it was a very practical concern for all who intended to live in the town and the systems for providing accomodation allowed the authorities a very practical control on the size and the character of the population. The newcomer had to make his appearance before the Bailiffs; the householder had to ask their permission to take in lodgers or inmates; and a prudent incomer would have to settle the circumstances of his accomodation before moving with his family and his possessions into the town.

Where each householder lived is not certain, for land and housing in Maldon was spread within the lordships of six or more manors and so it lacks the comprehensive rentals and surveys which survive for some towns. (One thinks here of the maps of 1591 by John Walker of Chelmsford and Moulsham which, with the complementary court records of the manor of Bishop's Hall, provide the basis of Miss Grieve's study of Medieval and Tudor Chelmsford). Many of Maldon properties' title deeds are privately preserved and unavailable to the topographer but fortunately there are three groups of material in the archives of the corporation which can be used to examine the circumstances in which this transient population housed itself rather than trace the histories and exact locations of individual properties.

The registration of deeds made in the conveyancing of properties inherited by females or which they held as dowers is a source of information about one special aspect of the property market, involving heritability and the movement of ownership away from the inhabitants of the borough. Such deeds, which were enrolled from 1574 in Court of Record registers, illustrate how the local custom called Borough English affected the inheritance of land and housing. In combination with short-distance out-migration it promoted the constant drift of title to property away from the town.

The second source is, it seems, peculiar to Maldon: a custom called Landcheap which was a tax levied on every purchase of land or tenements within the borough at the rate of ten pence for every *mark* of the purchase price. It was first written down among the Customs of the Borough in 1555 but the fifteenth century court rolls and the chamberlains' accounts record payment of this purchase tax and the Bishop of London's charter to the borough of 1403 specified that he had granted to the burgesses 'a custom within the town called landchepe' so, as its Old English

77

name − meaning land purchase − indicates, it was a manorial resource of considerable antiquity. As no other manor or town has (so far) been found which had this custom, it may be claimed as a unique source of information on not only transfers of ownership but more especially on current local market prices of land and housing in the sixteenth and seventeenth centuries.

Receipts of landcheap were often recorded item by item in the borough chamberlains' accounts and they often provide useful details: the occupations and domiciles of both vendors and purchasers; the actual price (which can also be calculated from the sum received); the names of the properties and their location; and − occasionally − references to special features of either the property or of the conveyance. Thus the 1572 account roll has a landcheap of 6s 3d for the purchase of a shop in St Peter's parish by Thomas Trappes of Danbury for £5. The shop was in the tenure of a blacksmith, John Mendham; the previous owner (the vendor) was John Sayer. Another landcheap, in the 1625 account, was for the purchase of a reversion and inheritance right in a dwelling house in All Saints' parish for £4 by Samuel Pratt, who also acquired by that transaction a tenement and shops belonging to the dwelling; and the memorandum adds that the reversion was to occur on the death of Margaret, wife of Robert Sandeford esquire but was purchased by Pratt from Thomas Rochell. Even though the series is incomplete and few details are given in the earlier rolls, sixty one accounts do provide full details of properties purchased between 1561 and 1658 and provide a good-sized sample of the market in real estate at Maldon across the period which Professor Hoskins signalised as The Great Rebuilding of England. It must be pointed out that sometimes the landcheap charged on the purchaser was reduced, in needy cases or by special favour, and that sometimes payment was partial, deferred or even refused, but the levy was always claimed and a record was almost always kept of the full amount which ought to have been paid. (See Figure 14.)

Not all transfers of property were covered by the landcheap records. There was no tax on the inheritance of property and the enrolled deeds in the Court of Record only partly cover such transfers, for they mostly concern female inheritance and wardship, not the simple inheritance of property by sons or other kinsmen. Much property was in fact inherited or was allocated by conveyances within families and this is a feature which helps to explain the apparent sluggishness of most house prices throughout the period 1550 - 1688 as seen in the Landcheap receipts.

The third source of information goes some way towards confirming this by providing a picture of the general pattern of property-holding in the borough. It is a group of drafts for a survey of the tenures in Maldon, undated but of the early seventeenth century, whose most probable purpose was to provide evidence for the Survey of Crown Lands which was begun in 1608 and, like this draft, was intended to

78

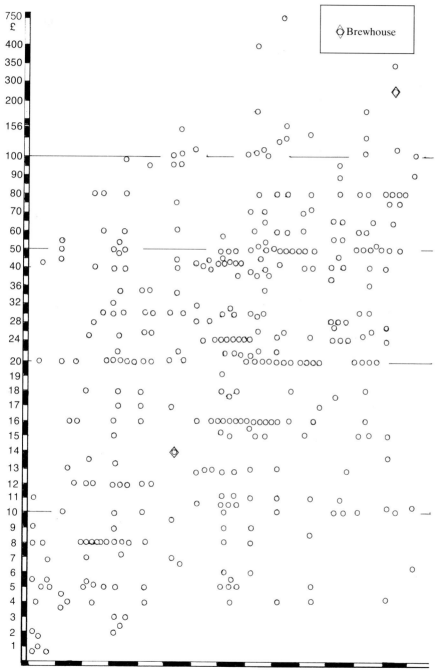

*Figure 14 Landcheap – House Prices*

declare the quality, quantity, rent and value of land and to provide a survey of all manner of tenures. Sales of Crown property in Maldon over the next ten years, which are recorded in the chamberlains' receipts of landcheaps from 'the King's Majesty's Patentees,' give some colour to the proposition that these were drafts for the proposed survey (which was never completed) and intended to provide proof that such lands as were sold might be rightfully declared to be held 'in socage' of the Manor of East Greenwich. A comparison of the landholders and tenants with entries for them in the parish burial and baptism registers, and the evidence of three conveyances of 1609, 1610 and 1614, shows that it was compiled in 1609 or early in 1610, when the commissioners of the Survey were still receiving reports from the localities.

Although it is incomplete, this Survey of Tenures remains a very large sample of the types of ownership and tenure prevalent in Maldon c1610. The items are collected by manors which in Maldon did not occupy discrete blocks of territory but had their tenements intermingled, so that the entries concern 192 properties dispersed across all the housing area of the town and all types of buildings, cottages as well as great houses. Some sixty years later 225 householders were assessed for the 1671 Hearth Tax so the extant portions of this survey may cover more than three quarters of all housing (perhaps as much as 85 per cent) in early seventeenth century Maldon, which is certainly more than an adequate sample. An analysis confirms what one would expect: the greater part of this largely transient population rented houses, and many of the owners were not inhabitants. Of the 192 houses listed in this survey, 75 per cent were owned by non-residents and approximately 68 per cent of the same houses were tenant occupied. The surveyors listed forty resident owner-occupiers but no less than sixty three non-occupying property owners, some of whom were owners of more than one tenement. Clearly the owner-occupier was a rarity in this town but this was not unique: at Chelmsford in the 1590s out of 144 dwellings 54 per cent were tenant-occupied, judging by Miss Grieve's meticulously analysed edition of John Walker's survey of 1591 and a manuscript survey (similar to this one of Maldon but much more detailed) of c1618-23.

Under the sub-heading 'The particular Tenements holden of the said Manor [of the Borough] in Full Burgage' this entry sums up the typical situation:

> 'Elisha Garrington and Alice [his wife] holdeth one messuage in the tenure of John Pratt, value:-£4; one other tenement in the tenure of Lowther, widow, value:- 40s; one other tenement in the tenure of Robert Pope, value:- 20s; and one parcel of land called Aldham's, value:- £3, in the same parish [of All Saints] but of whom, or by what services or rents the same or any of them are holden we know not.
> And this land-holding is worth per annum:- £10'.

It records a non-resident landowner, for Master Garrington was an ex-Alderman, who had removed himself and his family to Ardleigh, some twenty two miles away in 1611 (within a few months of this record being made). His tenants included a widow who was clearly known only superficially to the surveyors, whose name is not to be found in either parish or borough archives and who may not have been the inhabitant of that house at the time of the survey. Two freemen of substance were his other tenants. Robert Pope had married a daughter of Alderman William Bantoft in 1590, was a freeman and acted as Serjeant-at-Mace to the corporation. John Pratt was certainly one of the most prosperous of the town's tradesman and for some twenty years he had been one of the leading figures in the community, a Bailiff, a vigorous and controversial Puritan, a successful tailor whose cash bequests in 1619 totalled £460 and who was able to maintain one of his sons, Elisha, as a pensioner undergraduate at Emmanuel College in Cambridge. He was a property owner himself, yet in all his thirty nine or forty years living in Maldon he never lived in a house of his own.

Like many tradesmen John Pratt had come to Maldon as a youth from the nearby village (in his case, Purleigh), when he was apprenticed in 1579 or 1580 after the death of his father. He was married in 1585 − before the completion of his apprenticeship, it seems, − even though that was forbidden by the borough custom − he became a freeman the next year and he was the master of an apprentice from 1589. In those circumstances it is understandable that this ambitious young man originally had to take a lease on a home and workshop, that he may not have had sufficient capital to spare from the trade he was establishing to lay out on house purchase. And the building which he rented may have been more suitable than any which were available for purchase. It was in a prime position immediately to the west of the Moot Hall, in the centre of the Market, described in the conveyances of adjacent buildings in 1592 and 1605 as 'the house where John Pratt dwelleth'.

This was, at first, the situation for John Maldon, a haberdasher who as a young man came from Chelmsford when he was about 22 to set up shop here. He was a contemporary of John Pratt, he became a freeman in the same year, they were associated in the Corporation and in a puritan faction during the 1580s and 90s. The house he selected for his home and workplace was the cornershop where the Market Place met St Peter's Lane, built some thirty years before by a previous haberdasher, Henry Pynnell. Unlike Master Pratt, John Maldon was eventually able to purchase the building in 1598. It was expensive. The landcheap of £4 13s 9d 'for the tenement wherein he dwelleth' indicates that he paid Alderman Thomas Furnes almost £76, over double the average price in the 1590s.

There are plenty of other indications that this was a permanent feature of property

81

holding throughout the two centuries and not peculiar to the years around the time of this Survey. Thomas Porter, a tanner and head burgess in the Corporation 1559-62 and 1571-83, bequeathed to his wife his lease of their dwelling house called Scarlett's with the condition that she paid the rent and maintained the house in good repair 'at her own charges'. In 1588 the widow of Alderman Andrew Michaelson possessed seven houses whose tenants included four head burgesses. The Survey names as tenant-occupiers six existing members of the Corporation and three future members, including two who were Bailiffs of the borough in 1606, 1609 and 1610. A linendraper, Alderman William Francis, who was thrice a Bailiff, bequeathed to his wife in 1646 the lease of their dwelling. He had no other houses to bequeath, only land in the hamlet of Snoreham. Another linendraper, Richard Tennant, who was either a bachelor or childless widower, had goods and money to bequeath in 1657 but neither house nor land; his executrix was a widow in whose house he was dwelling at the time of his death. In 1663 two more head burgesses were tenants, according to the will of their landlord, the apothecary Ruben Robinson.

## KINSHIP AND PROPERTY

Because so many were so briefly inhabitants of the town leaseholding would naturally be commonplace but the custom of Borough English which had for long governed inheritance in Maldon was also a powerful influence on ownership and had always tended to keep housing off the property market. It may be observed in Figure 14 that only 4.6 houses, on average, were bought or sold in any of the years 1561 - 1670 for which transactions are recorded and in 1644 and 1656 there were no sales. In its simplest form Borough English was a type of impartible inheritance by which the youngest son inherited all his father's freehold estate:

'If the father die seized in house or land within the franchise of the borough, the youngest son of the first wife shall have the heritage'

says the first paragraph of the first Custom in the oldest surviving Custumal, of 1444. It involved both ultimogeniture and the impartibility of the parental estate, which, in combination, ought to have produced migration on a massive scale as elder sons without prospect of inheriting their fathers' possessions departed from their parental homes as soon as they could establish themselves independently.

In practice that was not so. There were modifications to the custom and it may be noted that there was a subtle adjustment built into the 1444 version: the inheritor was to be the youngest son of the first of a man's wives to have children − and children who lived. Thus he could be a younger son but not the youngest in a family where the man had married two or more times. There could be cases in which the eldest had the right of inheritance. And if a man had daughters only, his estate became partible, except that the youngest daughter was to have first choice:

'and if he have daughters all they shall depart [divide the property between themselves] but the youngest shall choose first'.

Where a man had several sons it was possible for him to make provision for them in his lifetime, so that only a residual estate would remain as the appropriate younger son's inheritance. That could be done by devising land or tenements to their use and by 1444 that had become a recognised practice in Maldon, the second paragraph of the Custumal decreeeing that

'it shall be lawful to every man that purchaseth any house or land within the borough for to devise the purchase; and that devise shall be shown before the Bailiffs at the next court after, or at the second time, else it shall remain to the heir'.

The last seven words show that this ordinance was intended to embrace settlements made for the elder (and sometimes the youngest) children during their parents' lifetime by enrolling in the Court of Record conveyances 'to uses' on their behalf.

From 1540 the Statute of Wills broke down the influence which Borough English had exercised over the distribution of town property because thereafter freeholds which had been acquired by a testamentary bequest could be impleaded safely in a court of common law. Previously freehold estates had (theoretically) reverted to the possession of whoever was Lord of that manor to which they belonged, to be redeemed by the customary heir from the Lord. Courts had not been able to countenance undisguised, outright sales or exchanges of freeholds. After 1540 they could and a major revision of the Custumal in 1555 amended the ordinance about devising property so as to admit that it would have no effect if any house or land which had been conveyed to the use of an elder or younger child was subsequently bequeathed:

'if any man have either lands or tenements in fee simple within the borough [and] will devise or divide the same to his children, or otherwise, if he do come into the court before the Bailiffs and there make any such devise, that then the same devise shall be good and effectual to him or them unto whom the devise shall be made ... So that the party after such devise made do not by his will or otherwise devise the same to the contrary. And in default of such devise or devises the heirs by the custom of the borough [are] to have the heritage'.

The revisers later inserted a statement that inhabitants could register their wills in the borough court but there remains no evidence that this was ever necessary.

The 1555 Custumal also omitted one clause of the older custom on Borough

English, which had decreed that when the heir was under age his mother could not continue to have the wardship of his inheritance if she remarried; and a precedent recorded in 1574 gave the inheritance of one under-age heir to his new step-father. In 1587 another precedent was set which modified the customary regulation for heiresses. Three married women were co-heiresses; instead of allowing the youngest to make first choice the Court of Record divided the estate into three shares of equal value and made the three women 'depart' thus:

> 'we did write the said three several parts ... in three several screws [of paper] and covered the said screws all over with wax and made them in three little balls and put them all in one bonnet in an indifferent man's hand ...'

from which each took her allotment.

Although the force of custom was broken before the first half of the sixteenth century was over, the past hundred years (or more) had stamped non-resident ownership firmly on the borough's property holding. Many of the tenements continued to bear the names of early fifteenth century owners (such as Aldham's, Crackbone's, Page's and Bawde's) although persons with that name had long since ceased to be inhabitants. Titles to property constantly retreated from the borough through migration, as with the house subdivided c1568 by Daniel Winterbourne: the halves were inherited by his two sons, one of whom had a son called John Winterbourne and he, in 1620, was a yeoman of Battle in Sussex. In that year the other son of Daniel died childless and so the other half of the subdivided building descended by inheritance to this yeoman of Battle. Since he sold the whole building to the feoffees of the new grammar school foundation established in 1609 by Ralph Breeder, the title to this estate happened to return to the town. But Borough English did not die out, for the conveyances enrolled in later seventeenth century courts of record sometimes include specific declarations of the grantees' inheritance as, or by descent from, youngest sons.

## THE HOUSING AREA

So far the controls on the size of Maldon's population which have been considered have been either administrative, as in the regulations for inmates, the review of inhabitants provided by the Views of Frankpledge and the orders made at the Quarter Sessions, or they have been abstract in the sense that property ownership and the availability of leases exercised an invisible but real control on the numbers and type of persons to be found in the town at any one time.

An equally powerful control, and visible, was exerted by the physical characteristics of the place. The upper limit of the population's size necessarily depended on the availability of land for building and on the existing stock of housing. Both were

84

very limited in Maldon at any time between 1500 and 1700, and so the topographical sources can tempt us into attempting to construct a profile of changes in population from the evidence of new buildings, the periods of most intense building activity, which should indicate growth in numbers, and the evidence of depopulation in references to decayed buildings, vacant house-plots, the amalgamation of houses to create single ones.

The town had much the same ground plan in 1700 as it had in 1500. Although there were many visual alterations, housing remained confined to, principally, the High Street, with another area alongside the roadways which descended the northern hillside to the Fullbridge and the Causeway. The four clusters of housing already described (in Chapter 1) remained almost as distinct and separate in the eighteenth century, as on Chapman and André's plan, as they had been in the fifteenth century. The reason for that may be partly that the population of Maldon failed to rise significantly but there was another reason which would have been obvious in the sixteenth and seventeenth centuries. The housing areas were hemmed in by pastures, orchards and market gardens which here and there reached right up to the streets to separate the groups of buildings quite distinctly. The ownership of these crofts, gardens, working areas, had effected a stranglehold on Maldon's housing space, for this land was too valuable to the butchers and yeomen to be given over to domestic buildings. They needed pastures for fattening the cattle they brought in for sale or slaughter from the grazing lands of the countryside. Market gardening put its own premium on cultivable land from at least the late sixteenth century, when references begin to occur to gardens or orchards as distinct tenements which had been 'taken out' of field areas.

Butchers occupied on leases the very extensive pastureland called Friars' Fields which stretched across much of the gentle southern slope of the town hill. Two enclosures called Mill Field and Tenterfield, fitted in between the houses along the middle stretch of the High Street and the north-eastern corner of Friars' Fields, had ceased to be used for a windmill or for cloth-finishers' tenters by 1630, when they were owned by Christopher Welles, a yeoman of Messing (a village twelve miles from Maldon) who was also a freeman butcher at Maldon. On this southern side of the High Street for over a third of a mile the only space which became available for house-building was the enclosure of the Carmelite Friary, which was dissolved in 1536. Between 1563 and 1574 its ruins were converted into one grand mansion house by William Harris of Mundon. Over the hilltop and on the sides of St Peter's Lane, St Helen's Lane and their continuation, Fullbridge Street, there were more fields and for much of their length these roadways had few houses. One side of Fullbridge Street was taken up by fields in which there were tan pits and glovers' worksheds, sited there for the spring water welling out of the steep hillside, and for the easy drainage of their trades' noisesome effluent into the river

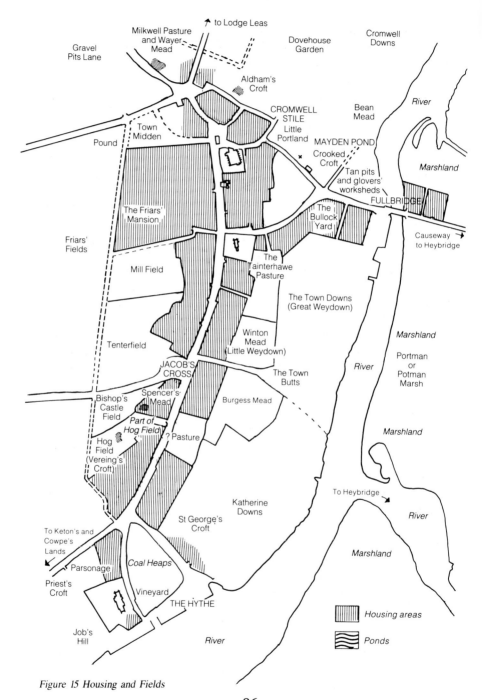

*Figure 15 Housing and Fields*

below. Meadows called The Town Downs — but no longer commonland — occupied the greater part of the northern slopes of the town hill and on its upper edge, behind St Peter's Church and the Market Place there were orchards, gardens and a pasture called The Bullock Yard. Winton pasture blocked any expansion rearwards of the housing along the High Street from St Peter's Church to the road junction called Jacob's Cross. In 1590 a butcher who leased two shops in the Butcher Row was tenant of Winton Pasture; by 1640 it had become an orchard. Next to that, across Butt Lane, was land set aside for the town's shooting butts and then for a distance of almost a quarter of a mile fields occupied nearly all the land between Jacob's Cross and St Mary's Church, clearly separating the Hythe from the rest of the town.

Lastly, the western edge of Maldon, on the crown of the hill, was sealed off with pastureland. Aldham's Croft lay directly behind the Market Place, very conveniently sited for dealers who gathered at the Butcher Row or in the Blue Boar Inn, whose yard led directly into Aldham's. It seems to have been a very extensive pasture stretching across a rear-access track of the Market called Sligges Lane — because of its miry nature (Sligges as in 'slough'), perhaps from the cattle which were driven along it — which the pasture's owner tried to enclose in 1569. Here, as in other pastures, an orchard was 'taken out' c1600, together with two gardens enclosed from the Blue Boar's land for market gardening. Lodge Leas, Milkwell, Bean Mead, Wayer Mead, Gravel Pits Field and the Town Dunghill (itself described as 'at the borough's end') completed the tight girdle of fields around Maldon, so that until the early 19th century the built-up area ceased abruptly on the very edge of the Market Place, from which the trader could break out immediately into the countryside.

Maldon had never conquered the rural origins of its four clusters of housing and even at the heart of the borough orchards and grassland were casually visible down its alleyways. Presentments at the Quarter Sessions invariably included complaints about bullocks, sheep, hogs (and, once, of a bull) wandering about the High Street and Market Place; of unleashed dogs; of grindstones, heaps of manure and piles of logs left beside the highway. Untidy farmyard conditions kept creeping out from behind the orderly urban facade which some of the townsmen sought to maintain. Maldon must have had an atmosphere similar to that of more recent American "frontier" towns. Its main road was lined with hitching rails; many houses had raised plank footwalks, so that pedestrians (especially the womenfolk in their ankle-length dresses) could avoid the mulch of manure and gravel that covered the street; smithies and stables, equivalent in function to our parking lots and service stations, were interspersed with houses and, with the inns and alehouses, were patronised by the drovers and grasiers who rode in from scattered marshland farms with herds of cattle or waggonloads of hay and grain. Everywhere there were the sights and sounds, and the reek, of cattle, pigs and horses, pervasive signs of the leaseholding interests which prevented the expansion of Maldon's housing area.

Thus hemmed in, the town impacted itself. Three strategies were available for the extension of housing. One was to rebuild so as to use more of an existing plot. Another was to subdivide a large house into two or more cottages, with perhaps some additional building within the site. The third was to spill out onto the common soil of the borough, onto the street or open space and this is well-documented. As in every other manor and town, an annual Assize Rent was levied for such encroachments, the amount varying in proportion to the amount of land occupied, and since the Chamberlains' Accounts always include a statement of their receipts of this rent, here is a frail thread of evidence which can be supplemented by other materials to suggest very broadly the major trends in the size of the population. In most years only a summary of the Assize Rental is given; itemised accounts exist only for 1507/8, 1536/7, 1539/40, 1550, 1573, 1597 and 1670, so over periods of varying length there is some indication of the prevailing pressures on housing. The latter gap, 1597 to 1670, is unfortunate because there was a policy in the seventeenth century of transforming the small fixed Rents of Assize into Ferm Rents which were larger and could be increased from time to time. Moreover, it should not be assumed that every encroachment was intended to ease overcrowding; some were made for the improvement of a building or to increase access to a yard.

So many of the house plots in the sixteenth century bore the names of persons active in the borough a hundred years earlier that the four housing areas within which new building activity had to occur must have been almost fully stocked by 1500. Thus, Pepper's, abutting on Aldham's Croft was named after a mercer of c1410 (Henry Pepir), and so on for the houses once owned, perhaps constructed, by John Baggeman, Richard Sergeant, Andrew Aylewyn, John Crackbone, Margaret Elmstead and others whose names occur in the court rolls of the first quarter of the fifteenth century. Baude's House and Crank's were the less fortunate products of this habit, both preserving the surnames of prominent burgesses of c1400. To this early stock the first surviving detailed Assize Rental adds five new dwellings which had been inserted before 1508. A few more tenements may have been squeezed into spare land between the older houses but if an average household size of 4.5 is assumed, then the fifteenth century had ended with a slight increase in possible housing size of no less than 22 persons. It seems likely that there had been no significant change in the size of the town's population.

And after 1508 pressure on housing apparently slackened. Until 1550 only two more encroachments for new buildings are recorded. A fall-back in population? Three acts of parliament, of 1541, 1542 and 1544, included Maldon among the boroughs to which special powers were given to halt their 'decay' and the bills requesting these acts had been so framed that individual towns could have themselves included by name if they so wished. An entry in the chamberlains' accounts for 1541/2 shows that the Bailiffs of Maldon had indeed taken steps to be included in forthcoming legislation: they had sanctioned payment of 3s 4d to the clerk of one of their Members of Parliament, John Edmonds of the Middle Temple, 'for a copy of an Act that year put into the parliament for the decay of houses in this town'. This was also one of the few occasions when the common council of Maldon made a point of electing one of their own freemen to parliament, in this case Henry Dawes, the learned son of John Dawes (a former merchant of the town) and a man familiar with public business. The common council wanted the powers offered by these acts for the repair of 'decayed towns'. Did they need those powers to halt a decline in population?

It is arguable that the number of taxpayers listed in the lay subsidy returns of 1524-27 understates the number of males in the borough just before 1540, perhaps by as much as 50 per cent, so that the population of Maldon in 1524 (when there were 194 taxpayers) might have really been as high as 2,000 persons. In 1547 the population may have numbered 1,200, according to the number of communicants claimed on the chantry certificates for all three parishes. So there could have been a very serious decline, by up to 170 households, soon after 1524. Professor Bindoff characterised the town simply as 'a small and declining port' in his edition of *The House of Commons, 1509-1558*. It would, however, be unwise to assume that the 'decay' which the burgesses of Maldon sought to combat with acts of parliament was of a demographic nature, or that many houses were unoccupied and falling into rack and ruin about 1540, even though the preamble to Queen Mary's first charter to Maldon, 1554, stated that the borough was greatly 'decayed'. The powers granted by these acts were retrospective up to twenty five years, so they did not necessarily refer to a sudden exodus of families in the 1540s; nor did they provide borough authorities with a means quickly to restore municipal vigour and prosperity. Largely the intention of the makers of these acts was to discourage landlords from seizing common rights in open fields and meadows, which could be done by leaving untenanted the town houses to which those rights belonged, but Maldon had only patches of commonland on the verges of its encircling agricultural land, with no rights of grazing or cropping reserved to any tenement, and those Assize Rentals show that whatever common soil the borough had was being occupied with new buildings. Moreover, only five sites are known to have become vacant or derelict in the sixteenth century and the only recorded implementation of the 1544 Act by the borough occurred no earlier than 1598! It is unlikely that the burgesses of the 1540s had any worries about derelict building sites in Maldon.

It is much more likely that (as is argued in the next chapter) it was some form of commercial reorganisation which they had in mind. It is not at all certain that there had been any serious decline in the number of householders between 1500 and 1540, because the lower limit for taxpayers in the 1524 lay subsidy was a valuation of 20s in either land or goods or wages per annum and the chamberlains' accounts indicate that at Maldon craftsmen's labourers were capable of earning much more than that in a year and unless there had been serious tax evasion the subsidy returns ought to be a reasonably accurate guide to the number of adult males in this town, indicating a continuing average of 1,000 inhabitants throughout the first half of the century.

It is also likely that the burgesses for Maldon, and the leading townsmen of the 1540s had firmly in their minds the use of the acts for the repair of decayed towns towards one particular building which was indeed derelict, and whose extensive site could be released for additional building plots at the very heart of Maldon. Darcy's Tower was the ruin whose future they contemplated: and with as little despair as would fill the heart of a modern developer with a city centre site coming almost within his reach. This building is now (and from 1576) the Moot Hall of the borough. It is, as it was in the 1540s, a tower, three storeys high, built massively of brick. Either in the middle or late in the fifteenth century it had been constructed as part of a scheme to build a fine mansion for the Darcy family whose great chantry chapel lay next door in All Saints' Church, and whose lodgings for their chantry priests (now the west wing of All Saints' Vicarage) occupied the north-west corner of the site for this great house. The Darcies possessed one half of the lordship of the borough and John Norden, writing in 1594 when the memory of their intentions was fading, commented that they once had 'a fair house' in the middle of the town 'whereof there remaineth at this day a tower of brick called Darcy's Tower'.

A pity John Norden could not have been more informative, for in its present state, much rebuilt in the early nineteenth century and hemmed in for two thirds of its height on two sides by housing, it is uncertain what kind of building this tower was intended to be. According to Norden it is the surviving part of an unfinished mansion and perhaps it was intended to be one of the corner towers for a Great House of the traditional courtyard plan. It does bear some resemblance, however, to the Hussey Tower built about 1455 south of Greyfriars' Lane in Boston, Lincolnshire, which is also a brick building rising three floors and with a spiral stair in an attached corner turret. (By coincidence that tower was also derelict in the mid-sixteenth century.) It seems most probable that the Hussey Tower was the solar wing of a larger building whose roof-line can be seen on one wall and an indenture of May 1539 for the sale of *Master Darcies cheyfe mansyon* to John Church seems to indicate a similar arrangement here: what was sold to John Church was a messuage or mansion, a chapel and 'other buildings' called The Tower but excluded from the sale was 'the tower of brick there builded' and this suggests

*Pl.4. Late-fifteenth century mastery of brickwork: the stairway of Darcy's Tower*

91

that there was once a timber framed manor house with, as part of a second phase of building, this brick tower which would provide the additional chamber accomodation needed by about 1485. If so, nothing so palatial as a huge courtyard house was ever planned and at some time between 1536 and 1560 a manor house of the Darcies behind the Tower may have been demolished.

Whatever the original lay-out may have been, by the 1540s the ground which the rest of this mansion might have covered was let out as garden plots, and the original building scheme had probably foundered in 1508 when Roger Darcy, one of King Henry VII's bodyguards, died. His only son was two years old and Maldon was never his home. Thomas Darcy, this little son, grew up in the royal service. He was knighted at Calais in 1532 and, as a Gentleman of the Privy Chamber, became one of the soldier-courtiers who surrounded the ageing King Henry VIII in the 1540s and then Captain of the Guard to the boy-king Edward VI. When John Dudley became the King's Protector, Darcy was appointed Lord Chamberlain of England (1551-53), raised to the peerage as a baron and made a Knight of the Garter. Unlike successful gentry and merchants, lawyers and royal counsellors of his and many other generations, he did not seek to establish for his family a great country seat at the earliest possible moment and he ran down the old Darcy properties in Maldon. The tower of their projected mansion might have become part of a very splendid building on the lines of that outstanding example of brick and terracotta Tudor architecture, the Marney Tower at Layer Marney, begun when Thomas Darcy was a boy by two other courtiers and close companions of Henry VIII. It lay on the edge of his estates, he must have known it. But Darcy's Tower remained unfinished, the rest of the house unstarted. His land sales and speculation in the 1530s and 1540s suggest that he was in need of funds to support his life at court. In 1544 he had also obtained a licence to alienate − that is, to confiscate − the endowments of six chantries whose priests had said Mass daily for his ancestors' souls in the parish church at Danbury and in All Saints, Maldon. (To be fair to him, in 1545 a commission reported that several chantries in Essex had been dissolved by other noblemen, merchants, gentry. This was four years before King Edward's government dissolved all surviving guilds and chantries.)

As his career reached its peak Sir Thomas sought at last for a suitable country seat. In 1550 he chose the former Abbey of St Osyth at Chiche on the north bank of the Colne estuary, which had been one of the finest monastic buildings in Essex. It was still in the Crown's possessions and he acquired it in exchange for many of his inherited properties, which included the tower and the Darcy lordship in Maldon. Thus he took his place in the House of Lords as Baron Darcy of Chiche and suddenly the neglected tower and all the site of the mansion became property which might soon be available for redevelopment.

Within the next thirteen years that is what happened. Deeds of 1562 show that two houses had been built by then around the corner of St Peter's Lane and the High Street. A confrontation on Corpus Christi Day 1558 between Master John Church, a Bailiff of the borough and a Romanist, and a group of dissidents took place in front of the house of Henry Pynnell which was the house on this corner and was described at its sale in 1566 as 'the lately built messuage in St Peter's parish'. Nearby, the Upper, Middle and Nether Houses had been built over a large part of the formerly open site by 1557, for a title deed of 1561 states that before 1558 The Nether House had been in the occupation of a brewer, Cornelius Peterson.

As for the Tower, it remained derelict, passing from one prospective developer to another, whose names are recited in the title deed by which it was eventually conveyed to the Bailiffs, Aldermen and Common Council in 1576. Soon after Maldon became a corporate town in 1556 it had set its eyes on Darcy's Tower as a suitable symbol of its new status. In 1562 a bequest of 20s 'to the town of Maldon' was made by one of the first members of the corporation, Master John Gaywood 'towards the purchasing of the Tower'. At the same time his brethren in the Common Council were seeking ways of forcing its absentee landlords into some form of restoration. That was the underlying purpose of a bye-law they enacted in March 1563 although it purported to forbid generally the destruction of 'any manner of mansion or dwelling house' on pain of a fine of 100 marks. Part of the page on which this ordinance is recorded has been torn away but from the beginnings of each line the missing portions can be reconstructed. As a preamble the ordinance recited the Corporation's powers under the three acts of parliament of 1541-44 but its substance was a requirement that the landlord 'of the said house called the Tower' (this portion of the text is complete) should make it 'one dwelling house, without any more defacing of it, within one year ... or otherwise he shall for none building thereof forfeit £40'. That sum would have gone much further than Master Gaywood's bequest towards the purchase price for the Corporation: eventually they paid £76 for the building, and if they could have convicted the 1563 owner of destroying it, the statutory fine of 100 marks (ie. £66 13s 4d) would have yielded them almost the ready cash. What they did with the building is described below (Chapter 5); what matters here is that the borough's concern to have its name in the acts for the repair of decayed towns arose not from any depopulation or dereliction but from its strategy to consolidate and improve a static economic and social position. From 1550 the increase in housing at the heart of the borough was evidence that this strategy was succeeding.

At least eight new houses were provided by the development of the ground on which the Darcy mansion might have stood. Also six new encroachments on the common soil are recorded in the Assize Rentals of 1536 to 1573, so that a minimum of fourteen new dwellings were added to the town's accomodation between 1536 and 1573: room for between sixty and seventy more men, women and children if the average per household was 4.5 or 4.75. For a population of 1,000 (as Maldon seems to have been by 1573) this suggests the town experienced an overall increase of 6% or 7% in its minimum size between the 1530s and the 1570s.

Then the pace of new building may have slackened. Between 1573 and 1597 only one item was added to the assize rental (and the effect of that was cancelled out by the conversion of another dwelling into 'a garden plot whereon was sometime a tenement') and between 1597 and 1670 only eight more encroachments, not all being new houses, can be traced. The conversion of assize rents into ferm rents may be obscuring our view of the housing trend but only fourteen other new buildings have (from various sources) been traced, each within the period 1590 - 1670. Groundspace was clearly hard to come by at that time and these houses were built on the selvedge of the housing areas.

A conveyance of a house in the New Inn Lane behind the High Street (in 1671) describes how it had been 'erected and made ... out of certain haylofts and stables which were part of the New Inn and other adjacent parts of the premises purchased by Timothy Rogers from John Maldon, haberdasher, and George Purchas, woollendraper'. Their names set the date of that new building back to about 1600. Not long before 1650 a building 'which was heretofore a stable and was sometime in the tenure of John Boswell' (deceased c1570) and near the Blue Boar Inn was, according to a deed of 1672, converted into 'the mansion house of Robert Walley, waller' whose will was made in April 1650. Another house (still standing, its timber frame at first floor level intact) was constructed in the mouth of a much used public trackway, now called White Horse Yard, leading out of the Market Place to the town midden. Another was built on the edge of the midden itself. Others were squeezed into gaps between the older houses, such as The Three Mariners (not an inn) which at some time before 1631 was built against the west wall of an 'ancient Hallehowse' called Ridler's, according to a conveyance of that date, and within the original house-plot of Ridler's. It was a compact little house, with a hall (the main room), kitchen and buttery on the ground floor and two chambers above them; and as the garden area was twenty one feet wide where it abutted on Ridlers, that is likely to have been the total width of this new house.

Only one of these fourteen new buildings of 1590-1670 was built outside the traditional areas (excepting one or two husbandmen's or labourers' cottages put up beside farm land well beyond the town itself) and this one was only a few yards beyond the housing area at the Hythe. It was constructed for a merchant, John Cade, c1600 and it survives as the rear section of the Jolly Sailor Inn, a small though solid house which Master Cade claimed had cost him almost £400. The explanation of so high a price for a simple brick, wood and plaster building may be that it included the purchase of land otherwise required for the storage of coal, lime, chalk and timber which were landed at the nearby quays. The price may have included Master Cade's additional purchase in 1598 of a malting house in the same parish (St Mary's) and very probably close to the house he built, which cost 100 marks (£66 13s 4d).

In one hundred years (from 1570 to 1670) Maldon's stock of new housing probably provided accomodation for between 66 and 80 more persons. That, as in the first two thirds of the sixteenth century, was a very modest rate of increase indeed: between 6.6 and 8.0 per cent, which corresponds well with the estimates of Maldon's population which can be made from more conventional sources. It illustrates the importance of the controls on settlement and shows how the unavailability of extra land on which houses might have been built helped to maintain a ceiling of about 1,000 on population size.

Whilst physical growth was thus limited, the standard of housing and accomodation was not. This slack time for the building of brand new houses was distinctly the time of the Great Rebuilding in Maldon as much as it was in England as a whole from the 1550s to the mid-seventeenth century. Expensive public building work was undertaken in the Market Place between 1550 and 1576 (which is described below in Chapter 5), with further improvements in the early seventeenth century, and the references in the borough records, wills and inventories to renovations, reconstructions and innovations, when collected, show that in the early years of Queen Elizabeth I's reign there was a new briskness about the Maldon scene, of straight new roof lines, of roof tiles as yet untarnished, newly sawn timber, crisp, fresh plaster on walls.

Behind the renovated houses and blocks of new buildings of the Market Place there lay the Friars' Mansion which one of the richest men in Essex, William Harris of Mundon, Southminster and Gray's Inn, and his son Vincent, created out of the ruins of the former Carmelite Friary between 1563 and 1574. In the year he bought the site William Harris ran up debts amounting to £927 6s 8d with five local men (acknowledged in the borough's Court of Record) and his son Vincent, who seems to have been the principal builder, referred in his will of 1574 to the debts incurred 'by reason of the great charges sustained in the building of my mansion house in Maldon'. For the payment of these building costs both William and Vincent Harris had mortgaged their great estate in Mundon and the mansion they created may have been a fine one if men of their great wealth had some difficulty in financing its construction. In the early years of the nineteenth century every trace of it was removed when the two elegant and vast 'Georgian' houses were built on its site.

Physical comfort, enlargement, renovation, modernisation were features of lesser townspeople's housing by the mid-sixteenth century. It was reported in 1567 of John Manning, who had purchased The Bull in the Mercery Row of the Market Place, that he 'from a ruinous estate hath repaired and new builded the same' [which was then re-named The Spreadeagle] in such wise as the same hath cost the said John Manning in ready money very nigh one hundred pounds'. His will (1582) tells how he had also wainscotted the interior and put in 'glass which is now standing and framed about the windows'. By then this house was tenanted. Its glazed window frames and the panelling were included in the rented accomodation: a condition of the rent being payable to Manning's widow, Margaret, was that she must not remove either and if she were to remarry, her husband was to enter into bond and give surety that he would also observe this condition. Similar conditions were laid down in the strict settlement devised by Christopher Living, a butcher, in 1616: 'the glass, wainscot and ceiling now being fastened, annexed and nailfast in, unto and about' his house was to be maintained and 'continued therewith from time to time for the use and benefit of' the persons on whom in succession the ownership of the building was devised. Staircases are several times casually mentioned as if they were not unusual in Maldon by the late sixteenth century. A witness in a court case of 1591 deposed that he had gone 'to the stairs door' in a friend's house; Widow Moore was allocated the use of 'the Stairs Chamber' in her son's house in 1619.

From the 1570s there are frequent references to the extension of houses and the 'enlarging of the groundsills' of Cobbes-at-the-Corner in 1575 by William Poulter, a master mariner, can still be seen, for this house (now The Rose and Crown) is still standing with only its side walls replaced and the change in roof-line where the building juts onto the corner of Butt Lane and the High Street marks this extension. The frontage of a house in Silver Street was extended three feet forwards and forty feet in length by Richard Josua in 1579 (but it is unlikely that the present frontage is the same construction). From about 1600 it became fashionable to create a new frontage by infilling the space below the jetty of the upper floor. Edward Rayner in 1623 encroached on the street for the 'enlarging of his shop towards the King's street so far as the chamber or loft over the said shop doth jetty over'. He was a metal worker, a brasier and pewterer. Master John Nash, a gentleman and for a while the town clerk, appears to have led this fashion when, c1598, he added thirty square feet to his front groundfloor room by filling in below the jetty. He also demolished an adjacent smithy and incorporated that space into his house. Where buildings were set back from the road extensions were bolder, with complete new buildings set onto the face of older houses, as when Thomas Trowers, a husbandman, added a new section reaching onto the roadway in front of his original house (in 1629). Porches were also added to some house fronts, another fashion begun by Master Nash in 1613.

The subdivision of ancient messuages into two or more tenements is of greater significance than these cosmetic and fashionable improvements, since its occurrence must surely highlight those years when the pressure on accomodation was greatest. Very often subdivision and extension took place together, with general improvements or modernisations being effected during the landlord's alterations. When a house was divided into two, three or sometimes four separate dwellings an extra bay or wing added and the floor area might be increased by moving the building line forwards to the roadway. Alternatively subdivision was preceded by an entire rebuilding of the whole site. A new entry passage and a parlour were constructed for Daniel Winterbourne when his property (facing the head of St Peter's Lane and beside Chequers Lane) was divided into two dwellings c1568. Two houses sold by James Seares, a glover, in 1624 were described in the deed as 'lately' newly built as extensions to his house called Smallware's. Another property was described in 1592 as 'the new house recently built' and it was already divisible into four tenements. One other was described in 1601 as 'late newly builded and now converted into three several tenements'. The housing whose occupants were technically 'inmates' was thus sometimes purpose-built, rather like the flats into which over-large mansions in modern towns are converted, and by no means a second-rate type of accommodation.

Along with these kinds of building activities there was a constant process of remodelling, renovation and modification. Wood and plaster was used for most buildings in the town until the late seventeenth century. It was the traditional method and it had certainly been the cheapest, Essex being a well-timbered area, and although making bricks was an established activity in this county long before 1500 they were used only for the grandest buildings in the Maldon area, as in the famous unfinished mansion at Layer Marney (c1520) and its neighbouring parish church tower and porch, as in the similarly incomplete Darcy Tower of Maldon, at Faulkbourne Hall near Witham (both of these begun in the late fifteenth century), and as in the miniature tower house called Beckingham Hall (c1546) and the great brick tower of its neighbouring parish church of Tolleshunt Major, and the fine tower of Sandon parish church (c1520). Wealthy patrons had these towers constructed, and the 'domestic' architecture of these examples was built for great landowners, the Lords Marney, the Darcy family, Stephen Beckingham Esquire. Thus the Canons of Beeleigh Abbey had their dormitory partly rebuilt in brick about 1500. What materials were used for the new Friars Mansion of Vincent Harris is unknown but it is unlikely that the materials of the medieval friary would have been suitable for re-use, except for boundary walls and infilling. It is tempting to suppose that by the 1560's the local families of gentry who had once been content with timber framed houses such as the Harrises' Mundon Hall, were taking up the tradition of earlier great landowners and building in brick. That seems not to be so: only the Mildmays' house called Great Graces in Little Baddow and the Harrises' Creeksea Hall of 1569 (near Burnham) were of brick. Timber and plaster construction continued to be the rule in this area. Spencer's (alias Harding's) in Maldon, although it served as the town house to a succession of gentry families, including the Harrises, appears from the Royal Commission on Historical Monuments' inventory to have been entirely a timber framed house with no significant modernisations of the sixteenth or seventeenth centuries.

Until the late sixteenth century brickwork was − for ordinary domestic purposes − confined to chimney stacks and the footings on which the groundsills of timber frames were laid, as in the 3s 3d paid 'for bricks used at the Cornhill to underpin the pattens there' in 1640, when the timber to make the 'pattens' cost 38s 8d, about twelve times as much as the bricks. One curiosity is the vaulted brick tunnelling beneath the fifteenth and sixteenth century houses along the east side of Silver St − popularly supposed to be part of a secret passage from All Saints' church to Beeleigh Abbey − which could have been a sewer or (this is slightly more probable) a wine cellar. Their location under the frontages of the houses seems to rule out the first explanation, whilst one of the landowners and occupiers in this street from c1550, Richard Josua, was a vintner. Like other brickwork in the town, it is unusual. Bricklayers are named as inhabitants of Maldon from about 1600 but buildings entirely of brick seem not to have been fashionable or usual in the town until the eighteenth century. One shop in the Butcher Row was so unusual that it was simply called The Brick Building, sometimes The Brick Shop: there appear to have been no others until the 1650s, when Nathaniel Osborne paid landcheap on his purchase of 'a brick house in St Mary's parish' for £64.

Yet one massive brick construction forms perhaps the best-known landmark of Maldon and may be the handiwork of those bricklayers named in the early seventeenth century. It is the rebuilt tower of St Mary's church which rises above the waterfront and replaced the medieval tower that collapsed in 1596. Licences for collections to help pay for it were issued in 1628. It is an echo of the late-medieval buildings of this area listed above: a church tower constructed under the patronage of the Bishop of London and the Dean and Chapter of Westminster and an interesting exercise in a 'Perpendicular' style which had proved suited to brickwork. After that the next complete use of bricks came to Maldon with Dr Thomas Plume's library and schoolroom which replaced the nave and chancel of St Peter's church in the late 1690's.

There was the advantage to wood and plaster that a building could be easily altered; it could even be moved, as in the borough chamberlains' account of the costs in 1639 for 'removing the Town Storehouse at Maldon Hythe from the place where it then stood to a more convenient place [with the charges for] setting, underpinning, tiling, boarding and re-seating'. To renovate, subdivide, modify such buildings was obviously cheaper than with solid brick and it was possible to proceed piecemeal at such work and with an extreme economy of materials. Crackbone's — one of the oldest houses at the western end of the High Street but, by the late 1950s too decayed to be capable of preservation — had as its nucleus a building of (apparently) the fourteenth century; wrapped around two sides of that was a fifteenth century extension with later additions. Nearby was a messuage described in 1670 as having formerly been 'divers cottages, shops and sheds' like the house of Robert Walley and the one made out of a hayloft and stable by Timothy Rogers referred to above; but a hundred yards away two shops had by 1681 been converted into one dwelling.

Externally these houses were probably always coated with plaster, as indeed was all the stonework of All Saints' church, with £30 paid in 1610 by the churchwardens 'for whiting the Church and Steeple on the outside'. In 1853 an architect commented that the 'grand south elevation' of this church was obscured by 'the illtreatment it has sustained at the hand of a parish plasterer'. This was the traditional and sensible method of weatherproofing buildings. The plaster protected the walls from rain and prevented the daub infilling of timber-framed houses from drying out and crumbling. None of this surface plastering has survived in Maldon, so one cannot tell if the walls were decorated with pargetting, such as survives on some buildings in Suffolk and north-west Essex, or if the house signs in Maldon such as the George, the Saracen's Head, the Blue Boar, the Star, the Three Mariners were in the 16th and 17th centuries depicted in this boldly moulded external plasterwork.

Internally the practical comforts of these dwellings would seem to have been considerable, judging by the bequests of treasured pieces of furniture, furnishings and plate or pewter included in their occupiers' wills and by a few descriptions available for the 1620s in the surviving inventories of St Mary's parishioners. Our guide on the great improvements in the English people's standard of living in the reign of Elizabeth I is the *Description of England* of 1577 by William Harrison. His observation that in his lifetime (ie. 1534-1577) housing had been greatly improved by the introduction of chimneys, window glass and by subdivision into several rooms has become the standard statement on the over-all change in domestic architecture and, as he was the parson of Radwinter in this county, all his description can be held to have special relevance to housing in Essex. Window glass has already been mentioned and although it is not often referred to in either the wills or inventories of property in Maldon, perhaps because it was a standard feature, the inference from John Manning's and Christopher Living's stipulations is that by the late sixteenth century glass windows had become as standard a feature of basic housing as piped water and sewerage are nowadays.

99

As for the frequency of staircases and thus of houses arranged into several rooms on two or more levels, it is best to go first to the Hearth Tax Returns from Maldon's three parishes in 1670 and 1672, at the end of more than a century of rebuilding, new building and subdivision of old buildings. These provide an unselective survey of a great part (if not all) of the accommodation available in the town and they appear to indicate that here people had a slightly higher general standard of comfort than the inhabitants of many other towns. The assumption is that the greater the number of hearths the more substantial the house must have been. One hearth is likely to mean at least one room, not every room necessarily having had a fireplace, and it is unlikely that a room in even a grand house in such a town as Maldon would have needed more than one fireplace. Therefore the number of hearths must usually represent the minimum number of rooms in each dwelling. The average number of hearths per household in Maldon was 3.2 in 1670 and 1672, whereas the average in other Essex towns lay between two and three. The difference can also be expressed by showing the percentage of houses in the main towns which had no more than one or two hearths:

> at Thaxted ... 80.3 per cent
> at Witham ... 76.1 per cent
> at Colchester ... 70.5 per cent
> at Chelmsford ... 63.7 per cent
> at Harwich ... 56.4 per cent
> at Maldon ... 51.5 per cent

Only one fifth of Thaxted's inhabitants lived in houses with more than two hearths; at Maldon just under one half of the population lived in houses with three or more hearths. There is no difference in climate between any of these towns to explain why there were rather more fireplaces in Maldon's seventeenth century homes, though coal may have been much cheaper since it was one of the port's principal articles of trade and transport must have added to its price inland (but coal was also imported in large quantities at Colchester). The principal reason for the slightly larger number of hearths in the average Maldon house by 1670 must surely be that the town was a favoured settlement for lesser gentlefolk who would expect and could afford accomodation in houses with several rooms and plenty of coal or wood fires. The standard reached by so many Maldon houses must also reflect the borough corporation's policy of preferring the immigration of those best able to maintain a comfortable way of life.

A few wills and probate inventories provide some indication of the standard of life which the the people of Maldon may have attained in the century and a half preceding the Hearth Tax returns. All kinds of newly fashionable items appear in some early seventeenth century wills, such as window curtains, mirrors, joined tables, cupboards and chairs. None can provide quantifiable information but William Harrison's observations on improvements in the standard of living in the mid-sixteenth century stressed the great increase in useful goods and furnishing as much as the increased privacy for members of the household which the creation of more chambers provided, so it is possible to compare bequests and inventories with his remarks and take a mental tour of some aspects of life in some of Maldon's dwelling houses.

First, a poor man in 1625: John Hunne was a weaver living with his wife only. (His son Robert, was a weaver in Danbury, his daughter Helen was married to John Houlden, joiner of Kelvedon.) Only two rooms are described in the probate inventory made after his death, a Workshop with his loom 'and other implements' and a Chamber, but there must surely have been a Hall, doubling as a kitchen and buttery. His house seems to have been one-storeyed, with half the inventory's total valuation (40s out of £4 5s 0d) provided by the simple furnishing of the chamber (a joined bedstead with a flock mattress, three bolsters, three blankets and three coverlets, one pillow, a warming pan, a chest and a bible). Seventy years before most people had slept on 'straw pallets or rough mats' (wrote Harrison) but John Hunne slept on a joined bedstead with a flock mattress. He and his wife had three bolsters and a pillow, with three blankets and a choice out of three coverlets where earlier generations were covered 'only with a sheet under coverlets made of dagswain or hopharlots [canvas] and a good round log under their heads instead of a bolster or pillow. If it were so that our fathers or the good man of the house had within seven years after his marriage purchased a mattress or a flockbed, and thereto a sack of chaff to rest his head upon, he thought himself to be as well lodged as the lord of the town ...' Hunne's lot in life had not been so hard. Furthermore, his clothing and the money in his purse amounted to 15s whereas the standard person of the 1540s and 1550s remembered by Harrison would count himself rich if his purse contained 'a noble or six shillings in silver' and in addition Hunne had an investment: half an acre of wheat 'on the ground' ready for harvest and worth 20s.

In the same parish lived Francis Hoye, further up in Hunne's trade, a shearman and living until 1627 in a rented house with his wife, four children and perhaps his mother. His house comprised eight domestic rooms and a Milk House, a Workhouse containing eleven sets of roving handles *with the stages, pearkes and other ymplementes* and some teasels, and his Shop which had other tools of his trade. His clothing and ready money amounted to £3 6s 8d, over four times as much as John Hunne's and his eight rooms were full of furnishings such as two glass cases, a 'press cupboard', five varieties of table, window and bed curtains and, especially for his children, there were three 'little low joined stools, one wicker chair ... two little chairs, three little children's boxes'.

Harrison thought house furnishings had 'grown in manner even to passing delicacy' but what might he have thought of Mistress Mary Muffett's bequests in December 1625? Her daughter-in-law received a little table and a joined table with a 'carpet' over it; a god-daughter received a silver gilt salt; three grandchildren got twelve table napkins each and one tablecloth each; her daughter had two chests from 'the little chamber above where I use to lie'. The state in which Mistress Muffett was used to live during her widowhood (and who Mr Muffett was remains unproven: if he was Peter, the Rector of Fobbing 1592 - 1617, whose brother Thomas wrote *The Theatre of Insects*, then his daughter may have been the girl frightened by a spider) would have impressed Harrison. Once upon a time, he said, costly furnishings 'great provision of tapestry, Turkey-work, pewter, brass, fine linen ... costly cupboards of plate...'. had been confined to great merchants' houses, knights, gentry and 'some other wealthy citizens'. As with the wealthier persons of humble social standing in the 1570s who were ambitious to 'garnish their cupboards with plate, their joined beds with tapestry and silk hangings, and their tables with carpets and fine napery', the inventory of this lady made in January 1624 catalogues a treasure trove in seven rooms.

Her Hall had a livery table (for serving food) with a cupboard, to go with the joined table with its green carpet; there was an hour glass, there were some books and on the walls were painted hangings, a looking glass and a picture. In the Parlour her joined bed's furnishings included down pillows, sheets and curtains, all valued at 14s, whilst in the Chamber over the Parlour, which was plainly used as a store-room, there was an even more sumptuous bed valued at £4 16s 0d, two great trunks and two great chests which on opening revealed linen fabrics worth £2 3s 4d, sheets, towels and tablecloths of holland worth £10, pewter candlesticks and spoons worth £4, a chamlett gown and petticoat, and a velvet hat in a hat case, worth £10 10s 0d. Elsewhere there were to be found spoons, bowls, a salt, a whistle, a thimble, all of silver, over £43 in ready money, a window curtain and a beard brush (presumably her late husband's). One wonders about the life of the servant who slept in the Maid's Chamber on a trundlebed, with a trunk and a little box for her clothes, and whose work took her to a Buttery filled by four kettles, two cauldrons, five pots, three possnets, two 'great pans' and four candlesticks, all of brass, and to a second Buttery with other cooking implements. In such a dwelling, as Mistress Muffett would have said as, in her violet gown and wearing her beaver hat she mounted her horse side-saddle, 'the wealth of our country (God be praised therefore and give us grace to employ it well) doth infinitely appear'.

The same thoughts ought to have passed through the mind of Benjamin Andrews in the years before 1630. He lived in a house of seven domestic rooms which were the Hall, with one Parlour adjacent (used as a bedchamber) and a little Buttery, another Parlour adjoining the Entry Passage which also had a bed but was apparently his kitchen as well, a Buttery next to that and two upstairs rooms over the Parlour and the Hall. His Shop is simply said to be 'next the street' and its contents give no clue as to his trade: seven 'old tables small and great', fire irons for cooking, a bucket and some timber. The contents of the house itself suggest at best a more masculine version of Mistress Muffett's domesticity. It had many bits and pieces of downgraded furniture mixed up with frying gear, battledore, old leather cushions, a beer stall and tilter, four bottles, one *ould picter in a frame* and only junk − a pair of bread scales, a little bag of feathers, six lead weights and an old bridle − lying in the Chamber over the Hall. Benjamin Andrews may have been a widower or a bachelor; he was arrested for debt at the instance of John Collett, draper, and Jasper Kingsman, innholder, and this inventory was made by the Serjeant at Mace of the borough for the attachment of his goods. He had committed suicide.

Wills without inventories cannot be of much help. Many of the contents of the testators' houses would not be mentioned, for a variety of reasons, and there was never a necessity to write down the rooms in which the items bequeathed were to be found. Edward Reade, a cook, mentioned only the Hall and the Chamber in 1598 but his bequests included wall hangings, settles, a joined table and forms, a little court table, two chests and a cupboard. Ten years before, his grandfather Edward Reade (also a cook) referred to the Hall, two Chambers and a Buttery and many of his bequests were his stock in trade − platters, dishes, fruit dishes, saucers, porringers, napkins, diaper tablecloths, hand towels − but the 'amendment of lodging' of which Harrison had written eleven years before had plainly occurred in the Reade household by then (1588). He had bed curtains of red and yellow say, fine bedding, painted cloths in his Chamber, hangings, chairs, stools and a table in the next Chamber, six silver spoons and 'a high candlestick with holes in the nose'. Ten years before that the ancient John Spuddell had very little to leave, save a canvas sheet (like the 'coverlets of dagswain' mentioned by Harrison) and a jacket but John Chandler, a shoemaker, had eleven pieces of pewter ware to bequeath and a featherbed, and Robert Stode (1569) had three dozen of pewter and two brass pots.

Lastly in this attempt at a walk around Maldon houses there stands on the north side of the river beside Fullbridge one whose structure has survived substantially unchanged from the later sixteenth century, except for a roof of new tiles and the insertion of modern widow frames. It was called Wrenche's and Thomas Wrenche, the last recorded man of that name in the town, was dead by 1409. So there was a building on this site from at least the beginning of the fifteenth century which had become by 1586 (as it was described in a conveyance from Richard Roberts to Edmund Hart, two glovers) an old, unoccupied dwelling house with two barns, a shed and an old house called *thould kytchyn*. There is now no trace of anything earlier than the existing house, the Welcome Sailor inn, which is an entire rebuilding at some time between Edmund Hart's purchase of the site and 1605, by which time it had become the property of another glover, Alderman Thomas Welles, and was inhabited by his eldest son John Welles.

The structure which has thus remained intact since about 1600 is architecturally unexceptional but interesting for its evidence of the standard of accommodation that artificers who were in an upper level of the borough's freeburgess group might expect. There were twelve rooms, their dividing walls certainly a part of the new construction. The ground and first floors each had four rooms and in the roof space were four more attic rooms, each of those fitted with two dormer windows. Two big chimney stacks of brick contain the flues of eight fireplaces and against the north wall are two original built-in stair vices. The house is simply a narrow, timber-framed box divided into six bays, its long sides facing north and south. The end bays form rooms almost square in plan on each floor and they are separated from the two central bays by two narrow sections each of which encloses, in the middle, one of the chimney stacks, on the north side one of the stair vices, and on the south side each of these narrow sections forms a lobby between the rooms on either side.

Compare that with this 1652 description of Paynes' Tenement: it had on the ground floor a Hall, a 'great Shop' and another Shop 'new erected'; and on the first floor four Chambers (two of which had been recently made out of one Chamber over the 'great Shop'), with a Garret room above them in the roof space. Wrenche's had eight hearths, in 1662 Robert Alcock, the owner-occupier of Paynes', paid tax on three hearths. The lay-out was different, since Paynes' was built or re-built in the mid-sixteenth century and had an entry passage through the middle of the building, like those described in the inventories of Francis Hoy's and Benjamin Andrews' houses, and (as in their premises) Paynes' included a workshop, whereas the Welles were glovers and had their working premises on the hillside across the river from Wrenche's where there was running water and access to tan pits.

The house that Edmund Hart built also gives us a summary of the housing trends in sixteenth and seventeenth century Maldon. It was clearly constructed so as to make subdivision possible and by December 1670 it was 'severed and divided into two several tenements or dwelling houses'. It was a grandson of Alderman Welles who capitalised on his inheritance of Wrenches. He was Thomas Welles late of Kelvedon, 'now' of Feering and a shoemaker, son of Christopher Welles of Messing, yeoman and butcher, who had been the youngest son of the Alderman and inheritor by the custom of Borough English.

CHAPTER 5

# COMMERCE

IN HIS *ITINERARY* John Leland noted his impressions of the principal characteristics of the market towns he had visited between 1524 and 1543 during his tours of England. What he would have written of Maldon (or may have done, for a note about the origins of the Darcy family exists in his surviving manuscripts) has to be imagined but the possibilities can be considerably narrowed down from local sources even though they are economically somewhat sterile. No subsequent traveller in Tudor or Stuart times made any useful comment on this subject but it is improbable that they would have found the inhabitants either reliant on the manufacture of textiles or occupied chiefly in shipping, the two areas of the economy which might most readily spring to mind. Instead, beer brewing, leather crafts, market gardening and perhaps tailoring are candidates for special notice but the overall impression which a perceptive visitor would probably have received, at any time in the sixteenth and for about the first third of the seventeenth centuries, would have been the great importance of the town to the commerce of the local region because of the facility provided by its borough court for deferred payments and for the guaranteeing of commercial settlements between traders over a wide area of the county.

In no way was any one craft preponderant in the occupational structure of this community. Maldon was not noted for textile production. Indeed, by the early fifteenth century, the quantities of Chelmsford and of Maldon cloths (as Dr Britnell has shown in his study of late-medieval Colchester) were insignificant when compared with the output of the truly textile-dominated towns and large villages in northern Essex and southern Suffolk; and during recessions in the clothing trades Maldon was not so greatly burdened with many unemployed workmen as were, for example, its neighbours Witham, Colchester and Bocking. Similarly the very flexible attitude of Maldon's magistrates and employers towards apprenticeship (as shown in Chapter 2) made for greater ease in riding-out economic storms, by the shedding of some part of the workforce. During severe unemployment in the textile trades, as in 1623 and 1624, the parish constables were diligent in bringing before the magistrates unlicensed inmates and 'idle' men who were ordered to depart the town. And the absence of craft organisation made for considerable flexibility in the occupational structure. In Elizabethan Bristol, as Professor Hoskins has remarked, 'there were over a hundred distinct trades for apprentices to choose from' and sixty-three in Northampton in 1524; eighty-two occupations (excluding those classified as Agriculture) existed in Maldon between 1560 and 1643 — as shown in Table 3 — but unlike Bristol there were no craft guilds here and the numbers of men in each occupation varied from year to year in the ebb and flow of inhabitants. The decenners' catalogues indicate that the numbers of wage-earners also varied considerably from year to year between 1569 and 1582; that would seem to have been the usual situation of the town's labour force.

From its administrative and legal records the impression to be gained is that the borough maintained the reputability of its trade solely by implementing statutory conditions on sales: by its officers' searches of the goods exposed for sale, by restricting private sales in shops or at the quayside so as to bring it all into the open market. The custumal was confined to regulating the marketing of commodities. There were no formal barriers regulating the entry of new men, except that two freemen were required as pledges for each man who sought to buy his freedom of the borough. There were no formal prohibitions on men taking up more than one trade. 'Foreigners' were to have lattices before their shop windows and to pay a quarterly fine but were not otherwise impeded in competing with residents. Only one attempt by Maldon craftsmen to exclude countrymen is on record, that of seven shoemakers calling themselves 'the whole and entire number and company of the art, mistery and science of shoemaking within this town' who petitioned the Corporation in 1581 that outsiders should be prohibited from 'selling their wares by retail or otherwise on the market days or any other days, other than in the open fairs' because these outsiders 'most unjustly and unlawfuly intrude themselves into the liberty of the borough and there do sell their wares on the market days to the great decay and utter undoing of us the shoemaker inhabitants'. This petition was unsuccessful. Nor was there an organised 'mistery' of this or any other craft in Maldon. The Corporation, chosen out of the entire body of resident and non-resident freemen, was the sole authority and the Bailiffs, by their 'communing' with newcomers and by the Quarter Sessions' deportation orders for undesirable competitors or unemployed persons, themselves exercised a very personalised regulatory system to protect the health of the borough's commerce. The present-day observer is really presented with two centuries of economic policy made and directed by the groups of aldermen who by turns acted as Bailiffs. To borrow a recurrent phrase in the chamberlains' expenditure accounts it was, or was intended to be, an economy 'at Master Bailiffs' commandment'.

Moreover, what has been written about short-distance resettlement patterns suggests that the continuously unstable nature of the town's population must have inhibited the establishment of any long-term family specialities; the frequent changes in membership of the freeman body must have prevented any manufacture or service from being monopolised by a permanent group of families. The interdependence of town and country meant that almost every activity in Maldon had its counterpart in the rural neighbourhood, or in the adjacent markets with which the town's trade was so closely connected, so that even in activities where the townsmen might have been predominant − shipping is the outstanding example − they were no more than activities common to the whole area.

It is difficult to draw up any satisfactory hierarchy of occupations for any period in Maldon. From about 1556 to about 1585 and from 1597 to the 1640's there are numerous attributions of trades or skills to inhabitants' names but the importance of any group of occupations in an urban community cannot be measured simply by numbers of persons. The trades which recruited the greatest numbers of apprentices were the ones best able to absorb a large workforce, but the occupations which required the greater expertise of a smaller number of persons (tailors, for example, or apothecaries, or shipwrights) were often far more influential and wealthy than handicrafts, exercising a controlling influence over the whole community which cannot now be discerned from an analysis of freemen's or apprentices' or corporation members' occupations. Maldon's enrolled indentures of apprentices are by no means complete records and so a fallible guide to those occupations which required the larger workforces. One has to fall back on numbers and to work from the indentures, the statements on occupations given in the borough courts' pleas, and stray references in Quarter Sessions presentments, wills, account rolls and the surviving miscellanea of the town clerks' files. From these Table 3 has been compiled. The numbers are for all stated tradesmen ('free' or 'foreign') and, it must be stressed, are not a definitive collection. For the purpose of comparison this Table has been drawn up to conform with the arrangement of occupations given by Dr J.F. Pound in his study of the social and trade structure of Norwich, 1525-1575, which has been widely adopted for surveys of other cities' and towns' occupational structures and itself is comparable with Professor Hoskins' ordering of the trades in Coventry, Northampton and Leicester c1524.

Apart from the inappropriateness of drawing comparisons between Maldon in 1560-1643, where there were only about a hundred self-employed males at any one time, and much larger communities over forty years before (in 1524) or a great city in 1525-1575, too strict an adherence to Table 3's numerical evidence would be misleading because the small size of this community meant frequent doublings of occupations. And further to confuse the situation, the pleas of debt reveal that there were some who followed one trade in Maldon, another occupation elsewhere: Robert Bryant, stated to be a yeoman of Sudbury and a shoemaker of Maldon (1608); Robert Nethersall, a yeoman of Brentwood and a vintner of Maldon (1624); and Thomas Shergate, a shoemaker of Maldon and a chandler of Leigh-on-Sea. These three cannot have been the only ones. As in other towns, some of Maldon's butchers were also innkeepers or alehouse keepers − to tide them over the periods in the year when meat was scarce or flesh-eating was forbidden- and bakers were often also brewers. But less expected cases of mixed employment also occur. John Dawes, a leading freeman of the 1520s was variously described in 1524 as a merchant adventurer, a haberdasher and a vintner. The activities of Thomas Furnes in the last third of the sixteenth century ranged from innkeeping to the promotion of bay-weaving, from being a wholesale vintner to

|  | 1560-1583 | 1601-1643 |
|---|---|---|
| **BUILDING & ALLIED** | | |
| Bricklayers & tilers | 3 | 9 |
| Carpenters | 3 | 4 |
| Glaziers & painters | 2 | 3 |
| Joiners | 5 | 13 |
| Shipwrights | 3 | 1 |
|  | 17 (6%) | 31(7%) |
| **WOODWORK** | | |
| Basketmakers | — | 1 |
| Coopers | 6 | 5 |
| Fletchers | 5 | — |
| Turners (inc. dishturners) | — | 1 |
| Wheelwrights | 1 | — |
|  | 12 (4%) | 7(2%) |
| **FOOD & DRINK** | | |
| Bakers | 6 | 7 |
| Beer brewers | 10 | 11 |
| Butchers | 9 | 30 |
| Cooks | 1 | 1 |
| Costermongers | 1 | — |
| Fishermen | 3 | 5 |
| Fishmongers | — | 1 |
| Innkeepers | 5 | 18 |
| Maltsters | — | — |
| Millers | 3 | 3 |
| Oatmealmakers | — | 3 |
| Saltworkers (Saltwellers) | — | 3 |
| Victuallers or tipplers | | |
| Vintners | 3 | 2 |
|  | 41(14%) | 84(18%) |
| **DISTRIBUTIVE TRADES** | | |
| Apothecaries | 1 | 6 |
| Barbers | 1 | 6 |
| Drapers | 4 | 1 |
| Grocers | 4 | 2 |
| Haberdashers | 2 | 11 |

*Table 3. Occupations at Maldon, 1560-83 and 1601-43*

|  | 1560-1583 | 1601-1643 |
|---|---|---|
| Linendrapers | 9 | 21 |
| Mercers | 1 | − |
| Merchants (inc. coal merchants) | 9 | 6 |
| Tallowchandlers | 2 | 2 |
| Woollendrapers | 3 | 9 |
|  | 36(12%) | 64(14%) |
| **TEXTILES** |  |  |
| Bay weavers | − | 4 |
| Clothiers | 3 | 12 |
| Combers | − | 1 |
| Dyers | 1 | 1 |
| Feltmakers | − | 1 |
| Fullers | 2 | 1 |
| Shearmen | 2 | 4 |
| Say makers | − | − |
| Silkweavers | − | 1 |
| Weavers | 9 | 22 |
|  | 14 (5%) | 47(10%) |
| **CLOTHING TRADES** |  |  |
| Hatters | − | 1 |
| Tailors & hosiers | 23 | 42 |
| Seamstresses | 1 | − |
|  | 24 (8%) | 43(9%) |
| **PROFESSIONAL** |  |  |
| Barber surgeons (or surgeons) | 1 | 1 |
| Lawyers and Town Clerks | 6 | 4 |
| Musicians | − | 2 |
| Physicians | − | 4 |
| Scriveners | 1 | 2 |
| Schoolmasters | 1 | 2 |
|  | 9 (3%) | 15(3%) |
| **MISCELLANEOUS** |  |  |
| Clockmakers | − | 1 |
| Limeburners | 1 | 2 |
| Horseleaches | 1 | − |
| Knackers | − | − |

*Table 3 continued*

109

|  | 1560-1583 | 1601-1643 |
|---|---|---|
| Ropemakers | – | 2 |
|  | 2 (1%) | 5(1%) |
| **METALWORK** |  |  |
| Blacksmiths and 'smiths' | 8 | 14 |
| Braziers | – | 2 |
| Cutlers (inc. sheargrinders) | 6 | – |
| Gunsmiths | – | 2 |
| Ironmongers | – | 2 |
| Locksmiths | – | 1 |
| Pewterers | – | – |
| Pinners | – | 2 |
|  | 14 (5%) | 23(5%) |
| **LEATHER & ALLIED** |  |  |
| Collarmakers | 3 | 9 |
| Curriers | 2 | 2 |
| Glovers | 9 | 22 |
| Harnessmakers | 3 | 2 |
| Saddlers | 1 | 3 |
| Shoemakers (& cobblers) | 25 | 34 |
| Tanners | 2 | 4 |
|  | 45(15%) | 76(16%) |
| **AGRICULTURE** |  |  |
| Gardeners | – | 8 |
| Husbandmen | 3 | 9 |
| Labourers | 13 | 7 |
| Yeomen | 13 | 24 |
|  | 29(10%) | 48(10%) |
| **TRANSPORT** |  |  |
| Carters (or carriers) | – | 2 |
| Mariners | 36 | 11 |
| Porters | 2 | – |
|  | 38(13%) | 13(3%) |
| **GENTLEMEN** | 10 (3%) | 10(2%) |
| ALL: | 291 | 466 |

*Table 3 continued*

a wool dealer. One freeman of 1625 was described as a butcher and a linendraper. And before going on to other combinations beyond the Food and Drinks trades, it may be noted that the innkeepers of Maldon were as impermanent and occupationally changeable as the rest. Thirty innkeepers and alehouse keepers were recorded between 1569 and 1576 but none were licensed for more than five successive years; twelve were innkeepers or tipplers for only one year; many were simultaneously craftsmen. In 1569 these licencees numbered twelve, of whom one was also a shipwright, another a fishmonger, two were tailors, two were blacksmiths, another a glover and another a shoemaker. They were so styled in their recognisances. In the remainder of the 1570's they were joined or replaced in the licenced trade by, among others, a limeburner, a shearman and a joiner, besides two more shoemakers, another glover, a collarmaker and a husbandman, all apparently combining their activities, not changing them.

Alderman William Eve was a grocer but his consignment of goods delivered at Maldon Hythe in 1569 indicates that he was dealing in a very miscellaneous range of commodities: dyestuffs, cotton, kersey cloth, iron (three tons), alum, canvas, oil (49½ gallons), bay salt, beside the currants, raisins and assorted groceries of his nominal trade. So the distinctions drawn in Table 3 between the grocer, the woollendraper, the ironmonger and the merchant have to be ignored in Maldon's case. Similarly Alderman Ralph Breeder, a haberdasher, bequeathed to his three menservants (1609) grocery wares, mercery, a stock of drapery goods and the contents of a 'salt shop' and his will also shows him to have further diversified into arable farming and dairying. Dr A.D. Dyer's account of the trades of Worcester in the sixteenth century shows that one can expect to find men such as these diversifying their trade: he has cited mercers (their speciality was the luxury fabric market) whose stock included grocery goods, haberdashery, all those sundries such as buckles and pins, lace and brushes which one would still expect to find in drapers' stores, and (like Master Eve's alum and dyestuffs) supplies for cloth finishers. It would be difficult to decide which of the occupations listed in Table 3 supplied the town clerks and the chamberlains of Maldon with those quires of paper, the vellum and ink bottles which regularly appear as purchases in their account rolls, and supplied them also to the townspeople, or stocked the strings for the cittern which three absconding apprentices strummed as they spent a night out on the saltings, if not shopkeepers such as these two men and their fellows.

An enquiry of 1608 on the stock of grain in Maldon described also the expected weekly output of bread and beer. Four brewers were named: for two brewing was 'their only maintenance' but the third was also a glover, the fourth was an innkeeper. The enquiry also lists a blacksmith, a bricklayer, a labourer and a shoemaker as regular bakers, whose joint weekly output for sale was reckoned to be about half as much as the production of the three full-time bakers. At the end of this enquiry comes one who exemplifies the difficulty in categorising the occupations of an unrestricted, opportunist, changeable economy in a transient social structure: 'Jonas Harrison doth both bake and brew, but we cannot learn what [weekly quantities]; and he both keepeth an inn and buyeth and selleth small wares; and use[th] such like means for his maintenance'.

In constructing Table 3 none are represented in more than one category. For each person it has been his principal, or most frequently attributed trade or profession, which has been counted. A standardised table of trades has its uses as a rough sketch of the town's economy. It can be usefully compared with the scalogram of Suffolk and Norfolk market towns drawn up by Dr J.H.C. Patten, which shows how few were those which had a range comparable with Maldon. It provided all the services and almost all the commodities which country people were likely to require, which they could at the time hope to find in a substantial market town but which they might not expect to get in lesser market places such as (in Essex) Burnham or Rochford, Dunmow or Coggeshall or Witham. Some Maldon traders did have shops or market stalls in other local markets: Richard Simpson had two shops, one in Maldon, another (less well stocked and apparently subsidiary) at Braintree in 1628; a blacksmith in 1577 had leases on two smithies, one in Maldon, the other at Tillingham; Rose Hearse had in 1609 been for long selling fish and oysters at Chelmsford market; a plea of 1627 describes Jeremiah Pledger as being 'a joiner of Chelmsford alias a joiner of Maldon' and Richard Collett was described in 1626 as a draper of Maldon and of Colchester; in the course of a lawsuit in the borough court (1600) against Henry Steven, a yeoman of Witham, it was noted that 'Stevens' wife told the under-bailiff of Witham they had a great deal of goods here at Maldon which they would shortly fetch away'; and all those *commorantes* or 'foreign' traders in Maldon by definition had premises or trading pitches in other markets. What matters is that all their trades, goods, services, were always available in Maldon's own market.

To this observation it may be objected that some trades are missing from the Table, or markedly under-represented. Why were there apparently no saltworkers in Maldon before 1600? The River Blackwater is one of the most saline in England, salt-refining along its shores has prehistoric origins and pure Maldon salt now has at least a European-wide distribution. Why were sawyers so few in a town whose houses were almost always timber-framed? Or why did carpenters and joiners apparently always constitute so small a proportion of the work-force? Obviously such deficiencies existed because many occupations were as suitably pursued in the country and along the area's riversides. Basket weaving and wood turning were rustic crafts; brick and tile-making required suitable clay beds; sawyers kept to the woodlands they tended, so that for the complete rebuilding of the Fullbridge in 1535 almost all the timber was cut and sawn in either Heybridge or Great Totham

112

at Thomas Sammes' Wood and for extensive repairs to this bridge in 1615 the Bailiffs drew up a contract with two millwrights of Danbury. The strange deficiency of Table 3 in fishmongers is partly because they were the same as the fishermen and also because it would be to Maldon that the fishermen of the villages along the estuary brought their catches for sale. And many townsmen (then as now) liked to combine their land trade with some profitable fishing: nineteen inhabitants were named in an Admiralty Court session of 1567 as unlicensed fishers; they included a shipwright, a surgeon, a grocer, two weavers, an applemonger, a glover and a currier. The borough's oyster fishery was always leased to outsiders.

Ship building was another craft which could be carried on anywhere along the creeks of the river. Other deficiencies seem to be the result of doubling-up, as with gunsmiths, cutlers and locksmiths who may often have been the same tradesmen − it was cutlers in Elizabethan times who were paid to maintain the borough armoury's guns − and similarly for blacksmiths and braziers. Those described as husbandmen, yeomen, or even as gentlemen, may have supplied a more diverse range of goods and services than foods and animals: Thomas Trower was described both as yeoman and knacker; Thomas Plume, Esquire, was a landowner who also traded in coal and one of his fields was called Gravel Pits Land.

For many of its everyday wares the town seems to have depended very considerably on visiting traders and peddlers. For example, pewter and brass candlesticks, drinking vessels and cooking pots were frequently included in townspeople's bequests but no pewterer is ever referred to and the term brazier is only to be found in the seventeenth century. The fines levied by the Clerk of the Market, however, frequently refer to defective pewter ware and to swords, daggers, and other metal goods. Moreover there were many everyday wares which had to be imported, then as now, such as glass, paper and books, musical instruments, pottery, paint, tar, oils, starch and (perhaps) soap, although many more items than it would be profitable to guess at may have been made, from time to time, by Maldon men working under different occupational labels.

## FOOD AND DRINK

Maldon's occupational structure between 1560 and 1643 compares interestingly with Northampton and Leicester in 1524 (as examined by Professor Hoskins in his study, *Provincial England*). In all three communities each major category occupied roughly the same share of all their trades, crafts, services, whilst their rank ordering points up the specialities of each town (see Table 4): victualling and the preparation and utilisation of leather.

| Northampton 1524 | Leicester 1524 | Maldon 1560-1643 |
|---|---|---|
| 1. Leather | 1. Food. Drink | 1. Food. Drink |
| 2. Food. Drink | 2. Leather | 2. Leather |
| 3. Clothing | 3. Clothing | 3. Clothing |
| 4. Textiles | 4. Building | 4. Building |
| 5. Building | 5. Textiles | 5. Textiles |
| 6. Metalwork | 6. Metalwork | 6. Metalwork |

Table 4. Occupations at Leicester, Northampton and Maldon.

The prominence of the food and drink trades may suggest that urban populations devoted too much of their labour to their own maintenance in the early sixteenth century and that this continued to be the case with Maldon into the middle years of the seventeenth century. Was this a feature of the urban crisis? If so Maldon's decline was continuing long after other medieval boroughs had picked themselves up and re-developed their economies. But when one examines the occupations within the Food and Drink category it becomes apparent that the suppliers of victuals were not particularly numerous in Maldon and that two other trades in this category stood out as exceptional in number, whose activities gave a distinctive character to this town's economy: beer brewing and butchering. This applies to the other categories as well. A more selective and detailed hierarchy of the 'top trades' of Maldon marks out these trades and suggests some movements within the occupational structure:

| | 1560-83 | 1600-43 |
|---|---|---|
| Clothing makers | 23 | 43 |
| Textile suppliers | 19 | 42 |
| Shoemakers | 25 | 34 |
| Butchers | 9 | 30 |
| Glovers | 9 | 22 |
| Beer brewers | 10 | 11 |

Beer brewing required considerable initial investment, much more individual capital than ale brewing, and it was capable of almost industrial organisation because (thanks to the hops, the ingredient which is the essential distinction between beer and ale, and is a preservative) each brew could produce several weeks' transportable supply. Moreover, greater quantities could be produced from the same amount of mash than of ale. Where the ale-founder usually had to sell each brew immediately, large quantities of beer could be stored, or could still be fit to drink after several days in transit by ship. When Richard Hart confessed to complicity in his servant girl's murder of her baby (his daughter, whom he had buried in a dunghill) in 1586, he asked the Bailiffs 'to have ten days' liberty to sell such beer as he now hath in his house, and from thence to surcease [brewing]'.

So the presence of a significant number of men involved in this trade at Maldon from the fifteenth century gives it a special interest. The coal trade which had already developed in the borough by 1400 meant that brewers here could obtain the fuel necessary to carry out their lengthy and necessary mash-boilings more cheaply than would have been possible inland: that and the considerable alien work-force which was present in fifteenth century Essex may partly explain why it became so much a speciality of the town.

It was not so novel an occupation in sixteenth century towns as used to be thought — bays and says, hops and beer did not come into England all in one year — but there is some evidence that Maldon, like Colchester, was one of the places to which this Dutch and Flemish activity did come in the early fifteenth century. The first plea in the borough court clearly referring to this occupation was between a Maldon shipmaster, John Bonayre, and a Colchester beer brewer, Thomas Wode, in 1446; within two years a Maldon brewer, John Deyre, was plaintiff against Simon Emenote of London (1448). As with Colchester, where some of the first beer sellers were of Dutch origin, aliens were closely involved in Maldon's early brewing trade, as is shown in an ordinance of 1463 which made an exception for 'the brewers' coopers' in a ruling that aliens and 'Dutchmen' were not to carry any kind of weapon other than their knives for cutting up food. There were, then, brewers at Maldon before 1460 who were employers of men from the Low Countries and whose production warranted the maintenance of their own barrel-coopers who apparently used distinctive long daggers which were essential to their craft.

These 'Dutchmen' were associated with the brewing of beer until the 1570s. Perhaps the last of them in the town were Peter Fox, stated to have been an alien, who was declared to have committed suicide in 1558, and Cornelius Peterson — a 'Dutch' sounding name — who was a self-employed brewer and in whose well the unfortunate Fox drowned himself. That they appear mostly as expert servants both to brewers and to coopers underlines the entrepreneurial element which distinguished brewing from most other occupations. It required considerable initial expense for its specialised equipment and also specialised buildings so that one should suppose investors were always involved in the establishment of the breweries which are referred to from time to time in the Maldon records. John Deyre and Thomas King, brewers in the mid-fifteenth century, are likely to be early examples of merchants who employed alien workmen to brew whilst they organised the supply of hops, of malted barley produced by farmers and maltsters (such as Terling and Thaxted suppliers appearing in lawsuits of 1421 and 1454), of barrels made by the coopers and their privileged alien workmen.

There were at least three or four brewers in business at any one time in the town, so there must have been at least that number of specialist buildings, each sited near a well or, preferably, a hillside spring. Once each brewery had been established its business stood a good chance of being continuous, so long as successive owners could find managers. One was in existence beside or behind Fullbridge Street by 1500 and may be the same as brew houses inferred from deeds to have been in that street over the next 150 years. A fresh water supply in Fullbridge Street would be readily available there, from the springs along the steep hillside. In 1503 it belonged to a widow, Isabel Peverel (who then sued its occupier for the last year's rent). In July 1574 Andrew Michaelson sued John Loughborough alias Brewer, who is stated to have been the manager (*ballivus*) of the plaintiff's premises in St Peter's parish, which was probably the one Mistress Peverel had owned and was by 1574 known as The Brewing House. When the manager took over, Michaelson's stock comprised 100 kilderkins, 100 firkins, all the necessary brewer's equipment and, as materials, 100 quarters of malt, 12 quarters of wheat, 12 quarters of barley and 120 tuns of hops. He seems to have been overstocked with hops but the pleas of debts in the borough court indicate that 100 quarters was a standard quantity of malt bought in at any one time by brewers. In 1569 there were complaints about Michaelson's products: his strong beer was selling (from the brewery) at 7 shillings a barrel but the Clerk of the Market judged it was insufficiently strong and should be sold as double beer at 4 shillings a barrel.

Whilst Bedfordshire, Hertfordshire, Cambridgeshire and Huntingdonshire were for most of eastern and central England the principal suppliers of barley and malt, Maldon brewers may have obtained their supplies from nearer home. Two of the deals made by or for Thomas Petchey 1567-69 were with a yeoman of Chafford Hundred (William Augure); one was certainly for supplying malt and costing £135, the other was with a local landowner, John Sammes of Langford (£10) and probably also for malt. It is noticeable that maltsters are absent from Table 3; possibly the brewers had their own maltings but only one is referred to in this town before the later seventeenth century, purchased in 1597 by John Cade for the high price at that time of £66. Perhaps such buildings were too much of a fire-risk among

116

timber buildings and malt was also regularly available from supplies brought in by merchants at the Hythe. Hops were also mostly imported, either from the Netherlands in coasters like the *Black George* of Ostend, or from Kent, or perhaps from parts of Essex and Suffolk. There was even some hop-growing in the town itself. Oatmeal was an ingredient of beer which Michaelson's stock did not include but this may have been purchased as required, for the market place had standings for its sale − six rents from oatmeal sellers were listed in 1599 − and some craftsmen may have prepared it as a domestic side-line, for the will of a blacksmith (Thomas Syttery) refers to a *wootemeale myll*, but by about 1640 a full-time miller was at work in Maldon, an oatmeal-maker named John Brown (died 1648) whose widow in 1655 bequeathed 'the Mill, being an oatmeal mill, and the mill house, near the Town Well in All Saints' parish'. This was sited a few yards from the centre of the market place and nearby there was (or had been, by 1648) a fulling mill. What motive power was used? Were there windmills on the backside of the market place? There is no clear answer to that question.

By 1600 a brewery much larger than those in the town itself had been built on the open marsh-side of the river, where Fullbridge House now stands. Sold to a linendraper, Matthew Coe, in October 1672 for at least £288, it consisted then of a dwelling, a brew house, a beer house and (by then) its own large brick malting house. In 1620 a lease of the great Portman Marsh from the Corporation described how the land was traversed by 'certain pipes or other conveyances to bring the water from the fresh river by or through the marsh ... on the north-west of the Causeway ... unto the brewhouse late of Edward Pike, deceased [1617] and now of Thomas Harris'. Just how the fresh river water was piped over level ground, and indeed across a space of at least half a mile from, perhaps, Heybridge Mill, must remain a technological mystery. When the brewer, Edward Pike, sold it in 1608 it was known as The Beerhouse and perhaps its subsequent ownership by Paul Dewes of Stowlangtoft (father of Sir Symonds D'Ewes), who was also a freeman and occasional resident of the borough, indicates the attractiveness of investment in Maldon's brewing trade in the late sixteenth century.

Compare the value of the Fullbridge brewery at its sale in 1672 (£288) with the price of dwelling houses at Maldon in the decade 1668-76: they ranged from thirteen shillings (£0.65) to £120, with £50 as the median price, excepting only the great Friars' Mansion which was sold for £350 and to which this brewery was the nearest in value. The two inns sold in that decade (The George and The Ship) were also above average price at £75 and £120 respectively. So beer had certainly made its mark on the town's economy by the late seventeenth century, with a history of steady growth throughout the period.

All Maldon's major brewers appear to have produced more than was necessary for local consumption. In an enquiry of 1608 on the consumption of corn supplies three brewing concerns were listed, consuming 40 quarters of malt barley weekly, which (at 18 gallons of beer per bushel of malt, as claimed by an early Stuart writer) would amount to almost 6,000 gallons of beer per weekly brew. Far more than the town's entire population could safely consume! At about 30 pints for each adult each week and allowing for considerable additional consumption on market days, there would still have been over half the brewers' production available for deliveries outside the town. In Henry VIII's reign many south-eastern ports did a thriving trade in exports of both beer and hops to France and the Netherlands, and a Burnham beer brewer (Thomas Ongham) in May 1569 was lading *The Harry* of Maldon for export 'across the sea', so it should not be surprising that in the middle of the century this borough's officials anticipated a regular export of beer: their chamberlains' accounts in 1568 specify receipts of toll for 'beer carried beyond the sea'. That cannot have lasted long, as warfare between England and Spain disrupted trade with the Netherlands from about 1580, but it remained a commodity on which tolls were charged at the town quay. Unfortunately the accountants usually presented a composite entry of the water bailiff's receipts but in four years (1565, 1566, 1568 and 1575) itemised accounts were presented which show the toll on beer carried from Maldon Hythe as respectively 22, 10, 13 and 12.5 per cent of all receipts for tolls on both in-coming and out-going foodstuffs and other goods. The continuity of the trade and the indications of production for distribution beyond the immediate locality at points across the two centuries at least suggests strongly that here brewing was a principal creator of modest prosperity.

The great number of butchers in Table 3 can partly be accounted for by the necessity of having all the meat consumed in the entire area prepared and sold under supervision and in publically controlled circumstances. For this the borough provided the Butcher Row and also 'the Bull Ring in the open face of the market' as it is described in almost the only direct reference to an essential feature of the horrors of the Tudor and Stuart flesh-shambles. Only in 'the common market assigned', as Maldon's earliest custumals insisted, might meat be sold and if a butcher did 'kill his beast at his house, [it was necessary] that he bring his flesh to the market with the skin, that the Market Looker may have the oversight thereof, whether the flesh be able to be sold or not'.

Numerous, frequently repeated injunctions – that bulls might not be slaughtered and offered for sale until they had been baited in the ring, that butchers were not to throw bones and hides into the churchyard behind the Butcher Row nor to trade from their own houses on market days, and that 'no butcher within this town dwelling or any other to the same town resorting shall from henceforth at any time hereafter blow their flesh, nor thrust up the kidneys of their flesh which they do kill or bring to sell' - emphasise the importance of the butchers' distributive trade for ensuring regular customers and the public responsibility of the Bailiffs

118

to maintain a wholesome, reputable meat supply for the whole market area of their borough. Here was a staple commodity whose distribution had to be maintained in one place, in the borough's market.

One of the gravestones in All Saints' church bore (until at least 1638) a latten plate of 1453 commemorating William Reade, citizen and butcher of London, and displaying his merchant mark, a butcher's pole-axe; another brass, commemorating Richard Wood, displayed the arms granted in 1530 to the Butchers' Company of London. Both are reminders that the butchers' trade extended beyond the sale of meat to supplying hides and tallow for the leather and other crafts in the area and in London, as well as in Maldon; and that one of the most lucrative aspects of the butchers' craft was cattle dealing, especially arranging for a steady seasonal supply of meat 'on the hoof' to the London market. Maldon's butchers, as has been shown (Chapter 4), owned or leased the immense field area surrounding and constricting the borough's housing space. A considerable proportion of the animals grazed there must always have been intended to be herded on from pasture to pasture until Smithfield was reached. Beyond the town, on the vast grazing-land of Dengie and Thurstable Hundreds, yet more and more contingents of cattle and sheep were fattened before butchers from London, Chelmsford, Colchester, Burnham and Rochford, and from Maldon bought them and contracted with the drovers to move them into the local markets or, more often, to London. There is no means of measuring the amounts supplied to the capital or its suburbs from the Maldon market but, as with beer, it is clear that the local population was incapable of consuming even a half of its stock and that neighbouring markets cannot have needed more than a fraction of the surplus. London, growing fast and spreading throughout the sixteenth and seventeenth centuries, offered a ready market and it is no more a surprise to find city butchers with a base in Maldon than in the 1860s to find agents of Chicago meat processers in Abilene.

Market gardening enjoyed the same ready trade with London's markets as the butchers and, most probably, the brewers. Numerous gardens unattached to any housing and separately leased, which could have been cultivated for market produce, are referred to in early sixteenth century deeds of the town. It is interesting that the fortune of the Appleton family of Dartford and South Benfleet was apparently built from large-scale trade in farm produce which they transported to the city in a fleet of hoys, of which their 40-ton *Mary* of Benfleet was the largest vessel of its kind in the Thames trade during the 1540s. One of the family, Roger Appleton, was well-enough known to Maldon's governing Catholics in 1558 to be elected an M.P. for the borough and his ship was trading within the Port of Maldon, so part of his cargoes may have come from here in the 1540s and 50s. The apples, pears, medlars and cherries of Maldon orchards (in 1574 the aldermen took a present of cherries when they spent an evening with their M.P. Vincent

119

Harris at The Friars), the root crops of its market gardens, were able to provide some part of the seasonal fruit and the 24,000 imported loads per year of carrots, parsnips and turnips which by Charles I's reign were being devoured by the population of London and Westminster.

The yeomen, husbandmen and labourers who formed 10 per cent of the occupational structure of Maldon no doubt contributed much of the supply of vegetables and fruit as well as the beer, cheese, grain, straw, hay, bullimong, timber and ostrey-wood, and coal which was shipped tide by tide out of the Port to London but the occupational term Gardener only makes its appearance at Maldon in a will of 1605 and a conveyance of 1614, coinciding with the incorporation of the London Company of Gardeners in 1605. About the same time references also occur to gardens and orchards which had been 'taken out' of crofts around the town in the latter years of the sixteenth century. Thus part of a large meadow had by 1593 been converted into an orchard and garden called Little Tainterhawe; an orchard was 'taken out' of Aldham's Pasture before 1600 and next to it were two gardens enclosed from land appurtenant to the Blue Boar Inn; an orchard and a garden were 'taken out of the land called Vereings alias Hog Field' before 1636; and by 1640 all the pasture called Winton had become an orchard. In 1681 a parcel of meadow was described as having been recently converted into a garden, then purchased from a Kelvedon shoemaker by Samuel Pond, gentleman, and in tenure of James Hawkes, gardener. There was also a field called The Hopyard in which a baker called Elias Luffkin built a cottage in 1592. One may presume that he devoted part of his time to the specialised cultivation of his hop bines for the Maldon brewers who, from about 1580, could no longer get their supplies from Flanders and otherwise had to buy from Kentish, Suffolk and Essex farmers. There may also have been an attempt to cultivate vines commercially: one close was known as The Great Vineyard and by 1670 Sir Robert Sprignell of Highgate had a vineyard near the Hythe, close to the saltcote there.

## THE LEATHER AND TAILORING TRADES

In any community the manufacturer of leather goods was sure of his trade; it was as important then as plastics are now in everyday life, for harness and fastenings, for waterproof, hardwearing garments, for innumerable types of containers and protective covers, for beds and chairs, drinking vessels and liquid containers, as vellum for documents and bookbinding. The salient feature of Maldon's leatherworkers is that a greater number of them were glovers or whitetawyers (31 during 45 years), working in the most expensive type of this material, than appears to have been usual in most towns. The number of shoemakers is also impressive, though not so intriguing. If all these men and their servants worked at a constant rate surely the town could produce more foot and hand coverings than its residents can have needed, whilst the frequent references to rural shoemakers suggests that their manufactures could have satisfied much of the market area's demand. If so, then the surplus production of Maldon's glovers and shoemakers went out either to London or, in peddlars' packs, to fairs across the country, and it is certain that the tradesmen themselves journeyed frequently to other Essex, Suffolk or Kentish markets.

The supply of materials came only partly from the town's own tanneries, where there were never more than two tanners working (their servants or labourers excepted, of course). A substantial quantity of tanned hides came in from village tanneries for sale at the three annual fairs and in the weekly markets, where Maldon tanners acted as the borough's Leather Searchers. There were few places in which tan-pits could be suitably located with ample fresh water, good drainage and a position down-wind from the housing areas, and in fact this trade (and gloving) was all sited near the Fullbridge, with drainage directly downhill into the river. Halfway up the steep hillside above Fullbridge John Welles had a shed, cistern and watercourse on land called Crooked Croft in 1605. Just above it was the Cromwell (formerly St Helen's Well) to which Thomas Cammocke had by 1599 added a cistern and piped water from a spring which was the original 'Crom Well' about six hundred yards away. For drawing drinking water this was an impracticable site but it could supply a regulated watercourse to the tannery and the glovers' and curriers' workplaces fifty or sixty yards below. The physical limitations go some way to explain why so few tanners were at work in a town so active in manufacturing leather goods.

There were, however, plenty of supplies of hides or skins from the butchers' trade and these few tanners were amongst the most prosperous of the borough freemen, as were the glovers who completed the preparatory work on their leathers in their own premises. Both trades required a considerable capital investment in materials - lime from the town's kiln, used in the initial removal of hair and fat, oak bark from local woodland for the tanning, as well as a large quantity of animal skins- and similar investment in 'plant' such as leak-proof tan pits, drying and storage sheds, a bark mill. Whitetawing or currying, which continued the tanning so as to make supple the best quality leathers, also required some kind of mill to work hammers. The Leather Searchers were always alert for insufficiently tanned leather, for in such a lengthy process, where the craftsmen had to maintain costly quantities of hides, so as to ensure a steady supply of good quality material, there was always a temptation to cut corners and raise some cash by offering quick sales at cut-rate prices. And the crafts had to cope with frequent changes in the elaborate regulations on the sale of hides and skins which could adversely affect their supplies.

All the leather crafts benefitted from a continuous and ever-growing demand for their goods; they had a wider range than inland towns, with both the agricultural sector requiring its boots and harnesses, saddles, fittings for ploughs and carts, and the maritime sector needing the fishermen's full-length boots and leather work for rigging, the wealthier urban and country gentry population's requirements for good shoes, hunting gear, bags, purses, knife and sword sheaths, fashionable saddles, and also (but less frequent in demand) the leather parts of the local militia's clothing and armour, such as boots, gloves, the pikemen's stout leather coats or 'jacks', straps for fixing together the various parts of body armour, belts, bandoliers, touch boxes, scabbards. This section of the town's craftsmen thus shared with the food and drink trades a never-diminishing market for their goods and, although some complaining by shoemakers has been noted above, they seem never to have found themselves facing any decline in demand from the markets they served.

The demand for clothing was also steady but, without the guidelines of statutory requirements and the necessary divisions between the crafts which help to make sense of the leather trades, much of what could be written about the garment manufacturing and textile distributing trades remains as surmise. There are few extant inventories; and wills do not offer reliable material with which to assess the prosperity of the town's tailors, drapers, haberdashers and mercers. Two of the wealthiest tradesmen about 1600 were a haberdasher (Ralph Breeder) and a tailor (John Pratt), according to their wills' bequests of cash: Breeder's in 1609 amounted to £1,431, a very large sum by all contemporary standards for a provincial haberdasher, and Pratt's cash bequests in 1619 amounted to almost one third that sum (£460), without taking account in either case of their legacies of houses, stock and household goods which have been referred to already in this study. Some tailors and drapers bequeathed virtually no money but often houses or land which they had purchased from their profits; most had perhaps settled money or possessions on their kin before making any will. We are thrown back on the numbers in Table 3 and if the entries in the main categories are adjusted so as to merge drapers, haberdashers and mercers with tailors, then together they may have taken up 14 per cent of all trades 1560-83 and 18 per cent 1600-43. Amalgamating them is supported by contemporary indications that one should not take the trade descriptions too literally: some apprentices were stated to be covenanted as both tailors and drapers; the probate inventory of Richard Simpson (1628) shows that he was a hatter (and reckoned as such when Table 3 was compiled) although usually described as a haberdasher. One of the Elizabethan tailors, Henry Capstack, came from Dentdale where stocking knitting was a standard secondary occupation and perhaps he should have been described as a hosier, a trade not mentioned anywhere in Maldon's records.

Within this grouping of trades there exist records of 124 indentured apprentices. 58 per cent of them went into tailoring and as their masters were also the largest group within this category of clothing trades it is clear that garment making was a speciality within this town, to which the drapers and haberdashers were appurtenant. Immediately to the north of the town one came into the textile manufacturing area, to Witham and Bocking, Coggeshall, Halstead, Colchester, Dedham, and then the Suffolk weaving at Long Melford and Lavenham, Boxford, Hadleigh, Nayland ... an almost endless list. Maldon's own textile production was a minor affair compared with their's and its situation prompts analogy with the clothing factories which much later sprang up around the mill towns of Yorkshire and Lancashire. The drapers and mercers and haberdashers bought in the materials, the tailors produced the made-up articles. It is probable that the local weavers and the small number of cloth-finishers in the district were entirely maintained by this tailoring trade. Whilst the Tainterhawe was a meadow used only for pasture (and one part for an orchard), the Tainterfield still had a 'tainter' standing in it as late as 1656; behind The Spread Eagle in the market place there was a fulling mill; there was always one dyer at work in the town; and some weavers were as prosperous as the major tailors. Minor the craft may have been by comparison with other towns in numbers of weavers and in output, it was responsive principally to the requirements of Maldon tailoring enterprises. One may note the number of clothiers and drapers who traded within the borough but certainly dealt with cloth produced over a large area. Between them clothiers, drapers and haberdashers employed 68 apprentices between 1566 and 1640, compared with the 32 taken on by weavers, combers, fullers and shearmen working in the borough. And there were two momentary developments in cloth making in Maldon which appear to have been in response to local initiatives. One was the appearance of silk-weaving, bay-weaving, felt-making from about 1600. The other was a sudden increase in the number of traditional weavers (of woollens) working in the town in the 1620s. This trend may have suffered from the slump in the clothing trades which occurred in the 1620s, for weaving does not figure prominently from the time of the Civil War.

But what market the tailors supplied must remain a matter of supposition and it may have changed over the two centuries. The will of one of the later master tailors, Benjamin Brockis (1654) refers to his shop-board, press and settle, one pair of shears, all his 'chessells' (scissors) and his 'drawing prints and patterns, with all the boxes containing them', which reads as the barest sketch of a business making clothes to order for regular customers. There were, and especially in the early seventeenth century, gentry and professional people − lawyers, clergy and their widows − living in or near to Maldon who may have bought their country clothing here, their other clothes in London, just as some groups of people still buy different types and qualities of clothing in different places. '...'Tis Term-time, and Michaelmas Term too, the drapers' harvest for footcloths, riding-suits, walking-suits, chamber gowns and hall gowns' says the scheming London draper to a young Essex gentleman in *Michaelmas Term*, whilst Maldon tailors may have found a good market in gentlemen's and women's wear for church-going, for hunting, for local assemblies. Where had Mary Muffett obtained the gown of violet colour, the holland apron edged with lace, the cloak faced with say, which she bequeathed to her friends in 1624, the fine camlet gown and petticoat that lay in a great trunk in her chamber over her parlour? There were 116 hats in Richard Simpson's Maldon shop in May 1628 of which 44 coloured hats were priced between eight and seventeen pence apiece but 34, mostly black, cost more than 2s 6d (about £0.12) each. Just how 'up-market' his trade was may perhaps be judged by comparing the average price of this Maldon stock – 5s 9d (£0.29) – with that in his Braintree shop, which averaged only 8d (£0.03) for three dozen each of black and coloured hats.

A further suggestion of a high-quality tailoring trade comes from five indentures of girls as seamstresses to Judith Hosier who was a silkwoman. They were taken into her trade singly over the period 1574-95 and were presumably engaged not for routine making-up of linen or woollen garments but for high-quality clothes of embroidered materials and, especially, ladies' wear. Silk-weaving may have existed in the town well before the first reference to it c1600.

However, the bread-and-butter trade must have been in cheap everyday garment manufacture and for each silkwoman's apprentice seamstress or embroiderer there must have been many women employed in the customary manner, doing piece-work in their homes. Since we know that the enrollments are an incomplete record of this town's apprentices, these indications of a lively and locally significant trade in tailoring and dressmaking must be seen in the context of a small town whose drapers, mercers, hatters, tailors and specialist weavers were significant only by comparison with the rest of the town's trade, where each appears as employer of only one, sometimes two or three servants and apprentices at any one time. In a community so closely knit with the surrounding area, ties of kinship and friendship or occupational connections may have been the principal attraction which brought these youths and girls into these trades in this town. The social reputation of the master or mistress with whom they would live was perhaps more important than the craft to be learned. 'We cannot lodge and board a dozen or fourteen gentlewomen that live by the prick of their needles but it will be thought we keep a bawdy house', the former Mistress Quickly remarked in *Henry V* but that could never have been suspected of these pious freemen of Maldon of unblemished repute in their country. Lads who worked with Master Maldon or Master Pratt were never in trouble; those who served Alderman Breeder benefitted greatly by his will; when Alderman Rudland's four teenage apprentices went on a mischievous rampage there was hell to pay.

## STABILISATION, 1540–1560

Was there only the 'invisible hand' of demand and supply guiding and shaping these diverse occupations in Tudor and Stuart Maldon? Was the borough simply a routine administrator of statutory legislation and conciliar proclamations on the limits within which each of these crafts and trades might operate? A communal strategy directed toward the stabilisation of the borough's commercial fortunes can be suggested and its actual existence has already been referred to (Chapter 4) in considering the evidence for a policy shared by some of the freemen to regenerate the town's housing, develop the open ground previously intended (perhaps) for the Darcy mansion, to acquire the Darcy Tower itself as their new Moot Hall. In the last years of King Henry VIII's reign and through that of his son Edward VI, from about 1540 until 1555 when Maldon received from Queen Mary I its second and much enlarged charter of incorporation, those ambitious townsmen thought out and pursued a policy which could strengthen and enhance what they would have called the *common weal*, the social and economic well-being of their borough.

In two ways their policy was old-fashioned; they sought to take over the remaining seignorial rights in their borough just as the twelfth century burgesses had negotiated concessions from King Henry II and in 1403 other burgesses had bought the right to exercise the Bishop of London's manorial rights; they also aimed at reinforcing their medieval inheritance of fairs, courts and customary laws. Their intention was to strengthen Maldon's traditional institutions, not to change its character.

There was nevertheless a very contemporary element in that line of thinking and that is not surprising, because these freemen included lawyers and landowners − John Church, Anthony Sparrow, John Boswell, Robert Gaywood − who were agents of men powerful in public affairs such as the Earls of Oxford and Essex. They were also acquainted with some distinguished Essex gentry who served from time to time as members of parliament for Maldon and were well aware of the Commonwealth ideas in circulation at Westminster. Henry Golding of Little Birch, for example, (M.P. 1559) was not only related by marriage to John de Vere, the 16th Earl of Oxford, and a counsellor in the Earl's household; he was also, in 1549, a very confidential servant of the Duke of Somerset, the Protector of King Edward VI, and thus certainly an associate of William Cecil, the Duke's secretary. Twice in this period (1542 and 1545) the freemen chose as one of their Members of Parliament the distinguished son of John Dawes (a former Bailiff of Maldon) and brother of a Vicar of All Saints, Maldon. This was Henry Dawes, whose intellectual ability and humanist talent is attested for us by his appointment as tutor to Gregory Cromwell, the only son of Henry VIII's great Secretary. After Thomas Cromwell's sudden fall from power and execution (1540) Henry Dawes maintained his association with Gregory, lived in the dead man's principal mansion − Launde in Leicestershire − and in 1544 bought from Gregory Cromwell a lease of the manor of Leigham's Court in Streatham. The point is that the ideas on reforming society which had so freely circulated in the great minister's household,

125

and which are generally identified as a 'commonwealth' philosophy of government, not only survived Thomas Cromwell's sudden and cruel death, they flourished ten years later in the court of Protector Somerset and right through the 1550s. Through Henry Dawes' association with Maldon until his death in 1550, and Henry Golding's thereafter, its knot of landowning lawyer freemen would be well briefed on Westminster's influential ideas on legal and administrative reform.

However, the careers of these influential men are a long record of management of noble estates, of conveyancing and acquiring lands to such an extent that the Harris family of Mundon and Southminster, the Osbornes of Tiled Hall, Latchingdon, were known to be among the richest in the county. Edward Bury (M.P. 1542) prospered in the service of William Parr, Earl of Essex (and in the 1540s lord of Little Maldon), as did the Earl's nephew, Nicholas Throckmorton, who was M.P. in 1545. William Harris, a distinguished lawyer of Lincoln's Inn, managed the sales of Sir Thomas Darcy's Essex estates throughout the 1540s (which included the exchange with the Crown of Darcy's Tower for St Osyth's Priory) and acquired much for himself in the process. John Wiseman of Great Canfield both served the 16th Earl of Oxford as Auditor of the de Vere estates (of which John Church was a Bailiff in Maldon) and practised as an Auditor of the Court of Augmentations which managed for the Crown, and also sold, properties seized from the Church. Richard Weston of Roxwell and Hatfield Broad Oak (M.P. 1555) was another distinguished lawyer, a Reader of the Middle Temple, who was retained by Maldon's Common Council and Corporation as Counsel in the 1550s.

When faced with men such as these, instead of seeing an idealistic devotion to the cause of the common weal one might well perceive 'nothing but a certain conspiracy of rich men procuring their own commodities under the name and title of a Commonwealth', as Sir Thomas More had written in *Utopia*. Distaste and suspicion of Masters John Church, Philip Goldborne and Anthony Sparrow by the younger and humbler freemen is implied in the one recorded criticism of them by townsmen in 1558: Henry Pynnell said

> "Anthony Sparrow is not an honest man".
> "Yes, I will say he is an honest man" replied John Bonner.
> "Aye, marry!" said Pynnell, "you must needs say so, for Masters Church and Sparrow are your men of law. But I care not a turd for Master Church — not him nor none of you all — for Anthony Sparrow is a false, forsworn knave ..."

Just how these 'men of law' interpreted the wording of the appropriate Acts has already been seen in the borough's involvement with the Acts for the repair of towns. No waste property, no neglected tenements (if there had been any) were taken into public ownership in the mid-century; their only visible concern was

126

to lay claim to the Darcy Tower (of which Master Church had been a lessee for a while). It has also been shown above how they responded to the Statute of Artificers (concerning apprentices) of 1563: servants were disguised as apprentices with little attempt to keep them for the statutory term or to bring them into the borough freedom. In neither case was the wording of an Act obeyed literally. It was adapted to the local situation. It was, of course, also the use of legislation to procure what seemed to be the best strategy for the well-being of the borough and it worked.

A distinctive feature of contemporary thinking on urban problems was the desirability of incorporation and this, too, happened at Maldon, with two charters granted — and the second of them naming these leading townsmen as the first principal officers of the new Corporation — in 1554 and 1555. In the same year as the first of these charters was granted, parliament passed a bill to remedy 'the utter destruction, ruin and decay' of towns which was considered to have been the consequence of a dispersal of crafts and trades across the countryside. The growth of rural trading was alleged to be causing the decline of urban markets and that may have been the meaning of the charter's statement that Maldon was a 'decaying' borough. There were political and religious factors which recommended their petition for a grant of incorporation to the court of Queen Mary (and these are considered below, in Chapter 6) but this Act's analysis of the 'decay' caused by a flight of industry and commerce to the countryside would have seemed applicable to Maldon, where the rural district swarmed with craftsmen whom the Act considered ought to have been plying their trades within the borough. It urged that speedy action be taken to strengthen the commerce of corporate towns and immediately the status of a Corporation had been conferred on them these Maldon townsmen pressed for a revision of their new charter in order to strengthen, enlarge and clarify the powers granted to them.

Did they next attempt to gather all those tanners, curriers, leather workers, tailors and smiths, maltsters and weavers into their borough? They did nothing of the sort. That would have been impossible, short of an entire reconstruction of the local community which no Tudor act of parliament could possibly initiate. Instead the terms of the charter granted in 1555 represent these men's response to local experience of the problem of commercial decay. They would not assert any monopoly but they would encourage commerce so as to bring trade and also money into the town. They would make Maldon the focus rather than the site of that busy wood-pasture land's economy.

There had been one fair annually at Maldon during the fifteenth and early sixteenth centuries. It had been held at many different times in the year. Now three fairs were granted (or two, if one of them proved to be 'to the nuisance of any fair near adjoining'), each of four days duration, which would be held in the Spring (24-27 March) and in late Summer (31 August to 3 September, 7-10 September). In practice there often appears to have been only one fair a year: either it was the Lady Day Fair in March or it was the Spital Fair which probably lasted over the whole period 31 August to 10 September and was held beside the former hospital dedicated to St Giles, whose feast day is 1 September. The intention was to increase the occasions when a larger than normal volume of trade could be attracted into the town, although never on the scale as the great annual Stourbridge or Bartholomew Fairs, and its function was similar to the Spring or Late Summer Sales in modern shopping centres, with supplies of specially-made sale goods brought in (by peddlars and itinerant fair traders in those times). Horse-sales − equivalent to modern car auctions − were always a feature of fairs but they were, above all else, occasions when country people could stock up for the winter months with essential goods at low prices and purchase cheap versions of luxury articles, or replace cheaply those items in daily use and worn out by spring time. Presentments in the Clerk of the Market's Pie Powder Courts and the receipts of fines detailed in the borough account rolls over the period 1555 to 1600 indicate some of the wares always to be found there: points and laces, haberdashery; knives and scissors, daggers and rapiers of Sheffield steel; pewter mugs, platters, candlesticks and chamber pots; boots, shoes, saddles, hides; linen and woollen textiles. The fairs were among the region's holiday occasions, when people from all over the local area renewed acquaintance, exchanged family news, arranged marriages and apprentice-ships. They were occasions for hiring servants too, and at Maldon's fairs these must have been the moments when may of those short-term decenners came into or left the borough. And for the distributive traders of the town these were, as in modern trade fairs, times for stocking up with basic goods at the end of Winter and just before Autumn and ordering supplies.

The 1555 charter empowered the new Corporation to revise the borough Custumal and to make additional bye-laws 'for public good of the borough' − a Commonwealth-style injunction − and for 'the private good of every man resorting thither'. This they did immediately, with an increase in the number of Constitutions, as they called the bye-laws, from twenty nine to ninety one clauses. Many were of course concerned with the details of government and behaviour but some were additions to older regulations of public trade and the outstanding feature of this new Custumal was its omission of serious restrictions on any of the rural traders coming regularly to market in Maldon, although the 1554 Act for the repair of decayed corporate towns sought to curtail the retail trade of outsiders in town markets. It must be said that the Act confined its sanctions to haberdashers, drapers, mercers and grocers, none of whom traded from the countryside: but there were 'foreigners' and non-resident freemen in these occupations who came to Maldon from the neighbouring market towns. The ninetieth custom ordained that freemen were not to buy victuals or 'wares' of any sort from any stranger or non-freeman until the Bailiffs had 'communed with him' and 'given him or them the liberty to sell at his pleasure' and that implies an intention to welcome all trade so long as there was official cognisance of it. In May 1569 the jury at the Quarter Sessions complained that a cooper who had been a resident freeman but had moved out to a neighbouring village continued to ply his craft in the town but a year later he was still being named for the same offence without any penalty being imposed on him. The Maldon response to the 1554 Act was to reorganise its trading regulations so as to encourage incoming trade by the guarantees of quality and fair-dealing which the powers granted to the new Corporation assured.

These two strategies put local money into circulation and this was the effect also of reinforcing the traditional use of Maldon's borough court as a registry of short-term debts. There were some eight types of lawsuit which had for over a century composed most of the business in its courts of record, of which the most frequent were actions for debts of fixed sums, followed by pleas of *detinue* (claiming wrongful withholding of money or goods) and by the three types of trespass cases, of which one concerned the act itself, another sued for compensation for damage committed during a trespass – *special trespass* – and the third concerned the damages allegedly caused by *detinue*. Actions concerning breach of covenant and actions of account (such as claims for payment of wages, spoiled goods or Andrew Michaelson's demand that his brewery 'manager' should render him an account) occurred more frequently in the later sixteenth century, as did actions for fugitive debt and the complex plea of *assumpsit* involving X impleading Y when Y has pledged that Z will pay £N to X, but has not done so. Each of these types of plea brought protection to trade.

The simple action for debt also had the effect of modern credit facilities. Coin was in chronic short supply in mid-sixteenth century England – perhaps rarely amounting to more than £1 in cash per person – so that a system by which a creditor could commence a plea of debt, delay the hearing from one court to another until the debt was paid and then withdraw action on payment of a service charge to the court (the rates were 6d for a resident, 12d for an outsider) provided a support for daily cash transactions and helped maintain regular trade at times when the volume of coin in circulation was low.

The deliberation with which the architects of Maldon's charter sought to strengthen the powers of the borough court to hear all such cases is shown by the detailed form of the grants made in their second charter of 1555. The magistrates were to have the right to hear in their Moot Hall 'all and all manner of pleas, as well real as mixed … as personal, of what sums soever, or of what kind or sort' and it was specified that they might 'hold and determine … and thereupon to render right' all the types of action outlined above and with no limit prescribed on the size of the pleas of debt they might hear. By contrast the charter of Aylesbury (1554) limited to £100 the sums which might be impleaded in its courts; those granted to other towns in the period 1553-56 make no mention, no specific grants or confirmations on the subject of pleas of debt, covenant, detinue or account, and since the contents of charters depended considerably on the negotiations undertaken by their recipients and their patrons at court, it is arguable that in 1554 and 1555 the freemen of Maldon and their friends among the local gentry were principally intent on acquiring these extensive concessions to their jurisdiction over commercial transactions because they grasped their vital importance to the economy of this town and its market area.

If John Leland ever did comment in a now-lost note on this town, it is very possible that he would have called it (as he did Swaffham) 'a very quick market', a lively centre of exchange. The activity of its courts was more important, more essential than any of its manufactures. One might go so far as to suggest that if all crafts had abandoned the town for the countryside, as contemporaries feared was happening, it would have remained an active and much frequented market because its specialist function in the locality was capitalist. There it was possible to raise loans, to transfer credits and debts or to contract for supplies with some certainty of future payment. It dealt in the precious commodity of security. Because the agency of freemen was necessary for the commencement of suits in the court, this facility acted as a counterweight to the dreaded flight of craftsmen into the local country by bringing them back to the market place in the pursuit of their trade, and thus channelling into (or through) Maldon a commercial share in the central, eastern and southern parts of the county. There are many suits in the court registers which were concerned with commodities and bargains which never touched the town market, as in a case of 1568 concerning building materials valued at £5 19s 0d which were to be sent from a brickmaker of East or West Hanningfield to a house in Rettendon, but the transactors had to make their way to Maldon if they wished to secure their bargains by this formal method although both Hanningfield and Rettendon were some ten miles from the borough. If the agreements were not honoured or the debt was not paid, then the fictitious lawsuit became a real one, as in the case above, where an agreement to supply bricks and tiles had allowed eight months for complete delivery and payment was not then made. (The plaintiff lost, because he was found not to have delivered the bricks or the tiles; he had added a suit of non-payment for a gelding sold to the defendant two years before, and which he was once again found not to have delivered.)

It was a very useful commercial service, fast and reliable in an age when fraud or sharp practice were quite easily carried on. Those who turned to other sources of cash, the travelling chapman, the bond drawn up by a scrivener, or dealt in the much more anonymous moneylending world of London (at that time), might find themselves defrauded as was a Maldon clothier, Thomas Clark, in 1572. His son went outside the borough courts and pawned 150 pieces of kersey cloth worth £300 to 'one Ferrant, citizen and merchant scrivener of London' for an immediate loan of £150. The cloths were to be redeemed at 20 per cent interest within three months but that was illegal, so Clark's son allowed the scrivener to draw up 'an absolute bill of sale and without any conditions, for that the said Ferrant said that he durst not meddle upon a conditional bill because of the Statute of Usury'. This could be a scene in a cynical Jacobean comedy, young Master Easy new up from Essex falling into the spider's web of a grasping City draper, and with no hope of redress: the 1571 Statute of Usury prohibited the taking of interest above the rate of 10 per cent annually; young Master Clark had nothing better than a receipt for an absolute sale of £300-worth of good woollen cloth for £150. And that was that.

Whilst resort to Maldon's courts saved men from such sharp practice there were limits to their usefulness and it is noticeable that the size of the average 'credit' did not rise over the period 1556-1628 (for which there survive reasonably numerous recorded cases) at the same rate as the prices of, say, wheat or textiles or as much as craftsmen's wages. By the end of the sixteenth century there did exist more financially sophisticated methods of raising money or making bargains, with access to Equity courts which were familiar with commercial needs. It was to such courts and facilities that young Master Clark should have addressed himself and no doubt one cause for the gradual falling-off in the use of Maldon's Court of Record was that London customers preferred dealing for their supplies of coal, firewood, dairy produce, vegetables and so forth in their city's own courts, or through scriveners, rather than in the remote court room of the borough of Maldon. This court could not provide the services of pawn brokers or bankers. It could not make available large sums of cash, it could not control the activity of its plaintiffs or in any other ways ensure the availability of long-term credit.

Thomas Petchey, one of the town's brewers, an innkeeper and a freeman of the borough, over-reached himself in January 1569 when he planned a brewing venture large enough to require the purchase of one hundred quarters of malt (cost: 100 marks or about £66 13s 4d) from a yeoman of the Thames-side Hundred of Chafford. He persuaded an alderman to stand surety that he would be able to pay for the malt but he also needed hops and here he made the mistake of making a private deal with the master of the *Black George* of Ostend, a Flemish coaster which had just arrived at the Hythe with a cargo of hops. This was pre-emption, for the master had not yet declared his cargo to the Bailiffs and they had not yet fixed a price on each of his goods. By sheer bad luck Thomas Petchey's schemes went awry: far away in Plymouth the bullion cargo of a Genoese ship in the service

131

of the King of Spain was seized to Queen Elizabeth's use; its original destination had been the Netherlands, as pay for the Spanish army there, and in retaliation at the Queen's action, the Duke of Alba retaliated by impounding the goods of English merchants in Flanders. At about that moment the *Black George* tied up at Maldon Hythe and Thomas Petchey climbed aboard to pre-empt his fellow freemen.

Before he could get his cargo secretly off the ship, the English government responded to the Duke of Alba's action by ordering all goods of subjects of the King of Spain to be arrested and impounded. That included the *Black George*. But as the Town Clerk and the Serjeants at Mace returned to the Moot Hall after formally boarding the ship and arresting its Master, they were met by Thomas Petchey demanding the release of his hops. Thereby he revealed his breach of the custom of the borough and (setting aside the increased tensions in Anglo-Spanish relations, the outbreak of further rebellion, bloodshed, disruption in the Netherlands with which the historian should properly concern himself) accidentally his career was ruined. Just before January 1569 he had been elected a head burgess or common councillor, his sons and his son-in-law had been admitted freemen without fee, he owned property and he had prospects of conducting a money-spinning brewing operation. Three months later he had been expelled from the corporation; being unable to brew he could not repay the loan for the malt he could not use, so the plea of debt before the Court of Record was now a true suit and he was forced to sell his four houses, including his own dwelling; and a further debt in April 1569 to a wheelwright of Feering indicates the beginning of a downward-spiralling career which ended with his prosecution for organising tennis matches behind his inn on Sundays during Divine Service. There was no mechanism of insurance nor any source for large-scale borrowing in the Maldon courts and the fate of this Thomas Petchey served as a lesson to all who kept their business within the borough's own facilities.

There was no possibility of finding here protection against the serious dangers and difficulties which beset any merchant or farmer or tradesman in the Maldon area: 'land rats and water rats, I mean pirates' who, as in Antonio's case in *The Merchant of Venice* had brought about the downfall of Master Henry Dawes' father in the 1530s, of whom it was related (in 1573) that this John Dawes

> 'made no testament nor executors etc. for that he had no goods or chattels whereof he might declare his last will, by reason they were perished and lost before his death, as well by shipwrecks on the sea as by many other his great losses and casualties and misadventures, very well known and approved by divers ancient and credible persons yet living in Maldon. By force of which losses the said John Dawes, being greatly indebted, was driven by mere necessity for the avoiding of imprisonment of his person for the

execution of his debts so far as his goods extended [to become] a privileged person and sanctuary man in the sanctuary of the late monastery of Beeleigh Abbey in Maldon, and so died the day and year above mentioned [1533]'.

Piracy hindered the coastal communications on which Maldon particularly relied and throughout both centuries warfare was endemic in the waters off the Essex coast. Like Chaucer's Marchant, John Dawes and many other Maldon traders after him

> *'wolde the see were kept for anything*
> *Betwixte Middleburgh and Orewell'*

for the waters off the Thames Estuary were rarely free of danger from pirates or enemy fleets, of which reminders recur in the records: orders for soldiers to embark there for France or the Low Countries in 1543, 1544 and 1551; a Fleming (*Dijrek Vansior*) captured at Maldon bearing letters addressed to the Duke of Alba in 1569; the preparations for the Armada; references to 'the goods which were the pirates' ' and 'washing the pirates' linen' which cannot refer to anything but some triumph in the Blackwater now lost to all but fiction; Goodman Rayner sent in 1626 hastily to Tollesbury 'to enquire touching a rumour of a fleet upon our coasts'; a Dutch pinnace loaded with armaments brought to the Hythe in 1629 'upon suspicion to be a Dunkirker'; the beacons which were lit whilst the population of Rochford Hundred fled inland and the county militia stood to arms when a peaceful fisherman anchored his boat off Wakering and was mistaken for a Dunkirk pirate in 1628; the battles against the Dutch off the North Foreland, in the Medway, off the Naze and near Southwold.

These events and scares could do worse than cause the loss of one ship. They could delay sailings, wreck covenanted agreements, clear the seas of trading vessels for an indefinite period. Hazards of that sort were as dangerous to the farmer who wanted to send his corn, butter or cheese to London, and to the merchant who had assumed a delivery date for a cargo at the Hythe, as were the Goodwins and other shoals of this area upon which ships foundered in storms. People said that piracy in 1628 stopped coastal and foreign trade and forced up food prices. The facilities for short-term credit at Maldon only protected the creditor against bad faith and could not act against factors as destructive of trade as these.

## MARKET AND HYTHE

As with housing, recorded changes in the buildings and facilities for public trading offer us a profile of the ways in which Maldon's commercial life was organised to meet local opportunities and adapt itself to changing circumstances. Here is the public face of the Bailiffs' and aldermen's economic policy for their borough.

At the beginning of the sixteenth century the market place had not yet taken on its final form, the 'spindle' shape of a long street, narrow at each end, bulging at the point of concentrated trading activity, which appears in the earliest (nineteenth century) plans of the town. By 1500, however, its essential components were in place. At the centre was the timber-framed Moot Hall, referred to as the Guildhall of the freeburgesses, with a 'solar' (an upper chamber), in the Bishop of London's charter of 1403. It was of the standard design: open on the ground floor to provide sheltered trading space but infilled with latticed butchers' shops and a prison cell known as the Lobhole. Eastward from this building there stretched two rows of permanent stalls, many already reconstructed in wood and plaster as workshops. One of these, the Mercery Row, ran parallel to the churchyard according to a rental of Mildmay properties dated 1548 which states, for example, that William Reynoldes of Chelmsford held the lease of a a shop 'being on the north side of the Mercery Row and in the south part of the churchyard upon the east end of All Hallows' church'. The other row of stalls or shops lay along the centre of the street and, with the shops under the Moot Hall, constituted the shambles or Butcher Row.

Some elaboration of the market facilities occurred at the same time as the housing development described in Chapter 4 began. Against the medieval Moot Hall a Market Cross was erected in 1540, an open-sided and roofed area with a stone-flagged floor which was usually known by the seventeenth century as the Cornmarket. A New Market Place was constructed next (1550-51), designed as a timber-framed lean-to extension of the Moot Hall's ground floor, and also with open sides and a tiled roof. Stables were built on the open ground immediately to the west of the Moot Hall. These all formed the quite small 'island' of market-infill buildings which now exists as an early nineteenth century rebuilding but with perhaps the original jetty of the south side of the old Moot Hall still visible. A Fishmarket of two or three stalls was set up nearby, alongside the church tower, not long before 1547.

At the same time that these installations were being brought into use the Bailiffs and aldermen developed a stricter policy of market control and at first they were intent on imposing narrow limits for the trading area. The revised Customs of 1555 had delimited the market for butchers as from the Moot Hall to the corner of St Peter's Lane but a new ordinance of 1562 re-defined and halved the area. (See Figure 16.) Instead of expansion, the new market buildings represent the leading townsmen's policy of reinforcing the old and perhaps creaking organisation of the borough. All vendors of 'small victuals' − dairy produce, poultry, vegetables and oatmeal − were now required to trade at the New Market Place only. There was, however, considerable congestion (which suggests that the diminution of the market place was only for administrative convenience, not because trade had declined); there were complaints and there was disobedience. So in 1569 the

134

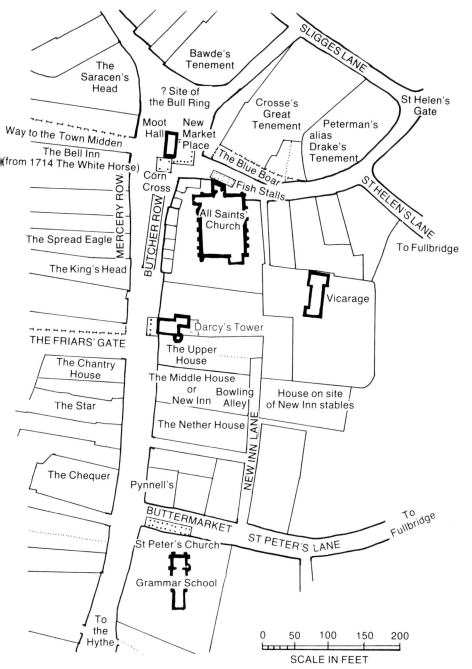

*Figure 16 The Market Place, 1500 – 1688*

135

Corporation agreed to revoke its restrictive ordinance because of the 'many discomforts and inconveniences borne by the populace of this borough, as is sufficiently shown in the serious complaints made by all the inhabitants from time to time'.

The Butcher Row was then re-extended. That marks the beginning of a phase of development in which the market place acquired its definitive shape. The most impressive event was the Corporation's renovation of Darcy's Tower in 1576, making it the new Moot Hall. A Buttermarket (or Long Market House, both names were used for it) was constructed before 1614 at the eastern end of the area, beside St Peter's church — by the nineteenth century the focus of the market had moved to this spot, changing the street name from St Peter's Lane to Market Hill — and by 1576 places all along the area of public trade had been designated for specialised trade: an Oatmeal Bin, an Applemarket, a Cornmarket, a Saltbin, the Fish Stalls, the Leather Stalls. At the same time (as has been described) housing continued to fill the sides of the market place and old buildings, such as the Spread Eagle and Crosse's Great Tenement, were being renovated. Drapers, haberdashers and shoemakers were opening their crafts in the new buildings, like Henry Pynnell the draper at the Corner House beside St Peter's Lane.

By 1576 the 'spindle' shape characteristic of many market places had been achieved. Congested with timber-framed, lath and plaster shops and stalls, festooned with coloured signs, it had many of the features to be seen in the mid-sixteenth century Flemish townscapes painted by the elder Pieter Bruegel. (Many of the types of people and many of their activities which he depicted might have been a part of the market scene at Maldon in 1576; a number of them were indeed 'Dutchmen'.) On one side rose the whitened walls of All Saints' church, its bulk enhanced by the low range of shops alongside, its fine masonry and bold buttresses set off by their plain frontages or glimpsed through the archway into the churchyard. The great timber spire with its attendant angle spirelets, bell cote and gilded weather vane loomed over the hub of Maldon's trade. Its sanctus bell (after the Reformation) struck the hours for a new clock on the church tower, and was still rung as in pre-Reformation days to regulate the opening and closing of the market on Sundays; the other bells in the tower tolled at the end of the Saturday Market to summon all to the Corporation's sermon. There, beside the old Moot Hall, were the bull ring, the stocks and the pillory. Printed proclamations sent from the royal Council were pinned to the pillars of the Cornmarket. Half closing off the view eastward rose the great brick walls of Darcy's Tower, the new Moot Hall, loop-holed and turretted, adorned with a wide timber gallery over part of the street to provide a sheltered space for linendrapers, a wooden dovehouse perched on its high roof.

One measure of market development would be the appearance of more inns. By its name and position the appearance c1578-80 of the New Inn seems significant.

It occupied one of the houses constructed in the middle of the century on the open ground to the east of Darcy's Tower and for its first twenty five to thirty years it had been called The Middle House. However, a certified count of the number of innholders, taverners and tipplers in 1577 (returned to an enquiry by the Privy Council) declared that the town of Maldon had only two innholders and one taverner but twenty three alehouse keepers or tipplers. The first three persons counted may have been the householders of the Star, Bell and Spread Eagle in the market place, who were applying to the magistrates for licences as victuallers in 1574, but the recognisances for alehouse keepers of the 1570s varied session by session from 10 to 15 and none of the information in the borough registers tallies with the official survey, on which little reliance can be placed. The King's Head, Bell, Saracen's Head, Spread Eagle and the Blue Boar became recognised inns soon after 1577 but the only inn created thereafter was this New Inn and the number of alehouses remained steady right through to the 1680s at least. When an army survey of beds and stabling available for quartering troops was prepared in 1686 (for the whole of England) most of the largest inns of Essex, measured by the number of beds and stabling they offered, lay beside the two principal thoroughfares running north from London toward Ipswich and toward Cambridge (see Table 5) and Maldon's position in the inn-capacity league was not impressive: fifteenth by the number of beds, twelfth in stabling. So much trade came and left by water − there were no more than two carriers at any time before the eighteenth century − that one should not expect inns there on the same scale as those filled daily with travellers at Brentwood, Colchester, Ingatestone and Chelmsford. Nor did the town have the demand for inns which Chelmsford shared with Colchester and Brentwood because of the business brought to them by the assizes, judicial commissions, the county lieutenancy and the archdeaconry courts. Travellers made few demands on Maldon. Most of those who came by land could reach it and return home within a day, and some may usually have lodged with relatives or friends. Instead, the inns here were of most use in the private trading which developed at Elizabethan and Stuart markets.

The Blue Boar is Maldon's epitome of Elizabethan market-place inns. It had once been a house named Crosse's Great Tenement and that building (probably constructed about 1390) survives at the rear of the present building. Its owner in the 1530s was that master-mind of the borough's survival, Master John Church, who was both the bailiff of the estates belonging to Beeleigh Abbey and also an agent of the Earl of Oxford. A large frontal extension of his house was complete in 1540 (when it began to be charged an assize rent) and it then received its new name from one of the most favoured badges of the de Vere household. Encroaching on the central soil of the market area it seems to have remained a grand dwelling house until the late 1560s but by 1572 it had begun its long life as the town's principal inn, for its owner, Thomas Furnes, was styled 'Innkeeper at the Blue Boar' in

|  | Number of Beds and Stables | |
|---|---|---|
| Chelmsford | 207 | 570 |
| Colchester | 198 | 362 |
| Ingatestone | 157 | 381 |
| Collier Row (and Romford) | 153 | 412 |
| Epping (and Coopersale) | 123 | 270 |
| Brentwood and Shenfield | 110 | 183 |
| Chipping Ongar (and Ongar) | 102 | 308 |
| Witham | 66 | 90 |
| Bocking and Braintree | 66 | 100 |
| Saffron Walden | 61 | 198 |
| Coggeshall | 61 | 89 |
| Billericay | 54 | 110 |
| Harwich | 47 | 13 |
| Waltham Abbey | 44 | 14 |
| Maldon | 42 | 100 |
| Dunmow | 41 | 111 |
| Harlow | 38 | 90 |
| Barking | 35 | 318 |
| Newport (and Audley 'Inn') | 32 | 107 |
| Ilford | 29 | 20 |
| Rayleigh | 27 | 21 |
| Grays | 22 | 22 |
| Rochford | 19 | 34 |
| Leytonstone | 17 | 57 |
| Southminster | 16 | 17 |
| Thaxted | 16 | 32 |
| Chigwell | 15 | 26 |
| Heybridge | 15 | 20 |
| Halstead | 14 | 30 |
| Gt. Baddow | 14 | 17 |
| Gt. Chesterford | 14 | 38 |
| Manningtree | 13 | 16 |
| Burnham | 13 | 23 |
| Danbury | 13 | 26 |
| Tiptree Heath | 13 | 21 |
| Dagenham | 11 | 14 |
| Horndon-on-the-Hill | 11 | 25 |

(Derived from Army Survey, 1686: P.R.O., W.O. 30/48)

*Table 5. Essex Inns in 1686: capacity for guests and horses.*

138

*Pl.5. Crosse's Great Tenement, extended in 1539 as The Blue Boar*

the record of his freedom of the borough in that year. Within ten years Master Furnes had developed other business activities, moved into a yet grander house and had a manager to run the inn. Its size and accomodation are inadequately recorded − and much internal alteration has obscured the structural evidence the building itself might have provided − but it was an important social centre; there the Bailiffs usually entertained their guests: it had a wine cellar; its landlords became senior members of the Corporation from Thomas Furnes onward. And it had a great asset: unlike all the other market place inns it had direct access to a large pasture called Aldham's, so it was ideally sited to take a leading part in the town's private cattle trading. This undoubtedly increased the inn's value. In 1629 Thomas Rochell sold it to its landlord, Alderman John Edwards, for £125, four times the price of the Spread Eagle, seven times that of the Star in 1607, two inns which had no pasture land directly adjacent to their yards (and one finds the Saracen's Head, which was on a very constricted site, buying a pasture on the outskirts of the borough) whilst Alderman Edwards' purchase − of a reversionary interest, not the freehold − reflected in its cost the combined value of the inn and Aldham's Land.

The inns, then, portray a restrained, modest development of marketing in the second half of the sixteenth century: nothing over-ambitious but a sound and measured consolidation of the traditional commercial life of this borough. On returning to the market place about 1625 there are signs which might be interpreted as the onset of a recession. The Butcher Row was demolished in 1620 as 'being noisesome and ruinous'. The old Moot Hall was dismantled the next year. Yet these events are better interpreted as a new phase of necessary reorganisation and improvement, for when the Butcher Row had come down the Corporation also ordered that the Corn Cross 'be taken down within convenient time and one arch be erected' at a maximum cost of £50, which was the profit on the sale of materials from the old stalls, and in its place there was to be 'one arch builded and erected for the enlargement of the said Corn Cross ... and one loft for four several chambers erected over the ... new arch'. When the upper parts of the old Moot Hall were dismantled the Lob Hole prison on the ground floor remained, newly roofed over. New stalls were also erected on the site of the Butcher Row. The rampage of Master Rudland's apprentices depicts this market place in May 1623 from a hooligan's viewpoint: they went 'up the town as high as the fishstalls, and [there] the said [Thomas] Birch overthrew the stocks; and coming down the street the said Birch took a stall near the Star and set it across the Buttermarket House, and overturned into the cartway two logs against the cooper's house'. As late as 1847 inhabitants of Maldon could remember a Lady Day Fair being held 'where the old Buttermarket stood' and September Fairs 'in the midst of the town where the butchers' shambles stood (and where the market is now held)'. So the Tudor installations for public trade remained, refurbished as necessary (not often through vandalism) long after the seventeenth century.

The utilisation of the Hythe or waterfront of Maldon mirrored the aldermen's policy on trade in the market place. As one area grew in facilities and architectural completion, so the other's commercial function dwindled. The Hythe in 1540-50 was only some 250 yards long by about thirty yards wide, including the surface of the wharves; no more than a riverside strip bounded by a pasture, a churchyard and the last steep dip of the town hill to the water, whose roadway was to be described in 1641 as 'dangerous for horse and man in regard of the straightness of the way and steepness of the hill when they [carts] are loaden'.

The Water Bailiffs' accounts include some details (despite their composite and summary format) which indicate the bulky nature of the goods to be found at the Hythe. Coal was a major commodity, heaped on plots leased by freemen from the Corporation and in the later seventeenth century also stored in yards behind the houses a little way up from the waterfront. Chalk, limestone, fulling earth, loads of timber and of 'ostrey wood' faggots (these latter mostly destined for London as firewood) were stored there, with mill stones and malt, oats, peas and a cattle-feed called 'bullimong'. It was essentially a storage place for goods coming in and goods waiting for transport down-river. Many of the ships or hoys were not of Maldon but a dispute over details of a contract in 1574 reveals a Maldon seaman, Robert Goddard, buying 160 cartloads of 'tallwood' for transportation by sea from the Hythe to Tower Wharf at London. Another Maldon seaman made a contract with a yeoman of Purleigh to take 3,000 bundles of firewood and 6,000 billets of wood to either Tower Wharf or St Katherine's Stairs in 1578, and much of the outward trade went to the City but Robert Goddard had, in 1575, disputed costs incidental to a voyage which had been made on his behalf to Newcastle-Upon-Tyne by another Maldon seaman, John Hills, (unfortunately an anchor had been lost at Hartlepool) and coastal voyages were clearly frequent although the coal trade was usually maintained by Tyneside colliers.

It is not entirely clear if the duties charged by the borough on goods were applied to exports as well as imports, and which of the goods referred to were leaving the Hythe. The Custumal refers only to measurage of goods 'coming to the said port' but according to the Water Bailiff's accounts for 1575, which were rendered in more detail than many, in that year 35 per cent of the receipts were from cheese, butter, beer which were certainly going from Maldon and dues were paid on 'wood to London'. He did not separate 'ostreys' (which would probably be shipped to London) from grain, salt and coal of which some was dumped for re-export, especially the coal. Another 35 per cent of his receipts were the harbour dues on carts brought for loading on the Town Quay and for 'groundage and bulkage'. Three bills of customs and duties gathered there show that in 1626 about 107 tons of malt and 92 tons of barley were brought in (which, with 10 tons of oats, indicate the great importance of beer brewing in the town), about 20 tons of rye and wheat, 2 tons of peas and 18 hundredweight of cheese (by the measure of Essex cheese at 300lb to the 'way'). The 4 tons of salt brought in may have been either bay salt from Ipswich or it may have been the produce of more local saltcotes. Coal (1,300 tons, measured by the Newcastle chaldron of 42 cwt., of which about one quarter went to Heybridge) was the main import, constituting over 80 per cent of the total tonnage that year and 319 cartloads of all these goods went out from the Hythe.

From about 1540, simultaneously with the development of the market place, a policy was adopted of running down any commercial activity at the waterside. A sketch plan dateable to about 1595 shows a maximum of fourteen dwellings there (possibly less, for some of the drawn elevations may represent only subordinate parts of dwellings) scattered along the road and a footway leading down towards the river. The plan also indicates some demolitions. One plot is marked as 'sometimes shops and warehouses, storehouses of the Earl of Essex'; another plot covering about a tenth of the area is described as 'a waste and void place'. The parish church

141

of St Mary lay stranded there above coal and chalk heaps, garden plots, a limekiln, a saltcote and a boat or ship-building yard; and when its tower and beacon light collapsed in 1596 the church lay for over twenty five years in partial ruin, adding to the ramshackle, tumbledown appearance of the place. Fifty yards from the water's edge one came to gardens, a vineyard, meadows such as Priest's Croft and St George's Croft, a zone of cultivation and husbandry separating the waterfront from the housing. Most of the Hythe was in St Peter's parish, the majority of whose parishioners had houses half a mile away, nearer the market; most of St Mary's parishioners also lived towards the western end of their parish, nearer the market. This was the one part of Maldon which most men left when they went home at the end of a day's work. By 1550 it had become an ideally secluded rendezvous for the Bailiffs to meet in the churchyard with an Imperial agent, Jehan Dubois, to plan an escape-route for the Princess Mary Tudor.

The death without male heirs of Henry Bourchier, Earl of Essex, (1540) was the occasion for this apparent dereliction to set in. The Bourchiers had been lords of the manor of Little Maldon and that included the Hythe. Subsequent lords appear to have neglected their rights at the waterfront and, just as the end of direct Darcy influence in 1550 appears to have freed the Bailiffs' hands in the development of the market area, so were they able to begin rationalising the function of the Hythe from 1540. The Custumal of 1555 imposed stricter regulations on the waterside trade in its revision of earlier ordinances. 'Stall boats' were only permitted to tie up there during the summer months. Townsmen were not to retail any fish, salt or coal there; instead, fish was to be sold only from the newly erected fishstalls in the market (just as 'small victuals' were only to be sold nearby in the New Market Place) and only before noon. The regulations also ensured that the traders should be drawn into the market: when a ship tied up at the Hythe its lead and line were to be brought by its master to the Bailiffs at the Moot Hall and to them the trader had to declare the nature of his cargo; before he might 'break his bulk' (unload) the trader had to receive a 'billet' from the Bailiffs who normally fixed a maximum price for his goods. In particular, coal was not to be offered for sale 'until the fellow make price with the Bailiffs'. All bargains concerning goods 'coming to the town by water' had to be recorded immediately by the Town Clerk (but sadly very few instances of such records exist) and a penny fee was to be paid to him for each, 'otherwise all such bargains to be void'. Of course, buyers of bulk goods made their deals on board the vessels, for they would have to appraise the value of the cargoes, but the regulations ensured a preliminary journey up the hill to the Moot Hall by the master and (if a different person) by the trader, and another journey by him and his customer when they had agreed on a sale. The Hythe was being restricted to the secondary role of a storage and goods-reception area. The Water Bailiff collected tolls there but the official table of customary dues was displayed at the Moot Hall. The down-grading of the Hythe was completed in 1576, when the Bailiffs moved the sessions of their Admiralty Court from the Town Quay to their new Moot Hall in the market place.

There were other quays too: at Fullbridge, higher up the tidal river (but there is no information about its installations, which must have been privately owned) and there were also wharves along the Blackwater branch of the river in the village and near the Hall at Heybridge. Here is a miniature version of that river and sea-borne trade of the Port of Maldon which has already been described and which helps to explain why the Hythe never underwent dramatic expansion. Just as in the Port as a whole, there were many small anchorages and lading places along the winding, marshy river system, lying beyond the boundaries of the borough. And Heybridge had a long tradition of rivalry with Maldon in the importing of coal and iron, the exporting of grain and dairy produce. Its situation was in some respects better: the description of the narrow and steep roadway to the Hythe quoted above comes from the petition submitted to the House of Lords in June 1641 by 'the inhabitants of that part of the county of Essex which is served with coal from the channel which cometh up to Heybridge by Maldon'; it was, they rightly complained, a 'tedious way to the quay of Maldon and dangerous for horse and man'. It had never been the policy of Maldon men to monopolise the river's trade except in the case of their neighbouring village of Heybridge. From the fourteenth century (at least) they had demanded tolls of every cargo carried past their Hythe into Heybridge Creek — 'no manner of vessel shall pass by the borough unto Heybridge to charge or discharge without making a fine' said Custom 21 in 1555 — and they would go to any length to maintain their right to this toll.

By 1600 the centuries-old dispute over these tolls revived as traders from various parts of the county began to assert that the borough had no right to charge them for their use of the more convenient lading facilities in that village. In 1611 the Corporation issued a new bye-law that for 'every vessel which from henceforth shall pass by the said Borough to Heybridge to charge or discharge any manner of sea-coals, wine, corn, iron, wool, cloth, fulling earth, fuel, timber or chalk, before the same vessel goeth away the owner or master thereof shall ... pay ... unto the Water Bailiff:

| | |
|---|---|
| for every chaldron of sea-coals | 4d |
| for every tun of wine | 4d |
| for every quarter of wheat and rye | 1d |
| for every quarter of malt, barley, peas, oats or bullimong | 1d |
| for every ton of iron | 4d |
| for every pack of wool or cloth | ½d |
| for every chaldron of fulling earth | 4d |
| for every load of fuel or timber | 1d |
| and for every ton of chalk | 1d.' |

The account roll for that year, which states that £3 9s 0d in damages and costs had been paid to Thomas Shele of Heybridge in a lawsuit 'about certain duties of sea coals', indicates that the village's traders had won a preliminary skirmish by a default of James Minckes, the borough's Water Bailiff 'and others' but the Corporation was determined to stand by its customary rights so that, as it was claimed in 1641, Maldon's coal merchants were able 'to starve the country by not parting with coal but at their pleasures and at their own rates'. In 1618 the Corporation decided to take drastic action to prevent ships slipping up-channel without paying toll. The Bailiffs imposed a Scot-and-Lot (a rate payable by all freemen) 'for and towards the making and setting up of a bar of timber and iron to cross the channel, to hinder and stay the passage of vessels by [ie. past] the borough to Heybridge until they have paid the duties and customs belonging to the said borough'. And they actually did it. The chamberlains' accounts for that year record payments for ...

> 'piling and crossing the channel near the limekiln';
> 'a chain weighing 101lbs for the crossing of the channel at the same place' two pale-posts 'unto which the chain at the said place was fastened' and ...
> 'watching at the piles for four sundry nights'.

A further £26 was 'lent and disbursed [by the Corporation's members individually] for and towards the defence of the customs and liberties of the same [borough] questioned withall before the Commissioners in Maritime Causes' because Heybridge responded by suing the borough in the High Court of Admiralty and the account rolls record the long and expensive legal process which followed. An initial fee of £3 1s 0d was paid to the Marshal of the Admiralty Court 'on the attachment of Master Bailiffs and Thomas Welles, one of the chamberlains of the borough, to answer a complaint made against them by some of Heybridge before his Highness' Commissioners for Maritime Causes, concerning some customs and duties demanded by them [the Bailiffs and chamberlains]'; 37s 6d was demanded on the appearance of the Bailiffs and the chamberlain in the court, 18 September 1618, and 36s 2d was paid 'at the same time for their food and horsemeat and horsehire for riding to London for the same Cause'. The Corporation's High Steward was the Master of the Rolls and it had its own Recorder, so its defence position was strong but costly. The account rolls specify 22s paid 'to Master Sergeant Chibborne [the Recorder of Maldon] for counsel on the customs of passage of vessels by this borough to Heybridge'; 6s 8d to George Cole, 'our Proctor in the same cause'; 1s to the porter of Sir Julius Caesar [the High Steward]; £7 6s 10d paid 21 October 'upon the second appearance, Master Chibborne's day for defending or answering for the borough' and 22s 'to Master Thomas Crewe, Counsel, for pleading at the same time'; 6s 'more for Master George Cole, the town's Proctor'. The customary encouragements were: 2 firkins of oysters for Sir Julius, 1 for Master Chibborne.

As the case dragged on into 1619, with yet more fees (44s 'to Master Sergeant Chibborne for his fee in Hilary Term to plead in the Court of Admiralty', 8d to Master George Cole, proctor, and 7s 6d 'for recording the appearance of Master Edward Hastler, Master John Clark and Thomas Welles in the same court at that time') the plaintiffs appear to have become impatient and to have wrong-footed themselves, for the 1619 account roll records payment of a 22s fee to the Recorder 'on his counsel concerning the Complainants' breach of the Commissioners' order, and for his going with the Bailiffs to acquaint the Commissioners with that breach' and the case was over. Maldon continued to exact its tolls and the Water Bailiff's station was moved about a mile down-river, eastward of the Hythe, to a place on the edge of Heybridge Hall Marsh called Borough Hills where the river channel (subsequently named Colliers' Reach) bends sharply around Northey Island.

At this point it is necessary to insert a digression, if only as a disclaimer on Maldon's part to any close connection between the borough and two now-famous riots in March and May 1629. At each time crowds of people, many of them women, descended on ships which were being loaded with rye and plundered them. It was, said Dorothy Berry after the March riot, 'the cry of the Country and her own want' which had provoked more than 140 women to follow a Maldon butcher's wife, Anne Carter, onto the ships (Flemish ones in this incident) to fill their aprons and caps with the grain the foreign merchants had bought locally. Two months later Mistress Carter was at it again, rallying almost three hundred men and women with the cry 'Come my brave boys of Maldon! I will be your leader for we shall not want [for bread]' as they boarded the ships of northern English merchants.

This was more than a matter for the Justices of the borough to deal with and the government issued a writ of oyer and terminer by which some of the rioters were tried and three of them were sentenced to be hanged. Anne Carter was one of those three and she was a Maldon woman but in both riots the mass of the crowds came from the region, from Heybridge and, especially, from the depressed weaving towns of Witham, Bocking and Braintree. What little is known of Mistress Carter (she had brusquely and impudently told Alderman Rudland that she would go to church on a Sunday if he would find someone to do her housework for her) suggests that she had a bitter contempt for Authority, a strong sense of grievance nurtured by poverty. And she had some confused historical notions, calling herself 'Captain of ...' perhaps 'the Commons' (the town clerk's report is damaged) and mis-quoting King Richard II's appeal to the peasants at Mile End. But this was not a Maldon riot. Furthermore — and this brings us back to the dispute over ships going to

Heybridge − the riots took place at Borough Hills, that isolated boundary place on the edge of the Heybridge marshland where Maldon's water bailiff now collected the tolls. So far as the borough and town of Maldon was concerned these disturbances involved mostly outsiders whose rioting occurred on the boundary of its territory and did not challenge its right to demand toll of every ship coming to and inward from the Borough Hills.

Eventually the disputes over the passage of ships to Heybridge brought about the petition to the House of Lords of 1641 (which failed) and it remained a matter of contention until the construction of the Blackwater and Chelmer Canal across the Hall Marsh created a by-pass of the borough at the end of the eighteenth century. A merchant named William Slater who regularly sold coal and iron at Heybridge Creek in the 1630s was described by the petitioners of 1641 as the only man 'who doth use to serve the country of Heybridge ... all men else being driven from buying of coal by reason of the turbulency of the Corporation' and whilst that allegation was not absolutely true (the 1639 Water Bailiff's account mentions 10 tons of iron taken to Heybridge for 'Battes of Braintree' and 19 tons of coal brought in by William Jarman and Widow Johnson of Heybridge and a saltweller, Adam Johnson, imported 4½ tons of coal there in 1642) this Slater was the only trader who persisted in using the Heybridge wharf and paid the tolls demanded by the Water Bailiff. He imported 662 chalder of coal, almost 1,390 tons, between 1638 and 1641 and although his vessel was seized by order of the Bailiffs for a short while he was quickly back in business. He imported 1,223 chalder of coal (about 2,568 tons) to Heybridge during the Civil War years, 1641-47, when it was a blockade of the coal trade during the Scots' siege of Newcastle that adversely affected his business, not the 'turbulency of the Corporation'. But the borough had survived a serious threat to its economy. Coal was one of its principal supplies and without a major share in its distribution the Hythe would have been no better than any of the smaller lading places on other Essex waterways.

Small though Maldon Hythe may seem to have been, it was the scene of continuous improvements. Just as extensions and developments followed on the expansion of the market place in the 1560s, so did the Corporation between 1560 and 1600 add three new wharves; it acquired extra rents from two quays, from additional coal heaps and from two new 'chalk platts'; and it established charges for rights of way, for enclosures and the movement of carts onto the quays. In the seventeenth century further improvements were made, such as moving the Town Storehouse completely from one part of the Hythe to another (1639) and dredging the channel, as well as regular maintenance of the timber quays. The chamberlains' receipts from rents there rose from a mere eighteen pence in 1537 − on only three items − to £2 4s 7d on nine rents in 1677. From the last third of the sixteenth century some habitation had begun to return. There was an alehouse − The George − until

146

about 1660 when it became a dwelling only, called Awnger's, whilst a medieval dwelling house named Cottingham's had become by the 1650s The Ship Inn. By then, too, distinctively labourers' housing was being provided, like three cottages made out of a storehouse just before 1661 and the deeds referring to these humble dwellings describe them as surrounded by yards and entry passages, storehouses and coalyards.

The Corporation could not do more. It could not gather into Maldon Hythe all the considerable but dispersed traffic of the Port, nor would it ever have dreamed of attempting that. Imports of victuals varied according to the seasons and the state of the harvest. Those factors they were powerless to determine or control. The fluctuations in the Water Bailiffs' receipts (see Figure 17) may reflect falls

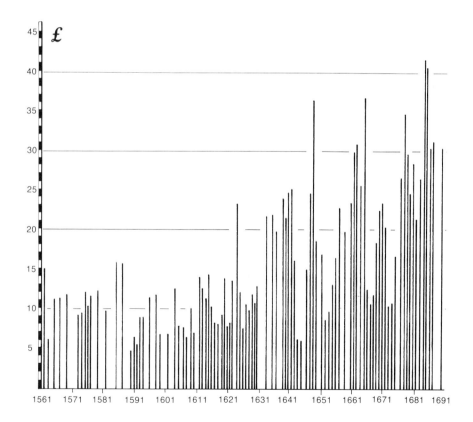

*Figure 17 Water Bailiffs' Receipts, 1550-1690*

147

in trade caused by outbreaks of plague — as in the reduced amounts for 1604 and 1624-5 — and the low receipts of 1664-5 must have been the direct result of a cessation of trade with London because of the Great Plague there. The depressed income from tolls around 1600 may have been caused by the silting of the river bed, that 'decay of the haven' to which people of that time gloomily referred.

What stands out most clearly from these accounts and all the other evidence of the Hythe's activities is that its trade was never in recession from the mid-sixteenth century. Having allowed for increases in the toll tariffs (details of which are incomplete) and the inclusion in the receipts of the tolls on Heybridge trade, the Hythe's traffic can be estimated to have at least doubled between 1550 and 1690. And the most significant component of that increase was certainly the town's coal trade. That is best demonstrated in the summaries of receipts for the Civil War years, showing the effect of the Scots' blockade of Newcastle and Tynemouth 1642-4. Although the term coal merchant never appears in the town's records of occupations, the ownership or leaseholding of coal heaps and ships shows us that those styled gentlemen and merchant, the major landowners (especially the Hastler family, the Plumes, the Robinsons, the Peacocks, the Sprignells of Little Maldon, Sir Thomas Gardiner, Thomas Goddard, John Cade, Robert Snape) were deriving much of their income from the distribution of coal brought in to the Hythe and their ability to 'starve the country' and control the price was what, as members of the Corporation, they had fought for and why they guarded so diligently the customary rights of the borough.

This topographical tour of Maldon's commerce and trades displays an economy which had never been intended to become a source of, let alone a guarantee of a general and increasing prosperity for an entire community. If one were to look for such a state of affairs it would be necessary to find first a settled, continuous community but we know that most of the people who traded in this market place and at this waterfront were transient. Those who were successful were investing in land or crops in the neighbourhood, in shipping, or — as with William Cornish, the immigrant linendraper from Garstang of 1560, whose son appears by 1600 as a citizen and draper of the City of London — they were encouraging their children to better themselves by yet more resettlement. So the economy of Maldon neither declined nor improved spectacularly. Instead, the reconstruction schemes of the mid-sixteenth century succeeded in giving the borough, as an institution, a special and a central place in the steady development of trade in the east coast region.

148

Whilst London continued to grow there was no fear of any long-term or irreversible recession in the commerce on which the borough reposed its fortunes.

CHAPTER 6

# THE COMPANY:
# A TREATISE ON MAGISTRACY

**B**Y NOW IT will have become evident that two authorities successively governed Maldon during the sixteenth and seventeenth centuries, the transfer taking place in 1554 and 1555 by two charters of incorporation (the second revising the first). In 1500 there was a common council composed of eighteen Wardmen appointed annually at a Court of Election from all the resident freemen. At the same court two Bailiffs were chosen to preside for the coming year over the borough and its council. This constitution had been established in 1403, when the Bishop of London demised all his jurisdiction and the demesne perquisites of his share of the borough in return for an annual ferm rent. That represented the penultimate stage in the evolution of this borough. The burgesses had over some four hundred years (to 1554) accumulated charters of privileges and obligations granted and confirmed by the principal overlords of the town, which were represented in the persons of the two, joint-acting Bailiffs whose predecessors had been bailiffs of the Crown's and the Bishop's manors; the burgesses had established a body of customs and held a range of courts and in 1525 the borough's right to exercise Admiralty jurisdiction was confirmed by another charter. Yet it was not a Corporation and, as has been shown in a discussion of housing and commerce, that was the objective on which the leading townsmen of the early sixteenth century, in association with the principal gentry of the area, had set their sights.

Their opportunity came with the events by which Mary Tudor became Queen in 1553. The leading townsmen had already commended themselves to her, for when she was sent to live in the manor house at Woodham Walter on the borough's western boundary in 1549 they had offered their respects with presents of fowls (the chamberlains' accounts for that year refer to payments 'in reward to my lady Mary's Grace at her last being at Woodham: that is to say, for eight capons: 8s 2d; for wild fowl: 6s; and for a turkey cock and a hen: 4s'). In 1550, when the princess was becoming very nervous of the intentions of the Duke of Northumberland, the Protector of the realm for her half-brother King Edward VI, the Bailiffs had certainly connived in plans which were made for her to escape by sailing for the Low Countries in a ship sent by her uncle, the Emperor Charles V. In the event she preferred to stay in England (flight might have compromised her claim to the Crown) but whilst the Emperor's ship rode at anchor in the Blackwater Estuary his agent Jehan Dubois made contact with her via the port of Maldon. He passed himself off as a merchant seeking provisions. The story is told in H.F.M. Prescott's 'Mary Tudor' where unfamiliarity with the local scene

150

led to an under-estimation of the local magistrates' involvement. The Bailiffs met him, ostensibly to fix a price and conclude a bargain on a cargo in his ship, as the Custumal of the borough required. They and Mary's representatives also consulted with him secretly in St Mary's churchyard overlooking the Hythe to arrange for her to pass by their jurisdiction unseen. Not long afterward, when King Edward suddenly died and Princess Mary escaped to Framlingham Castle to proclaim herself Queen, the Bailiffs declared their borough in her favour against Lady Jane Grey and joined the uprising which swept across East Anglia in Mary's support and brought down the Duke of Northumberland's fragile government.

It was specifically for its support that the borough was granted incorporation in 1554. The burgesses' ambition was partly fulfilled because of their recently proven loyalty, partly because a local gentleman, Sir Robert Rochester of Terling, was Comptroller of the Queen's Household, a Privy Councillor and had been especially close to her during King Edward's reign. It was he who presented the burgesses' petition for incorporation. Moreover, the leading townsmen such as Master John Church and Master Robert Gaywood, the civil lawyer John Boswell and the local lawyer Anthony Sparrow, were known adherents to the Old Faith, the English Catholicism of King Henry VIII's reign and of the previous nine hundred years. They would also be sure to have M.P.s chosen for their borough in the new queen's parliaments who would be loyal to that older faith. Their charter was one of several granted 'in consideration of their faithful adherence to the queen during the attempted rebellion by John, late duke of Northumberland and his confederates' as the preamble of Aylesbury's charter, dated 14 January 1554, stated. Lichfield in December 1553, Buckingham in January 1554, were granted charters for the same reason. Sudbury's incorporation (30 May 1554) referred to 'the relation of Sir Edward Waldegrave' of its burgesses' 'fidelity ... and of the strong resistance they made to the late attempted rebellion' and in June 1554 the incorporation charter of Maldon stated (after reference to the supposed antiquity of the town and its 'very ruinous and decayed' condition) that the queen had been 'informed especially by the mouth of her councillor, Robert Rochester, knight, Comptroller of her Household, of the resistance offered by the burgesses and inhabitants to the rebellion attempted against her by John, late duke of Northumberland, [now] attainted'.

In 1555 the townsmen and Sir Robert Rochester were able to negotiate a second charter from the Queen on the grounds that the previous one had been imprecisely phrased in respect of the nomination of the new common council,

> 'nor grant[ed] to the burgesses of the borough aforesaid any power or authority to name, constitute or choose amongst them any persons of themselves to be Bailiffs, Aldermen and Headburgesses ... that of them might be made and be one body corporate and politic, as in the same letters patent[of 1554] We meant to have been;

'and for that certain other doubts, questions and ambiguities in the same our letters patent might arise and already are arisen, We, that our meaning may more plainly appear ..'.

provided Maldon with a charter far more detailed and definitive in the powers it granted. It specified that the Corporation should have a prison and 'a tumbril, pillory, gallows, whereby offenders ought and shall be chastised, corrected and punished according to their faults, demerits and offences'. It added authority to hold a Saturday market and the right to appoint a Clerk of the Market with the guarantee that the royal household's own Clerk of the Market could not claim any jusrisdiction in Maldon. And it confirmed the Bailiffs their existing Admiralty jurisdiction.

The constitutional differences between the government of Maldon before and after 1554-5 need not take up space because the earlier administration which Maldon inherited from the fifteenth century had been in practice as effective as the new model, with a comprehensive jurisdiction over all the inhabitants even if it had acted by the assertion of powers which had not been precisely granted by charters. It always had a gaol and the chamberlains had paid for the construction of a 'jebbit' (gallows) and a pillory in 1551. There was only a formal difference between the methods of administration and the scope of government before and after 1554-5 except that Queen Mary's charter of 1555 amplified the powers which the Bailiffs had been exercising before. It put a sharper edge on their authority by moving specifically the judicature of first instance from the shire or the hundredal courts to the borough courts. The Bailiffs were now formally granted the right to hear and determine all manner of pleas in their court,

'...as well real and mixed, of what manner of lands or tenem ents soever being within the borough, liberty and precinct ... as personal, of what sums soever, or of what kind or sort soever they be ... [and] to hold all such pleas ... in the court aforesaid by plaints before the same Bailiffs to be levied and affirmed in the same court'.

Only pleas which involved the Crown or its ministers, or cases purely between non-freemen were excepted. It was a sweeping grant of competence to the borough courts which strengthened the authority of the Bailiffs and replaced assertion by specific grant.

Continuity there certainly was. The charter guaranteed a perpetual succession to the grants made by earlier lords of the borough and this continuity is symbolised in the continued use of a common and an admiralty seal made long before 1554. It was a mark of incorporation that the seal represented the action of all members as a single corporate person. At Maldon they continued to use the medieval common

*Pl.6. Queen Mary I and her consort Philip II of Spain depicted in the heading to Maldon's Magna Carta of 1555*

seal whose earliest known impression is attached to a 1370 transcript of a royal charter; a new seal was not made until 1682 and the Bailiffs also preserved the use of their splendid early sixteenth century Admiralty seal.

But there was development as well. Incorporation represented the final acquisition of real stability and security. Corporate responsibility replaced individual liability. The courts were strengthened by the formal delegation of judicial and coercive powers and especially by the automatic inclusion of aldermen in the Commission of the Peace. In 1500 the burgesses' rights had been obscured by the divided lordship of their borough as well as by the existence of other manorial jurisdictions within the same area but these complexities resolved themselves by chance during the middle years of the century.By 1560 the Crown had regained the lordship of both parts of the old Manor of Great Maldon (in which the borough was technically sited) from the Darcy family and the Bishop of London, so that all the burgesses became tenants of the Crown so far as their franchise was concerned and annually that was commemorated in the payment to the Crown of both the old ferm rents which had previously gone to the bishop and the Lord Darcy. A certain ebullience can be detected in the attitude of the burgesses and aldermen in the years following immediately on this urban coming-of-age. They acquired from the heralds a coat of arms whose design was derived from their common seal (the three leopards of England from the royal arms on the obverse of the seal, a sailing ship from its reverse). They opened a register or chartulary called the White Book and, when the new charter of 1555 was enrolled therein, the Town Clerk wrote above its text the title *Magna Charta de Maldon*.

## THE COMPOSITION OF THE COMPANY OF MALDON

A novelty of the new Corporation which must be pointed out is its adoption of a new name for its Common Council, which first appears in a new Custumal drawn up and revised by the first members of the Corporation in April 1555 in accordance with the 1554 charter, '...for the good rule and government of this borough according to the tenor, form and effect of the letters patent of our said sovereign lord and lady the King's [Philip II] and Queen's Majesty, granted unto them for the doing thereof as in and by the said letters patent more at large doth appear'. In the text of their Custumal appears this term for the Bailiffs, the Aldermen and the eighteen Headburgesses: they are 'The Company' and thereafter it appears frequently in the Corporation's records until the later part of the seventeenth century.

An analysis of the annual elections (which are recorded for all but seventeen between 1500 and 1688) suggests that this Company was not at all the oligarchy which one might expect a Tudor and Stuart corporation to have been. On average a freeman elected to its membership occupied a place for only 6.5 years in the sixteenth century, 11 years in the seventeenth. Nor was membership necessarily in one continuous session, so that it was more usual for men to be recruited to make up vacancies caused by temporary 'retirement' than to replace deceased or departed members. Thus, in the elections for the decade 1560-69 only 10 per cent of new members filled vacancies caused by death but almost 50 per cent held office for less than six years. In all, 48 men were needed to maintain at full strength The Company of 24 freeburgesses for those ten years.

It was also usual for aldermen to take a year off occasionally and the customary sequence of their official life ran thus: alderman, Bailiff, Justice of the Peace, alderman, year off, alderman … and so on. Nine aldermen were normally needed to maintain the necessary annual establishment of two Bailiffs, two J.P'.s, four aldermen and one 'off duty' alderman. Among the eighteen headburgesses there was considerable movement in and out of The Company, reflecting the pattern of migration among the town's population at large. Thus Humphrey Hastler was a headburgess in 1568 and again in 1570; the next year he was reported at the Court of Election to have left the town but he had returned by 1575, when he again took up a place in The Company. One of the wealthiest freemen in Maldon from about 1550 to 1600 was Richard Josua (or Joseway), a vintner, who spent sixteen years in office but in three spells: one of twelve years and (after no less than eighteen years but it does seem certain to be the same man) two more pairs of years, 1586-87 and 1590-91. One man was permitted to stand down for one year; another served two years, was 'pardoned' the next and then served for a further six years. These years out of The Company were usually granted to suit the requirements of the men's occupations, as when William Poulter, a ship master, was elected a Bailiff (1557) but excused since he was about to be 'engaged in his affairs overseas'.

It follows that in any given year The Company was drawn from far more than twenty four contributory families. A little exercise in political arithmetic shows how broadly based the 'ruling group' (if that can be allowed as a true description of it) really was. Between forty and fifty families were involved in the composition of the common council in any decade so, in a population of probably no more than 1,100 and assuming an average of 4.75 persons per household, there was a ratio of fifty common councillors to 250 householders. That is, about one householder in every five could have a place in The Company for at least one year in any decade.

Since only freemen were eligible and they appear to have numbered 100 in an average year, about one half of them in any ten year period were liable to be elected. In fact recruitment for The Company spread so wide a net over the borough's male population that the wardmen of the early sixteenth century and the headburgesses in the subsequent Corporation cannot justifiably be regarded as the ruling group.

155

Maldon would have held a unique position indeed among the towns of Tudor and Stuart England had the reality of power within that community really been vested in so great a proportion of the townsmen as one fifth of all males or one in every two freemen. Certainly an Assembly of the House (as Corporation memoranda sometimes styled formal deliberations) was a gathering more truly representative of the freeman body than might have ben expected for a borough of those times, yet whereas membership of The Company was widely recruited, so were the occasions for an individual's participation in the true decision-making process thinly spread. In fact the ruling group was tucked away within The Company and far more restrictive in its membership.

An inspection of the corporation lists reveals successive inner groups, men who served for long and continuous periods and were thus distinct from the ordinary headburgesses or wardmen whose membership often lacked continuity and consequently lacked experience. Thirty seven freemen can be picked out who were especially distinguished by their length of service, like Thomas Plume who had one year as a headburgess, immediately on his departure from Danbury to live in Maldon, and then twenty seven years (1624-53) as an alderman. He finally had to ask his Company for permission to retire on the grounds of extreme age and ill-health. These thirty seven formed no more than 9 per cent of the total personnel of The Company between 1567 and 1692 (those were the years in which they themselves served) yet they occupied exactly one third of all the available places in the common council. These were the men on whom the effective government of the borough really depended, for they had the experience necessary to make decisions, the knowledge of precedents, a familiarity with court procedures, an awareness of probable future contingencies. Power rested with them because they were the most experienced, not necessarily because they were the oldest or because they were the most discreet and able, as prescribed in the 1444 Custumal, although long service would normally mean that Bailiffs such as these men posseessed all these qualities.

Custom and procedure ensured that these men held the initiative of action because the government of the borough was in practice at the will of the two annual Bailiffs. Of course that was never specifically stated and in theory it was not so. It was a principle that the whole assembly acted in concert as The Company. It was a matter of common belief, an accepted ideal, that they should be at all times a fellowship acting in a spirit of brotherly accord. There were no opposition parties within borough governments, there was no concept of minority dissent. A fifteenth century ordinance which the Corporation inherited from the previous Common Council forbade any of its members to *make stryffe or debate among his felawshippe in tyme of councell of comounyng* and ordered the ejection of any member who was 'contrary to the common will'. There certainly were serious differences of opinion within The Company, especially in the 1590's (which are examined in Chapter 7 below) but the main concern of all was to compose such discords, as by re-establishing the communal feasts which customarily concluded the Quarter Sessions in the borough 'for a means of the better enjoying and continuing of common amity and brotherly kindness and unity in and with the whole Company, society, body of this House, one member with another'. That was written in 1598 and remained the ideal for the Corporation for many years to come but its writers included Alderman William Vernon (32 years in office), one of those thirty seven long-serving men who have been picked out as the true rulers of Maldon. His brother aldermen, who were the other writers of this homily, would have agreed with him that real authority stemmed from the exercise of the Commission of the Peace and was thus confined to four men each year: the two Bailiffs and the out-going Bailiffs who were always appointed to continue for another year as Justices of the Peace.

## THE DISCIPLINE OF THE COMPANY

The Custumal of the borough, the memoranda of its assemblies, the oaths prescribed for its various grades of officers and inhabitants provide administrative evidence of the control exercised by the two annual Bailiffs. One of the oaths has already been cited − that for new decenners − by which each adult male inhabitant swore obedience not to the Common Council or to the Justices but to the Bailiffs alone. Within the Common Council before and after incorporation the same subjection to the Bailiffs applied. In some corporations the common councilmen were termed Assistants and although they did not use that name that was exactly what the headburgesses of Maldon were. In the meaning of the French word *assister* they did 'assist' at assemblies of The Company simply by being present. Their duty was to assent, to give consent by silent presence. When the Corporation was created a regulation was introduced into the Custumal for its internal discipline by which the initiation of policy and discussion was reserved entirely to the Bailiffs, who were always 'to show first their opinion'. Hence it was out of order for anyone else to propose a motion for discussion. Furthermore, the promulgation of decisions was entirely the business of the Bailiffs, because it was customary for the ordinances of the Common Council to be published as Orders of the Justices of the Peace at the Quarter Sessions. In those court sessions the subordinate position of the headburgesses was formally demonstrated when they presented the decisions of the Common Council in the form of a petition. Then, in their capacity as Justices of the Peace, the Bailiffs and Aldermen ordered that the request be allowed and observed. From at least 1555 every ordinance which was formally declared to have emanated from the Common Council was first moved by the Bailiffs, then accepted by the Bailiffs in the Quarter Sessions and finally made lawful by a declaration from the mouths of the Bailiffs enthroned upon the Bench of their court.

157

Any notion of taking the initiative and making policy which a new member of The Company might have entertained when he first donned his gown and made his way along the High Street to the Moot Hall would have been squashed when he took his oath of office. In fact it was not even a real oath. He was merely required to assent to a charge delivered to him orally by the Town Clerk, which instructed him in each point of his duties. He did not even give his assent individually, for the text of the charge is clearly written for group delivery:

> 'You shall well and truly occupy the office of Headburgess of this Borough for the year following and truly and duly be here at every Quarter Court and there and then true and due inquisition make with your Company of all such points and articles as shall be showed unto you on the Queen's [or King's] behalf, and for the good rule of the borough; and a good and true verdict thereof make and present, according to the Custom of the Borough. So God help you'.

That is all. No reference to participation in council, only of attendance at courts as a juror.

Aldermen fared better but though their Charge was individually administered it made plain their subordination to the Bailiffs:

> You shall well and truly exercise and execute the office and room of one of the Aldermen ... and be always present and ready to aid and assist the Bailiffs and your brethren Aldermen and Common Council to the best of your wit, cunning and power for the better maintenance and execution of Her Majesty's laws, statutes and customs within the said Town and Free Borough ... And [you shall] be present at all the General and Quarter Sessions of Her Majesty's Peace within the same ... and at all other time and times when you shall be called and summoned lawfully unto the Moot Hall ... then and there to confer with the Bailiffs and Common Council for and about the commonwealth of the town, if you be not letted or hindered to come to the Session or Council by sickness, impotency or other such reasonable cause. So God help you'.

Two texts of the Oaths of Officers exist — c1555 and c1604 — and only in the earlier one are there any which are worded personally, as true personal oaths, except that the Aldermen's and Bailiffs' oaths were always personal. In 1555 personal oaths were provided for the decenners and freemen but even they became group charges in the 1604 text. The headburgesses received group charges in both texts. But when the Bailiffs, the consuls of the borough for the year, took office each always swore a personal oath which proclaimed him the *advocatus* of the sovereign:

158

'I shall well and truly govern and maintain the town, the franchise, the right, the profits and the welfare of the same ... I shall well and truly keep the Peace of our Sovereign Lady the Queen ...'

Nowhere was the authority of these men more clearly expressed than in an Exhortation which was to be delivered by their Serjeant at the commencement of every session of their Admiralty Court. At first the sessions had been held in the open air on the Town Quay at the Hythe but when the new Moot Hall was opened in 1576 the Bailiffs moved their sessions there and it was apparently then that their office was invested with gestures of civic grandeur and they chose to be openly equated with the Lord Chief Justice and the Lord High Admiral of England. In their alternative role as joint-Admiral the two magistrates entered their court in procession, preceded by their Serjeant carrying an oar instead of the mace, and when they had taken their seats he summoned with three 'Oyes' all who 'had to do before her Majesty's Bailiffs and Admirals within the Liberties'. Then the Order for Keeping the Court required him to address the jury with a homily which was based on the argument that the sovereign − 'the head of the commonwealth and from whom all Justice as from the original fountain floweth' − required the rule of law on the seas within his or her dominion as much as upon the land; that the Lord Admiral of England had the same function 'for the execution of her laws upon the seas' as the Lord Chief Justice had on the land; and that his power was possessed and exercised within the boundaries of the Admiralty of Maldon by the present Bailiffs.

'Within this Liberty her Highness' Bailiffs are the Admirals and have the power of the Admiralty within the Liberty, as by the express words of the Charter, in as ample and large manner and to all intents and purposes as hath the High Admiral of England'.

The effective concentration of power in their hands is also to be seen in the borough account rolls which (unlike the treasurers' accounts of some towns) record every item of expenditure. Two chamberlains were appointed each year and the entire management of the borough's finance was technically their responsibility. Yet although they received all the income due to the borough, accounted for all expenditure and acted as quartermasters for the town militia, their office was not of aldermanic rank, they rarely received any training or held the office sufficiently regularly to develop any expertise in financial administration. (However, from 1626 to 1631 the same two men were, sensibly, continuously in office.) Their final account roll was written up for them by the Town Clerk. They were never called on to make good any deficit from their own pockets (whereas in many towns the treasurers were expected to make good the year's balance from their own resources) and from 1521 the medieval practice ceased of issuing the out-going chamberlains with a quittance after the audit. They were not responsible for the Corporation's

*Pl.7. The Bailiffs' seal as Admirals of the Port of Maldon*

finances, the Bailiffs were: the Bailiffs gave the orders, The Company assented, the Chamberlains paid out the cash. Apart from fees, rents and minor recurrent items all the expenditure which the Chamberlains recorded in their lengthy and fascinating account rolls was normally warranted for the purpose of audit with a standard phrase, repeated item after item, 'at Master Bailiffs' commandment'.

But like their chamberlains the Bailiffs were never expected to subsidise the expenditure which they authorised. For a Tudor or Stuart community this is an odd and thought-provoking feature of the account rolls. It was usual, it was expected, that the rich held the principal offices and in return dipped into their own money chests to cover expenses beyond the resources of the corporation or vestry or guild or company. They were expected to be liberal in such support and to provide munificently and voluntarily for the public benefit, to be charitable, to provide feasts and entertainments. Never at Maldon did the Bailiffs pay out of their own

160

funds for a single musician's or a company of players' performance. Master John Bush, a Bailiff in 1535 was repaid 12d 'that he gave to the King's Juggler'; the chamberlains provided the 3s 4d paid 'to my lord of Oxford's bearward' in 1561; the 2s 6d given to '[  ] Oteley for sounding his trumpet' in 1603 'upon the proclaiming of the King's Majesty' and the sums donated on numerous occasions to bell ringers and especially to the players' companies visiting the town, came from the borough chest. When the Bailiffs patronised the Latin or Greek play produced and acted by their town's grammar school in 1623 it was the chamberlains who provided the 2s 2d 'for wine and sugar given to Master Danes and other gentlemen when his scholars did last act a comedy in the grammar school'.

There is no doubt that most were quite capable of finding the money for such expenses and that they were always among the wealthiest men not only in the town but in the district. For the early sixteenth century that can be demonstrated from the lay subsidy returns, when the three taxpayers in 1524 who were or had been Bailiffs (Thomas Wyborough, John Dawes and Richard Benham) were in the top 6 per cent of the assessments, with the first two unusually highly assessed at £260 and £215 in goods. Six of the Bailiffs of 1540-50 are to be found in the 1544 subsidy return and five of them were in the top 12 per cent of the borough taxpayers. Whilst later subsidy assessments provide no trustworthy guide to the relative fortunes of the Corporation's members, three local assessments for rates are of some use. One of 1566 gives by far the highest assessment to the two Bailiffs and one of the aldermen; another of 1569 also rates the Bailiffs and aldermen most highly. The most useful rate allocation (or Scot and Lot) is of 1619 because it was levied on as many people in the town as possible, free and 'foreign,' and consequently the rates were not levelled down as much as in other more selectively applied rate demands, so that the amounts charged run in much finer gradations. All the aldermen of 1619 were in the top 13 per cent of the rateable population and they formed the richer part, too, of that top section. Though there was some overlapping (since some resident gentry and yeomen were not members of The Company, nor even freemen) the assessments for rates indicate that the aldermen formed the wealthiest section of the town's population, with a *per capita* rating of £9.06, far above the majority of the headburgesses, whose rating was £3.07 a head, and nine times as wealthy that the rest of the freemen and some of the 'foreigners' who together formed 81 per cent of the assessed inhabitants but whose *per capita* rating was only £0.8.

It is also clear from other sources that many of the aldermen were rich compared to other townsfolk. John Church, a Bailiff eight times between 1533 and 1588 was a gentleman servant to the de Vere family, Earls of Oxford, an agent for their estates in eastern Essex and until 1536 he was also the manager of the temporalities of Beeleigh Abbey, rich enough to lease the Maldon home of Sir Thomas Darcy (the

Darcy Tower), and one of the undoubted creators of Maldon's incorporation. After his time the borough's affairs were largely in the hands of Master William Vernon of Little Beeleigh, a gentleman landowner, whose pre-eminence in The Company lasted from about 1565 until his death in 1611. He and his colleague Thomas Eve, a wealthy merchant, continued John Church's schemes to make Maldon a notable town: they brought to the borough the ownership of Darcy's Tower and superintended its conversion into the new Moot Hall; they were the Bailiffs when the register of apprentices' indentures was begun, when court cases were arranged to create precedents to protect the rights and autonomy of the borough; and Master Vernon was one of the few local men ever chosen to be one of the borough's M.P'.s. That was for the session of November 1588 to March 1589, when he was elected instead of a nobleman's nominee because, as a draft letter of explanation to this nobleman (whose identity is not known) states,

'. . . having some consultation amongst ourselves it was then thought very requisite that for some necessary causes for the good of our poor town (too long now by letter to trouble your Lordship withal to declare) that some fit person of the inhabitants within the said borough (and to be taken out of the society of our Company) should be elected to supply the place of one of our burgesses [in parliament]'.

Seventeenth century aldermen were often gentry and most were landowners. They traded in coal, iron, chalk, cattle, ships; they sent their sons to schools such as Merchant Taylors' and to the university, and had them instituted to local vicarages and rectories. They were all capable of bearing the 'port' of high office and authority. William Vernon's successor as the leading personality in The Company seems to have been John Soan who was only thirty one when first elected an alderman. His and William Vernon's are the only monuments to these magistrates of the sixteenth and early seventeenth centuries which have survived in Maldon, both in All Saints' Church. Master Soan's (of 1636) records his 'pious and religious service to his generation' for twenty seven years as an alderman and seven times as a Bailiff. At his death Thomas Plume took over as the clear leader of the aldermen, guiding it through the most difficult of times, through the Civil War and almost right through the Commonwealth.

So the arrangement current during the period of this study, of paying the running expenses of office from corporate funds, is a very curious feature of the Maldon system. In the matter of money the Bailiffs preferred to emphasise the unity and common liability of The Company rather than their own great local power. Perhaps it is a reminder that even this tiny ruling group within a Company of ever-changing personnel was itself impermanent and expected to be so. Only a few of the aldermen in any decade could claim very long experience; most were appointed when they were in their early thirties and needed guidance; and as the Bailiffs exercised their powers jointly it is likely that an older man paired with a comparatively new 'Other Bailiff' would always be the true maker of decisions and would have the final word in any discussion. Sometimes both Bailiffs were new to their office and then the advice, warnings, predictions of a senior alderman would carry great weight. Thus Master Church or Master Vernon, Alderman Soan or Alderman Plume would continue to govern behind the scenes in the years when they were neither Bailiff nor Justice of the Peace. Thus in 1585 William Vernon had been an alderman for over fifteen years, two of his colleagues had been in office for five years and three were elected only in that year. In such a situation Master Vernon's authority and his opportunities to direct the incumbent Bailiffs and Justices whilst not exercising either of those positions himself was clearly considerable.

There was also the Town Clerk who, in any borough, was close behind all successful government. Particularly active Town Clerks held office in conjunction with these leading aldermen. During the heyday of Bailiffs Eve and Vernon they and their borough were ably served by that John Barnardiston to whom we are indebted for compiling those catalogues of decenners in the 1570s. A touch of the civic splendour Vernon and Eve sought for the Corporation was reserved for him at the formal occupation of the new Moot Hall, when £2 10s 0d was paid to 'Master Town Clerk towards the making of his violet gown'. In the time of Aldermen Soan and Plume the able industry of Thomas Cheese and Nowell Hammond as clerks is shown in the numerous bundles of their files and in their beautifully written, handsome registers of court business. Until 1567 the necessity of employing a full-time clerk does not seem to have been appreciated at Maldon, except by the clerks themselves, for the brief tenures of office by the six who occupied the post between 1550 and 1566 suggests that they found intolerable the clerical burdens imposed by the newly invigorated commercial and communal life of the town. Until 1567 they were local attorneys who combined their official work with private practice as scriveners, notaries, stewards of estates, surveyors and auditors. Blaise Salter was Deputy Town Clerk in 1562 and also the Customer for the Port of Maldon. Anthony Sparrow, who had an extensive private practice as an attorney and estate agent, was sometimes Town Clerk, sometimes a deputy, over the years 1544 to 1566. Master John Barnardiston, a member of the Barnardistons of Kedington in Suffolk, was the first clerk who appears to have been prepared to specialise in borough administration. He began in Maldon that enduring tradition of the Town Clerk as a solicitor with an advisory and executive influence in the Bailiffs' decisions and activities. He was the expert on procedure, precedent and capability. He was Steward of the Bailiffs' leet courts, the registrar of their Quarter Sessions, Courts of Record, Admiralty. He wrote the chamberlains' accounts and kept their cash. He composed the Bailiffs' letters replying to royal commissions, gentry, nobility, preachers, to the Privy Council. It was his task to know the location of evidence in the borough's muniments which legal counsel needed to consult when there were lawsuits for or against the Corporation. They were thus necessarily the close and daily associates of a small group of aldermen and because of the confidential or secret information which they possessed about the Coporation's rights and obligations, because they were the best qualified to judge how The Company stood financially at any time in the year, and because of their legal knowledge, they could be the most influential men in the borough community. And because each was the servant of The Company, the payments had to be expressed as 'at Master Bailiffs' commandment' when they were in fact decided by or had been negotiated by the Town Clerk.

## THE PARAMOUNT AUTHORITY OF THE COMPANY

Local government proceeded by the assertion of rights and, if necessary, by the prosecution of such claims in lawsuits. Town charters were not blue-prints of routine urban administration, nor were they detailed constitutional instruments. Their value lay in the correct deployment of their clauses to rebut attacks on corporate decisions or to argue the validity of particular courses of action. Consequently the text of the charters and of the customs of Maldon were kept closely guarded. They were referred to as 'the secrets of the borough' and whilst they had sometimes to be produced in a court for examination by counsel and were available for consultation by officers of the borough, care was taken that no unauthorised 'foreigners' might see them (unless they went to the extraordinary trouble of searching out copies of the texts among the Charter Rolls and Patent Rolls at Westminster or in the Tower of London). All the charters of Maldon were stored in a locked chest in a locked room called the Charterhouse within the Moot Hall. Freemen swore to keep these 'secrets of the borough' and when one of them in 1673 borrowed from one of the chamberlains the White Book of Maldon, in which were copies of all the charters and also of the customs, and left it for several hours in the house of a non-freeman, he was disenfranchised 'for breach of his oath, thereby discovering the secrets of the said borough'. A century earlier Anthony Sparrow was dismissed as Deputy Town Clerk (1566) because he was considered unfit 'to have the records and books of this borough under his custody and by reason of his office to know the secrets, truths and counsels of this borough'. The impediment thus thrown in the path of those who opposed any of the Corporation's privileges is indicated by the request of some Heybridge men and other county petitioners who in 1641 desired the House of Lords to obtain for them the right to examine the 1555 charter.

It was in The Company's interest to preserve an uncertainty about the true extent of its franchise whilst by precedent cases designed to convince everyone of the reality of its claims, and by activities and declarations it arrogated a wide range of powers over the lives of the town's inhabitants, free and 'foreign', which were not specifically laid out in its charters. The Borough of Maldon was, said the magistrates, a Liberty, immune from any external authority lower than the Lord Lieutenant and the Privy Council. To uphold this they could cite the *Ne Intromittent* clause of the 1555 charter:

> 'so that our Sheriff ... Escheator ... Clerk of the Market of our House ... Admiral ... Steward and Marshal ... nor any of them may enter nor may sit within the borough, liberty and precinct to enquire of any things or matters that to their office appertaineth or belongeth ... and it is lawful for the Bailiffs, aldermen and headburgesses to resist any invasion of their rights without our [the sovereign's] impeachment, or of our heirs, or of any person whatsoever ...'

That clause had been in the 1554 charter and immediately after it had been granted the Bailiffs had fought and won a test case when one of them and two of their constables were prosecuted by the Royal Clerk of the Market. This clause and another which confirmed the admiralty jurisdiction of the Bailiffs, were the basis of The Company's protest in 1635 against an infringement of their franchise by the deputy of the Earl of Warwick (who was Vice-Admiral of England), who proposed to hold his own court in the borough. The Town Clerk pointed out that

> 'Admiral[ty] jurisdiction within the liberties of the incorporation of Maldon hath always been exercised by the Bailiffs ... beyond all memory and the late King and Queen, Philip and Mary, by their charter did grant and confirm admiral[ty] jurisdiction to the Bailiffs ... with a prohibition and restraint to any their admiral or any of his ministers to intermeddle within the same liberties ... all which rights they had long before, beyond memory and always exercised without interuption'.

The Earl commented to his deputy (William Pulley) 'I am very unwilling any liberty within their corporation should be infringed and therefore I would have you defer to keep the Admiral[ty] Court for that corporation till I be further satisfied in that point', for he was himself a freeman of Maldon, as the Bailiffs reminded him, by virtue of having been once one of its M.P.s. Even so the matter went before the High Court of Admiralty in 1636 at the same time as the corporations of Harwich and Colchester were defending their jurisdictions against writs of *Quo Warranto* and in 1637 another summons came for the Bailiffs to attend this Vice-Admiral's Court in the King's Head Inn within their own borough.

The intrusion of rival jurisdictions was always a threat. The first question put to each jury in the Admiralty Court asked 'if any burgess or resident of Maldon hath impleaded or sued any other burgess or resident before the Lord Admiral or any other judge for offences on the sea' and for more than a century before its incorporation formally granted the borough immunity from the proceedings of external courts the burgesses had been guarding their own jurisdiction. Inserted into the 1468 text of the borough customs is this order (an example of the clumsiness of much English prose before the mid-sixteenth century):

*Pl.8. Muniment chest remaining in the Moot Hall*

*Ner non' freman of the bourgh shall sue non freman of the bourgh out of the bourgh wythowte he sue hym first in the bourgh to the ende of his ple[a]*

nor might he continue a lawsuit in other courts without licence from the Bailiffs *and a great fyn*. In 1568 the continuing duty of every freeman to maintain this *Ne Intromittent* privilege was driven home with a charade acted out in the open court. One of the two Bailiffs for that year, the powerful William Vernon, was himself cited in the Quarter Sessions for having impleaded another freeman in a court outside the borough. Found guilty, the sentence passed on him was that he should be deposed from his office as Bailiff and as alderman, then deprived of his place as a headburgess, then expelled from the franchise of the borough and suffer imprisonment. None of that actually occurred but it appeared that Master Vernon was saved only when The Company had been petitioned by the Recorder and two peers of the realm — no less — to show its clemency, and only after a third peer who also happened to be present, the Earl of Sussex, had offered arbitration.

If Maldon men were required to have recourse to the courts of their own magistrates and to prevent external jurisdictions being exercised within the borough, they were also forbidden to assist at courts outside its liberty, even the County Assizes. In 1567 Humphrey Hastler was presented before the Maldon Quarter Sessions because

'he did offer and put himself upon a jury or inquest at the last assizes or sessions holden at Brentwood contrary to his oath made by him when he

166

was sworn a freeman and headburgess for to maintain the liberties of the borough, so that being demanded he should have prayed to be discharged for that he ought not to be put in inquest out of the town of Maldon'.

To preserve this immunity The Company had to ensure that its own courts were fully employed. Among the chief occasions for the assertion of its authority were the Quarter Sessions, where the business of the borough's court leet was combined with the work of the Commission of the Peace. The Sessions, as has been shown, were meetings of the common council, an Assembly of the House but with the Bailiffs and two of the aldermen fulfilling principally their roles as Justices of the Peace. The Town Clerk in his violet gown sat with them. The Recorder, a judge, came to preside over the Sessions. The headburgesses formed the jury and presented their inquest, drawn up during the preceding days. At the conclusion of the court, the Bailiffs (consulting with the Recorder) issued their Orders and then the entire Company retired for a good dinner to demonstrate their solidarity of purpose. The business they had done in their courts in the century before the incorporation of 1555 had often been much the same but the details are clearest in the presentments and orders of the incorporated borough sessions.

The juries always presented a wide range of offences and problems, from trading offences to matters of public health and public amenities, from vagabondage to purely borough affairs such as the decenners who had defaulted at the View of Frankpledge or the defamation of the Corporation's officials during the execution of their routine duties. Breaches of the peace formed a curiously small part of the Quarter Sessions business, apart from the perennial cases of card players on the Sabbath, gossiping women, scolds, hedgebreakers (mostly elderly women gathering firewood,it seems) and perennial *brethelde brawlers* as the 1444 Custumal had called worthless persons who would not *be justified by the Baillies for ther brawlyng*. Year by year acts of parliament added to the presentments which had to be made to justices in their Quarter Sessions. Here they licensed alehouse keepers and fined those customers who played Irish game, ninepins, stool ball, sladethrift, span-groat, slide-groat, tray-trip, tennis or bowls. They took recognisances from victuallers not to sell meat in Lent or other times of fasting, and also dealt with the butchers who from time to time sold putrid meat ('cow's flesh as yellow as a pagell or kite's foot' − as a cowslip − was one accusation of 1568) or slaughtered bulls for meat without first having them baited. They received reports from the parishes' Surveyors of Highways on the landholders who were failing to scour ditches and householders who were 'in default of their work on the highway' or had refused to pay their rate to the surveyors. The constables here presented their complaints of householders who had refused to take their turn in the Night Watch and males who had neglected to practice archery. The justices applied the sumptuary laws which attempted to regulate expenditure so as to preserve social graduations;

167

they fined servants for wearing such finery as 'great and monstrous breeches', long cloaks and ruffs of excessive size, and other men for using handguns for wildfowling, ferrets for rabbing. They applied the Statute of Artificers to tradesmen who retained servants from week to week, not by a year's contract, to those who sent away maids before their term of service was finished, to men who failed to obtain a licence to keep a maidservant, to young unmarried craftsmen who practised their trades in Maldon peoples' homes. Those who were absent from Divine Service were breaking the Act of Uniformity; those who neglected to wear woollen hats made in England were (in the 1560s and 1570s) prosecuted under another act for the preservation of the clothing trades.

Business peculiar to the borough had once been the principal subject matter of its courts, although many of its customs or bye-laws were based on statutes, such as the Statute of Winchester, 1293, concerning the harbouring of vagrants and aliens. After incorporation complaints against inhabitants concerning local amenities (defective drainage, refuse dumping, dirty slaughterhouses, dangerous wells, rickety buildings, stray animals, unleashed mastiff dogs), defaulters, encroachments and slanders against officials, were still comprehended in the Quarter Sessions and there the jury still gave notice of land and houses sold during the previous three months, so that the chamberlains could levy the appropriate Landcheap on the vendors; the Water Bailiff still presented his quarterly receipt of tolls and The Company heard the Orders which the Bailiffs formulated as a result of what they had heard during the court's proceedings. It was usually at the Quarter Sessions that new freemen were admitted and took their oaths; and new decenners were also sworn in on these days.

The Company's influence between these busy quarter days was continuously exercised by a range of other courts. The Admiralty Court did for the riverside what the Quarter Sessions did for the land; there were Petty Sessions, a Pie Powder Court during the borough's Fairs and a Court of the Clerk of the Market for weekly markets, and the regular, sometimes twice monthly sessions of the Court of Record at which most apprentices' indentures were witnessed and enrolled copies were registered. This court spent much of its time hearing the actions for debt which have already been described and the similar civil actions of detinue (the wrongful detention of money or goods), trespass and special trespass, which involved either real damage done in the course of a trespass or damages alleged to have been caused by the detention of money or goods. Actions over broken agreements, claims for damages or for payment of wages were heard — though all too frequently the clerk omitted any description of the cases — and at the same time the aldermen and, of course, the ever-active Bailiffs carried out the formal but customary questioning of wives to record their assent to conveyances of their property by their husbands. The bundles of Town Clerks' papers display yet more work which showered down on these aldermen, such as writing enquiries to other magistrates to check on strangers in the town, answering enquiries by the Privy Council about vagrancy and alehouses and the condition of the town's armour, weapons and stores of gunpowder. Frequently, too, they were with the Town Clerk in the Moot Hall to interrogate vagrants and unmarried mothers.

No wonder the Bailiffs never (or very rarely) subsidised the borough from their own resources. So much of their weekdays must have been swamped by official duties that they must often have relied greatly on their families and servants to carry on their personal trade. Alderman Ralph Breeder was a very wealthy bachelor haberdasher and his gratitude to the people who maintained his household and business for him isdisplayed in his bequests of £40 plus leasehold land and seven acres of coppice to two of his maidservants and his entire stock of grocery, haberdashery, mercery wares, drapery wares and 'shop wares' to his three capable servants, each formerly an apprentice with him, to the value of at least £100 each in 1609. They had filled the role of sons to their old master.

Did such men ever regret the eagerness of Master Church, Master Gaywood and their Company in the 1550s to reinforce with its incorporate status the Liberty of their borough? It seems not. For there was more. An amalgam of civic pride and the new religious attitudes which were produced or encouraged by the Elizabethan settlement of religion prompted these officials to treat the separate parish institutions as departments of their corporate government. This attitude is illustrated by an ordinance of 1569 which divided the whole town into four wards named after contemporary aldermen, which it was proposed should supersede the parish divisions and their saints' names: 'Item, the said borough town and all the hamlets, parishes and limits within the same always hereafter shall stand divided into four several wards in manner and form following ...' The ward boundaries had no correspondence with the existing parish boundaries. In fact this ordinance was never enforced, the Corporation continued to appoint constables for parishes, to divide its lists of taxpayers and report its searches for vagrants by parishes, but the existence of such a scheme is an example of the trend of thought at that time. And there was bound to be confusion over the relationship between borough and parish because the statutory duties imposed on parish officials (and the creation of such officials by statutes), on the Surveyors of Highways, the Overseers of the Poor, the Churchwardens, made them accountable to the magistrates, who were the aldermen, in the borough courts. Moreover, the town's small size precluded any separation of the borough and the parish officials; all had to be chosen from the same limited pool of manpower. Most of the parishes' records are lost but it is clear that their officers frequently doubled as officials of the borough. Anthony Sparrow was not only a deputy Town Clerk but also, c1553-1566, a headburgess, a churchwarden of St Mary's parish and (after misdemeanours) one of his parish's

Surveyors of Highways. An apprenticeship indenture of 1610 includes the names of four Overseers of the Poor who were at the same time sworn members of The Company.

All Saints' and St Peter's parishes were united as one vicarage with a lay patron; St Mary's parish was served only by stipendiary curates. There was little chance that the incumbents might stand against aldermanic control of their civil affairs, particularly when their vestrymen were headburgesses and aldermen. All Saints' and St Peter's lay within the Archdeaconry of Essex but St Mary's was in the peculiar jurisdiction of Westminster Abbey; the neighbouring parishes to the north of Maldon were within the Archdeaconry of Colchester. This was a place where a man might easily evade prosecution in the ecclesiastical courts by moving his inhabitation. An Office (the church courts' civil law version of a common law prosecution) of the Archdeacon of Essex against 'Peter a Fleming' was discontinued in 1575 because the accused lived outside the court's jurisdiction, in St Mary's parish. Thus the clergy were divided, their Ordinaries were remote and slow moving, whilst the Corporation was present, united, ambitious to extend the capability of its own courts and jealous of any other authority intruding its jurisdiction.

Archdeacons did hold their courts sometimes in All Saints' church but often they heard cases concerning non-Maldon people, while similar cases involving inhabitants were tried in the borough's court which applied its own customary punishments for immorality. A woman of Little Baddow tried by the archdeacon in All Saints (1574) for adultery and pre-marital intercourse received the standard ecclesiastical punishment of a penance, humiliating but otherwise painless. A Maldon girl, however, accused of fornication at the Quarter Sessions (1592), was sentenced to suffer the nasty and traditional borough punishment of The Cowl: she was carted around the town tied astride a pole or 'cowl-staff' even though she was pregnant. The custumal prescribed a mysterious punishment called 'Bearing the Mortar' for some moral offences. It was ordered for William Man and his daughter-in-law (1591) as the penalty for their incest: 'they were both punished by riding in a cart upon the market day throughout the town in the open market and the said William Man wore the mortar all the while' according to the Town Clerk's note. The Corporation could even excommunicate inhabitants. Three cases can be found in the borough records (1570, 1571) which were based on a statute of 1551 ordering the excommunication of anyone who struck or laid hands on another in a church or churchyard. There were two grades in this ancient ecclesiastical penalty and Maldon's Bailiffs did not restrict themselves to the Lesser grade, which forbade the culprit admission to the sacraments; they were prepared to deliver the full sentence of the Greater Excommunication which excluded the culprit from all contact with his Christian brethren:

*Ipso facto facit excommunicatus et exclusus de solidate et consocietate Christiani congregationis.*

170

# THE LIMITS OF POWER

Discretion in procedure and in sentencing posed continuous problems for The Company's aldermen. The more extensive their claims to jurisdiction the more frequently they found caution to be necessary. It was noted in Chapter 1 that the magistrates exercised discretion in applying the current law on vagrancy: some vagrants were punished and expelled, others were treated with a degree of mercy, according to the apparent merits of each case. But discretion could easily be mistaken for partiality in all kinds of minor matters, as when Thomas Trowers complained that he was the victim of discrimination because whilst he was fined for dumping manure on the highway, one of the magistrates was not: 'It is a blind jury,' he said, 'that can spy out my dunghill and not see Master Snape's clayheap,' so he 'did pout and scoff at the jury of the Clerk of the Market as they passed by' his dwelling house and that landed him in court charged with defamation of The Company.

When it was dealing with with allegations of fraud, assault, smuggling, fornication, sacrilege, sorcery and murder The Company had to proceed with considerable caution and rightly so, for the magistrates' sentence might have to be the death penalty. Which cases should they themselves determine with their Recorder's assistance? Which would it be prudent to refer to a court outside the borough? Although they possessed a gibbet there survives no evidence that it was ever used. Only two executions are known to have been performed in Maldon in the sixteenth century. The only one to be found in the borough's archives was the burning of a man which is recorded in the chamberlains' account roll of 1548-9 as payments 'for line that was occupied at the sufferance of Gale' and 'to make a fire about the execution of the said Gale'. The other, the execution by burning at the stake of a Protestant named Stephen Knight, 28 March 1555, is referred to only in John Foxe's *Book of Martyrs*. Certainly neither of them was a Maldon inhabitant, nor were they tried in Maldon; and in Stephen Knight's case the town was one of many to which Protestants were taken so as to give the greatest popular impact to the bishop's and government's policy of stamping out heresy in Queen Mary I's reign. 'The said Gale' was most probably one of the Anabaptists, a sect loathed by Protestants and Papists alike, whom the Protestant Bishop of London of Edward VI's reign believed to be troubling both Essex and Kent with heretical and radical preaching. It is most probable that he, like Knight, was brought here so that his 'sufferance' might warn the market crowd of the fate in store for heretics.

So far as can be seen all cases which were likely to end in capital punishment were quickly transferred to an external court. A case of rape was submitted first to the Archdeacon of Essex and then to a county magistrate at some expense to the borough. At least four cases of sorcery were transferred to either the Essex Assizes or to the Privy Council because each involved accusations of premeditated

171

murder. In the chamberlains' accounts for 1621 the procedure for a case of murder is clearly documented: a baby was found dead near the Portman Marsh, beside the causeway between Fullbridge and Heybridge; when its unmarried mother was arrested as its murderess she was first held in the town for questioning and then (at a cost of 25s to the borough) transferred to Colchester Castle to await her trial at the Assize Court in Chelmsford. The Assize records show that Maldon inhabitants were normally tried at its Chelmsford and Brentwood sessions for all the offences punishable by hanging or, worse, by hanging, drawing and quartering. None of the chamberlains' accounts indicate that the executions took place on Maldon's gibbet. The limit to the Bailiffs' and aldermen's power was marked by the distinction between, on the one hand, the little groups of men and women seen leaving the town under the sergeants' and constables' guard, bound for Chelmsford and Colchester, and on the other hand the drunkards, whores, vagabonds, unruly apprentices, loud-mouths and scolds who were penned in The Cage, pilloried, flogged, branded in the market place, imprisoned in either the Lob Hole, the Moot Hall's gaol or the Brick Prison, or were half-suffocated in the ducking stool which stood over the common sewage outfall at the Hythe.

The magistrates' treatment of accusations of witchcraft displays the caution with which they approached any matter liable to end in an execution. They clearly preferred to be sceptical of the evidence brought before them, as when a freeman (Edmund Hunt) was found to have consulted Dr John Dee at Chelmsford about methods of detecting buried treasure in Beeleigh Abbey's ruins and, more particularly, in a far sadder case when the accusations were that Alice Chandler, a seamstress, had murdered the eight-year old daughter of Francis Cowper (a fletcher) by sorcery and that Ellen Smith had attempted the death of John Eastwood and also had caused the death of Goodwife Webb's little girl. The magistrates heard the evidence (or allegations): when John Eastwood had sent packing the son of Ellen Smith, who had come begging 'for an *almose*', he was soon after seized with violent pains and the next night he and a neighbour saw a rat run up his chimney 'and presently it did fall down again in the likeness of a toad; and taking it up with the tongs they thrust it into the fire and so held it forcibly [until] it made the fire burn as blue as azure'; that as the Widow Webb's daughter died she cried out 'Away with the witch!' and soon after Goodwife Webb saw 'as she thought, a thing like to a black dog go out at her door, and presently at the sight thereof, she fell distraught of her wits'. They may have been as little inclined to take this kind of talk seriously as they were to believe the evidence offered by Ellen Smith's own twelve or thirteen-year old son, who told them that his mother kept three spirits − 'the one called by her *Great Dick* was enclosed in a wicker bottle; the second, named *Little Dick* was put into a leather bottle; and the third, named *Willet* she kept in a woolpack'. They had the house searched and noted that whilst the bottles and the woolpack could be found 'the Spirits were vanished away'. Their answer was to transfer the case to the Assizes. Alice Chandler and Ellen Smith were sent to Chelmsford in April 1579, where they were found guilty and hanged.

172

Thirteen years later the magistrates had been listening to the Town Preacher, Master George Gifford, and they had probably read his first book on the subject, *A Discourse of the Subtill Practises by Witches and Sorcerers* published in 1587. In it (as in his *Dialogue Concerning Witches and Witchcrafts* of 1593) he taught that whilst witches really did exist they were no more than the instruments by which the Devil enticed people into wicked acts. The evil lay as much in the things people did to witches, in the willingness to accept superstitions, as in the sorcery. So when Margaret Wiseman of Maldon was accused in 1592 − by seven men and five women − of using 'the wicked art of withcraft, sorcery and charming, to the great offence and terror of many' the magistrates sought out six females of some social standing and associated with George Gifford who would appear as compurgators with her in the archdeaconry court. They also found three freemen to act as sureties for her good behaviour and bound her over to stay at home 'to live Christianly, honestly and orderly, and to behave herself'. When gossips continued to persecute her, the Bailiffs put the matter in her husband's hands: why, they asked him, had he not reported that 'he had seen a broom in his house sweep the house without any hands?' and they took his word as sufficient that he had never witnessed such a thing, had never said so to anyone and had never had cause to say such a thing. The discretionary limits on authority included the aldermen's respect for the health of their own souls.

## FINANCIAL RESTRAINTS

Maintaining and improving public facilities were as vital to the reputation of The Company as its coercive powers. Maldon would indeed have been in decline if its corporation had failed to maintain the roads and bridges, its quay and storehouse, the market stalls and shops, and its Moot Hall. If its magistrates could not display munificent hospitality on the scale which the commonalty, the clergy and gentry alike expected of an incorporation its reputation would have been seriously weakened, as an alderman pointed out in about 1591:

> 'when certain players played on the Lord's Day at night ... and Master Bailiffs rebuking them for the same, Master Morris [the alderman] spake openly in the Hall that before times noble men's men had such entertainment when they came to the town that the town had the favour of noble men; but now noble men's men had such entertainment that the town was brought into contempt...'

It was essential for The Company to ensure it could cover the great and ever mounting cost of governing an urban liberty. And all manner of emergencies, from flooding or storm damage, riots and rebellions, to expensive lawsuits and threats of foreign invasion, might at any time impose expenditure so heavy as to wreck the delicate financial state of the borough and prevent its proper maintenance of these public functions and facilities. And however great the blows fate might strike, the noblemen's companies of players kept on turning up, expecting their 'rewards' of 30s (or more) — until the exasperated Bailiffs in 1632 paid the last troupe 'not to show their play' — and the duck, teal, oysters, sugar loaves, barrels of wine, lavish 'diets' at the Blue Boar, still had to be lavished on gentry as New Year gifts and on dozens of grave divines for sermons preached on market days.

Expenditure always matched income. In some years there was a small credit balance, in others the chamberlains declared a deficit which, it will be remembered, was not made good from private purses. Sometimes the accounts nearly balanced exactly. There was never a case for supposing that one emergency would be the only call that year on the income so far received. Resources were always stretched. The problem was the unpredictability of any year's income and this was more of a problem at Maldon than in many other boroughs because a very large proportion of its sources were not fixed sums such as the customary rents by which most corporations were financed. After Arrears or Cash-in-Hand statements the first entries in the 'Charge' (or income section) of the chamberlains' accounts were always for the Assize or customary rents and the Ferm Rents from the leasehold property owned by the corporation. At Bath the city chamberlains had no standard sources of income except assize and 'increased' rents; at Cambridge in 1519 the rental constituted 80 per cent of the town treasurer's receipts and 87 per cent in 1590; at Saffron Walden rents were 67 per cent of the Holy Trinity Guild's receipts in 1546 and at Stratford-upon-Avon 96 per cent of the revenue was provided by rents. Maldon's assize rental was composed of tiny amounts — from one penny to two shillings per annum — and its total shrank from £1 3s 3d in 1507-8 to about seven shillings in the 1660s. The ferm rental was also small. It did rise from £15 (total) in 1576 to £76 by 1686 but that was done by transferring charges from the fixed assize rental and the increased income did not greatly affect the proportion which rents formed of the total annual receipts. Furthermore, the corporation made no purchases of land or buildings even though they were empowered by the 1555 charter to acquire fresh property up to the value of £40 per annum. In fact the increased receipt in Ferm Rents was due to increases in only four major items whose yield rose from £18 9s 9d in 1598 to £64 by 1664.

Table 6 gives the percentage each type of income formed in a number of accounts drawn at random over the whole range of account rolls from 1500 to 1688. The contributions of each source — admission fees, Landcheap, estreats of courts and so on — to the yearly revenue varied considerably from year to year. Rents were never the mainstay of the borough income and the yield of all the other sources depended on factors which could not be accurately forecast. Landcheap receipts rose and fell with the market in land and houses in the town, from 2 per cent of the total income in one year to 34 per cent in another. The proceeds or 'profits'

174

| | I | | II | | | | | | III | | |
|---|---|---|---|---|---|---|---|---|---|---|---|
| | 1 % | 2 % | 3 % | 4 % | 5 % | 6 % | 7 % | 8 % | 9 % | 10 % | 11 % |
| 1508 | | 11 | 55 | 5 | 5 | 11 | 11 | 2 | | | |
| 1512 | | | 35 | 7 | | | 38 | 3 | | | 15 |
| 1524 | | | 55 | 15 | | 10 | 20 | | | | |
| 1537 | 5 | | 66 | 7 | | | 19 | 5 | | | |
| 1562 | | | 6 | 4 | 11 | 3 | 10 | 1 | | 31 | 33 |
| 1575 | | 38 | 17 | 2 | 16 | 13 | 14 | | | | |
| 1576 | | 13 | 10 | 13 | 11 | 7 | 14 | | 1 | | 25 |
| 1578 | | 25 | 26 | 10 | 3 | 13 | 17 | 3 | | | |
| 1581 | | 65 | 9 | 5 | 2 | 5 | 9 | 1 | | | 3 |
| 1586 | | 12 | 22 | 2 | 10 | 13 | 32 | 1 | 1 | | 5 |
| 1590 | | 5 | 17 | 2 | 26 | 4 | 18 | | | 9 | 19 |
| 1595 | | 12 | 25 | 8 | 17 | 13 | 22 | 1 | | | 1 |
| 1598 | | 7 | 23 | 7 | 34 | 8 | 12 | | | | 9 |
| 1604 | | 2 | 40 | 7 | 4 | 18 | 27 | 1 | | | |
| 1608 | 10 | | 38 | 5 | 8 | 13 | 26 | | | | |
| 1616 | 32 | | 33 | 6 | 11 | 7 | 13 | | | | |
| 1624 | 7 | 19 | 36 | 7 | 19 | 6 | 6 | | | | |

Table 6  Variations in the Sources of the Borough Revenue, 1550–1690. (Each source is expressed as its percentage of the annual total.)

Section I: (1) Cash in Hand; (2) Arrears on the previous account.

Section II: (3) Rental; (4) Freedoms; (5) Landcheaps;
(6) Water Bailiffs' Receipts; (7) Estreats of Courts;
(8) Customary Tolls.

Section III: Extraordinary Revenues: (9) Benevolences; (10) Scot and Lot;
(11) Miscellanea such as special fees, sales of timber and sale of felons' goods.

Table 6 — continued overleaf

| | I | | II | | | | | | III | | |
|---|---|---|---|---|---|---|---|---|---|---|---|
| | 1 % | 2 % | 3 % | 4 % | 5 % | 6 % | 7 % | 8 % | 9 % | 10 % | 11 % |
| 1625 | 10 | | 50 | 2 | 8 | 6 | 6 | | | | 18 |
| 1629 | | 8 | 47 | | 20 | 8 | 14 | | | | |
| 1633 | | 33 | 36 | 5 | 7 | 12 | 7 | | | | 1 |
| 1638 | | 29 | 26 | 2 | 29 | 8 | 5 | | | | |
| 1643 | | 20 | 57 | 2 | 6 | 5 | 8 | | | | 2 |
| 1649 | 8 | | 49 | 6 | 10 | 10 | 6 | | | | 9 |
| 1655 | 12 | | 57 | | 8 | 10 | 9 | | | | 2 |
| 1660 | 37 | | 44 | 1 | | 12 | 7 | | | | |
| 1662 | 27 | | 36 | 5 | 12 | 13 | 7 | | | | |
| 1672 | 25 | | 41 | 6 | 17 | 4 | 4 | | | | 5 |
| 1686 | | 15 | 54 | | 5 | 17 | 8 | | | | |

*Table 6 continued*

(from *proficua*) of the courts similarly varied from 4 to 38 per cent of total income, depending on circumstances beyond the chamberlains' or aldermen's control. The number of freemen admitted by the payment of the full fee, the number of persons who were fined in the borough courts (and how much their fines were depended on the nature of their misdeeds or errors), the number of fines called 'withdraughts of action' when pleas of debt were cancelled, the number of packhorses on which toll was charged, the amount of business done by the water bailiff in collecting tolls and measuring quantities and in anchorage fees, were the facts behind the sums of money coming into the borough chest. Chamberlains would have been cheered by increasing numbers of foreigners commencing pleas of debt, since they paid twice as much as freemen for licence to withdraw their actions. When commerce and trade were flourishing, with many vessels coming to the Hythe with coal and iron, wheat, barley, hops to unload, timber and beer and cheese to take on board, the water bailiff's receipts were considerable. Much of the borough's income was at the mercy of economic conditions in the wide world beyond Maldon.

176

There were advantages to such an income structure. This was a small market town but its gross receipts were comparable to those of larger ones such as Leicester, Bath, Stratford-upon-Avon and indeed the corporation was sometimes very rich, with gross receipts averaging just over £90 from 1558 to 1600, nearly £130 between 1601 and 1641 and almost £200 between 1642 and 1689. Cash supplies were also more frequently available in Maldon's situation than in those towns which relied on rents paid perhaps only in one lump sum at the year's end or at Michaelmas and Easter. The serjeant-at-mace presented his receipts of court fines (the Estreat of the Courts) quarterly, as did the leather searchers, the clerk of the market and, above all, the water bailiff. Freemen's fines were paid straight into the chest, or sometimes paid in installments but never entirely deferred. Landcheaps were probably collected from the vendor as soon as possible after a sale. So there was usually a reasonably healthy proportion of the year's income available at the beginning of each quarter from which to pay at least the immediate costs presented by an emergency. And there was a feature of their income about which auditors and chamberlains kept very quiet: a considerable portion of the borough income was derived from outsiders. Every property sold by a non-resident − and they were a sizeable proportion of all owners − every foreigner withdrawing his action for debt, and these were also numerous (and paid more than an inhabitant) and all the fines imposed on peddlars or on visiting tradesmen from other market towns, and the customary fines paid by the foreigners or *commorantes* for their shops, was very literally income. A considerable share of the water bailiffs' receipts was obviously provided by visiting merchants or ship masters and especially by those who wished to unload or load outside the borough at Heybridge. These latter persons, the men of Heybridge too, and their customers, were continuously aggrieved by the higher prices forced on goods bought and sold there. They may also have suspected that they were indeed lining the coffers in Maldon's Moot Hall with their silver.

Inside every freeborn Englishman there was (as now) a conviction that he should not be taxed. The Crown was traditionally expected to 'live of its own' which meant paying all the costs of government out of its 'proper' or customary revenues; taxation counted as 'extraordinary revenue'. So, too, for The Company. From time to time it had to demand that its freemen should pay Scot and Lot, assessed as a rate depending on the sum needed, but it always knew that this had to be a last resort. When expensive repairs to the Fullbridge were urgently required in 1618 the Town Clerk composed a preamble emphasising the legality of The Company's demand for payment of a scot and lot; it was levied, he said 'by virtue of our Charter granted by King Philip and Queen Mary ... for the making of byelaws, ordinances and constitutions for the public good'. In 1568 a levy of two shillings per freeman was prefaced with a clear explanation of the circumstances, a declaration that there was insufficient money in the borough chest to meet the emergency and an announcement that the advice of the Recorder had been obtained (which would dissuade the unwilling from seeking legal advice with a view to non-payment).

They seem always to have met with trouble in exercising their customary right. In 1615 £5 1s 4d had to be found to cover the charges of both Bailiffs, two aldermen, the Town Clerk and one of the serjeants for

> 'riding unto and being at London in Michaelmas Term last past to consider and advise with Master High Steward, Master Recorder of this borough and others their learned Counsel about the validity of the ordinance and rate made and taxed by the corporation for the new making and repairing of Fullbridge, the Causeway called Heybridge Causeway and of other decayed and ruinous [bridges] near to them late wasted and impaired by inundations of water, being opposed and much hindered by Robert Snape, one of the freeburgesses of this borough and other inhabitants of the same'.

Even the most careful, solemnly phrased demand failed to bring in its full, expected total. In 1568 there were 98 chargeable freemen but two refused to pay (and did not), six more had not paid when the clerk wrote out the final account, ten had to be excused on the grounds of poverty, seven died before they could pay and against the names of another four neither a contribution nor an explanation is written. Instead of the £9 16s 0d which The Company needed at that time, the chamberlains presented an account for £7 17s 8d, a loss of nearly one fifth of the estimated yield even after additional names had been entered in the list of scot and lot payers.

There were few alternatives to this levy on the freemen in emergencies. The traditional English (and continental) reliance on donations from the chamberlains and magistrates was not observed in Maldon, as has been shown. One similar expedient was for officials to forgo their fees, as at Bath in 1598 where the Mayor did not take his £40 and it was credited to the city income, but the Bailiffs of Maldon received only £2 apiece per annum and even if all the officials of the corporation had returned their fees to the borough chest the total would have been no more than £17 at that time. Only once, in the accounts of 1546-7 where the fee of one of the Bailiffs is omitted, has any recourse to that method of enhancing the income been noted and possibly there was another reason. It is possible that sometimes chamberlains or Bailiffs supplied bridging loans at no interest to make up temporary deficits but only a cash book would show that kind of subsidy and this type of record was not preserved once the final account had been written and audited.

Sales of rents were another traditional source in urban finance but as Maldon possessed only four properties whose rents were large enough to attract an investor such a method of raising a wind had to be weighed against the effect on its remaining

178

income from rent in the years ahead. The borough did sell three houses outright in 1562 (which suggests that buyers of rents were not forthcoming at that time) but the only other example of asset-stripping of this kind is a sale of one small piece of waste land beside the town midden for £2.

The evidence for loans is also slight. On three occasions other public funds in Maldon were raided. Eventually such money had to be refunded but £70 borrowed in 1565 from the churchwardens of All Saints parish was not repaid in one lump sum. It was demanded by the churchwardens in 1568 when the huge wooden spire of their church required thorough renovation but the scot and lot levied for this purpose was only enough to cover the repair costs, not to repay the principal entirely. Sad to relate, The Company also supplied itself with money bequeathed for the relief of the poor, with a series of accounts in the early years of the seventeeenth century recording interest charges paid 'to the Overseers of the Poor of All Saints' parish for the use of £8 of the gift of Richard Josua deceased'. In 1686 there was a loan £120 from a widow of bearing an interest rate of 6 per cent, but the only other examples of loans which have been found were smaller, bore no interest charges and were made by members of The Company. £15 13s 4d was raised by seventeen members of The Company in April 1564 and in 1595 the chamberlains were paying back £21 6s 8d loaned by another twenty members. In addition to its scot and lot in 1618 another loan was raised by The Company, 'money lent and disbursed by them to the borough and to be repaid by the common purse of the same for and toward the speedy turning of the water into the usual channel which now runneth into a back creek near Blackwall'. The borough had little to offer as security on loans apart from timber growing on wasteland around its boundaries or the annual lease of its oyster beds in the outer Blackwater Estuary, which was one of its few lucrative rents. Apart from parochial funds there were certainly few pools of capital available and reliance on such a source was unwise because it could create an accumulated debt too large to be easily paid off.

Lacking any of the more sophisticated methods of finding funds quickly the chamberlains had to fall back on the scot and lot, but rather than do that too often they would first save money from one project and spend it on another, robbing Peter to pay Paul. Sometimes they even went cap-in-hand to their neighbours. The 1534-5 accounts list sums raised from the villages and some individuals north and south of Maldon for the complete rebuilding of Fullbridge which was undertaken in 1535. Once The Company made the mistake of supposing that foreigners would be only too pleased to be associated by subscription with the famous corporation of Maldon. This was when it was converting the Brick Cross in its market place into a gaol (1567) and the register containing the list of freemen paying their scot and lot for this also has three pages set aside for foreign receipts. Headed 'Be it remembered forever...' these pages are divided into sections to record *Contribuciones honorabilium* and *Contribuciones venerabilium*. Though the clerk

179

went so far as to write in the names of the members of parliament and of other county gentry who had been associated with Maldon in the past, only one of them subsequently contributed. These pages have remained almost blank to this day, a memorial to Maldon's post-incorporate optimism and to outsiders' indifference.

Caution always governed The Company's policy on its expenditure. Whilst everything was paid for from the borough chest, each official avoided extravagance and civic ambitions were kept within strict bounds. There are few references to regalia (and there was a notable absence of gifts of plate in the wills of aldermen); the maces of the two Bailiffs' serjeants appear to have been those inherited in 1555 from the old borough and the oar carried before them as Admirals was clearly not one of those ceremonial silver pieces to be seen in some other borough regalia, for it was bought at Colchester in 1562 for two shillings. The florid silver-gilt mace which is now in use was only acquired in 1687 (and its head is partly later, of Queen Anne's reign after 1707), costing £55 6s 0d but made out of the older ones and marking a break with tradition because it was for the new office of Mayor which was (temporarily) substituted for the two Bailiffs' offices. The officials' fees were also kept at a minimum; Table 7 shows that they doubled at incorporation, but they were then paid out of a greatly increased income; the High Steward's fee was not introduced until late in the sixteenth century and the stability of the fees from 1555 is noteworthy. Only the serjeants and a beadle (who was not a fee-ed servant of the Corporation) were provided with liveries and badges. A medieval custom of making a livery allowance to the Bailiffs and the chamberlains was discontinued early in the sixteenth century. Minor officials were paid only for specified tasks. Thus the Bellman was paid for the number of times he cleaned the street outside the Moot Hall or helped to re-turf the shooting butts; the constables, the bellman and watchmen were paid for extraordinary tasks such as 4d paid 'to Gilmour to make proclamation for every man to keep in their dogs in the time of the infection' in 1604 and giving warning to the townsmen 'to shun receiving or lodging of any persons coming from Colchester or other infected place' during another outbreak of plague in 1626 (for which the bellringer was paid 8d) but when 20d was paid to watchmen 'at sundry times to watch' in 1604 they were replacements 'of such as were departed the Town in the time of the sickness of the plague' and the account roll infers that the Night Watch would have been expected to patrol unpaid had its members been present. The Company did not maintain its own Waits – the costs of 'rewards' to the professional companies of actors who turned up were enough of a burden – and they took their guests to the Blue Boar Inn rather than have their own cook; they did not maintain a Surveyor, nor a Chaplain (except in 1570 when they paid a salary to Master Edmund Chapman); instead the Bailiffs personally supervised their few woodlands and farms, assisted professionally by their Town Clerk, and paid for each invited preacher to eat and drink with them after their sermons.

|  | | 1535 | 1562 | 1575 | 1615 | 1624 | 1681 |
|---|---|---|---|---|---|---|---|
| High Steward | | | | | 100s | 100s | 100s |
| Recorder | | | 20s | 40s | 40s | 40s | 40s |
| Attorney | | | 13s 4d | 13s 4d | 13s 4d | 13s 4d | |
| Each Bailiff | | 13s 4d | 40s | 40s | 40s | 40s | 40s |
| Each Chamberlain | | 5s | 6s 8d | 6s 8d | 6s 8d | 6s 8d | 6s 8d |
| Serjeant-at-Mace | | 13s 4d | 13s 4d | 20s | 20s | 20s | 40s |
| Second Serjeant | | | 15s | 20s | 20s | 20s | 40s |
| Each Constable | | 2s | 2s | 2s | 2s | 2s | 2s |
| Town Clerk | (1) | 40s | 80s | 80s | 80s | 80s | 80s |
| | (2) | | 6s 8d | 6s 8d | 6s 8d | 6s 8d | 6s 8d |
| | (3) | 3s 4d | 10s | 13s 4d | 13s 4d | 13s 4d | 13s 4d |

Note. The fees of the Town Clerks were (1) an Annual Fee; (2) a fee for holding the Courts of the Clerk of the Market and Admiralty; and (3) for making the Chamberlains' annual account roll for the audit at the end of their year in office.

*Table 7. Corporation Fees*

The limitations on its exercise of power were not so apparent to the generality. Outwardly the Corporation maintained a proper and fairly imposing dignity. Their original Moot Hall and then their great brick Moot Hall were soberly impressive. When the Darcy Tower was converted into this new Moot Hall in 1576 over £20 was spent on building an extension (it appears to have been over the street, where the present 'Georgian' porch is) and on glazing, wainscotting, plastering. In 1614 £6 1s 10d was 'laid forth and bestowed about the repairing and beautifying of the Moot Hall, galleries and other houses of the said borough' during general repairs and redecoration to Corporation property. In its Hall the town and royal arms were emblazoned above the Bailiffs' seats, with a curtain of green say to protect the gilding and the oil colours from the sunlight. *Parfumes* were regularly bought to sweeten the Hall and in 1564 the chamberlains bought four '*halpenny potts* for to set flowers in at the Moot Hall'. They bought a chamber pot for it in 1666 and from 1685 purchased pipes and tobacco for The Company's delectation. State

*Pl.9. Crown of the borough's mace made in 1687, inverted to show the Stuart Royal Arms (James II) on the cap*

occasions were given a light brushing of splendour, as by hiring trumpeters when James I in 1603 and Charles I in 1625 were proclaimed king, and musicians to enhance the ceremony of oath-taking of one of the M.P.s elected for the Short Parliament. No outsider would see the anxious conferences of Bailiffs, chamberlains and Town Clerk, the casting-up of cash books in the face of emergencies. What was visible, the courtesy of gifts to visiting notables, the expensive and recurrent reconstruction work on wharves, bridges, causeway, the daily examples of work done 'at Master Bailiffs' commandment', the charity provided for genuine pauper vagrants and other travellers such as soldiers, were matched by the sight of the Bailiffs' weekly procession through the market place accompanied by their serjeants and the beadle, attended by Clerk and Aldermen, their appearance in court associated with the Recorder and the magistrates, flanked by all their brethren of The Company to do justice and to enquire and to order all who were within the Liberty of their borough.

## AUTHORITY UNDERMINED

Restiveness under so narrowly based a system of government is understandable. The inhabitants were not nurtured to acceptance; the Custom of the Borough so frequently brandished at them was not the customary law of their parents and grandparents, since so many of them were, at any one time, emigrants of other communities. To them the authority of The Company was arbitrary, its powers were of an uncertain and undeclared extent, based on charters and records which were locked away behind the blank, brick walls of Darcy's Tower, guarded with oaths of secrecy by a permanent few and expressed by an intrusive system of policing. Maldon's inhabitants never entirely succumbed to the dictates of their magistrates who were often tradesmen rather than the gentry who sat on the Bench in other areas' sessions. Throughout both centuries they were being brought to court for the offence of Opprobrium because of their defiance of petty rules and tyrannical behaviour, or because of their obstructiveness, their abuse of officials, by blankly and openly ignoring the bye-laws, and by that most effective form of revolt, mockery and jest. Such tactics were not confined to any one class. Gentry and artisans, freemen and 'foreigners', residents and visitors alike abused The Company in language uniformly coarse and injudicious:

> 'You are a liar and an *unhonest* man and you have spoiled the town... too young [to bear office] ... a jackanapes ...a creeping churl ... a rascal and a fiddler ... a false, forsworn knave ...'
> 'Knaves, villains and slaves'.
> 'The whole Company of the eighteen headburgesses ... a company of perjured knaves'
> 'He did not care a turd nor a fart' for any member of The Company, remarked a saddler in 1660.

'Thief, whore's-son, false, forsworn, cuckold, knave, back-biter, bawd' were the descriptions expressly prohibited in the 1444 edition of the borough customs and repeated in the 1555 version.

To guard their dignity the 1555 custumal ordered that the Bailiffs must be accompanied by at least four headburgesses and both market lookers, by all the constables and two aldermen when inspecting the Fairs held in the borough. The greatest were as liable to receive defiantly dismissive insults as were the much abused nightwatchmen and the constables. When one of the headburgesses, John Maldon, called a gentleman resident in the town a drunkard and 'a common haunter of inns' the accused sent him a playing card — the knave of clubs — and called him a 'a coxcomb and a fool and an ass'; he had, said the accused, seen men more honest hanged. When this same gentleman, John Shipton, was presented before the Quarter Sessions of Michaelmas 1618, charged with being drunk in public, he told the assembled court 'that there were none but boors and clowns within the said town and that there was none there fit to govern; and that afterwards he would spit the Bailiffs in their face and give them a box of the ear — but he would have his guard about him'.

Much obstructive behaviour was not precisely directed at The Company. It was rather the protest of the many young persons living as servants in Maldon against Authority of any inconvenient kind. Adam Bradhedd, who was a blacksmith's workman, regarded the night watch duty as an unnecessary nuisance: when he was on duty himself, on Sunday 7 June 1635, he 'broke up the watch and went away between two and three of the clock before the arisage of the sun' and the night before one of the constables who had gone 'to search for any idle, wandering and disordered persons' and came to William Payne's house,

> 'it being about ten of the clock in the night season and the Watch long before was set, he and his fellow constables heard a noise …and seeing what the cause was they found there … then tippling and drinking, Adam Bradhedd … [with] two of Master Rucke's men … And this informant and his fellow constables and the watchmen causing the company to disperse and go to their masters' house[s], the said Adam Bradhedd refused until he had drunk up his drink; and called the constables *Busy fellows* and [said] that they came to places where they were not welcome before they were sent for; and [he] washed one of the watchmen's nose in a wench's breech'.

Drink encouraged these youths to speak out of turn. A Mundon blacksmith, William Newcombe, was put in the stocks one market day in June 1624 because he was drunk. John Edwards the younger, the son of the landlord of the Blue Boar, came to the stocks and asked Newcombe to drink a pot of beer with him. A bystander heard him say that 'Master Bailiff Pratt was a knave and a rogue to put the said

184

Newcombe in stocks, seeing he was not drunk for he that was drunk could not stand nor go' and then say 'that he cared not if Master Pratt stood by and heard him, and wished the pox of God to take all the Bailiffs in the town. And the said John Edwards being told that his mother had sent for him, he wished the pox of God to take her and the devil confound her. And this examinate saith he verily thinketh the said John Edwards had been a-drinking hard'.

The restiveness of the inhabitants under The Company's rule arose from more than youthful rebellion or tongues loosened by boose. Those who knew they would not be inhabitants much longer had little to lose by insulting a constable. Disappointment through failure to find the prosperity and security or social advancement which had brought people to the town may have encouraged critical comment about the way the place was controlled. And the small scale of Maldon may itself have contributed. Possibly it was too small a place to bear so complete an array of authority as that which The Company claimed to possess. The inhabitants lived in one or other of four clumps of buildings which were each quite small in area and within each rich and poor lived intermingled. The aldermanic class had no chance of withdrawing itself from public gaze into some special 'West End' preserve. The Company's members were surrounded by their subjects; every foible, every slip or error could be scrutinised by curious neighbours. It was all too easy for grievances to arise, as with Thomas Trowers' complaints mentioned earlier in this chapter. Some aldermen did not possess the reticence, the honesty or the self-control necessary to retain their integrity or to uphold the authority of their Corporation in this little town. Personal foibles could attract mockery, as with Master William Burles (six times a Bailiff) of whom it was remarked that 'he did gorge and fill himself full of varieties of meats and victuals; and when he had so filled himself he would come out of the door like a hog and ready to vomit up that he had eaten'. Some headburgesses had to be expelled from The Company for drunkenness, for being like Michael Marchant, tanner, 'a common gamester and frequenter of inns and houses of common resort, drinking and spending much time there in derogation of the reputation of his place [in the Corporation]' and especially because such behaviour led the person to be 'vehemently suspected to have disclosed the secrets of his fellows of the House'. The 'common fame of incontinency with one Anne Gates, widow', and 'like common fame that he hath attempted the chastity of the wife of one John Carden, deceased' led to the expulsion of a headburgess in 1647.

Such personal deficiencies of conduct were and always will be commonplaces in the discussion of public lives; petty scandals, in most cases, which have always been grist to the mill of gossipers. At worst they highlighted unfairness and hypocrisy. In the barber's shop, that grave preserve of masculine matters, talk could become more dangerously productive of unrest than in an alehouse or at a shop door. The justices became seriously worried in 1623 by the activities of Thomas Eastwood, 'a disorderly person' who

> 'amongst other his disorders in his barber's shop and elsewhere hath spread abroad many opprobrious speeches and false reports of John Soan, one of the aldermen of this borough, the which do tend to his contempt in his place of government; and the said Thomas Eastwood still continueth in his disorderly courses. We therefore taking into consideration how persons of his quality do labour for their bad ends to disgrace government and governors do require you and every of you [the constables of St Peter's parish] to arrest the said Thomas ...'

because he was telling clients that he had heard 'a proctor or solicitor of London speak of Master John Soan of Maldon, that Master Soan was forsworn and that if he had been followed [brought to trial] he might have lost both his ears'. (The solicitor was, Eastwood insisted, named Lyons, who dwelled at the sign of The Seven Stars in Lombard Street.)

Petty matters everyone? In 1587 Elias Nicholls was much angered when some of his goods were distrained by the serjeant of the senior Bailiff when he had been found guilty of 'divers contempts and breaches of laws'. In his fury he not only uttered 'opprobrious speeches against Master Bailiffs' but also 'seditious words dangerous to the state of the town', in which he threatened horribly 'that he and others would make such a hole or breach in Maldon as never was made there before'. By accident or design Elias Nicholl touched The Company at its tenderest spot with these few words: '... such a hole or breach as never was made there before'. He did not manage to achieve what he had threatened. No outsider and certainly no petty delinquent within the borough could manage to pierce the Corporation's armour. On its rock of charters founded it might perhaps for ever laugh at all its foes. But, and perhaps within Elias Nicholl's lifetime in Maldon, that breach was quite suddenly made from an inadequately guarded direction.

CHAPTER 7

# RELIGIOUS CHANGES
# AND DISSENSION

IN MANY ENGLISH boroughs the last years of the sixteenth century were marked by quarrels and controversies. Governing bodies were opposed by the commonalty in some places; factions appeared within corporations in others; at Doncaster the election of a mayor in 1590, at Ripon the choice of a 'wakeman' and irregularities in the recruitment of aldermen in 1598 were in dispute between the commons and their ruling groups; the Warden of the Cinque Ports was in dispute with the commonalty of Sandwich over the composition of that town's common council from 1593 to 1605; there were troubles in Leicester from the moment of its incorporation (1589) about the allocation of leases of new town land, culminating in a Privy Council enquiry of 1593; and at Newcastle-Upon-Tyne these latter years of the century witnessed a struggle for power between an inner ring of burgesses (mercers and coal merchants) and a larger group of less wealthy men who found themselves without influence in the management of the Tyne coal trade.

So also were there 'popular quarrels' at Colchester and Maldon in the 1580s and 1590s. On first inspection they appear to have been a minor local version of the tensions which had developed within the Church of England between those who, in line with the wishes of the Queen and her Council, intended no further Reformation in the structure or the doctrine of the Church and, on the other side, that well-organised and determined network of laymen and clergy on whom was to be fixed the label 'Puritan'. But theological debate had no strict confines in sixteenth or seventeenth century minds and in these 'popular quarrels' clashes over personalities were mixed up with ecclesiastical squabbles and controversy, sectarian conspiracy merged with social grievances concerning law and order, common rights and private ambitions.

> 'In the two towns of Colchester and Maldon I found great quarrels and contentions, both in their civil bodies and among their ministers, the people divided and the priests taking part on both sides, and *at war with themselves as well in matter of popular quarrels as points of doctrine*'.

This was the report sent in 1595 by Dr Richard Fletcher, the Bishop of London, to Sir Robert Cecil on the past ten years of dissension in both places. 'All which' he claimed, 'I so travailed in that I put moderation to their perturbations and peace to their places'.

Apart from those urban disputes which happen to touch on issues of general economic concern − such as the coal trade of Newcastle or the settlement of Dutch weavers at Halstead − the substance of many of these quarrels is apparently of only parochial interest. But their general drift has a much wider significance for they are often the only evidence of clashes between established authority and public opinion. Dissension momentarily disrupted the well-ordered surface of urban life and through the cracks it is possible to glimpse some of the tensions of contemporary society and just a little of the private opinions of the townsmen. In the case of Maldon there is sufficient information about the troubles of the borough to mount an investigation of the relationship between the Corporation and the general population (the 'commonalty') and to see a little more precisely how much correspondence there was between the theory of The Company's power and the actual practice of government.

In associating a survey of the processes by which the Protestant Reformation occurred in Maldon with this study of dissension it is not my intention to allege any necessary connection between religious beliefs and social disturbances, or that religion was the divisive factor. Indeed the most general observation must be that major religious changes occurred with impressively law-abiding co-operation; factions and quarrels broke out only at what appeared (to contemporaries) to be the end of religious reforms.

## RELIGIOUS CHANGE IN MALDON, c1530 - c1560

About the year 1595 Master George Gifford was occupying his mind in that ever-green pastime of placing notable recent events into the sequence of apocalyptic marvels and mysteries set out in the *Book of the Revelation to St John the Divine*. In the course of his sermons he reminded his congregation in All Saints' church of the origin of their Protestant faith:

> 'Yea, it is evident that the sixth trumpet was sounded long since because it draweth well towards four-score years since this Angel came down from heaven with the little book open in his hand, and that the light of the Gospel began to peep out and to disclose the foulness of popery. For in the year 1516, or in the year 1517, Martin Luther began to call some matters into question'.

King Henry VIII conducted a campaign against Papal jurisdiction in his realms which had no connection with the German Reformers' assault on the doctrinal and jurisdictional base of Papal authority but by his death in 1547 the Protestant position was gathering considerable support in influential places in England and by 1559 reformers could claim considerable success. By the 1580s the English had become a predominantly Protestant nation but not as violently as in parts of continental Europe, and with not so radical a change as, for example, in the Genevan

188

city state of John Calvin. In the piecemeal restructuring – by legal processes as much as by preaching – of Englishmen's religion an immense change occurred which was as almost imperceptible to them as it remains to an observer of ordinary people's lives four hundred years later.

Physical changes – the dissolution and demolition of institutions and buildings (abbeys, chantries, shrines, sacred images), the restructuring of churches' interiors – and doctrinal statements can all be charted easily but the earliest stages in the growth of Protestant beliefs are bound always to be elusive for the local historian. The convictions on which they were based were essentially personal, internalised, traceable only occasionally when conflict with authority produced written reports. Lollards preceded Protestants in England's religious movements dissenting from the orthodox Catholicism of the later Middle Ages. None of them have been traced in fifteenth or early sixteenth century Maldon. By the late 1520s the doctrines of Martin Luther certainly were being studied and were winning converts in East Anglia and the first hint of his teachings reaching this town ought to be the appointment of Dr John Bale as Prior of its Carmelite Friary in 1529. His autobiography states that his conversion to Protestantism had begun at Cambridge University immediately before he came to Maldon. From his one year living in the borough there survives a notebook but it contains only jottings about previous friars made for his projected history of his Order – no heresy there. Whilst it cannot be established that Lutheran teaching was ever expounded from the pulpit of the friars' church, a very slight case could be made out for the Town Play, Maldon's 'native' religious drama, as the earliest local vehicle of Protestant ideas. Bale was a playwright – moralities and interludes – and it was stated in 1536 that he had already composed a cycle of three plays for John de Vere, the 15th Earl of Oxford, whose family's influence in Maldon has already been referred to. One of Bale's plays composed before 1536 was *The Thre Lawes* and at Doncaster in 1535, to whose friary Bale had gone from Maldon in 1530, a suspected heretic had confessed that 'one Bale, a White Friar', had taught him 'about four years ago that Christ would dwell in no church made of lime and stone by man's hands' and in the play lines 1369-70 are of comparable meaning:

*Not yet, as they call it, a temple of lime and stone*
*But a livish building, grounded in faith alone.*

It is the assertion of 'faith alone' which is noteworthy and in *Johan Baptystes*, one of Bale's cycle of three plays for the Earl of Oxford, there is a dispute between a Pharisee, a Sadducee and John the Baptist on the respective merits of Good Works and Faith Alone as the means of Salvation. Priestly opposition to the Lutheran doctrine (that Good Works were in themselves of no help to Salvation) is emphasised in the play by the Pharisee's and the Sadducee's agreement that '*This fellow [John*

189

*the Baptist] preacheth new learning ... his doctrine peradventure might hinder else our livings'*. Perhaps the borough adopted this cycle for its Town Play which seems to have been performed at three-yearly intervals. No text survives and the only descriptive material about it is in the Book of the Play, the accounts for a particularly spectacular production staged in the ruins of Bale's old friary on Relic Sunday in July, 1540, but possibly the references to armour borrowed for 'them that bore harness', 'two calf-skins for him that played John Baptist', 'dyeing of Christ's coat' and guns and six-and-a-half pounds of gunpowder (perhaps for thunder when God speaks at Christ's Baptism?) are indications that *Johan Baptystes* was part of the lavishly produced drama to which the borough's Common Council treated its populace and neighbourhood once every three years. Yet Bale could not safely do more than present a theological discussion until King Edward VI's reign began in 1547 and there are no clues in this topic to the actual reception of Lutheran doctrine by anyone in Maldon. The Bailiffs in 1540 were most probably orthodox believers; they most certainly would not want to risk the penalties current in Henry VIII's England for the dissemination of heretical opinions.

There may have been youngsters in Maldon during the 1540s who, like William Maldon (of Chelmsford) tried to study the new English translation of the Bible, began to make unorthodox remarks about traditional beliefs and practices, and fell foul of their conservatively minded parents as he did. But again, no record of them has survived. It is also frequently suggested in studies of the English Reformation that Lutheran doctrines entered the country by way of the east coast ports and since Maldon housed aliens who were mostly Flemings and 'Dutchmen' it does seem probable that some of them may have introduced a knowledge of Martin Luther's teachings to some of Maldon's inhabitants. One of them, Cornelius Peterson, did make a prominent member of Colchester's Dutch community – Winken Grenerise – his executor and Colchester was infected with heresy by the 1540s, but there is once more no certainty that this was how the Protestant Reformation began to take root in Maldon.

Apart from John Foxe's *Acts and Monuments* of 1563 (better known as *The Book of Martyrs*), which merely involves Maldon as the place to which one Protestant victim of Queen Mary I's reign was brought for execution, information about the earliest reception of Protestant beliefs comes either from ecclesiastical courts' records or from the testimonies of a few extroverts such as Chelmsford's William Maldon. Signs of unorthodox beliefs are very much wanting in the town before 1558 and the evidence of the townsmen's wills is that they were as conventional, obedient to the law rather than to their consciences, as were the inhabitants of most towns in England. The preambles of wills, in which the testators made the bequest of their souls, have for long been used as indications of religious outlook. They vary during the Reformation period from the traditional Catholic piety of

190

the bequest to 'Almighty God, the Blessed Virgin and all the saints' to the more probably Protestant bequest of the person's soul to 'Almighty God, trusting to be saved by His mercy from Hell' in which the emphasis is on Justification by Faith alone. Thus Francis Gowton of Maldon in 1482 bequeathed his soul to 'Almighty God, His mother Saint Mary and all the saints of Heaven' whilst in May 1600 George Gifford, 'preacher of God's Word in Maldon' began his will with an invocation of Jesus Christ only, 'in whom I have believed, whom I have professed and whom I have preached and taught according to the gift and grace of God bestowed on me'.

Statements so patently Protestant as that can only be found from the 1580s and there are none which give even a broad hint of Reformist beliefs before the 1560s. Until then the majority of the inhabitants' bequests of their souls were typically neutral and in most cases their other bequests to religious purposes were limited to what custom required by way of mortuaries and small gifts to cover 'tithes forgotten'. As wills were written by and in consultation with a clerk, only the boldest of Protestants would deliberately declare his unorthodoxy during the first half of the century. The positive evidence of the pre-1560 Maldon wills (which were, of course, only made by people of some substance) is of support for the traditions of the old faith. In 1536 John Cheyney, a tailor of All Saints' parish, bequeathed 4 pence to the altar, another 4 pence to the Guild of St Katherine and requested Robert England 'to see me honestly brought to the ground and my Month's Day kept ...' A few townsmen displayed a more generous but still conventional piety. John Messing of St Peter's parish (1532) gave 5 shillings for tithes forgotten; he made gifts to all three of the town's religious brotherhoods − 6 shillings for repairs to The Star, ('the house of Our Lady' as he called it, which he held on lease from the Guild of the Assumption), a candlestick and basin to St George's Guild, 13s 4d 'to the new building of the Guild of Saint Katherine' − and made bequests to the friars of Maldon and Colchester ('one honest friar of the White Friars of Maldon, of the election [choice] of mine executors to sing Mass in the said parish church of Saint Peter for my soul, my friends' souls and all Christians by the space of half a year', 5 shillings to the Grey Friars, of Colchester) and 10 shillings to Beeleigh Abey for a Trental for his soul − and, furthermore, money to be distributed to the poor of all three parishes 'where as is most need' at his burial and to five paupers every Good Friday 'as long as my wife liveth, if she be able'.

These were legacies within the framework of medieval Catholic piety: works of charity, including the maintenance of religious property and the provision of requiems which implies belief in Purgatory for the souls of the deceased. Richard Benham's will (November 1536) betrays the same anticipation of Purgatory in his request to be buried in the churchyard beside the stairs of the Charnel House which is still beneath the south aisle of All Saints' and as close as was possible to the

191

*Pl.10. The accumulation of medieval piety at All Saints' Church: Darcy's chantry occupied the three south-eastern bays; St Katherine's Guild built the north-east chapel; the housing of the charnel house stairs is half-way along the mid-fourteenth century south aisle*

statue and altar of Our Lady of Piety which were within that aisle. Like John Messing's will that of John Pagett (1529) disbursed money on repairs to church buildings, Masses and what he called *deadis of charite* but he was probably wealthier than Messing and could afford to subscribe not only to the gilding of Our Lady's tabernacle in St Peter's church but also towards the construction of Saint Helen's chapel which must have been a project at least in the planning stage at that time (and of which there is no further mention as a building in any extant record).

Between 1500 and the 1570s there were extremely visible and unavoidable changes in religious practice. They were the outward signs of doctrinal reform and were all required by law. None appear to have caused the unrest or rebellion which occurred in areas more remote from London. None of the Maldon churchwardens' account books have survived but what the parishioners paid for and experienced were certainly the same changes as those recorded by the wardens of St Andrew's, Heybridge, and which occurred throughout the realm. The Royal Supremacy was acknowledged. The English Bible would have been placed in each church from 1539, with public readings such as those which took place in Chelmsford and inspired the Protestant convictions of young William Maldon. The images, such as the Blessed Virgin Mary in St Peter's and Our Lady of Piety in All Saints' church (over the crypt doorway), first lost their votive lights, then were themselves

192

taken down. The interior walls were whitened, texts and the royal arms replaced the old 'superstitious' frescoes; the Rood was removed from each chancel screen (but replaced in Queen Mary's reign); altar stones were replaced with the wooden communion tables which the first Book of Common Prayer (1549) called 'God's Board'. According to the inventory of St Mary's church, made by a royal commission for church goods in 1552, £17 1s 10d had been spent since 1547 by the churchwardens in whitening the walls, in replacing glass and putting up the king's arms. (The commissioners' reports on the other two churches are now incomplete.) An English Common Prayer took the place of the various Uses with which many Maldon people had been familiar in their far-off birthplaces. A brief and partial return to the old ways in Queen Mary's reign, but also the introduction of the Roman Missal which was unfamiliar to all, was followed by a subdued return to many of the requirements of the Henrician and Edwardian reforms in 1559.

The impact of change was lessened by the length of time in which they occurred. Visible, structural alterations were frequently balanced with restatements of traditional beliefs and many inhabitants may not have experienced any of the distress which alterations such as these, affecting beliefs and religious habits, can have. Yet these were, in total, revolutionary religious changes and it must surely be insufficient to assume that here they were met with complete apathy. There were pious men and women of this town who gradually found themselves denied their accustomed intercessions at the images of Our Lady, St Roger, St George, St Katherine, were required to take communion in both kinds, could no longer avail themselves or their children of the ceremonies with which they had been baptised, the oils with which their parents had been anointed before death. Consider the religious experience of John Spuddell, mid-century serjeant at mace to the Bailiffs, who was born about 1491 and could in 1570 recall Maldon's 'house of Friars long time before the dissolution [1536] and divers Priors ... Dr Bale ... and one Prior Brook, the predecessor unto the said Bale'. Step by step during his middle age change had swept away the devotional habits and state of mind in which he had been nurtured. Monks and friars, chantry and guild priests, chantries and obits and bede rolls, pilgrimages to the heart of St Roger Niger enshrined in Beeleigh Abbey, the indulgence (remission of penances) granted to those who made their offerings in the Jesus Chapel there: all vanished one by one without hint of any local protest, without overt resistance.

By the 1560s two completely ruined and partly demolished religious houses — Beeleigh Abbey and the Carmelite Friary — and one of the three parish churches, the partly wrecked interiors of the other two churches, gave daily witness that the old faith had been irretrievably lost. By the 1570s one is presented with a town government supporting and entertaining the militant Protestant events known as the Prophesyings and in the 1580s active in the protection of a preacher, Master

George Gifford, well-known for his Calvinist leanings and prominent among East Anglia's and London's Protestant extremists. By 1590 it has become a town whose government is willing to connive in conspiracy to thwart the wishes of its bishop and of the High Commission. Apathy and willing obedience to religious change imposed by law have become a commitment to demanding, or even forcing yet more reform in opposition to the law.

To explain how such a change occurred in this town it is essential to refer to the migratory nature of Protestantism, which has been its recurrent characteristic: the Marian exiles who fled to Switzerland and southern Germany, the Puritan colonisation of New England, John Bunyan's 'Christian', the gatherings of Congregationalists, the itinerant Methodist preachers; It was very much a necessary characteristic of early Protestantism in the Essex of Queen Mary I, when people from many parts of it and the neighbouring counties made their way to Colchester (eighteen miles from Maldon) so that it became 'like unto a city upon a hill and as a candle upon a candlestick gave great light to all those who for the comfort of their conscience came to confer there from divers places of the realm' according to Henry Orinel or 'Crinel' of Willingham. His story, which has been fully discussed in Dr Margaret Spufford's *Contrasting Communities*, displays numbers of men and women engaging in theological debate at night in the 'common inns' of that large town in 1555, who had come from 'divers parts of the realm' and were apparently prepared to wander elsewhere in search of their faiths. Did secret Protestants at Maldon do likewise? It is more likely that people kept unconventional notions to themselves in this small but well-policed community, where John Boswell (one of the Bailiffs) was a principal hunter of heretics in the county, or that they journeyed as privately as possible to secluded 'safe places' or sought the greater anonymity of inns in more populous towns like Colchester, Ipswich, London, or perhaps went out to ships moored in the Blackwater, where itinerant preachers such as Trudge Over The World (finally caught near Colchester) preached and Protestant clergy conducted the services of the 1552 Book of Common Prayer.

The historian is less likely than the Marian bishops to catch sight of these early, covert Protestants as individuals. However, their migrant religious habits can be linked with the known migrant character of Maldon's population. As immigration brought in new groups of fairly young people, the differing attitudes towards religion overlapped. Few were life-long inhabitants like John Spuddell; their religious experience had not been nurtured in local customary devotion. At the beginning of Elizabeth I's reign the aldermen were certainly Romanists. They were the older generation and certainly the wealthiest. It will be remembered that incorporation was achieved in and through Maldon's support for Mary Tudor's accession. The first aldermen of the borough were active promoters of the Counter-Reformation which was attempted in her brief, sad reign. Master John Boswell was a practising civil lawyer, active in the ecclesiastical courts and he had assisted Bishop Bonner's inquisition against Protestants throughout Queen Mary I's reign. Master John Church was devout and related by marriage to Edmund Tyrell, one of the fiercest persecutors and burners of heretics in the county. And Edmund Tyrell was one of the pro-Catholic gentry chosen under the aldermen's patronage to be members of parliament for the borough from 1553 to 1558. Yet by the end of Mary I's reign and despite the burnings of convicted heretics throughout the county some kind of Protestant opinion did exist in the town, among the commonalty and the newer freemen. They managed to exist uneasily alongside their actively papist seniors and magistrates. An examination of twelve witnesses in June 1558 shows us Master Church walking the High Street to enforce the solemn observation of the Feast of Corpus Christi and meeting an unmistakeable demonstration of anti-Romanist feeling. Finding the shop of Henry Pynnell open and a group of men standing around its door he challenged Pynnell with the question which extended and in modern English would be: "Don't you know what day this is?"

"It is Thursday," replied Pynnell;
"I know it is Thursday" said Church "but it is more, for it is Corpus Christi Day".
"Corpus Christi Day?" then said Pynnell. "Whether is Corpus Christi a man or a woman?"
"It is the Feast of the Body of God".
Then said Pynnell to John Church "It is the feast of the Romish Mass and as for you − you are more the Pope's friend than the Queen's".

Ten months later, in April 1559, forty four people, including eleven married couples with their maidservants, were reported to have gone 'out of the town at Easter and *received* without any lawful authority'. That is, they had gone to a parish church in the country (or perhaps a house) and received Holy Communion in both kinds before Midsummer 1559 which was the date fixed after Easter of that year when the Book of Common Prayer was officially to be brought back into use. Henry Pynnell was a fairly recent immigrant (free 1552); his wife was among those going out of town at Easter and among the others were young freemen and future freemen such as Thomas Spigurnell (free 1552), Robert Albert (a tailor from Little Dunmow, free 1564), Nicholas Moore from Plympton and William Abraham from Sudbury (shoemakers and both free in 1560) and a Dutchman, Harman Hendrijk, all immigrants and probably young people.

Co-existing with them were immigrants far less passionate for reform who kept themselves within the law but may rarely have developed close ties with Maldon's religious institutions. One in-comer who was a pious man in the manner of the old faith, William Stokes, made his permanent gift for his soul's health to his native

195

parish church of Bevercoats in Nottinghamshire – a silver salt weighing about 14 ounces, to make a chalice. Alderman Robert Gaywood was unlike most of his contemporaries in being the son and grandson of Maldon people; unlike all his contemporaries he requested burial alongside his father and – this too was unusual – was to have on his tombstone a brass of himself, his wife and his children. Others required their burial outside Maldon: Francis Gowton, 'merchant man of Maldon' in 1482 had desired burial in 'Our Lady churchyard in Antwerp' and Thomas Withers, a chantry priest in Maldon, requested interment at Little Waltham Church 'near unto the font' whilst distributing his goods and money to St Paul's Cathedral in London, to the College at Pleshey and to his friend Master William Dowman at Pocklington in Yorkshire.

The attitude of many during the period 1530-1560 is most probably reflected in the churchwardens' accounts of neighbouring Heybridge, where changes in religious practice conformed rather parsimoniously with the legal requirements of the time; just so with the people of Maldon, even in those most personal matters of baptism and burial. One of the Bailiffs, Richard Brett, and also Alderman John Hastler, made wills in November 1558 and June 1559 which did not include arrangements for the traditional funeral rites at their burials in St Mary's church, although both were drawn up before the new Book of Common Prayer was brought into use. Another Bailiff, Robert Gaywood, made his will in November 1559, after the 1552 Prayer Book had been re-imposed by the 1559 Act of Uniformity. He gave instructions which show that he preferred the traditional funeral rites of the old faith, with lighted tapers around the hearse, held by fifteen 'honest men ... during the time of the administration and other obsequies' – which suggests that he expected Mass to be said – and his will also assumed performance of the Month's Mind but he added this proviso: 'I will that at the day of my burial [there shall] be provided such honest help and service as the law will suffer, as they can be gotten or provided, with clerks to minister such service as at that time shall be appointed to be used and done at the funeral'.

## TOWARDS A GODLY MAGISTRACY 1562 - 1582

Because there were so few continuous families and the population's turn-over in each decade was so extensive, the rate of change in religious attitudes could be rapid. Within ten years of Elizabeth I's accession and the inception of her government's religious settlement the Old Guard of Queen Mary's reign was dead whilst more and more in-comers who were young or in early middle age made up a population which had little knowledge of the old ways of worship and had sometimes been taught only the new language of Protestant religion. At the same time the new Corporation began to explore the extent of its authority and discovered that it could assert itself within the parochial structure of the town and, in 1562, ordered its chamberlains to collect all the vestments, disused for the past three years, from the three churches, make them into costumes for the borough play and then sell the materials for its own funds, less £5 to All Saints' vestry. Thus within three years of Elizabeth I's accession, Maldon's magistrates had not only decided that Protestant worship and doctrine had come to stay but also that they could ignore the rather vague ornaments rubric of the 1559 Prayer Book, which could be taken to prescribe the use of such eucharistic vestments as had been worn 'in the second year of King Edward VI'. By contrast, nine years later (1570) the churchwardens of Masham in the recusant heart of Yorkshire were compiling an inventory of vestments and other items necessary to the liturgy of the Old Faith, and which they kept in private storage.

From 1566 clergy who were committed to the Prrotestant cause were available to succeed the older generation of priests. The vicars of All Saints before then, from 1551 to 1566, were not apparently ardent for reformation: John Dawes (vicar 1551-61) was the son of John Dawes of Maldon and like his brother Henry (the M.P. for the borough) he was a learned man — a Cambridge Bachelor of Civil Law — but he was also a pluralist, holding the benefices of All Hallows Barkingchurch in London from 1542 to 1565 and of Rivenhall in Essex 1560-65 and he had inherited his brother Henry Dawes' wealth in 1550 so he was able to keep his distance from his cure of souls. His successor lasted one year and the next, Nicholas Johnson, resigned to become rector of Woodham Mortimer and seems to have been also landlord of the Saracen's Head Inn in Maldon where in 1580, it was alleged, he and Humphrey Poles practised sorcery by making a wax image of the Queen.

By the time Johnson resigned his cure of souls in Maldon the patronage of All Saints' and St Peter's vicarage had passed into the possession of Thomas Franke of Hatfield Broad Oak. He was desirous to promote men of Protestant convictions. Thus the first certainly Puritan clergyman appeared in the town.

This was Robert Williams, the vicar of the two parishes 1566 — 73, and with him came the alliance between a preaching ministry by the clergy with the magistracy of the Aldermen. It was he who first among the town's clergy deliberately conveyed an exercise of ecclesiastical authority to the Corporation. In his vicariate the Bailiffs judged three cases leading to the sentence of the Greater Excommunication which should have been taken before the Archdeacon in his court and a case of transvestism which should properly have been judged by the Archdeacon was heard and punished by the borough court. In his time as vicar the Corporation also proposed replacing the town's parochial divisions by wards named after its Aldermen (1569) for administrative purposes. Master Williams cannot have wished to see his parishes entirely subsumed by the civil authority for like most vicars at that time his stipend was small and he was very dependent financially on his right to the Lesser Tithes of his two parishes. But in 1568 he took before the magistrates, instead of his Archdeacon, an action against Alice Cole, widow, for disputing tithe payments to him. She, incidentally, alleged in her defence that

> 'he useth his parishioners at Maldon very extremely, wresting and wringing from them unreasonable tithes not due and he made me also to pay him for one tithe pig: 5s ... The vicar unreasonably asketh tithes of winter milk and colts and of cows which men kill in their houses, which never were paid nor asked before within the parish'.

The traditional complaints against the parson and his tithe were the same, whatever the colour of his dress. Tithes were one survival of the medieval and Papist structure of the Church that no Puritan ever demanded to be abolished.

Another notable change during his time as vicar occurred in the cultural links between the settlements of the area. Early Elizabethan Puritanism's Prophesying Movement replaced the traditional religious drama, the 'native' plays performed by many communities. Both of these activities, plays and preaching, reveal that interdependence of town and country which has been seen in their population structure and economy; the difference was that the old 'scenic apparatus' of the pre-Reformation Church was replaced with professional sermons. There had been in the fifteenth and sixteenth centuries several 'native' plays which from time to time went on quite extensive tours: the borough chamberlains had made payments in 1469 to the performers of the Stow Maries Play and the Players of Sandon, Ulting and Woodham Ferrers; in 1530 the Heybridge Play went to Maldon and then out as far as Tollesbury, Coggeshall, Terling, Felsted and Woodham Ferrers. Maldon's own dramatic production in 1540, referred to earlier in this Chapter, involved payments to a Chelmsford scenery painter, a London 'professional' (*Felstede of London* who was its producer) and two men from Prittlewell and Rayleigh (for unspecified assistance), whilst there were contributions in cash towards the cost of the production from a Londoner, a Chelmsford man, another at Hazeleigh, the inhabitants of Chelmsford and of Great Dunmow which amounted to 21 per cent of the total receipts. On the occasion of its last performance, in 1562, its producer (*Burles the propertie plaier*) came from Chelmsford; the next year some of its wardrobe was purchased by two Braintree men for £3 6s 8d; and in 1564 Master Richard Josua purchased the remainder of 'the players garments' for £9. After that Maldon's drama was entirely supplied by professional touring companies performing secular pieces; in place of the old religious plays and spectacles as a vehicle for the sharing and the inculcation of ideas and attitudes, the wealthier and literate among Essex men now placed sermons and lectures as their group activities.

Prophesying was a radical and formative preaching movement within the Church; groups of clergy held public sessions in which sermons were preached with moderators to lead discusssions of the preachers' techniques and of the content of their sermons. The laity were admitted to these highly professional assemblies, which were potentially a powerful method of advancing the reformers' cause, though a Prophesying can only have appealed to a minority of the community, whereas the drama had attracted large audiences. In the 1560s and 1570s six centres of Prophesying were established in Essex, one at Colchester, the other five all within Maldon's market area, at Romford, Horndon-on-the-Hill, Brentwood, Chelmsford and the borough itself. As with the drama, the borough provided a location but it did not supply the expertise, nor all the performers nor all the auditors. Its market day sermons were similarly attended by those who had come to the market itself and, as in many other places, the congregations included numerous outsiders who gadded about the county following their favoured ministers from one pulpit to another. Indeed, George Gifford's supporters claimed in 1595 or 1596 that there was 'a concourse of people' coming to the market only on days when he was preaching. Trade followed the sermon: 'many of them are greatly decayed and become poor for want of the concourse of people on these days, by whom they were wonted many ways to gain money' reported the curate of St Mary's, Maldon. Gifford himself described how sermons by popular preachers drew crowds from many parts of the countryside to markets. In *The Countrie Divinitee* (1582) he makes the Atheist in his dialogue complain how 'now they run in the weekdays and beggar themselves' and how people even went off to other towns to hear sermons when they should have been at work.

Thus All Saints' church became from 1566 The Company's assembly place for weekly sermons and the Bailiffs and aldermen began, in effect, to act as the patrons of its pulpit. From this decade the Sermon became the cardinal feature of Maldon's religious life. One of Vicar Palmer's humbler parishioners (Nicholas Smith) told him in 1592 that 'he never denied to pay towards the reparations of the church, or anything that is due, but he is willing to pay so that he were placed in some convenient place near the preacher'. The two successive vicars of All Saints, Robert Williams and Fabian Withers, paved the way for the powerful preaching and successful ministry of George Gifford by their committed co-operation with The Company in organising an impressive programme of sermons. They and at least some of the Corporation were attempting to create a replica of Geneva in Maldon.

Their programme had a notably radical start in 1570 when Edmund Chapman preached as the town Lecturer, for he had been a Fellow of Trinity College, Cambridge, and he preached the doctrines favouring a further and presbyterian reformation of the Church of England as it had been taught in Cambridge by the eminent Dr Thomas Cartwright. The university's missionary efforts in Maldon were supplemented in that year by a visit from 'certain scholars being Scots students at Cambridge' who were paid 3s 4d. Thereafter the chamberlains' account rolls list a stream of preachers to whom the borough gave dinners and expenses in return for their sermons. A Master Simpson preached there six times 1570 - 1574; Master Betts, Master Lawrence, Master Wood, Master Malson 'and his colleger' or student-preacher, were each paid for sermons in All Saints 1570 - 1573 and Master Waters, 'the preacher of Kel [ ve ] don' twice in 1573. The Company also became patrons of the Prophesyings until the Queen's disapproval of those events led her to suspend from office the Archbishop of Canterbury, Edmund Grindal, because he refused to forbid them. The use of All Saints' for the Prophesyings in (especially) 1573 and 1574 indicates both the vicars' and The Company's prominence in the Essex Puritan movement. Archdeacon Walker chose the second day of the 1573 Prophesying to preach there against 'our play'. That must have been a specific play objectionable to Dr Walker and currently being produced in the town, for the Borough Play had been stopped eleven years before. The same year the Bailiffs gave the chaplain of the Puritan Earl of Sussex a dinner costing 9s 4d, three times the average sum spent on preachers' dinners, for 'his most learned sermon made in the parish of All Saints' on Midwinter Day.

## GEORGE GIFFORD: MAGISTRACY AND GODLINESS

Fabian Withers (vicar 1575-1582), the second of these co-operative clerics appointed by Thomas Franke, is an examplar of the vigorous Protestant clergy who were beginning to exercise immense influence in Essex and in London. Such men were graduates, many had wealthy or influential connections, which gave them sufficient independence to risk the consequences of nonconforming, and they were married men in or approaching middle age. The son of a city merchant (Lawrence Withers, Salter and Alderman of London), Fabian had been educated at Christ's College, Cambridge, 1544 - 1548, and was the elder brother of Dr George Withers, rector of Danbury (Essex) and Archdeacon of Colchester from 1570 to 1616. Fabian was the senior of four clergy in Alderman Withers' descendants: beside himself and his much more distinguished brother George, his own son Samuel went to Christ's College in 1572 and his nephew Thomas Withers was there from 1582 to 1589. Like Robert Williams he employed curates to help him exercise his ministry, mostly young graduates who, as soon as they had been ordained, spent one or two years in a kind of apprenticeship to their profession and in preparation for the bishop's examination which preceded their ordination as priests. Only one of these needs to be mentioned, the great George Gifford, who succeeded Withers as vicar in 1582 and whose arrival brought dissension to the borough.

George Gifford was surely picked by Fabian Withers as his best immediate aide and as possibly his most suitable successor. Unlike other curates he had been a schoolmaster (at Brentwood), he was married, had one son and was 33 by the time he came to Maldon in 1581, a priest of three years standing. He did not have wealthy or influential family connections – he was born about 1548 at Dry Drayton on the edge of the fenland between Huntingdon and Cambridge, almost certainly the son of a yeoman – and Dr Margaret Spufford's observation (in *Contrasting Communities*) on the spiritually 'tough and strong ground' of Dry Drayton's inhabitants at that time, which its distinguished Puritan minister of 1570-91, Richard Greenham, described as the 'intractableness and unteachableness of that people', highlight the practicality, the familiarity with the life-style and preoccupations of ordinary men and women which can be sensed in his published work. Like Withers, he was a graduate of Christ's College in Cambridge and as many of that and other colleges were beneficed in the eastern counties and London they were often able to return to the university at the great annual Stourbridge Fair (to stock up with goods for the winter) or, as Masters of Arts, for the academic Commencement ceremonies. Members of the college could thus keep in touch and become acquainted with the more recent graduates of their Society. That may be how George Gifford came to be known to Fabian Withers and perhaps he was also recommended by Fabian's brother, the Archdeacon of Colchester and rector of Danbury.

His impact on Maldon was immense, even though it was also to prove divisive. He was a skilled and diligent preacher who wore considerable learning lightly, as a reading of his published sermons will quickly show. Like many of the successful Puritan preachers, especially the next generation's Stephen Marshal (born not far from Dry Drayton at Godmanchester, a weaver's son and in the 1620s and '30s a Maldon householder), he had a gift of using the everday language of his congregations in his sermons. So influential as a preacher was he that Archbishop Whitgift in 1589 publically prohibited him from entering any pulpit of any church in London. Twenty years after his death he was remembered in Maldon as 'the faithful preacher of the Word of God in this Incorporation'. To this talent he added a gift for pastoral work so that in his lifetime many testified that (in the words of Thomas Purchas) 'Master Gifford is his father in God, for that he hath begotten him by the Gospel to God'.

But from the start of his clerical career he faced, as had Fabian Withers, a campaign organised at Court and among new bishops to bring to heel the reforming activities of the more extreme clergy. The Queen's anger at Archbishop Grindal's defence of Prophesyings led the bishops to impose restrictions on preaching, so that the absence of payments by The Company to visiting clergy for nearly thirty years from 1576 reflects how successful that policy of repression was. Gifford's appointment as a curate at All Saints was one way by which an additional preacher for the town could be found but only with episcopal approval, which probably explains the chamberlains' note in 1581 of entertainment given to commissioners at an enquiry 'directed from the Bishop of London touching Master Gifford and Master Withers'.

Approval had been given even though the new curate was already known to be a radical who would not comply with the Prayer Book's rubrics on vestments, kneeling to receive communion, the blessing of rings in the marriage ceremony, making the sign of the cross in baptism, but above all was known as a principal activist in the Essex Puritan movement. Although he lacked family connections he did have the companionship of three members of his college days: Robert Wright, who had become chaplain to Lord Rich, the greatest landowner in Essex and a supporter of the Puritans' cause; Richard Rogers, who was vicar of Wethersfield; and a younger man, Ralph Hawdon. All three were close at hand, for Lord Rich's household lived frequently at Rochford, Wethersfield is some fifteen miles away from Maldon and Ralph Hawdon (vicar of Rayleigh) came to live at Langford on the edge of the borough itself. In 1582 Gifford attended a meeting with Rogers and many other clergy in Wethersfield parish church which was the inception of the famous Dedham Conference of ministers; he led the Braintree Classis (a 'cell' within the Conference organisation); in 1585 he and Robert Wright attended the House of Commons to lobby Members of Parliament on behalf of the ministers who (like himself) had been ejected from their benefices. All his life George Gifford retained that migratory habit of the Protestant extremist, riding from and back to Maldon about the affairs of the Puritan classes, to Cambridge, to London, Dedham, Braintree and to any meeting of the Elizabethan Bishops' opponents. Archbishop Whitgift told Lord Burghley in 1584 that 'the said Gifford is a ringleader of the rest [of the nonconforming clergy of Essex] ... His deserts may be such as will deserve deprivation'.

Fabian Withers resigned the vicarage within one year of Gifford's arrival and Richard Franke, the new patron of the living, duly nominated him as successor. Instituted 30 August 1582 he lasted two years until (as will be shown below) his Puritanism caused him to be deprived of the benefice. But he had by then built up a body of committed supporters ('Master Gifford's favourers') and most, if not all, in The Company were determined to stand by him. He became a privately retained preacher of the town, with some official recognition allowed (in that he was licensed by the bishop to preach and was permitted a share in the occupation of the vicarage house) and remained until his early death, aged about 52, in 1600. Although, according to his will, he had this share in the vicarage house he purchased land in St Mary's parish in 1587 and had by 1596 acquired a house in that parish. That placed him in the peculiar and remote jurisdiction of the Dean of Westminster Abbey and gave him a base for his activities as convenient as were the Minories in London for other Puritans: there he was outside the jurisdiction of the Archdeacon of Essex and that may explain why causes which were twice commenced against him in the Essex Archdeaconry Court for nonconformity (1592 and 1595) were allowed to lapse.

When he was deprived of his benefice in 1584 his principal supporters in Maldon appealed to Lord Burghley and the Privy Council for his re-instatement. Their principal argument was that Master Gifford had 'builded us up to obedience both towards God and towards her Majesty, and towards all the ministers of justice under her'. The late seventeenth century historian John Strype, who acquired the manuscript of this petition, paraphrased it in his biography of Archbishop Whitgift, published in 1718. Gifford, he wrote, 'was much valued there for the good reformation he had made in that market-town by his preaching; where very notorious sins reigned before his coming; and others had been by his diligence nourished and strengthened in grace and virtue'.

What the preacher could inject into his community was Zeal, for Tudor and Stuart government necessarily stood or fell by the efforts of its humbler levels of administration. A parish constable, a borough magistrate, even the lowliest of the decenners could make or mar the maintenance of law and order by his attitude. Gifford's mission was to convert men's complaisance into zeal for the law, to persuade all who had taken any oath of office or the oath of a freeman or decenner, not to compromise with wickedness in any form. Professor Collinson has shown how Puritan preachers of that time applauded and encouraged such conmbinations of Clergy and Magistracy. He has cited a sermon by Laurence Chaderton of Emmanuel College which listed the evils with which The Company of Maldon also dealt in the Quarter Sessions − 'conjuring [spirits], witchcraft, sorcery, charming, of blaspheming the holy name of God, ... profaning of the Lord's Sabbath, disobedience to superiors, contempt to inferiors, murder, manslaughter, robberies, adultery, fornication, covenant-breakers, false witness ...'. Chaderton called for the Church of England to be remodelled as a presbyterian organisation so that clergy could more directly assist the lay justices (at Maldon the Bailiffs) who were 'the Lord's servants in magistracy'. Thirty six years after Gifford's arrival in Maldon Samuel Ward, the Town Preacher of Ipswich 1605-1640, was still proclaiming the same principle: magistrates and the ministers were 'the principal lights ... these two optic pieces ... guardians and tutors' of the commonwealth; ministers of religion were 'God's Trumpeters and Drummers' to the lay magistrates. In the combination of Master Gifford (the 'tutor') and The Company (the 'guardians') the commonwealth of the borough of Maldon achieved by 1584 a model of the Puritan preachers' ideal which was also the fruition of the former co-operation between the Bailiffs and the vicars of All Saints.

The times were propitious for his preaching. Within a day's sailing from the Black-water Spanish armies were at war against the Dutch rebels; Philip II's assassin struck down the Calvinist Prince of Orange and Englishmen, afraid for their Queen's safety, formed the Bond of Association to defend her against any similar attempt on her life by emissaries of the Pope or the King of Spain. By 1588 England was openly

*Pl.11. Dr John Whitgift, Archbishop of Canterbury 1583 – 1604*

at war with Spain; it was in danger of invasion by Spanish forces and, many feared, of treachery from its Catholic sympathisers. The conspiracies against the Queen's life and in favour of the Catholic Mary Stuart, Queen of Scots, which were unmasked in the 1580s heightened the tension. 'We are now in peril of goods, liberty and life by our enemies the Spaniards; and at home [by] Papists in multitudes, ready to come upon us unawares', wrote Gifford's colleague Richard Rogers.

Godly and thoughtful men saw enemies everywhere: papists, heretics 'and other enemies to God and Her Royal Majesty' were alleged by the supporters of Master Gifford to be delighted when he was deprived of his vicarage in 1584. Zealous government was preached as loyal and righteous government. The preacher depicted the magistrates' work as part of a struggle between the forces of Antichrist and Reformers and in his *Sermons upon the whole booke of the Revelation* which were published in the last year of his life (1599) and had been preached in All Saints' church he continued to set Maldon within his panorama of contemporary Europe. He observed sure signs of an impending Doomsday; the Holy Spirit was at work in the persons of godly reformers; the Pope and his seminary priests, casting off all disguise, were discernible (to him) as creatures of the Bottomless Pit.

'The Dragon, the Beast and the false prophets have sent forth their messengers, even their unclean spirits which are like fogs, into all lands unto the kings of the Earth to stir them up unto battle. The Jesuits, the Seminary Priests, are dispersed into all countries ... All these things come to pass in the days that we live in. Now of late years there entered (as they call it) into the Holy League, kings and princes, binding themselves with solemn vows to do their uttermost to destroy and to root out all that profess the holy gospel of Jesus Christ: here is great conspiracy against the Church. And, by the singular blessing of God, our noble Queen hath been − and is − the greatest defender and protector of the holy worship and true worshippers that is under Heaven. The Churches in other countries have by her aid been much supported and relieved in their distresses. The Romish Beast and his company have espied so much and do make full account that all their wars and enterprises against the Church are to small purpose unless they could first supplant and destroy her Majesty. And to effect this their wicked desire they have invented all the ways and means which possibly they can. Their Pope (who is the standard-bearer in that apostacy) did long since [1572] excommunicate her Highness. He hath from time to time sent forth his Jesuit priests and others, to work all manner of treacheries and traitorously to murder her royal Person ... The King of Spain, who hath given his power to the Beast, sent his forces Anno 88 for to invade her land ...'

## MASTER GIFFORD'S FAVOURERS

It would be unlikely that Maldon's Preacher expected to convert all its inhabitants, just as it is unlikely that he expected all of them to be regular or frequent attenders at church. In his manual for preachers of 1609, *The Shepeard's Practise*, Richard Bernard pointed out 'that Christ came to bring a sword and not peace: not that a Minister should set his people by the ears; but that he should speak the Word so as by God's blessing it might make a spiritual division amongst them'. In Gifford's ministry the dissensions began which, eleven years later, Bishop Fletcher claimed to have pacified and to some extent Gifford did 'set his people by the ears' and created a communal faction if not Bernard's 'spiritual division' amongst them. There were some who were very strongly supportive of him and when they had to be petitioners on his behalf to the Privy Council, their somewhat colourful reference to the 'rioters, dicers, quarrellers, drunkards and adulterers' who openly rejoiced when he was deprived of his benefice in 1584, was an admission that his ministry had already been divisive: 'they stick not openly to fill our bosoms with all contemptuous and bitter speeches, mocking and taunting us with our profession'. Two years later (1586) the Corporation needed to elect two Puritan spokesmen as the borough's M.P.s, and in part that was done in the hope of Gifford's re-appointment as vicar: only 43 freemen voted, which was only about 50 to 60 per cent of all the freemen; and the votes cast for the two Puritan gentlemen amounted to only some 33 to 40 per cent of the total number of votes cast. All three candidates were Puritan and it would seem that a very large number of the freemen preferred not to vote for any of them.

In 1584 George Gifford was one of many Essex parsons who refused to subscribe his name to any of the *Articles Touching Preachers* issued by the newly enthroned Archbishop of Canterbury, Dr John Whitgift, who required all the clergy to whom they were offered to state (by subscribing their names to the second of three statements or Articles) that they were willing to conform themselves to the rubrics and forms of service in the Book of Common Prayer. Gifford's prominence within and without the borough made him well known to the High Commission as one of those who preached that the Church of England of his time was 'but halfly reformed' in matters of doctrine, in its continuing traditional organisation with priests and bishops and canon law, and in its enforcing of the survivals of medieval Papalism, the vestments and ceremonies and customs required in the instructions or rubrics of the prayer book. It was against such clergy that the Archbishop's *Articles* were aimed, to break their organisation. William Tay, the vicar of Peldon (a few miles north of Maldon), urged his brethren of the Dedham Conference to beware of 'Antichrist tyrannising the Church by our bishops'. Some thought that a compromise should be sought but Tay was adamant they must recognise the wickedness of the designs of 'certain men crept in unawares' and prayed that each member of the Conference might be given 'the courage and fortitude to stand in the truth and to quit ourselves like valiant men in the Lord His cause'. When put to the test Gifford and most others in the Conference refused point blank to put their names to any of the *Articles* and so he was soon afterwards deprived of his benefice: thrown out of his vicarage on the orders of the Archbishop and the High Commission.

The Corporation (and others) were outraged. The Company was at the height of its power, and so sure of its authority that it began a long and in the end inglorious campaign to have him reinstated. A petition, the *The Complaint of Malden to the Counsell*, was sent to Lord Burghley, pointing out how grievous a blow had been struck at their authority. It failed. They tried again with another petition, this time on behalf of other deprived or suspended ministers and addressed it to their bishop, Dr John Aylmer. It failed. Parliament had been summoned so they next tried to bring pressure to bear through the two Members whom they elected: Edward Lewkenor of Denham, one of the most prominent of Puritan gentlemen in Suffolk; and William Wiseman of Mundon, a former alderman of the borough, who was an agent of the Puritans' patron in Essex, Sir Robert Rich. Although the House of Commons was well supplied with sympathisers for the deprived and suspended clergy their cause was not provided with adequate parliamentary experience and the forcing-through of reforms never occurred.

These failures did nothing to cool tempers. When their diocesan himself, the Bishop of London, came to the borough in his Visitation of 1586 there was, he believed, a plan to humiliate him in All Saints' church — he had been informed that a man had been hired who would burst into the church dressed as a fool or jester, snatch off his 'Canterbury Cap' and hurl it into the assembly — 'whereupon', he informed Lord Burghley, 'it is not to be doubted but a dangerous tumult would have arisen'. And for the next parliament, 1586-7, Master Gifford's 'favourers' (and as has been noted above, only those voted) elected Puritan members again. They gave 22 of their votes to Master Lewkenor and preferred John Butler of Thoby (father-in-law to Alderman William Vernon's son) by 13 votes to their previous M.P., William Wiseman's 8. By then forty ministers, most of them living within Maldon's market area, had been suspended from office and the Essex M.P.s were deluged with petitions from outraged parishioners. These were organised by the Dedham Conference, which decided that Maldon was to have one petition by itself — an indication of how strong Puritan feeling there was considered to be. But again the M.P.s failed to achieve anything. Their chief objective turned out to be so radical a Presbyterian proposal for far-reaching reform of the Church of England (Sir Anthony Cope's *Bill and Book*) that the Queen prevented a full reading of the Bill and frustrated the Commons debate. Master John Butler also lost his nerve and 'brake his faith' by not speaking in support of Peter Wentworth's attack on the

Queen's behaviour towards her parliament. At least he stayed a free man: Lewkenor joined Wentworth, Cope and three others in the prison of the Tower of London before the parliament was over.

Meanwhile further schemes were afoot in Maldon. First, the parishioners who were supporting Master Gifford had managed to persuade their bishop, Dr John Aylmer, to licence him as an unbeneficed preacher in Maldon, for there was no official objection to his theology, which was sound, and when he was simply preaching there was no requirement that he should wear a surplice; and he was not licensed to officiate in any of the services of the Book of Common Prayer, so he could not break any of the laws to which he so much objected.

Secondly, they enlisted the aid of the new patron of All Saints' Vicarage, Richard Franke, to make a very curious choice of a new vicar. This was Mark Wiersdale, who not long before had been described in an archdeacon's visitation as 'no preacher', who had had left Cambridge University without graduating and been ordained a deacon only two years before this appointment. He was extremely young and poorly qualified; an unlikely substitute for a patron of Puritanism to choose in any circumstance, one would think, but South Weald, where he had been appointed curate, is not very far from Hatfield Broad Oak, so his patron would have known full well that young Mark Wiersdale had been suspended from his curacy 'because he is no preacher and a nonconformist'.

Perhaps a device was in train to get round Gifford's deprivation. Here was a devout young Puritan who might, after a decent interval and when the laws ecclesiastical had been appropriately reformed in the next parliaments, resign. Then the patron could once more present Master Gifford to his rightful place. In the meantime he would maintain the reforming movement in this town with a gifted pastor and preacher at hand to assist or more probably to direct him. In fact he was gone within three years and he seems to have been a hot-headed, contentious young man who would not have been tolerated by the Corporation if it had not been necessary to keep him in Maldon long enough to let the matter of the Archbishop's *Articles* fade away. In 1585 he got himself into serious trouble − almost − by attempting a debate on the validity of the Queen's royal style and title during the archdeacon's visitation. 'The Queen is not Queen of France or Ireland', he said like a schoolboy initiating a schoolroom debate, and persisted even when others in the church warned him that his speech might be considered seditious, because 'whatsoever did diminish any part of the Queen's style was in the danger of a praemunire'. It was indeed capable of being construed thus but the Bailiffs immediately intervened, made their own enquiry and absolved the young man from any charge of uttering treasonable opinions, so that both the Privy Council and the High Commission decided they could not successfully pursue the matter.

The Archdeacon, however, could take action and prosecuted him 'for that he doth not say Service upon Wednesdays and Fridays' which Wiersdale said was unnecessary, especiaily as he preached instead; 'for not praying for the Queen according to her Injunctions'; for not wearing a surplice, to which he gave the standard Puritan response that 'he had none offered to him' by the churchwardens; not giving thanks for women safely delivered in childbirth; not 'marrying with the ring' and not making the sign of the cross with water at baptisms. To the last accusation he replied that 'he could not tell whether he had used ring or cross'. To these sulky and uncooperative replies the archdeacon's court responded with a disciplinary sentence: he was to confess his guilt before his congregation during Divine Service. It is doubtful if the aldermen and headburgesses, or many others in that congregation, would be shocked at his confession: Gifford's supporters still needed him. In 1587 he did resign the vicarage, and according to *The Seconde Part of a Register* he did so with a request that Master Gifford might be offered the benefice once more.

Although one should treat any conspiracy theory with caution there does seem to be a case for supposing that the young man had in this instance acted faithfully on orders given by godly persons and with the connivance of the patron, Richard Franke. If there was a conspiracy, it misfired. *The Seconde Part of a Register* states that Richard Franke immediately presented George Gifford for institution as vicar but the Bishop of London refused to accept this nomination.

Through the technical lapse in the patronage (for no acceptable candidate was presented) it was possible for the bishop to nominate the new vicar. His choice, Master Robert Palmer, the vicar of Great Waltham near Chelmsford, was provocative. He was one of the last persons in the Church of England whom the godly of Maldon wanted to be charged with the cure of their souls. He was a career clergyman, who became a pluralist by holding the vicarage of Great Wakering in south-east Essex simultaneously with the vicarage of All Saints' and St Peter's Maldon; and he had a legal instead of a theological training, having left Magdalene College in Cambridge to complete his studies at the Middle Temple. In their eyes he was plainly in the pocket of a bishop who persecuted and obstructed true pastors and had undermined the authority of The Company of Maldon. Such a man was unlikely to connive at any scheme which would put Master Gifford back where some of the townspeople and many troublesome Puritans throughout Essex wanted him, in All Saints' Vicarage.

There was one comfort left: the bishop's licence for Master Gifford to preach was still in force so the new vicar had to accept the existing scheme by which he and Master Gifford were to be alternating preachers in his pulpit, in his church, to his parishioners. To some extent the dissension which began to tear the town apart from the moment Master Palmer was instituted was created by his own determination not to yield one more inch to these devoted supporters of this anti-vicar.

## MASTER PALMER AND THE COMPANY

Although the contrasts between George Gifford and Robert Palmer, the new vicar installed by the Bishop of London in 1587, are of interest, it must be emphasised at this point in the narrative that the two men were not personal enemies. Whilst that is to the credit of both, it would appear that by their personalities each gained a following and that created the unmistakeable polarisation of Maldon's small community in which dissension flourished. For where Gifford was a restrained and prudent man − 'in his life he was modest, discreet and unreproveable' − and thus the associate of earnest, godly men and women, Palmer was boisterous and flamboyant, 'a common bowler for money day by day' (as it was alleged against him in the court of the High Commission in 1594) and not only in public places such as the New Inn but at his own alley which he had opened for like-minded sportsmen in the vicarage orchard. He was a 'good fellow', the acquaintance of drinkers and games-players, 'a gamester at tables and cards for money' not only in Maldon but also at Romford where he was reported to play cards with another scandalous cleric, John Frith the rector of Hawkwell. He was, said the godly, intemperate in his speech, given to loud talk and oaths, and many a Puritan list of unsatisfactory clergy consists of similar descriptions of those whom the precisians condemned as the 'dumb dogs that would not bark', and served as a prologue to more serious charges.

Let it be remembered that he had been a student of the Middle Temple, for London's inns of court around the Temple were as much places for the education of gentry as they were schools of law. To Master Gifford's supporters Robert Palmer was a 'scandalous minister' like those who were scheduled in the Puritan black-lists of non-preaching, worldly and ignorant clergy; his behaviour may have been what others expected of a gentleman. All that is left of his own work in Maldon is the very carefully compiled transcription of his parish registers, done in 1598-9 from the poorly maintained records left by his four Puritan predecessors. All the allegations against him are to be found in the Cause Papers presented by his Puritan accusers and there is no other material which can directly confirm his opponents' accusations. Only once among George Gifford's printed works can a remark be found that might have been a covert shot at Palmer. It is in a sermon which was preached at All Saints after dissension and faction had simmered down, in the later 1590s:

> 'nowadays we have some Gospellers which can laugh even heartily at the committing of great sins and enormous offences: it is a sport to make men

— or to see them made — drunken. If I should enter into all particulars I should be tedious. Ye may easily see what manner of professing the Gospel hath invaded our Churches and how far it hath prevailed ... All seemeth now happy, "The Gospel, the Gospel" is in every man's mouth; but the Lord will spew out of his mouth all lukewarm Gospellers, all that be neither cold nor hot ...

but this is perhaps no more than Gifford's description of a type to which a captious listener could, if he or she had wished, compare the laughing, shouting, bowling and drinking vicar. Equally Gifford's comments in his book or discourse *The Countrie Divinitie* are so like the allegations made against Master Palmer that one might suppose they are the curate's description of his vicar:

'the drunkards meet together and sit quaffing, and the minister (which should reprove them) to be one of the chief: when he should be at his study, to be upon the alebench at cards or dice'.

But that was written in 1581, before Master Gifford had arrived in Maldon and six years before Master Palmer was appointed vicar.

For his part, the new vicar was potentially a dangerous man not only to Gifford but to all of Gifford's widespread network of correspondents and associates. Behind his noisy affability Robert Palmer's accomplishment was as an ecclesiastical lawyer. More than six years elapsed between his induction as vicar of All Saints and the outbreak of his quarrel with The Company and for part of that time he acted as an Official of the Archdeaconry of Essex. His curate meanwhile was a leading participant in movements which the Privy Council and the High Commission were anxious to track down and to silence. Let there be no misunderstanding: George Gifford's activities were, especially from 1588, very dangerous to himself, as any reading of Professor Collinson's detailed account of the Elizabethan Puritan Movement will prove. His associates' houses were raided, papers were taken, ministers and preachers were imprisoned and questioned. The most extreme among them made matters worse by their famous and scandalously witty Marprelate Tracts which encouraged the idea that all Puritans were actively seeking to destroy the traditional structure of the Church of England, its bishops, their archdeacons, the ecclesiastical courts and their lawyers. What the Directory or 'Book of Discipline' might be which these country clergy and reform-minded academics discussed, who had compiled it, how these favourers of a presbyterian Church government met, who organised them, were questions to which the Bishops and the Privy Councillors wanted clear answers. And whenever they got answers, Master Gifford's was among the names of the organisers.

The strange features of this witch-hunt are, first, that George Gifford was never imprisoned, nor subjected to any formal proceedings; and second, that Master

211

Palmer never moved against the curate of his church who was so clearly active in the East Anglian reforming movement. Yet from 1591 to 1593 Palmer was the Assessor whenever the Archdeacon of Essex sat in person in his court; he acted as judge when the Archdeacon was absent; he was empowered to hold synods of the clergy in each deanery within the archdeaconry; he could conduct visitations; he could induct parsons to their benefices; indeed he was expected at all times to exercise the authority of the Archdeacon's office, to maintain the canon law and the laws ecclesiastical of the realm. As the Archdeacon was 'the Bishop's Eye' so was Robert Palmer the Archdeacon's and the Bishop's Eye planted within the town of Maldon, yet apparently winking at the matters in which Master George Gifford was plainly implicated that so moved his masters.

Instead, and only after four years had passed, he struck at Master Gifford's protective patrons, The Company, the magistrates. The Corporation's proprietorial attitude over his church was the issue and he turned on these men only when he had been appointed the Archdeacon's Official. And he may have been pushed into action by one of his card-playing cronies, Master Frith of Hawkwell who arrived in Maldon on a market day in January 1592 and announced to Alderman William Bantoft that he was going to preach the sermon in All Saints' Church. It was Master Gifford's turn to preach, he was told, and he was warned that there was an arrangement for the vicar and curate to preach on alternate market days which had been sanctioned by Archbishop Whitgift. But during the service, with the Corporation in its accustomed place,

> 'when the psalm was in singing before the Sermon (and the same more than half being sung) and Master Gifford was gone out of his seat to the pulpit, the said Master Frith came into the church and entered into the pew [reading desk] where Divine Service is used to be said.
>
> 'And presently, so soon as the psalm was ended, Master Gifford standing in the pulpit ready to begin his sermon, the said Master Frith began to make a speech with a loud voice where he stood, whereat the Bailiffs and other the people there assembled (being ignorant of his pretence) were greatly astonished, supposing him to have been out of his wits rather than otherwise ...

From his pulpit Gifford requested the Bailiffs 'that the said disturbance might be removed' but when they ordered Frith to be quiet he insisted that it was he who was going to preach and that the Bailiffs had no jurisdiction in the church 'For', said he, 'Master Palmer who is vicar and hath more authority here than Master Gifford, had appointed me to preach ... and when he was taken off to the Moot Hall for interrogation by the magistrates he continued to argue that within the church itself laymen had no authority and that 'if he were as Master Palmer is, Master Gifford should not preach there at all'.

212

Eleven months later the same principle surfaced again, when the vicar sent a joiner to fix a lock on the pulpit door. On the day that was done George Gifford was the appointed preacher and in fact he had to deliver his sermon from the prayer desk but that was the end of a troubled day. Before the service began the vicar was in the church and 'one Sturgion coming into the church of All Saints ... asked Master Palmer ... whether he would preach that day. The said Master Palmer made answer that he would not make him account', no doubt sensing some mockery of his position by this Samuel Sturgion, a young husbandman of Beeleigh. At that moment 'there came into the church one Richard Williams and John Pratt, who rang the bell to a sermon'. The vicar went to them and told them to stop. He seized the bell rope and the confusion which occurred as a result (which will be readily understood by any who have had to do with church bell ropes) led to two separate accounts by witnesses.

(A) 'Then the said Richard Williams said though he forbade them to ring, yet they might toll and − Master Palmer holding the bell rope in his hand − took the same and tolled certain times, and said that Master Gifford had showed forth an order from the Lord Bishop of London that he might preach then'. The vicar angrily declared that that man would not preach in his church, 'nor none such as he was, except he did wear the surplice, minister the sacraments, make the cross in baptism and subscribe [to the *Articles Touching Preachers*] as he [Palmer] had done'. That declaration, on the day he had the pulpit locked, suggests that at long last the vicar had decided to make himself master in his own church. He may also have been afraid of the Corporation's reaction to his intended 'coup'.

Witness (B) testified that as the two ringers tried to toll the bell by stretching their arms over the vicar's head, they somehow pushed his hat down over his face: 'with his [Pratt's] over reaching of him he pressed and beat down a little his hat; and thereupon the said Master Palmer went forth the church and said that he was pressed down and beaten out of breath, when in truth [this is the opinion of the scribe compiling this, an accusation against the vicar] it was no such matter ..'.

By the time Master Gifford mounted the stair in front of the Corporation and the assembled people of the town, to find himself publically locked out of the pulpit, his vicar had met his own crisis and what has just been described from an edited version of two witnesses' depositions was reported thus by the Bailiffs themselves:

'You attempted to break an order set down by the Lord Archbishop between you and the town preacher for your course of preaching; and the Bailiffs − being requested by him to see the order quietly observed, and they telling

213

you they would do so — you went out of the church and slanderously diffamed them, [saying] that the church doors were beset and that the Bailiffs put you in fear of your life'.

John Pratt has already appeared in this study as a prosperous tailor, as a leaseholder and property-owner, as an immigrant who had become a leading member of The Company by 1592, who was soon to be an alderman and a Bailiff with a son studying at Cambridge University. Here he is in his younger days, already one of the godly followers of Master Gifford. He was open to the charge of assaulting a clergyman who was at that time an Official in the 'bawdy courts' of the bishops who sought to entrap and silence such ministers as his chosen pastor. It was a clear case for Pratt's excommunication and for this offence he was committed first to the town gaol and then to Newgate Gaol where he gave bond for his future obedience to the laws ecclesiastical. His case was not formally recorded by the town clerk and the sentence on him is known only from a chance observation in 1594. Possibly another townsman, John Morris, referred to him (also in 1594) when complaining about the partiality shown by the Bailiffs in the exercise of their authority, 'for that they would not remove persons excommunicate (as they said) out of the church and imprison them', to which the Bailiffs replied that they 'had neither sufficient notice nor lawful warrant so to do'.

In the Corporation's version of the bell ringing incident there is also an interesting 'addendum' in which the Bailiffs alleged that management of the belfry was no business of the vicar and another of his accusers' allegations suggests that he had experienced other tiffs with The Company about the ringing his church's bells:

'You ... have quarrelled and with unseemly speeches reviled many, as namely Richard Josua, being Bailiff, terming him *ould rotten wolfe* with other bitter reproaches, when he the said Bailiff did but deny (for some just cause) the ringing of an eight-of-clock bell in the parish of All Saints, when you — having nothing to do in the matter — would appoint it to be rung'.

Between Master Frith's demonstration (January 1592) and the December 1592 bell ringing episode there was a Midsummer bye-round concerning an ageing wool comber of Maldon, Thomas Harding, who acted also as an Apparitor of the Essex Archdeaconry courts (that is, he delivered summonses to appear in the court). He had fallen foul of Alderman William Browning during a silly argument over the alderman's opinion of the militia who had been assembled at Tilbury in the Armada Year 1588. Harding alleged that the alderman 'did report that there were none at Tilbury Camp but rogues and rascals' and since Harding himself had been one of the soldiers he had retaliated by calling Alderman Browning 'a rebel and not the Queen's friend'. For this clear case of Opprobrium he was gaoled. When

Robert Palmer as Official held court at Great Baddow, Midsummer 1592, his apparitor was still in prison and in his place there came Edmund Hunt who announced this to the court. A man from Great Waltham (Robert Palmer's former parish) asked if this Master Browning was still a Bailiff or a Justice and when Hunt said 'Yea' the response was:

> 'Then if he spake such words he is neither meet to be a Bailiff or Justice but deserveth rather to be hanged'.

In December 1592, immediately after he had used his Official-ship to break the order for his and Gifford's preaching and confront The Company Robert Palmer mounted his main attack on them with a strange argument about 'popular election of ministers' which seems to have been his public assertion that he had a larger following in Maldon than the town preacher. He was reported to have argued 'that ministers ought to be chosen by the voices of the people, asserting moreover — very dangerously against the peace of the Church — that such ministers as were not chosen by the voice of the people were no ministers to them over whom they should be set'.

This was taken as an attack on The Company's patronage and protection of George Gifford. In many towns it had proved to be an obstacle to the Puritan movement that the parishes were usually impropriate to laymen who exercised their right of presentation without reference to local wishes. By their arrangement with the Franke family, the lay impropriators of All Saints' and St Peter's parishes, The Company had from 1582 possessed the power of presentation. Now a vicar 'intruded' by a bishop over The Company's heads was rousing the disaffected in the town to stir themselves against a clique of Puritans.

## MASTER PALMER'S SUPPORTERS

He must have aroused an immediate response from his auditors, for the Bailiffs later argued that he had been forced to retract his words. 'Since the first of December 1592 you have not only denied that doctrine in the pulpit (which had been well) but denied that ever you taught any such thing. And so many that heard you teach it were persuaded that you make no conscience of lying, that durst so openly tell so manifest a lie. And since that time also you have in private speech confessed that you did indeed preach for popular election, saying that Master Calvin led you awry...'

To his side the vicar gathered several men disenchanted with their Corporation. One was a former Bailiff, William Soan, who had been ejected from The Company in 1586. Another was mine host of the New Inn, John Spigurnell, in whose house

Palmer was wont to play cards. Master John Morris, a clothier, a Yorkshireman, a member of The Company 1567-1583 and in that time thrice a Bailiff was another supporter, and John Lock, a scrivener who had been disbarred from presenting pleas in the borough court. All these were also supporters of one Walter Lovell, for whom the Bailiffs were to have a particular dislike (as will be seen) but each had his own grudge against the Corporation and each added to Master Palmer's grievances his own charge of mis-government, partiality or separatism. In Master William Soan's case he had been ejected from The Company immediately after being a Bailiff (1585) and then, as usual, one of the Justices of the Peace. Apparently he believed he knew better than the elders of that society how borough government should be conducted and in 1586 he 'writ a discourse according to his fancy and the same sent to Master Vernon and Master Garrington, then Bailiffs, who (seeing his vain folly) returned him answer according to the same'. What a pity this treatise on magistracy has not survived. Its rejection hurt his pride and thereafter he devoted his energies to the frustration of the course of government: whilst still a justice he ordered the delivery from gaol of a man imprisoned by the Bailiffs and,

> 'for that he could not have every matter ordered and disposed to his liking, grew so haughty and contemptuous, stirring up such trouble and contention amongst The Company at every meeting, not only to the great disquietness of the whole town, that the said Company dismissed him of their society and put him out of the Town Hall'.

He had also obstructed the View of Frankpledge by refusing to let his servants and children attend and he was also given to calling members of the Corporation 'asses' and 'dolts' and publicly 'wishing the government of the town were in other men's hands'. Above all he fell foul of The Company's 'father', Alderman William Vernon who, despite his seniority had been treated to a dissertation on how the borough ought to be governed and had been publically called a knave by Master Soan.

John Morris had also been accused of contemptuous behaviour after his removal from the Corporation. His remarks about the excommunication of John Pratt has been noted above, and also his argument that the Bailiffs had brought the town into disrepute by rebuking a company of actors for an unlicensed performance on a Sunday evening, and it was on that issue that he and The Company had parted. When he had said his piece on that matter he had stormed out of the Moot Hall but as he went he was clearly heard to say of them 'A sort of precisians and Brownists' and he also laid the blame for the antagonism towards Master Palmer on the Corporation:

> 'Master Morris saith that when the prayers are read in the church no man answereth [Amen] for that he sayeth in his opinion if any should do so they should be scorned by Master Gifford's favourers'.

216

So also said John Spigurnell of the New Inn, in whose estimation 'there is a great faction in the town of Maldon, that the like is not in any town in England'. That situation he blamed on 'Master Gifford's favourers ... whereby it appeareth he directly chargeth the Bailiffs and governors to make the factions, being [themselves] Master Gifford's favourers'.

Such attacks chimed in with the vicar's personal crusade against the men who wished to dispose of his belfry and his pulpit as if those were their own property. The moment for him to speak out again came in January 1594 when the annual Court of Election had just been held. One of the Bailiffs chosen then was old Alderman Vernon − no friend to Master Palmer's supporters − and the other was a newcomer to the borough and by reputation a Puritan, John Brooke.

On the Sunday which followed this Court of Election of 1594 Master Palmer's sermon to the Corporation made direct and specific criticisms of the Bailiffs who had been chosen. A joiner named Jeremy Pledger testified that the vicar announced 'that they had chosen one that was a schismatic, and that there many more in the town of Maldon,' while the bell-ringer Richard Williams, a headburgess, affirmed that the vicar had said 'that such as were chosen Bailiffs were young men, greenheads, schismatics, and many more in this place were schismatics and factious persons.' In the summary of the articles deposed against Robert Palmer before the High Commission soon after this sermon this charge was summarised thus:

> 'the Sabbath day next after the Bailiffs were chosen [he] reproved the choice of the said Bailiffs and, charging the town with Anabaptism and faction, he charged one of the Bailiffs to be not only young and intemperate but also a favourer of such factious persons.'

The composition of The Company at this time will be examined shortly in the light of those remarks on its membership. For the moment it must be noted that this sermon must have been heard by a great part of the residents of Maldon. The accounts of the dispute point clearly to one man as the objective of the vicar's accusations: Master John Brooke, who had only entered the Corporation in 1592 and was already a Bailiff. He was named as a schismatic. With Brooke, however, the vicar associated poor George Gifford, whom he termed in the course of this outspoken sermon 'a hypocrite ... one that dealeth knavishly ...a maintainer of factious persons ... an intruder.' And the collection of his remarks presented for the High Commission's consideration ends roundly with the statement that 'many other in the town of Maldon, which are obedient to the laws [the Bailiffs and aldermen] you term schismatics and factious.'

All the vicar's epithets: 'schismatics,' 'young men,' 'greenheads' (that is, inexperienced), 'intemperate' and 'factious' correspond interestingly with the early seventeenth century definitions of Puritans as those who refused to conform without question, or to accept the settled establishment of the Church of England, who campaigned for reforms and were 'ever discontented with the present government.' John Morris' jibe at The Company – 'a sort of Precisians' – carried the same social and political implications rather than the ecclesiastical meaning of observing scrupulously the outward forms of religious affairs, for he had been referring to the Bailiffs' inhospitable attitude towards noblemen's companies of actors. Palmer also called The Company 'hypocrites' which was another frequent accusation: 'the hollow crew,' 'the counterfeit elect,' whose characteristics have formed a literary tradition from Malvolio down to Mr Slope. The comments on The Company as 'a few base aldermen' and 'such as loved not gentlemen' also echo contemporary allegations that Puritans were base-born and they bring the matter home to the composition of the Corporation and its pretensions within the borough.

Professor Collinson and Dr Paul Slack have drawn attention to very similar situations arising out of two later and better known confrontations, in Norwich around 1607 and at Salisbury in 1633, each between a Puritan magistracy and consortia of disaffected townspeople with gentry and others of the neighbourhood. In each case it was the magistrates, with their preachers, who were accused of being factious. Tradition has almost conditioned us to suppose that Puritans were instinctive revolutionaries. They were not necessarily so, especially in these early years. Two of Master Palmer's epithets can be certainly be ignored: The Company contained no Anabaptists, the universally feared extremists of the Reformation, it contained no Brownists, followers of Robert Browne who were prepared to separate themselves from the Church of England and adopt a fully Presbyterian structure of congregations with elected ministers. George Gifford was the man these Maldon Puritans followed and he was certainly no Separatist, even though his ideals for a reformed Church, the subject-matter of the meetings he held with the Braintree Classis, the Dedham Conference, at the private assemblies of ministers in London and Cambridge, were the goals of the presbyterian movement of Elizabethan England. But 'he never used conventicles but ever preached and catechised in the church' wrote John Strype, and in 1590 and 1591 he had attacked the movements towards independent congregations in three pamphlets:

*A Plain Declaration that our Brownists be full Donatists*
*A Short Treatise against the Donatists of England*
*A Short Reply unto H. Barrow and J. Greenwood.*

Nevertheless he did favour the creation of Puritan cells, such as now existed within The Company and among the townspeople of Maldon, which would form a church within the Church, be the leaven in the lump.

218

An analysis of a list of the voters when John Brooke was elected an alderman (September 1592) and of the depositions made by sixteen witnesses before the High Commission in 1594 — interrogatories *ex parte* Palmer — combined with the evidence of bequests not only shows who the people were against whom Master Palmer had launched his attack from the pulpit, it also indicates a very clear split between those who were members of The Company, or associated with them, and a quite distinct group who were indeed inclined to Separation. Twenty two men and one widow formed a closely associated religious family who each, or in two's and three's but never altogether, met with George Gifford for prayer and bible study, and sometimes for supper, who each provided support for godly widows, bequeathed each other rings for remembrance, bibles, books of sermons or commentaries, and witnessed each others' wills.

Five members of the Corporation of 1594 and three future members belonged to this group. The most prominent of them was John Maldon, who appears as having the most extensive links with all the other twenty two. He was thirty years old in 1594 and had been brought into The Company when he was twenty eight. It may be remembered from earlier parts of this study that he was an immigrant haberdasher from Chelmsford and the founder of an influential freeman family in the borough. John Pratt, the tailor and the man principally accused of assaulting the vicar, was another of the group and also a young man. These two at least qualify for the epithet 'young men' and 'greenheads' but many of Gifford's flock were elderly, and they were the most influential. In particular there was William Rochell, a headburgess in 1593 and 1594, whose will (he died in 1594) included legacies to George Gifford, 'preacher of Maldon,' and to Gifford's 'shadow' Ralph Hawdon of Langford, to John Pratt and Alderman Brooke, and to Henry Hart and John Clark who, like Rochell, were newcomers to The Company. This William Rochell had obtained his freedom of the borough by his marriage to the widow of Alderman Richard Josua — the 'old rotten wolf' of Palmer's sermon — and she was the daughter of that Alderman Bantoft who had tried to prevent Master Frith's interruption of George Gifford's sermon. When Rochell died his widow made a third marriage, this time with a Suffolk gentleman named John Martin. He in turn became a member of the Corporation (1595) and — outdoing John Brooke — he was immediately promoted to be one of the two Bailiffs, to accompany his father-in-law William Bantoft. Like Rochell this Martin made bequests to Gifford and Hawdon and must be counted as one of the godly of Maldon in this particular group. It must be noted, too, that despite seniority in age, these men were also 'greenheads' in government, for the longest-serving (Andrew Momford) had been in The Company for only eleven years, whilst Ralph Breeder, one of the Bailiffs of 1592, had served only seven years, Thomas Walker (the other Bailiff of 1592) had served three and Richard Williams, the bell-ringer with Pratt, was fifty four years old in 1592 but a headburgess for only three years.

219

*Schismatic* can be more fitly presumed to apply, in its religious sense, to a second group of Master Gifford's followers, eight men whose replies to questions revealed little association with the first group and little with each other except that they had all prayed with one of their number, Anthony Topley or Topliffe. They met in two's or three's haphazardly, as when Anthony Topley invited Richard Scott to accompany him 'by chance, once or twice in the evening before he usually went to prayer' or when he 'did bid one Henry Matthews to supper one night with him, and that after supper he stayed until that he had said prayers; but denieth that ever there were any more at one time than the said Richard Scott with him.' In fact Topley declared that he usually prayed alone ('unless at one time when he was not very well he desired the said Richard Scott to pray for him'). Remarks made by one of the vicar's supporters, William Soan, indicate that Topley was regarded as independent of the larger group, saying to him when he heard that Topley was being produced to testify before the High Commission 'that he had joined himself with a sort of factious fellows' and remarking on another occasion to Topley 'when he [Soan] hath perceived anything done or ordered by the governors to his misliking, that he knew who did pain that to be done, saying it was G.G. dwelling above.' In fact Richard Scott, a Wakefield man by origin, was most probably the leader in this little group. In 1603 he and a Thomas Powell were brought before the Archdeacon of Essex as 'vehemently suspected to be Brownists' and as having failed to attend Divine Service in their parish church for six months, nor to have received Holy Communion once in the past year. And indeed Richard Scott eventually took an oath of allegiance to the Crown (in 1613) by which he declared himself to be a Brownist.

In examining the vicar's claim that the Bailiffs and aldermen and the rest of their Company were factious sectarians, it can be seen that he was quite wrong. The only followers of Master Gifford in 1592, 1593 or 1594 who were likely to be Separatists were these eight men led by Topley and Scott, and none of them were members of the Corporation.

Nevertheless, the vicar's supporters shared his particular dislike of the new alderman, John Brooke, and well before the sermon they had been openly alleging that he was an enemy of the Established Church. Both John Morris and William Soan were cited as encouragers of one Walter Lovell, 'a troublesome and quarrelsome and contentious fellow' who was wont to call The Company 'cannibals' and 'scrape balls.' (He was in fact described as a gentleman and a surgeon in the record of his bail of £20 for good behaviour toward John Brooke and John Pratt, no mere' fellow.') In May 1593 this Lovell had been standing at the street door of his house as Alderman Brooke came by. When the alderman drew level, Lovell 'seemed to make a leg or curtsey unto him divers times' and when Brooke asked what was meant by that, Lovell had replied 'I am as honest a man as you.' Brooke remarked that unlike Lovell, he was no quarreller nor 'brabbler' and Lovell then said

> 'You are a knave, a Puritan, a Precisian and a Brownist, and there be many such Brownists in this town.'

All this was confirmed by John Stretton who just happened to look out from his shop in time to witness the surgeon using 'very hot speech' to the alderman. (Indeed, how many at other doors entertained themselves with this piece of alderman-baiting?) When Stretton enquired why he had behaved thus, Walter Lovell repeated his accusations,

> 'For,' saith he, 'there are divers of such fellows in the town who will be rooted out ere it be long.'

Having voiced the opinion of one section of the townsfolk, having 'endeavoured to stir up strife between the townsmen and the government' and having accused a headburgess of assault within his church, Master Palmer rounded-off with a complaint to the Archbishop himself. That forced The Company to take action against him because, first, he accused the Bailiffs of threatening him physically ('the Bailiffs had put him in fear of his life and had beset the church doors for him') and, second, he implied their disloyalty to the laws ecclesiastical in his allegation, similar to the observation of John Morris, 'that there was an universal dumbness in the church at time of Common Prayer and that none in the church answered [Amen] unto the prayers that were read.'

Thus dissension came to a head in the winter of 1594. Its roots stretched back to the 1580s, it had brewed steadily since 1592 and now The Company turned upon its critics. They complained to the Privy Council, which ordered the matter to be investigated by the Archbishop in the Court of High Commission and it is their accusations to that court which have supplied part of the information about the course of these troubles.

## THE COMPANY AND THE TOWNSMEN

Whilst they were opening proceedings before the High Commission the aldermen also prepared a case against their disaffected townsmen, not only Masters Morris, Soan and Spigurnell but others who had taken the opportunity to pile more grievances onto the complaints of separatism. In particular The Company had to deal with a cousin of John Spigurnell, one Thomas Spigurnell, who was the stipendiary curate of St Mary's parish and whose professional fitness it was at pains to belittle. The Corporation's description of him as 'sometimes apprentice with a book-binder, after a vagrant peddler, then a ballad-singer and teller, and now a minister and alehousekeeper in Maldon' occurs in the case they built against him:

> 'A Brief Collection of such slanderous matters arising against the present governors and government of the said borough, devised by certain common disturbers of the peace and quiet estate of the same, pretended to be informed unto certain persons of worship within this County (by way of complaint) to seek reformation but rather, more probably to be conjectured, tending to stir up the commons of the town to oppose themselves against the same governors and government and to cause a tumult and uproar within the same town, set down in writing and attempted to be put into practice by Thomas Spickernell ...'

Here they listed three aspects of this priest's agitation, by which they thought he had attempted to overthrow them.

His first allegation was that the common pastures — the Portman Marsh and the Town Downs — had been enclosed against the wishes of the townsmen and were being, he claimed, leased deliberately on very low rents for very long terms. True or not (and he could only claim that this policy had begun some sixty years before) such a complaint was likely to incite riots against enclosure, for his accusers claimed that he had told the freemen how they could 'of their own authority enter and dispossess the tenant [of the marshland] and use the same as in old former times.' His additional claim that the Bailiffs had closed off rights of way across the Downs was, they argued, 'tending thereby (as it may be presumed) to procure the under sort of the people unlawfully to assemble, and with violence to un-close and lay open the same ground.'

Actions such as that had taken men before the Court of Star Chamber. In addition Thomas Spigurnell was alleged to have spread about the town two further grievances calculated to disaffect the 'under sort' of people. He complained about the officiousness with which officers of The Company were exercising their authority. 'There is no penal statute' he was alleged to have said 'but the same is executed upon them to the uttermost;' they levied excessive fines on 'foreigners' for the right to trade in Maldon and upon inhabitants for 'hogs going in the streets and for many other small matters and trifles.' He also pointed out (quite correctly) that the feasts which The Company held at the Quarter Sessions, and with commissioners after the fixing of subsidies, were paid out of public funds. This was a shrewd blow if the poorer people stood outside the Blue Boar Inn (as the people of Casterbridge gathered to watch Mr Henshaw's mayoral dinners) to gaze as the corporation and their preacher or commissioner guests feasted within and, long-standing custom though it was, the Bailiffs recognised that this comment was likely to 'inflame the hearts of the commons of the town with ire and move them to murmur and grudge against the governors' as this collection of slanders puts it. (It may be noted that one bill from the Blue Boar, for the dinner given to three subsidy commissioners in 1625, amounted to £4 2s 3d and contained twenty two items.) A haberdasher, Edmund Hunt − he who had provoked comment by outsiders at Great Baddow − added the weight of his opinion to the general resentment in June 1594 by saying that 'the cheer of the town was lost and the liberties of none effect' and so had the disbarred scrivener John Lock 'used the means to persuade the people that the cheer of the town was lost and the liberties of no force; very dangerous to the stirring up of lewd persons to resist authority.'

So far the term 'The Company' has been used as if its members did all stand together. Now it seems that they did not. Elias Nicholl's 'great breach' really had come to pass. 'Two or three' headburgesses (whose names are nowhere given) joined forces with eight disaffected freemen and disassociated themselves from two more lawsuits which their Company had just begun in its own defence. One was the suit against Master Palmer, the other was against Jasper Smith who had accused the magistrates of imprisoning him unjustly. 'Finding themselves grieved with many things' these headburgesses had written a complaint to the Privy Council because they were convinced that both lawsuits had been commenced by Master Vernon and Master Brooke for personal reasons, 'out of pure malice' and 'not for any just cause.' Thus they called into question the principle of corporate responsibility which should have been one of the great strengths of The Company. Indeed, that ubiquitous authorisation 'at Master Bailiffs' commandment' in the chamberlains' account rolls had always pointed to this weakness in the Corporation's management of its affairs, especially as now the Bailiffs began to change their tune and claim that they had only acted under the advice of all their Company, 'being the common council of the town' which had 'the whole of the ordering and disposing of the matters and affairs that are to be dealt withal within the said borough.'

The really dangerous effect of these men's disaffection was to open the very Secrets of the Borough for outsiders' inspection and it is not surprising that there are now noticeable gaps in the borough archives − court registers, chamberlains' accounts − which must have been brought out of the Charterhouse within the Moot Hall for inspection by a commission of four local Essex gentry appointed by the Privy Council to examine the accounts for the six years last past (1588-93). Worse still, the commission upheld the dissidents and concluded that some part of the legal costs of these actions had been unjustifiably borne by the common chest although they were essentially personal lawsuits. The Bailiffs were ordered to repay an appropriate sum to the chest.

According to the writer of the memorandum which relates this episode these disaffected persons numbered only eight out of eighty freemen, only two or three in The Company's twenty four men. A memorandum on the activities of Masters

223

Soan, Morris, Lock and John Spigurnell nevertheless admits to the existence of a much more considerable disaffection at large in the town and even threatening, with the aid of dissenters among the 'governors' to overthrow the common council. They had 'fained to themselves a counterfeit corporation' which, 'the more to deface the lawful government of the town' they claimed already gave them 'a greater Hall than the Bailiffs [had].' Thus in the Spring and Summer of 1594 did the vicar's assault-by-sermon of January extend dissension from a quarrel between himself, the Bailiffs and the town preacher into a threat of civil disobedience, open contempt for the common council of the borough and secession among the ruling group. Worse still, it had become news throughout the town's market area. In places where they talked men were discussing the great breach in the proud borough's Company of governors. Master Gifford saw parallels between the events of his own time and those in *Revelation*. How did he and his favourers see this part of the text? 'Babylon the great is fallen, is fallen, and is become the habitation of devils, and the hold of every foul spirit ... Come out of her, my people, that ye be not partakers of her sins and that ye receive not of her plagues'. In manor houses and in hunting parties where country gentry met, at parish gatherings after Divine Service, in market places and among the merchants of London the imminent fall of The Company was the latest news:

> 'and what they [the counterfeit corporation] have consulted upon in their assemblies that might tend to the disgrace and reproach of the governors and government, and slander of the town, hath been published in the pulpit, prattled in alehouses, affirmed to personages of honour and worship, and reported both in city and country'.

When Bishop Fletcher reported to the Queen's Secretary of State, Sir Robert Cecil, on these troubles he commented that there were two issues, one ecclesiastical and the other civil. From such contemporary materials as have survived it has been possible to flesh out the complaints of the townsmen against The Company and the split within the freemen over the lawsuits raised by the Bailiffs, which were the lay quarrels; and the attempt by Master Palmer to gain full and entirely ecclesiastical control over the affairs of his parish church, which was the religious quarrel. When the vicar transferred his animosity from Master Gifford to the Corporation, mounting an outright attack on its procedure, its membership, its authority, he managed to overlay the two issues and this too the bishop had noted. The clergy, he said, took part on both sides 'as well in matters of popular quarrels as points of doctrine'. Having been a town preacher himself (at Rye, 1575-81) Bishop Fletcher probably understood instinctively the nature of Maldon's troubles but some three hundred years later the causes of dissension are of at least as much interest as the narrative. These localised disputes and protests were considered by contemporaries sufficiently dangerous to the fabric of society for the Privy Council to concern itself in their speedy settlement, regarding the factious disputes at

Doncaster, for example, as 'a most un-Christian thing' which might even 'overthrow the town'. So we are not inclined to accept the good Bishop's mollifying comment to Master Secretary Cecil as a sufficient explanation. The reasons for the clerical storms in Maldon have been already considered; what about these disaffected headburgesses and aldermen? and why did that obscure clerk's, Thomas Spigurnell's, agitation work so well?

One of the traditional causes of unrest and riot can be ruled out immediately. The harvests of the early 1590's (one has to base this on what is known of the national trend) had been satisfactory, there had been enough grain and prices had not risen sharply. Dissension had rumbled on in Maldon's streets and churches during a recovering agricultural period between the two very bad harvests of 1586 and 1596, so high food prices, near-starvation for the poorer people (and it has been suggested that their number was slight in this town) would not seem to have caused the outburst of defiance and agitation against The Company. Nor would sharp changes in seasonal food prices have explained the strangely drawn-out nature of the troubles. It is also unlikely that there was any substance to Spigurnell's allegations about the enclosure of common pastures, except that enclosure, signifying robbing the poor of their rights, was a potent rallying point for any social disorder, an expression of communal unease, of suspicions that the powerful and the privileged were failing to uphold the trust imposed by their offices, that a conspiracy of rich but ignoble and tyrannical men was about to sacrifice the status of the community, trample on the rights of the commons, for their own selfish ends. Spigurnell's allegations were listened to by people who were mostly immigrant within the last twenty to thirty years: they did not know what had been the state of the common lands sixty years before; but they could believe that for a long while the members of The Company − men sworn to secrecy on admission to its membership − had been systematically going about to deprive people like themselves of their customary rights.

It has been seen that there had always been a current of defiance and criticism of the Bailiffs and their officers, of Opprobrium, but whilst it had been usually directed at individuals by individuals, now there was a chorus of complaints; where once it had concerned isolated incidents, private outrage, now it concerned communal grievances and it was a group of 'governors' at whom the complaints and contempt were directed. The protests were also concerned with a wider range of grievances: that the magistrates were far too rigorous over trifling breaches of the bye-laws; that The Company feasted itself out of public money; that it defrauded people of their common rights and victimised the poor, such as elderly widows who foraged for firewood from the hedges; that it inhibited the trade of 'foreign' newcomers by imposing fines heavier than was customary for the right to open shops; that it was bent on destroying the good name of the town. Injustice, arbitrary fines, haughtiness, corruption were the themes then, as ever, buzzing in the taverns and over the shop-boards and in the homes of Maldon's inhabitants.

225

To this add the charge that the Corporation was filled with 'intemperate' and 'factious' young, inexperienced men who were recent newcomers. Of all the Corporation's members the men who most fitted this description in the experience of the ordinary townsman were the Affeirors. Their's was an office in which young headburgesses had scope for some independent action; their duty was to sit in committee after the Quarter Sessions to assess the fines payable for each of the day's convictions. Within the bounds of custom they settled amercements as they saw fit and the charge delivered to them when they commenced work defined their duties thus:

> 'truly to affure and set all manner of amercements; to high no man for malice; to low no man for love; but to set every man after the quality of the trespass'.

A zealous group of Affeirors hoping to find the ultimate deterrent for the regular petty offender was thus able to increase amercements according to its judgement. Here is an explanation of the complaint about levying excessive fines 'for small matters and trifles'. Master Gifford's auditors who were in The Company saw their chance to act in the cause of the reformation of society and to them the fines they set may have seemed commensurate with the wickedness of the offences; 'the zeal of Thine house has eaten me up' these godly young affeirors might have said; that sage Town Preacher of Ipswich, Samuel Ward, pressing the case for an uncorrupt and assiduous magistracy at all levels of government (in *Jethros Justice of Peace* preached in 1618) warned the next generation against any manner of slackness:

> 'What can the Superiors do if the Inferior inform not? what can the eye do if the hand and foot be crooked? ... If Pleaders and Attorneys will colour and gloze, if the Clerks and Pen-men make false records, may not any of these disturb or pervert Justice? If the least finger or toe of this body be distorted − I mean Jailer or Serjeant − or any other that should execute Justice be remiss and slack, then must the Dutchman's proverb be verified: "Look what the Bell is without the Clapper". Thus we see in this curious clockwork of Justice, the least pin or wheel amiss may distemper and disorder all'.

How did their victims view their decisions? 'Hypocrites' was one of the abusive epithets cast at this Company by Master Palmer. Moreover, their zeal carried them beyond the influences of social rank; they set their fines as zealously on their superiors, the gentry resident in the town, as they did on the poorer inhabitants. When Master Harris' bull got loose in the High Street from its pen at The Friars Mansion he was presented along with humbler offenders. This Thomas Harris, a gentleman indeed, an M.P. and certainly the wealthiest inhabitant of the town, was presented at a Quarter Sessions with such ne'er-do-wells among the poorer folk as the constables had arrested 'for that he the said Thomas Harris was drunk within this borough, saying as he went down [the] street from Master Bailiff, "Here is a Bailiff indeed, a hog-grubber to shut his doors against a poor man". For which offence of drunkenness the said Thomas paid five shillings to the use of the poor of the said parish of St Peter's'. The comments of Master John Shipton about the magistrates being 'boors and clowns' when he too was charged with drunkenness, suggests the response of this class of inhabitant to the presumptions of these young tradesmen. Whilst they were in office a gentleman was advised to be on his guard. And it was not an egalitarian society: the presence of wealthy men and women with perhaps several in their households meant trade for all, for the butchers, the shoemakers, glovers and tailors, vintners and brewers, cutlers, gunsmiths, glaziers and painters. A group of Affeirors who 'loved not gentlemen' was bad news. In return the gentry defended their touchy sense of honour by openly declaring their contempt of this low-born Company.

As for the dissidents within or recently departed from the Corporation's ranks, they may well have sensed the existence of an inner group, the new blood which was thrusting them aside to take over the aldermanic bench so that its rigorous policy towards wickedness might be the more quickly and thoroughly implemented. The voting when Master John Brooke was elected a Bailiff on the death of old Richard Josua may have looked rigged to them, as it does now; a rushed affair engineered to secure the place for these young men's candidate. For when the voters are measured by their length of membership of The Company, Brooke's supporters were by far the most recent:

| CANDIDATES | Votes given | Total Number of Years Served | Average Length of Membership |
|---|---|---|---|
| Thomas Welles glover | 2 | 16 | 8 |
| Thomas Hutt clothier | 3 | 14 | 14 |
| John Brooke yeoman | 9 | 47 | 5 |
| Members Not Voting: | 7 | 100 | 14 |
| All: | 21 | 177 | 8 |

*Table 8 Voting Measured by Years of Membership of the Corporation, 5 September 1592.*

Four of the non-voters were aldermen, three of them with over twenty years' service each, one of them Bailiff William Vernon whose abstention is most noteworthy. The other three were headburgesses, of whom two had, it states on the voting list, not been given warning to attend the meeting, whilst John Spigurnell of the New Inn, whose vote certainly would not have gone to Master Brooke, had been absent 'on his urgent business' when the voting took place.

There had surely been much to be said in favour of either Thomas Welles, for nine years a headburgess and minor official, an established glover and leather trader with two sons in the business, or of Thomas Hutt, who had been a headburgess for ten years and had become a clothier rather than the shearman that he was when admitted to the freedom. Tradition would have prescribed either of them rather than John Brooke to fill the vacancy on the aldermen's bench. But neither of them can be found to have had any personal attachment to Master Gifford. As with the nominations of George Gifford and Mark Wiersdale to be Vicar of All Saints', a conspiracy theory looms over the intrusion of Master Brooke, of manoeuvering to push aside the older members of the Corporation who would have retained a share in the magistracy of the borough for men not absolutely affiliated to a reformation of manners which young and ardent followers of the town's Preacher were anxious to enforce. If so, then a need for devious procedures may indicate how weak in Maldon the Puritans actually were.

## ECCLESIASTICAL OUTCOME

The final concord effected for these troubles would be less than adequately documented if there had not survived an account by an independent and well-qualified local witness who had good cause to provide his superior with a commentary on the situation after 1594. It is a letter written by William Arthur, the stipendiary curate of St Mary's Church, to his master the Dean of Westminster on New Year's Day (25 March) 1596. He reported first that the Bishop of London had established a rota for the preaching of the two clerics and that Gifford's special Wednesday sermons were to be discontinued; and unlike the Bishop's claim to have 'so travailed' at his Primary Visitation in 1595 that he had 'put moderation to their perturbations and peace to their places', this informant considered that the Bishop had barely managed to stop the dissension from growing yet more extreme:

> 'my lord of London in his late Visitation compounded rather than cured (and that with very much ado) the envious brawls and controversies between Master Palmer and Master Gifford, with these conditions and orders prescribed and to be kept on both parts, viz:
> that they should by turns preach on Saturdays, Sundays and Holy Days

228

and that when the one did preach on Sundays the other should catechize
[in] the afternoons, et cetera;
Master G. his wonted Wednesdays sermons utterly to cease;
By which order his L[ordship] no doubt hoped to remedy the schism and
take away the dangerous factions here among us, but how happily may it
please your worship now to hear ...'

The personal quarrel between the two clergymen seems to have been settled largely
to Gifford's material benefit, for his will shows that Master Palmer had been
required to concede to him some part of the vicarage house and some share of
the benefice's income, since Gifford bequeathed to Alderman John Brooke (no
less) his lease, held 'by demise and grant of Robert Palmer, vicar of All Saints'
and Saint Peter's ... of and in the vicarage house, tithes, profits and other things
thereby letten and devised', though this will also shows that Gifford was not resident
there since he bequeathed to his wife Agnes 'the messuage where I now dwell'
with the proceeds of its sale after her death to the benefit of their children.

Clearly Master Palmer came off poorly; he remained as Vicar on rather less than
two thirds of his original stipend; he had no better than parity with Master Gifford
as preacher in the town, but 'if Master Gifford preach[es] the church is full, but
if the other − not half so'; and very quickly his old adversaries, the Puritan group
− led by no less than five of the six Aldermen, Masters Brooke, Breeder, Burles,
Garrington and Vernon (who were all appointed overseers of Gifford's will) −
began to pester the vicar to permit George Gifford to preach in All Saints' church
on Wednesdays, 'promising Master Palmer money for his consent, which he utterly
refused' whilst they rejected his wry offer to seek the Bishop's permission to deliver
a mid-week sermon himself. ('To preach on those days himself to his own flock
that desired so much teaching; which they as obstinately refused except Master
G. might do it'.) Foiled, they began to concoct yet another stratagem to get around
those episcopal regulations which since 1584 had deprived Master Gifford of his
own benefice and pulpit.

Their scheme was the principal reason for this curate's letter to the Dean, for these
importunate Puritans turned their attention to St Mary's Church, asking Master
Arthur to permit Master Gifford's Wednesday sermons to be preached there.
Moreover, chance put in their way an opportunity of which they thought to make
much capital. The tower of the church collapsed, destroying the roof over some
part of the nave:

'as men never satisfied ... they have been as earnestly in hand with me to
suffer him to preach weekly in St Mary's, as it were in despite of Master
Palmer (I will not say of my Lord [Bishop] himself), and offering upon

that condition ten pounds or a main sum toward the setting up again of our steeple stairs and church roof, born down with the fall thereof the very Wednesday before Shrove Sunday last, which is thought will cost some three score pounds to re-edify, a charge (except your Worship stick both a good and great stock therein) will never be gotten out of the parishioners' purses ...'

Except for Master Thomas Hutt − now at last an alderman (the only one not of Gifford's flock) and in 1596 one of the two Bailiffs − the parishioners refused to contribute towards the repair work and rebuilding unless their favourite preacher was accommodated with its pulpit. The curate listed their alternative suggestions: 'some bid "Let it all fall, that the parish may fall to Master Gifford"; other[s] would have it (to save their own purses) the churches sold; other[s] say "The vestry [should be] pulled down to help"' and one of the aldermen (un-named) who was paying only 6s 8d annually (£0.33) for his lease of a house owned by the parish, and who was sub-letting it for no less than thirty shillings (£1.50), 'and such in reason as I think should be most liberal' offered a contemptible 3s 4d (about £0.16) towards the rebuilding. 'Which (their request) if I should rashly have yielded to [it] I feared would breed a worse schism and faction than ever we had'. The stratagem failed. Gifford remained deprived and if not silenced then severely muzzled as a preacher. The rebuilding of St Mary's Church − for which funds might have been raised plentifully had it become Master Gifford's auditorium − was not undertaken until the 1620's.

Additionally the curate mentioned in his letter Gifford's friend Ralph Hawdon who was a member of the Classis Movement in Essex, a graduate like Gifford of Christ's College (though slightly junior to him) and a member of Gifford's Maldon circle. He was also a pluralist and an absentee cleric, for he was Vicar of Rayleigh − some fifteen miles south of Maldon and across the River Crouch − from 1594 until 1609 but until 1600 he was living two miles north of Maldon as vicar of Langford, and in 1600 he became Vicar of All Saints'. However, the godly of the borough and district do not appear to have held that against him. In 1594 William Rochell bequeathed £10 to 'Master Raffe Hawdon of Langford' and Hawdon's signature appears among the witnesses to that pious old man's will; he was also given £5 as 'Master Ralph Hawdon of Langford' in the will of John Martin (1599). George Gifford was similarly favoured with bequests by Rochell and Martin and it seems the two clergymen were in some kind of partnership, expressed thus by William Arthur: 'the fantastical sort run by flocks two or three miles off to one Ralph Hawdon, another Gifford (so known to be this two-seven years) or rather the same as well in consent for his part as conceit for theirs', to whose sermons Gifford's followers went whenever Master Palmer had his turn for preaching.

In 1600 George Gifford and Robert Palmer both died and by their almost simultaneous decease the *impasse* resolved itself. On the one hand it might seem that the Puritans won decisively, for the patron of All Saints' and St Peter's Vicarage was still the Richard Franke who had presented Gifford and Wiersdale in the 1580's and who was son-in-law to our Puritans' Alderman William Vernon. The Bishop of London had no cause to object to his nomination for Master Palmer's vacant benefice and Ralph Hawdon took the long-coveted place. As Elisha's mantle fell to him, so did the gifts, the patronage and the respect which the pious townsmen had formerly bestowed on their great preacher Gifford.

And to the Corporation there was delegated for the next sixty years the effective patronage of this benefice. Such a prize was sought after but unattainable in many other towns. (Of course, it was a make-shift, second-best approximation which lasted only as long as the real patron would permit.) In 1619, as in 1600, the Corporation was privileged to make its own choice of minister and the two candidates who underwent 'interviews by sermon' were no less than a Fellow of Christ's College at Cambridge, Israel Hewitt, and the 'plain and powerful' John Rogers, Vicar of Dedham, one of the most celebrated of Puritan preachers. Maldon's Corporation paid their travelling expenses and dined each after hearing his sermon; 3s 4d was paid 'to Peter Christmas [a freeman] for horse hire to ride after [ie. fetch] Master Hewett, a preacher' and 6s 8d was paid to the landlord of the Star Inn at Maldon 'for the horsemeat of the said Master Hewett'. Six of The Company voted for the great thunderer of Dedham Vale; the other eighteen approved the less electrifying style of Master Hewitt, who was presented to the living, and right through his ministry, 1620-49, his material needs were assiduously superintended by the Corporation.

Indeed, there was a financial sting to this delegation of patronage. In return for the opportunity to judge between one of the most celebrated preachers in all Essex or Suffolk and a Fellow of one of the principal bastions of Puritanism in the University of Cambridge, they had to be prepared to guarantee continuing financial assistance. In 1650 the stipend of the combined vicarages was valued at £50 per annum. That was somewhat better than the national average of £43 10s 11d for vicarages but the man appointed here had to minister to two parishes and in the past had often maintained a curate to assist him. Master Hewitt retained his fellowship of Christ's College for a full year after his election as vicar and from the outset some of the parishioners subsidised his stipend: in 1623 £5 was given to him out of the borough chest 'by the commandment of Master Bailiffs and consent of the whole House toward a certain yearly contribution (meant to be given to him if it could be raised and continued) which is much diminished by the death of many which did freely give while they lived'. In 1641 they donated £3 2s 6d 'in consideration of his great pains and [in] token of their great loves and good affection towards him', and a further £10 was settled on him in 1644 in return for

*Pl.12. St Mary's Church Tower, rebuilt after 1628 following its collapse in 1596*

his series of sermons known as the Saturday Lectures. He was also paid to preach sermons preceding the Quarter Sessions courts.

John Simpson, who became c1619 the curate of St Mary's, was also able to share the bounty. Until 1642 he had to make do with chance additions to his stipend from the gifts of gentlefolk (John Tanner, a lawyer, bequeathed him ten shillings for preaching his funeral sermon; so did a yeoman, Thomas Diglitt, who referred to him as 'Preacher of St Mary's'; and Mistress Mary Muffet bequeathed him twenty shillings in gold currency to preach her funeral sermon in All Saints' Church, whilst bequeathing Mistress Simpson a holland apron edged with lace); then, during the Civil War, the Corporation began to pay him: £5 in 1642 for delivering the Saturday Lectures for six months; £2 10s 0d in 1643 for 'one quarter ended the 5th day of February last'; £2 10s 0d for the next quarter of the year.

In the aftermath of the Civil War, when both Hewitt and Simpson, were growing old a scheme was drafted to use some of the income from St Mary's Parsonage (which was a farm, not the curate's land, and had been sequestered in 1646 from Westminster Abbey's estates) to provide £150 in augmentation of both men's stipends. This was the borough's wish but the Parliamentary Committee for Plundered Ministers decided to settle a large sum on a Town Lecturer instead, rather than increase substantially the two resident clergymen's incomes. They considered Hewitt too old to give sufficient pastoral value for the extra income he was asking them to allot to him, and Simpson (though 'a godly man') they found to be 'not only aged but in respect of other weaknesses and infirmities disabled from the service of the said cure [of souls]'. After Hewitt's eventual resignation in 1650 the Corporation agreed to pay the removal costs from Romford of John Horrocks, who had just been named by the Committee as the new Town Lecturer and whom it had appointed Vicar, and also to pay for renovations to the Vicarage House, up to a total cost of £14.

Through all these men's ministries visiting Puritan clergy were regularly invited to preach to the Corporation and market folk, and to attend the Combinations of Clergy which the Corporation was pleased to subsidise. The chamberlains' accounts of the first half of the seventeenth century contain in effect a roll of those whom the Corporation was pleased to honour, names reflecting the flowering of learned and pious Anglican Protestantism in Essex and southern Suffolk: Ezekiel Culverwell of Great Stambridge (brother-in-law to Lawrence Chadderton, Master of Emmanuel College); John Rogers of Dedham; William Negus, deprived of his Rectory of Leigh on Sea in 1609, then Town Preacher of Ipswich; Purchas, Perne and Rowbotham, Joyner and Wilmot; and Master Daynes, 'Minister of God's Word at *Bakles* in Suffolk', to name but a few. For each there was wine and sugar: a quart of sack, a pottell of claret, a quarter or a half a pound's weight of sugar. Before 1600 George Gifford was the only clerk in holy orders who was also a freeman of the borough. By 1630 there were twelve, half of whom were sons of Maldon freemen and the other six had each for at least a few years made their homes in the borough and ridden out to their parishioners at Stowe Maries, Althorne, St Lawrence, Mayland, Little Baddow. For them Maldon was a professional gathering place. They were all Cambridge graduates of roughly the same age and perhaps with common interests. By living in Maldon they could help to organise the Combinations which were gatherings of clergy to hear and discuss both the techniques and the divinity of each others' sermons, occasions which had reappeared after Queen Elizabeth I's death but which were not the older Prophesyings in spirit. In Maldon, too, they could meet with gentlefolk of their own class to read and to discuss, to ride and hunt perhaps, with whom to sup.

# A 'PESTILENT NEST' OF PURITANS?: MALDON, 1600 - 1642

In many market towns of eastern England the ambitions of the Elizabethan Puritan movement were as nearly attained as in Maldon. There were local variations and each situation to some extent reflected the changing attitudes and fortunes of those powerful patrons by whom Puritans had for more than thirty years been encouraged and protected: the Hastings family in Leicestershire, Sir Edward Lewkenor, Sir Robert Jermyn and Sir John Higham in Suffolk, Lord Robert Rich, the Barringtons and Mildmays in Essex. Between such personages of great potential influence and the Corporation of Maldon there lay their agents, seeking always the maintenance of the patron's local interest. A Puritan Corporation meant (from 1584 to 1611) an assured seat in parliament for Sir Edward Lewkenor, John Butler, William Wiseman, Thomas Mildmay of Moulsham, Sir John Sammes of Langford. Thomas Cammock had the interests of his master, Lord Rich at heart whilst he was a resident of Maldon in the 1580s and '90s and somewhere behind the story of his elopement with Frances Rich, to which her brother was so strangely acquiescent, there must originally have been some allusion to his close association with this powerful patron. Puritanism began to flourish here in the 1570s when the town clerk was Master John Barnardiston, born at Kedington where, in the next generation, John's nephew Sir Nicholas Barnardiston made 'Ketton' a 'Town and Corner' where 'the Magistry and Ministry joined both together and concurred in all things for the promoting of true Piety and Godliness'. Puritanism in Maldon rose and faded parallel with these larger political interests.

Maldon had no endowed Lecturer, as some towns did, although its beneficed clergy did fulfil the role of a salaried town preacher and were often styled as such; a string of visiting divines, guests of the Corporation, also supplied a programme of Lectures. Like many of the smaller English towns, it tried to organise some private arrangements to augment its beneficed clergy's incomes, so that it could attract — and also retain — well-trained and well-spoken-of preachers. Many towns also sought but could not obtain the advowsons of their parish churches. Here the Corporation did not possess any right of presentation to the Vicarage of All Saints and St Peter but in effect it had control of the patronage (as has been seen) at no more cost than occasional 'sweeteners' such as the sugar loaf costing 22s 6d 'sent and given to Master Richard Franke, Esquire, Patron of the parishes of All Saints and St Peter' in 1621. There was also an endowment securing a salary for the Master of the town's Grammar School (by the will of Alderman Breeder, 1609). This was controlled by the Aldermen and Bailiffs — who were trustees of Breeder's Charity during their terms of office — and as they were all apparently Puritan in the first half of the century, the movement controlled the school.

So prevalent in early seventeenth century England were such attitudes about local government, manners and Protestant religious practice, that the Puritanism which one could be tempted into describing as the reigning force in so many Jacobean and Carolean market towns may have been far less a conscious policy than it now appears to have been. Corporate activity, as recorded in the surviving files of Maldon's town clerks, was directed first and foremost by statute law enacted during sixty years or more of social reform encouraged by the royal Court. The preaching of Williams, Withers and Gifford to the magistrates of Maldon from about 1566 to 1600, and as urged by Samuel Ward of Ipswich in 1618, echoed and emphasised government policy; it was successful, acceptable, because they confirmed what the ruling class wanted to believe about how their people should be governed.

Here was a town under the unexceptional control of a Puritan ruling group, whose slight abnormalities were the product of local circumstances. And, as elsewhere in the eastern counties and the midlands, its Puritanism fell short of the ideals of Elizabethan agitators. Any success which the campaign of Master Gifford's devotees might appear to have won was very limited. He had never been restored to a benefice and his own insistence on the maintenance of a national Church, his opposition to Separatism, undermined his and many of his colleagues' schemes for the establishment of a Presbyterian Church under the monarch's Supreme Governorship. By the time The Company's action against Master Palmer reached the Court of High Commission, in 1594, all of Gifford's colleagues had been forced to admit defeat. Nine had been tried in the Court of Star Chamber, the Dedham Conference had broken up. In the next ten years hope of a revival in Presbyterian fortunes faded, for although Robert Devereux, the new Earl of Essex and the Queen's favourite, posed as the great patron of the Puritans — Gifford's sermons on the *Book of the Revelation* were dedicated to him, as were many other publications by Puritan divines – he was executed in 1601 and before that the supposition that he would become the most powerful exerciser of patronage in the realm had become unlikely. When Queen Elizabeth I had died (and also these Puritans' arch opponent, Archbishop Whitgift), remaining hopes that the new king, James I, might be sympathetic to the Puritans' principal aims were dashed at the Hampton Court Conference where he rejected their appeal for a reform of the Church along Presbyterian lines. The ministries of Hawdon and Hewitt, those Maldon Combinations and the revival of sermons by visiting clergy, the enrollment of ministers of religion among the freemen, were a faded image of the kind of Christian community which George Gifford had intended.

Moreover, the movement lost its impetus. It was no longer the most radical party. The Separatists, such as (in Maldon) Richard Scott the Brownist, had taken over that role; Arminian theology was, by 1600, putting the older Calvinist doctrines on the defensive. Presbyterian leanings also became very muted. One reason for that was the success with which King James' bench of bishops (many of whom were themselves steeped in Calvinist theology) won over these radicals, so that Nicholas Bownd, pastor of the Puritan church of St Andrew in Norwich was able to publish (in 1604) an assurance to his Bishop that he and his congregation were very content 'to yield obedience to your Lordship's godly proceedings'. That sentiment was very different to the threats of disorder which hung over Bishop Aylmer's Visitation of Maldon in 1586, (even though one may suspect that a proviso lurked in the last two words of Bownd's compliments to his Bishop).

A second reason, the local one, seems to be that Master Gifford's favourers had flung themselves and their Corporation headlong against the Establishment in the 1580s and no one came off the better for persistent defiance of authority in that Queen's reign. One senses that they had learned a hard lesson and it can be seen in the chamberlains' accounts that from the time of Bishop Fletcher's Visitation (1595) The Company was at pains to show courtesy and to do honour to the officials of the Church. That may have been partly due to the acceptability of visitors such as the distinguished, locally born Samuel Harsnet (the son of a Colchester baker) who was Master of Pembroke College in Cambridge as well as being the Archdeacon of Essex. At his visitations in 1606 and 1608, sugarloaves and pottels of both sack and claret were bestowed on him by the Bailiffs, but the chamberlains recorded him as 'Master *Hassenet*', ignoring his office. In the 1624 account roll the emphasis was again placed on local distinction by the money spent on wine and sugar given 'to Master Doctor Sammes and the ministers at the Lord Bishop's Visitation'. But there were also gifts of wine and sugar and 'other courtesies' for Dr Stanhope, the Bishop's Official in 1608, for Dr Savage 'coming to the town in his visitation' in 1610, 1613, 1616, 1620 and – note the phrasing of this – no less than £8 13s 0d

236

'for the diet of the Right Reverend Father in God, the Lord Bishop of London [Dr John King] and of his officers and attendants coming in his Visitation of this town this year' (1612).

Right up to the outbreak of the Civil War these 'courtesies' were scrupulously observed.

Thwarted and compromised, Puritanism was also frustrated by the essentially personal nature of Calvinist piety. A group identity of a sort was preserved by the habit of 'gadding about' to this or that minister's sermons, by styling each other 'goodman' or 'goodwife' and by the groups which met for private worship, study and discussion just as the first Puritans of Maldon had done with Master Gifford; but such associations were essentially restricted to literate and educated men and women. Their formation was based on the social links of kinship, marriage, commercial association, rank and mutual concerns; they were prone to disruptive quarrels, easily fragmented and weakened by population mobility and, of course, by deaths, just as in 1589 the Dedham Conference was declared to have come to an end by 'the death of some of our brethren and their departure from us to other places'. The leaven in the lump tended to become a clique bonded by perceived similarities in conviction, by family obligations, by a belief that they were indeed the elect, God's peculiar people. But we must not fall into the trap of stereotyping these people and as an antidote, we may look at a Puritan group through the will, made in 1619, of John Shipton which opens a little window on the life-style of those whom Robert Palmer twenty five years before had called 'factious'.

What a curious personality appears in the diverse written references to John Shipton himself. His brother Thomas was a London grocer who managed his finances and he appears to have been himself wealthy, distributing £430 in cash among twenty six kinsfolk and close friends. He had also been brought to court and accused of public drunkenness (once only, so far as we can tell) and it was another Puritan, John Maldon, who named him as a haunter of inns and a common gamester. In return John Shipton had behaved offensively to the 'base Aldermen', the 'boors and clowns' who sat in judgement on him; he was sensitive about his gentility. Perhaps this experience had been his moment of conversion (as for young William Perkins at Cambridge, when he heard a woman point him out to her child as 'drunken Perkins') for John Shipton possessed a small library of Protestant Divinity by the time of his death and had surrounded himself with clergy to study those books effectively.

That he and his circle should be styled Puritan is confirmed by the books' Calvinist subject matter. By 1600 the doctrine of Predestination which was the corner-stone of John Calvin's theology (that Christ's death was an atonement only for the sins

237

of God's elect, of those predestined to salvation) was being defended by English Puritans against the arguments of a Dutch Calvinist, Jacobus Arminius, that He had died to atone for all mankind, that free will had been given to men by God's grace so that they might find their way to eternal salvation. William Perkins of Christ's College, Cambridge, attacked the Arminian thesis (to which Arminius wrote a reply). So did Dr George Abbot (Archbishop of Canterbury 1611-33) whose decision to send representatives of the Church of England to the Dutch Calvinist Church's Synod of Dort, where Arminianism was denounced, earned him much favour with Puritans. Another prominent defender of Calvin's doctrine was John White, rector of Barsham in Suffolk.

A man does not give his friends books of which he disapproves and John Shipton's bequests included these three anti-Arminian writers' books. There was John White's *Defence of the Way to the True Church*; books vaguely called 'Master Perkins' Works in three volumes' may have been the three volume edition of *The Workes of that famous and worthie Minister of Christ in the University of Cambridge, M[aster] W. Perkins, newly corrected according to his owne copies'* published at Cambridge in 1608; and he had 'three works of Master Doctor Abbot's, the which were by me lent to Master Toftes of Norwich, grocer' and which now found their way into the study of the learned vicar of Mundon, Andrew Cook, B.D.. The curate of St Mary's Maldon, John Simpson, received 'all Master Downham's works, the which I have' which refers to the anti-Arminian writing of Dr George Downham, Bishop of Derry from 1616. Calvin's own writings figure among these bequests ('Calvin upon the Old and New Testaments') and his successor Theodore Beza's 'Testament with the great Annotations'. The most valuable item in Shipton's library was 'Master [John Immanuel] Tremelin's Bible', the standard international Protestant translation into Latin from Hebrew and Syriac texts, which was given to John Danes, the Master of Maldon's Grammar School. It, too, was a Calvinist production. Add to these the works of late-Elizabethan Puritans, of Nicholas Bownd the Sabbatarian, Thomas Brightman, 'all the works of Doctor Willett the which I have with me ... Porlock upon the Thessalonians and Colossians ... all the works of Master Doctor Reynolds and Master Doctor Whitacres the which I have ...' and one has an outline of the viewpoint shared by the men and women to whom these volumes, already frequently loaned, were bequeathed.

A visit to the great Library which the son and grandson of members of this group, Dr Thomas Plume, gave to Maldon in 1704, is an exploration of the mentality of the seventeenth century Church of England which these people knew and had come to accept. On its shelves can be found copies of many of the publications mentioned in John Shipton's will and those described in the will of Thomas Cheese, a professional scrivener and the very competent town clerk of 1623-25: 'Master *Marlorett's* exposition upon Saint John's Gospel', Theodore Beza's 'Paraphrases

238

*Pl.13. An assembly of sixteenth and seventeeth century British and European scholarship: Thomas Plume's Library*

upon the Psalms' and Calvin's sermons on the Book of Job. The Plume Library was not assembled from Maldon people's bookshelves (indeed it was partly created by bulk-purchasing in London auctions in the later seventeenth century); it contains many works by Roman Catholic European scholars and polemicists but most of its titles were published in the period 1600-50 and the appearance of 'Sleydan's Commentary' in the booklist of Thomas Cheese hints that these Puritans were prepared to read impartially the works of all scholars. For 'Sleydan's Commentary' was a Roman Catholic history of the religious wars in Germany in the reign of the Emperor Charles V, of which an English translation was published in 1560. There can be no doubt that Thomas Cheese was a firm Protestant; so was the recipient of this book, Alderman John Soan; and so was Master Christopher Hanworth to whom it had previously been loaned.

John Shipton's will indicates the composition of a Maldon Puritan group which would study and circulate books such as these in James I's reign. Its basic component was the family, in this case his own of eleven: himself, his wife and mother, two sisters-in-law and two brothers-in-law, one sister, one brother and two nephews. There were also four of the borough aldermen and the widows of two leading personalities in the years of faction, Mistress Agnes Gifford and Mistress Elizabeth Pratt (sharing £10). In addition there were eight locally-beneficed clergymen and some friends such as Edward and Mistress Alleyn of Hatfield

Peverel. It is interesting to find in his circle the aldermen to whom he had once been so abusive: Master John Brooke, John Clark, Bailiff William Francis, Bailiff George Purchas and that it included John Soan, who was the son of that William Soan who had been so opposed to Alderman John Brooke c1592-4 and a supporter of Robert Palmer. In bequeathing a trust fund of £10 John Shipton required these four aldermen to use it 'as I have made known to the said John Soan of my mind touching the same'.

Three features of the Puritan movement in early seventeenth century Maldon are perhaps illustrated by this will. The first is that many members of Shipton's circle, including him, had entered the town subsequent to the years of dissension. Secondly, there were close links with other Puritan centres and groups. His brother was a London grocer; he had loaned his copies of George Abbot's books to 'Master Toftes of Norwich, grocer'; by his sister's marriage the Alleyne family of Hatfield Peverel and their minister, Master Stable, were members of the group; Master Andrew Cook was the vicar of Mundon; at his death Mrs Susanna Shipton married the vicar of Wethersfield, none other than the highly successful preacher Stephen Marshall who was to be a preacher to the House of Commons at the outbreak of the Civil War and who, by his powerful sermon *Curse ye Meroz*, would rouse many of the undecided to Parliament's side in 1642. By his wife Susanna, John Shipton was also related to the sons and daughters of Alderman John Luffkin (died 1618 'being very aged and stricken in years') whose will followed the pattern of this group's bequests in its legacies to Master Ralph Hawdon, to Master John Soan ('my good neighbour'), Mistress Gifford and the poor of all three parishes. The Luffkin family also spread this group's links into Kelvedon parish. It would be better to see them as local rather than resident Puritans: as in everything else, the borough's religious identity was merged with its neighbourhood and its market area. A *Treatise on Drunkenness* by the Ipswich preacher Samuel Ward refers to Ralph Hawdon (Gifford's successor) in such a way as to imply that any of his auditors at Ipswich, where this was originally preached as a temperance sermon, would know of this vicar of Maldon. And one phrase shows that Ward himself had been acquainted with the vicar and knew someone else closely in touch with the Maldon area: citing the case of 'five or six that plotted a solemn drinking at one of their houses' in Dengie Hundred, 'laid in beer for the once, drunk healths in a strange manner and died thereof within a few weeks', Samuel Ward stated that this had been told to him 'by one that was with one of them on his death-bed to demand a debt, and often spoken of by Master Hawdon, late Preacher of Maldon, in the hearing of many ...'

The third feature of Maldon Puritanism c1600-25 pointed to by Shipton's will is the drawing together of former opponents, as if some reconciliation, a movement away from extreme positions, had occurred. That corresponds with the acceptance

240

of bishops and their officials, and the open conformity to the Book of Common Prayer and to canon law. This group was not, however, a long-lasting association within the town and although in their successors it might have seemed possible a new generation would establish itself permanently, that proved not to be so. This new generation is better described as Calvinist rather than Puritan. It included locally admired (and doubtless admirable) young preachers trained at Cambridge, who came back to their old homes as resident freemen of the borough as well as beneficed, graduate clergy. William Nash, for example, was the son of a town clerk (John Nash, died 1621). He was probably at school in Maldon and after studying at Trinity Hall and St John's College in Cambridge until he was 25, returned to be rector of Stow Maries and curate of Cold Norton. However, he lived in Maldon as a resident freeman (and his son William was baptised in St Mary's parish, 1623). Others of this second generation, the children of the Elizabethan Puritans, were prosperous tradesmen so that a 'native' Calvinist society appeared to be well-established in the borough by the mid-1620s but with what success may be seen in the Pratt, Maldon and Gifford families.

The family of John Pratt numbered ten persons at his death in 1619. It included his three sons by his second marriage, of whom Elisha was an undergraduate at Emmanuel College and eventually Vicar of St Lawrence parish near Maldon (where Parliament's Parochial Inquisition of 1650 found him, aged 49, to be 'a very honest and painful minister'), whilst Jeremiah and Samuel Pratt maintained their father's merchant tailoring trade and sat as aldermen and Bailiffs of the borough. With an even more impeccably Protestant pedigree the Maldons retained their presence in the town both as tradesmen and as gentry, and one of them a locally-beneficed clergyman who was also a non-resident freeman. George Gifford's family was born during the years he was in contention with the Bishop of London and the Archbishop, 1586-99 (apart from his eldest son, George, born before he came to Maldon). At his apparently sudden and early death the preacher left four, possibly five sons aged one, six, eleven and about 20 years respectively, one married daughter (Mary Leake) and an eight-year-old daughter. Of this brood his second or third son, Samuel, became a graduate clergyman and a non-resident freeman who got himself local incumbencies – he was Vicar of Althorne and Rector of Snoreham – within easy riding distance of his home town. Three sons remained in Maldon as tradesmen: George, the eldest son, was a saddler and only became a freeman when he was 40 (in 1622); his brother Jeremiah had been apprenticed to a Maldon tailor (Robert Pope) and his other brother, William, became a linendraper and a freeman. As with John Shipton's circle, this generation failed to achieve permanency in the borough. It was dogged by sickliness and early deaths. George Gifford's sons Jeremiah and Samuel died without heirs, aged respectively 19 and 50. John Pratt's sons, also named Jeremiah and Samuel were 28 and 33 at their decease. The Maldons did maintain a long-living family but most of the

241

children and grand-children spent long periods away from the borough, as did John Maldon I and his eldest son, Jacob, who each retired to Chelmsford when ill-health overtook them.

The part played by migration in the depletion of the town's Puritan community was sometimes as absolute as death. Alderman Thomas Ruck requested the Corporation's permission to vacate his office in 1638 because he was about to go with all his family 'to parts beyond the seas' and on 29 March, 1638 he

> 'and Hawkins his servant and Joseph Hills [a Bailiff in 1634] and Wayte his servant took every of them the oaths of Supremacy and Allegiance to his Majesty before the Bailiffs and Master Thomas Plume, one of his Highness' Justices of the Peace within this borough, in the Moot Hall of the same; the said persons being bound for the plantations in America called New England'.

Altogether sixteen persons left the borough in this migration and it may be noted that none of them had been its inhabitants for more than ten years (except perhaps 'Hawkins' who cannot be identified). Alderman Ruck had lived in Maldon since 1628/9 and was one of those gentry immigrants like Thomas Plume or John Shipton. He took with him to Massachussetts a wife and four sons aged two to nine years. Joseph Hills, a woollendraper, was another immigrant, with a sister and brother-in-law in York, and he had paid the exceptionally high entry fee of £8 to become a freeman in November 1631; his family, at migration, numbered seven (his wife, three sons and three daughters aged between two and twelve years). John Wayte was also an immigrant, the son of a Wethersfield tanner and apprenticed to Joseph Hills only seven months before this voyage to the far side of the known world. Like earlier Puritan members of the Corporation both Ruck and Hills had become Aldermen very quickly after arriving in the town. Clearly they found its Puritanism as insufficient as Governor John Winthrop —

> 'All other churches of Europe are brought to desolation, for which the Lord begins already to frown upon us and to cut us short ... and who knows but that God hath provided this place to be a refuge for many whom he means to save out of the general calamity...'

— and shook the dust of prelacy off their wandering feet by emigration to literally a new England. There they founded the township of Malden in Massachusetts, where godliness in religion and magistracy might be constructed anew on the banks of the Mystic River: a new Maldon beside the new Boston, Chelmsford, Dedham, Braintree ... in a new society.

Emigration to America was a special characteristic of East Anglian and Essex population movement in the seventeenth century but if more Maldon families crossed the Atlantic then they only did so after first moving out of the town and into some part of the market area, as did Hester, baptised as the daughter of a Thomas Welles (a butcher) in St Peter's parish 21 July 1611, who married Hugh Mason in January 1633 and with him sailed from Ipswich to New England soon after.

Back among the remaining resident Puritans the most propitious event in all these family histories was the marriage of Jeremiah Pratt's widow, Elizabeth, to the wealthy gentleman-immigrant Thomas Plume. One of her sons, Samuel, remained in the borough all his life, to become an alderman and a Bailiff like his distinguished father; but it was her younger son by her second marriage, Thomas (born 1630), whose career marks the final and complete landslide of Maldon Protestantism into complete conformity, for this Thomas Plume was ordained a priest of the Church of England and administered the Holy Communion by the Prayer Book rite in Greenwich during the last years of the Commonwealth, was the editor of two bishops' biographies, became Archdeacon of Rochester and rebuilt St Peter's church in Maldon to house the Grammar School and the great library he had accumulated for the use of the gentry and clergy of the Maldon area. Hard to think that one of his great-grandfathers had been a Presbyterian conspirator and an assaulter of a priest.

And as a further indication of the sea-change which took place among Maldon's Protestant, Calvinist congregations one can look to the life of George Gifford's eldest son, also named George. He may not have been very clever, for he had no share in his father's books and he appears only as a saddler (but without a recorded apprenticeship) who did not become a freeman until he was at least 40. He was pointedly left out of Ralph Breeder's munificent legacies to Maldon Puritans (the £20 bequeathed to Mistress Gifford, George's mother was to go to William and Jeremiah, the two youngest of her sons, if she died) but that may have been simply due to age: by 1609 George Gifford II could look after himself. It must have been by virtue of his parentage that he was appointed a headburgess but he was never elected to any responsible office within the Corporation. The most interesting feature of an otherwise utterly undistinguished life is that during the Civil War, in October 1643, he was ejected from The Company and so was at the least suspected of disloyalty to the Parliamentary cause. He would then have been 61 or more and the most probable explanation must be that he was objecting to the Solemn League and Covenant which was taken by the House of Commons in September 1643 and refusing to make his Protestation of acceptance of the League and Covenant. Yet the intention of this agreement with the Scots was to establish in England that Presbyterian form of church government for which his father had campaigned; its signatories bound themselves to the reformation of religion 'in doctrine, worship, discipline and government according to the Word of God and the example of the best reformed Churches ... the extirpation of Popery, prelacy (that is Church government by Archbishops, Bishops, their Chancellors and Commissaries)'; and the Parliament adopted a Directory of Church Government which was based on the Book of Discipline which this George Gifford's father had discussed in private conferences from 1586. Like young Thomas Plume, George Gifford II must have been a Royalist in his sympathies. In reward he was restored to membership of the Corporation in 1660 by a writ of Charles II. Another difference between him and his family's associates, was his long life: he was last listed as a headburgess and freeman in January 1671, aged at least 89.

'Where are all these pestilent nests of Puritans hatched but in corporations, where they swarm and breed like hornets?' Archbishop Laud was asked in 1640. Had this question been put to Archbishop Whitgift in 1590 it would have been reasonable, on looking at Maldon's Company, to agree that Puritanism was a flourishing force in this borough but in 1640, on the eve of the Civil War? The Puritan Moment occurred in the 1580s and 1590s; since then a conventional Calvinist-inclined Anglicanism had prevailed; in forty years high mortality and a migratory habit in its adherents' families − a mirror of the characteristics of population change − had dispersed and thinned-out the Puritan community within this town. Like the allegation that 'it was the universities that preached your Majesty out of his kingdom' which was made after Charles II's Restoration in 1660, (that is, that graduate Puritan preachers unable to find benefices and forced into Lectureships and chaplaincies had incited the Great Rebellion of the 1640s), this allegation that corporate towns were nurseries of revolutionaries was an attractive explanation for the outbreak of Civil War but it proves not to have been truly applicable to the borough of Maldon.

Against the background of the fading, dying Puritan-orientation within Maldon's oligarchy let us set the Humble Petition submitted by Enoch Grey, Minister, to the House of Commons in 1646 or 1647. He was the rector of Wickham Bishops, three to four miles from Maldon and in July 1638 he came to preach in the town. His complaint some seven or eight years later was that the two Bailiffs and an alderman had prevented him from preaching, arrested and imprisoned him, refusing to accept bail. According to Enoch Grey's petition they accused him of sedition, began proceedings against him before the Bishop of London's Commissary, Dr Aylett, and when he escaped from the borough gaol 'set watches and made searches in the town for your Petitioner, made stay of your Petitioner's horse, bound him over to the Sessions' and 'obtained the Lord Chief Justice Bramston's warrant for the attachment of your Petitioner as a felon and traitor'.

His statement was as vividly related as every other petition handed to the parliament and his solicitor did add the phrase 'should some circumstances in particular fail in proof' to a long tale of hiding and pursuits, of grievous material and physical harm done to Master Grey and his family, and of miraculous escapes – as when the Lord preserved him in Sandwich 'and· thence, by stupefying the Watch, graciously afforded a third and glorious deliverance' – but the preliminary facts in his statement were true enough: he named Jeremy Browning and Thomas Clark as the Bailiffs of Maldon and Alderman Thomas Plume as the magistrate who arrested him, and they certainly were the two Bailiffs and the Justices of the Peace in 1638. (They had recently administered the oaths to the emigrants to America.) These three must have known this local minister perfectly well, and his views, so it is interesting that they took so strong a line of action against him. Sermons in Maldon had evidently lost their old radicalism by 1638. Loyalty, a law-abiding community, was this Corporation's policy at all costs, as it evidently was in Sandwich.

The county of Essex may have been one of the Puritan strongholds of England at the outset of the Civil War. Maldon's puritanism had for over forty years been dispersed into it. Whether Dr Richard Fletcher was right to take credit for snuffing out the troubles of the 1580s and 1590s, or if it was the decease of George Gifford which brought the Puritan Moment to an end in this borough is immaterial. By 1642 a nest of these puritan 'hornets' it was not; its moment of dissension had been brief and was long past when the county militia was called to arms.

245

## CHAPTER 8

# MALDON IN RETROSPECT

THIS STUDY HAS worked at two levels. At one the major event was the rescue of Maldon from the late-medieval decline which threatened many English towns, a rescue attempted by the reinforcement of its urban and commercial institutions during the middle third of the sixteenth century. But the tides of migration undercut that attempt, for at the other level a surge in the recruitment of inhabitants, in which many were long-distance immigrants and which for a brief period produced an almost cosmopolitan community, was followed by a sharp contraction of the range of recruitment. In the mid-sixteenth century the alien, 'Dutch' element in the population disappeared; from about 1600 the numbers and social standing of the immigrants born outside the county dwindled; by about 1660 the dependence of the borough on locally-born men to maintain itself was almost complete. At one level there is to be seen an attempt to create a distinctively urban, autonomous community; at the other there is an increasing integration of town and country.

The modern observer is thus faced with two Prospects of the borough. On parchment it appears to have been a powerful civic organisation. The array of charters, regalia and official titles, the impressive range of its administration suggest that it was a minuscule edition of the greater towns of provincial England, Physically it appeared to be no more than four small, impacted huddles of buildings which a smother of gardens, orchards and pastures practically camouflaged as a scatter of rural hamlets. That is how contemporaries also saw it. They too were in two minds about its urban status. William Camden visited Maldon shortly before 1576 and he was very disappointed:

> 'I saw nothing memorable, unless I should mention two silly [plain] churches, a desolate place of White Friars and a small pile of brick built not long since by R.Darcy ...'

He was certain that this place was the site of Camulodunum and so the oldest recorded town in Britain but despite his disappointment at the absence of any relict features of a Roman town he was constrained to allow that 'for the number of the inhabitants and the bigness' − that is, although its population and the built-up area was small − 'it is worthily counted one of the principal towns in all Essex and in the records is named The Burgh of Maldon. It is a haven, commodious enough and for the bigness very well inhabited, being but one especial street ...'

Neither view can quite be discounted. It was indeed a small place but not quite as small as many contemporary market towns and its population constituted a larger concentration of craftsmen, specialists and professionals than could be found in the surrounding country townships. The Company which ruled it really did have immense power within the borough boundaries and it was a rich Corporation but the ambitions of the leading townsmen of the 1550s and 1560s put a continual strain on its resources and in the end failed to take full effect. The dissension of the 1580s and 1590s shows that the community found it hard to respect the weight of corporate authority which bore down upon it and outsiders began to challenge the Corporation's claims and privileges. Even the occasions of most self-consciously urban activity, the plays, the Prophesyings and the market-day sermons commissioned by the Bailiffs and Aldermen, the Combinations of clergy, the parades of the trained men of the town militia, all relied on the participation of outsiders. An event as peculiar to Maldon as its pre-Reformation Play, its native drama, depended on outsiders as the accounts for the two very spectacular performances in 1540 show. Attracting audiences numbering over 1,500, the production was subsidised by outsiders, the scenery was made by a Chelmsford painter, a London 'professional' was producer.

## SED QUIS CUSTODIET IPSOS CUSTODES?

Every account roll of the borough chamberlains includes expenditure for the entertainment of either noblemen or, more often, the gentry of the neighbourhood who were invited to feasts on the occasions when plays were performed before The Company, who were present with the Corporation at sermons and to whom the Bailiffs sent New Year presents and other occasional gifts of wine, sugar loaves, oysters, fowl or fish. This was not gratuitous courtesy: the recipients were the greatest landowners of the town's most immediate market area, men of power and responsibility in the local community. Since Maldon depended on recruitment from its neighbourhood and because many former freemen eventually lived within the country domains of these gentry, they were naturally persons of great importance to the inhabitants of the borough. From the middle of the sixteenth century they often resided in Maldon and one reason for its standing within the county must be that a corporate town was essential to the exercise of the gentry's social rank. Only with a corporate body which was, in a sense, possessed of equal gentility (it had a coat of arms, its aldermen were Justices of the Peace and the representatives of both the Lord High Admiral and the Crown itself, it could boast as much, or more, antiquity as they), could they properly associate themselves. The gentry accorded dignity to the Corporation by accompanying it to church, by assisting at its Sessions of the Peace as co-adjutant magistrates, by sitting with it at feasts and plays; the Corporation augmented the gentility of its guests by the dignity of its officers and the civic ceremonial of its public appearances.

Tudor governments lived in readiness for rebellion and those Essex gentry who were involved in the affairs of Westminster saw a good reason why a borough of

Maldon should exist and why its Corporation should be invested with so much authority. One of the principal motives for granting charters of incorporation in the middle years of the sixteenth century was to establish loyal and dependable royalist bastions in the provinces. For its part the common council of the earlier Maldon government had accumulated weapons and armour in its Moot Hall and rated its townsmen for the supply of new harness of war and sent out fully equipped squads of soldiers when armies were being raised to meet the danger of rebellion or foreign invasion. When Kett's Rebellion broke out in Norfolk in 1549, armed men were prepared 'to go towards Kett' but on the government's side. When Mary Tudor proclaimed herself Queen in 1553, as has been seen, Maldon men were among those turning out in full armour to support her cause. And the chamberlains' accounts of Elizabeth I's reign, and the reigns of her two successors, have frequent lists of expenses incurred by the borough in responding to the requirements for men and arms in royal service.

To the Crown and to the gentry who controlled the county for the Crown, it was necessary for the borough of Maldon to exist. In a sense, its survival as an urban and almost completely self-governing community was due to that necessity rather than by virtue of its commercial success. And throughout the latter half of the sixteenth century the influence of the gentry grew, they acquired an increasing interest in its affairs as well as frequently taking up residence in it so as to maintain a presence. This growth of interest was in step with the increasing importance of purely local recruitment of new inhabitants and it can be traced in the elections of members of parliament for the two borough seats in the House of Commons.

Like most borough seats those of Maldon were normally taken by county gentlemen who had little material interest in the town itself. Only six were ever residents, only two were members of its common council at the time of their election and the statutory regulations that M.P.s should be resident burgesses and be paid a daily allowance during sessions of parliaments were never fully complied with. M.P.s were made honorary freemen at the time of their election and paid their own expenses, two of them even recording an undertaking to bear the costs of their office themselves. Before 1559 it seems that there was a very wide franchise in the elections, in which all the freemen and also the 'commonalty' of the town could participate to elect their representatives 'by most voices and greater number' and often the Members were men from the further parts of the county, some even from outside it, and men with experience as sheriffs and tax assessors. In Queen Mary's reign they were, however, a weighty group of Essex landowners, traditional Catholics hand-in-glove with the 'men of law' who governed the borough. Support for the government brought Maldon its charters of incorporation; the government got the compliance of the borough in its Counter-Reformation policies; and gentry with extensive interests in Essex affairs got their seats in parliament.

248

From 1559 the situation took a slightly different turn. The break-up of the medieval estates in the borough — Darcy, de Vere, Bourchier, the Bishops of London — has been shown to have given the new Corporation its chance to create its own authority. From the townsmen's viewpoint the granting of great powers and explicitly detailed rights was essential to guard against the possible aristocratic backlash which some boroughs experienced (such as Thaxted, where John Cutts in 1566 forced the new Corporation to surrender most of its rights to him and even to pay compensation for revenues previously lost to him) and, indeed, during the period 1590 to 1645 Maldon's Corporation did have to fight off challenges to the rights it claimed — to charge Landcheap on the purchase of a manor, to charge tolls on ships passing its Hythe to load and unload at privately owned wharves.

It has been pointed out that despite friction of that sort, the incorporation of a borough usually improved the relationship between boroughs and gentry. The two powers in the land co-existed and co-operated. And so they did at Maldon, where the 1560s brought new groups of immigrant freemen to power in the borough and saw the establishment of the local gentry, all recently risen from yeoman stock or themselves immigrant to the area. The borough eventually became Puritan because the gentry of the local community willed that it should be so. It was also the high period of The Company's power, marked by an attempt to bring parliamentary elections firmly within the control of the Corporation and so, in practice, under the control of the Bailiffs. An ordinance of January 1559 in the common council alleged that because previous elections (as of the now discredited Marian M.P.s) were said to have been made 'rashly', without regard to the candidates' gravity, sobriety or good wisdom and by 'especial secret and sinister love singular', the Bailiffs and Aldermen decided that they, with two head burgesses and twelve *burgesses of the comminaltie* (freemen who were not members of the Corporation) should make the future elections.

That did not take permanent effect, for although attempts by the first High Stewards of the borough (after 1590) to nominate Members were politely evaded, there were more than twelve freemen participating in some elections of Queen Elizabeth I's reign. In practice Essex gentry, often connected with the borough or with its freemen, obtained the seats. Four inhabitants of Maldon (who were immigrant gentry) were elected between 1572 and 1600; the Recorder of the borough took one place; others went to Sir Edward Lewkenor of Denham near Bury St Edmunds because he was a protagonist in parliament of the Puritan cause favoured in the Maldon area.

When Lewkenor died in October 1605 a new climate had begun to influence the Corporation's policies. By then the consequences of the dissension considered in the previous chapter had forced the aldermen to restrain their ambitions and the Privy Council had begun to manage more carefully the composition of the House of Commons. It wanted to nominate Lord Howard de Walden for Lewkenor's vacant place, a man who had no association with the Maldon area. The Bailiffs had to inform the Council that the election was not entirely in their gift and that already, within eight days of Lewkenor's death, several people had, as they wrote,

> 'made means for the place, and there being a gentleman within three miles of our town, one Sir John Sammes, a man well esteemed of, had procured many voices for his electing, and in all appearance was like to have the place . . .'

Of course Sir John Sammes (of Langford and Little Totham) stood down 'as not willing to oppose himself against so worthy a man as my Lord of Walden' but the Bailiffs had to persuade him. They were, they reported, 'driven to some hard exigent' by the Council's request.

Thereafter the gentry of Essex, particularly members of the Mildmay family of Chelmsford and Moulsham, Little Baddow and Danbury — and property owners in the borough as well as the greatest family in the area apart from the Harrises of Creeksea, Woodham Mortimer, Margaretting and Maldon — assumed open management of the elections. There are two clear reasons why the Corporation's control should have waned. First, parliamentary politics became much more complex from about 1620 as the Commons began to fight for the initiative in policy-making and attitudes towards representation altered so that Members of the Commons began to demand wide franchises in borough elections. Secondly, after the spate of critical complaints in the 1590s of The Company's high-handed attitude by which they had turned elections into nominations, the Bailiffs and Aldermen were constrained to sound the opinion of the freemen and other concerned parties more widely and openly. At the same time the range of immigration at Maldon began to contract and the influence of long-distance immigrants decreased. An undated letter (of 1624 in fact) directed to the High Steward, Sir Julius Caesar, from the Bailiffs illustrates the electoral situation. It is a rough draft of the Corporation's reply to his request that he and Sir Henry Mildmay should be elected for the next parliament. This reply is so full of erasures and rephrasings that the Bailiffs must have experienced real difficulty in telling him the truth, that they had lost control of Maldon elections:

> 'The contents of your honour's letter we have made known to our brethren the Aldermen and Common Council but the electors (being all the freeburgesses, and many of them now affected to men of quality near to our township) are desirous to gratify them with place with us. In which regard we, finding question of your honour's satisfaction for our accomplishment

of your honour's letters, thought it our duties to give speedy advertisement thereof ...'

A memorandum lists eighty nine freemen who had voted for Sir Henry Mildmay in April 1625 and for Sir William Masham in June 1625, showing that the parliamentary franchise had indeed ceased to be the same as nomination by the Bailiffs.

From the 1620s the subjection of the borough to the will of the leaders of the local community is exceptionally clear. One of its M.P.s in the Long Parliament was Sir John Clotworthy, who has been singled out in the principal guide to the composition of the House of Commons at that time as the clearest example of a 'carpet bag' politician. He was a Devon man and the Earl of Clarendon commented in his *History of the Great Rebellion* that Clotworthy's election at Maldon was procured by 'powerful persons'. It is likely that the other M.P., Sir Henry Mildmay, who was Master of the King's Jewel House and High Steward of Maldon, arranged the event. The two men have been judged possibly the most unattractive of all the scoundrels who intruded themselves into that Parliament in 1642. In some towns the Civil War which broke out between the King and his Parliament eventually polarised former antagonisms between members of the ruling oligarchies but in Maldon the Corporation which had experienced so powerful a bout of division and bitterness in the 1590s now remained passive, except that the demotion of Bailiff James Starling was called for by an ordinance of the Parliament in 1648 and that during the war discreet absences from the town by some of its members and the demotion of George Gifford indicate that some people were unwilling to follow the policies of their Members of Parliament.

The greatest part of the borough's military expenditure between 1642 and 1648 was for self-defence, for artillery and road blocks and the construction of ramparts 'at the upper end of the town' (but where exactly is not stated), except for some assistance to forces raised by Sir Henry Mildmay to fight for the Parliament. The greatest part of the money allocated for military purposes was spent during the siege of Colchester (1648) and then, it would seem, purely out of self-interest. Oysters 'and other things presented to the Right Honourable the Lord Fairfax at his being at the town the last summer', wine and 'other things' given to 'ministers, colonels, captains and soldiers' as the New Model Army passed through to the beleaguered town of Colchester (which Royalists from Kent and parts of Essex had occupied in a fresh outbreak of warfare) are thus discreetly summarised in the account roll. And, as happens to communities when armies come into their neighbourhood, there was the expense during the siege of providing men, food, provender and wages for the *'leaguer before Colchester'*. Throughout a troubled twenty years, warfare followed by an experiment in republican rule, the Corporation conformed itself entirely to the requirements imposed by circumstance. Hardly had the martyr king's head been stricken off than they were having their maces altered and the new State Arms painted in their Moot Hall. As Charles II landed at Dover in 1660 they were taking down those Commonwealth Arms, putting back the Stuart kings' arms and re-altering the maces. During the Protectorate of Oliver Cromwell they dutifully apprehended men wanted by The State for interrogation but in 1660 they whose town had once sheltered Isaac Dorislaus, Counsel for the Prosecution of Charles I, were active 'to make stay of one who, it is supposed, was one of the late King's judges, whose name was thought to be Cornelius Holland'. They proclaimed equally the accessions of His Royal Highness Richard Cromwell, the Lord Protector, and of King Charles II with suitable bell-ringing and celebrations.

From 1660 all remaining pretence of the borough's independence was removed. The Corporation retained only nominal control of parliamentary elections. The gentry now permeated its ranks to make secure their hold on electoral procedure, so that one baronet who was not a resident freeman (Sir William Wiseman of Rivenhall) was three times a Bailiff and a Bramston of Roxwell was twice a Bailiff. From 1660 to 1688 the admissions of freemen show the decline in the relationship between the borough and the community: the number of applicants for the freedom increased in election years (in each of which there was an average of forty eight enfranchisements) and declined to an average of only eight in other years. More and more non-residents claimed the freedom in right of their wives. The number of resident craftsmen seeking enfranchisement for the sake of their trade declined. The situation was unexceptional. Many boroughs like Maldon 'got down on their knees, in full regalia' to offer their charters to the Crown for remodelling five or six years before 1688. Maldon docilely accepted four successive new constitutions, each of them nominating new officers. And the men who grumbled at the alterations were not the Corporation members, the freeburgesses or the townspeople but − again, as in many other places − the county gentry who, for a moment, were ousted from their posts as fee-ed officials of the borough.

John Horrocks, Vicar of All Saints and Town Preacher during the Commonwealth, felt the change in local politics more sharply than other townsmen. He had come in 1650 at the warm invitation of the Corporation. In 1662 he refused to subscribe to the Act of Uniformity and, like Gifford in 1584, he was ejected from his benefice. Like Gifford he too stayed in the town and settled himself in St Mary's parish. The Corporation, however, had been purged, the crypto-Royalists had been reinstated and where The Company of the 1580s and 1590s had given powerful support to their preferred minister, that of 1662 bent its local authority against him. There were other Dissenters in Maldon who, with Horrocks, refused to accept the re-establishment of the Church of England in its ancient form and absented

*Pl.14. James II, King of Great Britain 1685 – 1688*

themselves from their parish churches in defiance of the Act of Uniformity. They, and Horrocks and his household were accordingly prosecuted and after he had been gaoled in the Moot Hall prison, tried − and assaulted in court by one of the Bailiffs − he was run out of town on horseback 'with a sergeant on each side of him thro' all the town like a common criminal'. It must be added that Master Horrocks maintained himself very creditably thereafter as a schoolmaster, setting up one of the early Dissenters' Academies (his was in Bermondsey) which became a force in practical education in eighteenth century England.

The dissension of 1660 - 1668 was quite different in kind to the disputes of 1584-1600 in Maldon. Gifford and his godly disciples had been presbyterian by inclination but they were decidedly not separatists. Horrocks and his faithful flock were practising presbyterians and they were separatists who became The Meeting and eventually the Congregational Church which began to flourish under toleration in the next century. Gifford had the support of many of the Essex gentry. Horrocks suffered because a new generation had taken over the direction of affairs in the borough.

## A FINAL PATTERN

In its local context the history of Maldon explores a slow process of disintegration. Instead of the autonomous urban society which could have grown within the framework of franchise and corporate government created − or reinforced − in 1554 and 1555, the townsmen were never a distinct community and their economy was always interdependent with the region of its principal market influence. Once long-distance migration ceased to be significant in the composition of the town population the links provided by birthplace, kinship, marriage and common interest with the surrounding area began to erode its peculiarly urban and independent characteristics. Where aldermen had once set about creating a miniature Geneva they later preferred to be ciphers who administered their borough according to the preferences of the landed gentry of east-central Essex. Of all its functions only that of sending representatives to the House of Commons had increased in importance but that passed from the control of the Corporation to an electorate composed (by 1688) largely of non-residents.

In 1688 the borough lost and then regained its mid-Tudor constitution. Only eighty years later, in 1768, the charter was lost for good. The process of dissolution was complete. Over a technicality the Court of Chancery was induced to declare an election of the two annual Bailiffs invalid and ordered a new election. Supinely the common council and the freemen failed to obey the instruction. A judgement of *ouster* was issued by Chancery and the Borough of Maldon ceased to exist.

Significantly the borough representation in parliament continued, the only function for which Maldon had been valued by its masters for over a century.

The property, the archives, the rights to markets, fairs and fisheries were promptly mortgaged to the Town Clerk but when the records were returned to a new Mayor and Corporation which was chartered in 1810, the letters patent of Henry II, of 1171, and the charter of the Bishop of London, of 1403, from which were derived the joint office of Bailiff, were lost and have never been recovered.

# Appendix I

# HIGH OFFICERS OF THE BOROUGH OF MALDON

The first two offices in this list — the High Recorder and the High Steward — were not created at the incorporation of the borough in 1554-5. A Recorder, who was a sergeant or counsellor-at-law, the person "learned in the law" whom the 1555 charter specified to preside with the justices at the Quarter Sessions of the borough, was appointed from 1562 at least (which was the first occasion on which one is referred to) but the charters of incorporation did not specify the appointment of any permanent Steward. The High Recorders named between 1584 and 1607 appear to have had honorary appointments but the dissension within the corporation in the 1590s and the lawsuits involving the privileges of the borough during the early 17th century may have presented the Bailiffs and Aldermen with the necessity of acquiring a powerful patron who could be attached by an official fee and the freeburgess-ship to give protection and influence in the Westminster courts. Whilst there was such an officer bearing the title of High Recorder, the judge who provided the practical legal assistance was styled his Deputy.

## HIGH RECORDERS

Robert Devereux, Earl of Essex, 1584 - 1601

Sir Thomas Mildmay of Moulsham, 1601 - 1607

## HIGH STEWARDS

1610 - 1636
Sir Julius Caesar; Chancellor of the Exchequer from 1606; Master of the Rolls from 1614.
The Letters Patent of the Corporation (of 3 December 1610) appointing him High Steward are enrolled in D/B 3/1/34 f.98v.

1636 - 1660
Sir Henry Mildmay of Great Waltham and of Graces, Little Baddow; Master of the King's Jewel House to Charles I; M.P. for Maldon 1621 - 1622, 1625, 1640 - 1660.
The Letters Patent of the Corporation (of 2 May 1636) for his appointment as High Steward are enrolled in D/B 3/1/20 f.57r.
His appointment lapsed at his degradation and sentence of life imprisonment in 1660.

1661 - 22 January 1688
Sir John Bramston of Skreens, Roxwell.
The following three High Stewards held office by the new charters forced on the Corporation of Maldon by James II during 1688. After the 'Glorious Revolution' Sir John Bramston was re-instated in his office.

256

January 1688 - 20 March 1688
William Attwood, esquire.

March 1688 - 20 June 1688
Sir William Wiseman, baronet, of Rivenhall.

June 1688 - 22 October 1688
Sir John Rotherham of Gray's Inn, serjeant-at-law and Baron of the Exchequer.

# RECORDERS

In 1562 ...
John Lathom, gentleman.

In 1565 and 1567 ...
John Reynolds, gentleman.

1569 - 1584
Thomas Gent, esquire, of Steeple Bumpstead; barrister of the Middle Temple; M.P. for Maldon 1572 - 1583; serjeant-at-law (from 1584); a Baron of the Exchequer from 1586 and a member of the Court of High Commission for Ecclesiastical Causes.

1584 - c1596
James Morris, esquire.

c1596 - 1607
William Wiseman, esquire.

1608 - 1618
Charles Chibborne, esquire, of Messing; serjeant-at-law; died 1618.

1619 - 1632
John Wright, esquire, of Romford; Bencher of Gray's Inn and a Clerk of the House of Commons. Letters of Sir Arthur Harris and Sir Julius Caesar recommending his appointment in 1619 are in bundle D/B 3/3/397, items 10 and 11; his election (11 November 1619) is recorded in D/B 3/3/217/4. He died in 1632.

1633 - 1635
John Bramston, esquire, of Boreham; serjeant-at-law. Born (1577) at Spencer's, the Maldon home of his parents' friend Christopher Harris of Mountnessing. He was father of Sir John Bramston, the High Steward of 1661 - 88. Resigned the office of Recorder on appointment in 1635 as Lord Chief Justice of England.
Note of his election, January 1633, as Recorder in D/B 3/1/20 f.21v.

1635 - 1645
John Porter, esquire, counsellor-at-law.

1646 - 1652
Euseby Wright, esquire, counsellor-at-law.

1652 - 1659
Colonel Joachim Matthews, who died in May or June 1659.

1659 - 1662
Tristram Conyers, esquire, counsellor-at-law.

1663 - 1678
Francis Bramston, esquire, of the Middle Temple; serjeant-at-law; Baron of the Exchequer from 1678; younger brother of Sir John Bramston, High Steward, and younger son of Lord Chief Justice Bramston.

1679 - 20 January 1688
Moundeford Bramston, esquire,; counsellor-at-law; nephew of Sir John Bramston, High Steward.

20 January 1688 - 20 March 1688
John Rotherham (junior).

20 March 1688 - 22 October 1688
William Attwood, esquire, formerly High Steward.


## TOWN CLERKS

1504 - 1514
Richard Pynde.
A Freeman of Maldon from 1485. Elected Town Clerk at Epiphany, 1504 (D/B 3/3/61).

1514 - 1543
Philip Goldborne.
Subsequently commemorated by the bound collection of court papers and lists of his time, *Registrum Goldborne*, which is now D/B 3/1/2. A Bailiff from 1543, he was debarred by the Custom of the Borough from holding lesser office thereafter.

1544 - 1547 and 1551 - 1553/4
Anthony Sparrow
After 1554 he served occasionally as a Deputy Town Clerk and was removed from that office 15 January 1566 as unfittted 'to have the records and books of this borough under his custody and by reason of his office to know the truths, judgements and counsels of this House' (D/B 3/1/5 f.131v).

1548 - 1550 and part of 1555.
George Alleyne, gentleman.

1551 - March or April 1557.
John Machyn, gentleman.

April 1557 - 1558.
Humphrey Pike (or Pake or Peke), gentleman.
Elected on the death of Machyn: D/B 3/1/5 f10r).

**1559 - 1564**
Jerome Songer, gentleman.
Appointed for the year 1559 (D.B 3/1/5 f.33v). Stated in a lawsuit of April 1560 to be a resident of Witham.

**1565 - 15666 or 1567**
William Ayloffe, esquire.

**1567 or 1568 - 1584**
John Barnardiston, esquire.
A Freeman from 1564, when he was stated to have been born at Kedington, Suffolk, and to have (in 1564) three children. He had five more children 1564-1577, all baptised in St Mary's parish, Maldon: Vincent (August 1564); Judith (November 1565); Joan (August 1567); George (July 1569) and a second George (May 1577).

**1584 - 1586**
Robert Sharpe.
Buried in St Mary's parish, 28 April, 1586.

**1586 - 1604**
Michael Henshawe.
Died of plague, March 1604.

**1604 - 1621**
John Nash, gentleman.
He died 10 February 1621 (E.R.O., D/B 3/1/19 f.133r).

**1621 - 1625**
Thomas Cheese, scrivener.
Elected Town Clerk 12 February 1621 (E.R.O., D/B 3/1/19 f.133r).
He lived in Maldon from at least 1586 (when his daughter Sarah was baptised in St Peter's parish) and became a freeman during the 1590s during the period for which no memoranda of enfranchisements survive. His retirement from the office of town clerk was requested by the Corporation in January 1625 because of his age and infirmity and Thomas Plume, gentleman, was appointed his deputy, but the old man apparently refused to give way, for he appears as Steward of the next Court Leet to be held (D/B 3/1/19 ff. 192v - 193r and f.197r). He was buried in St Peter's parish 19 November 1625.

**1625 - 1634**
John Bentley, gentleman.
Previously appointed as attorney in the Borough Court of Record, October 1625 and elected as Town Clerk 28 November 1625 (D/B 3/1/19 ff.202r,205r). Buried in St Peter's parish, January 1635.

**1635 - 1660**
Nowell Hammond, gentleman.
Buried in St Mary's parish, 1661.

**1661 - 1669**
John Coe.

**1669 - 1675**
Thomas Ashpoole, gentleman.

1675 - 1702
William Carr, gentleman.

## BAILIFFS

Names are given in order of their first appearance in the lists of Bailiffs. Their first and last years of office are given, followed -in the case of men who served more than twice- by a statement of the number of times they held office.

The names have been grouped in four slightly overlapping periods; 1500 - 1560; 1557 - 1609; 1594 - 1661; 1648 - 1688.

(a) 1500 - 1560

1. Thomas Wyborough 1500 - 1530 (14).
2. Thomas Dale (I) 1500.
3. John Stukk (I) 1501 - 03 (3)
4. William Harding 1501, 1502.
5. John Ormesby 1504.
6. Robert Goldborne 1508, 1509.
7. John Dale 1508 - 1519 (5).
8. Thomas Gaywood 1509 - 1518 (6).
9. John Dawes 1511 - 1525 (5).
10. Reynold Fowle 1514, 1519.
11. John Nash 1515 - 30 (6).
12. Richard Beynham 1522 - 1532 (7).
13. John Bush 1526 - 34 (4).
14. Thomas Solme 1527.
15. John Basse 1532, 1539.
16. John Church 1533 - 1559 (10).
17. John Robardes 1535.
18. John Richmond 1535, 1536.
19. John Sherman 1536 - 47 (5).
20. John Stukk (II) 1537, 1538.
21. Edward Shovelard 1540 - 42 (3)
22. Reynold Smith 1542 - 47(4).
23. Robert Gaywood 1543 - 59 (5).
24. Philip Goldborne 1543-47 (4).
25. William Poulter 1548 - 1560 (3).

(b) 1557 - 1609

26. John Hastler 1557. 27. Richard Brett 1558.
28. Edward Coker 1558 - 1578 (6). 29. John Boswell 1560, 1564.
30. John Cooke 1561. 31. William Hale 1561 - 70 (4).
32. Richard Josua 1562 - 91 (4). 33. John New 1563.
34. Edward Garringtom 1563 - 71 (3). 35. Thomas Eve 1564 - 81 (5).

36. William Vernon 1565 - 1602 (10). 37. Andrew Michaelson 1567, 1571.
38. Richard Roberts 1568. 39. Thomas Spigurnell 1568 - 76 (3).
40. John Southern 1571 - 83 (4). 41. Thomas Clarke 1572.
42. John Morris 1574 - 82 (4). 43. William Bantoft 1575 - 95 (4).
44. Thomas Furnes 1576 - 85 (3). 45. Thomas Smith 1580, 1584.
46. George Frend 1582 - 93 (3). 47. Blaise Salter 1583.
48. Richard Pellet 1584. 49. William Soan 1585.
50. Edward Garrington 1586. 51. William Browning 1587 - 1601 (4).
52. Thomas Walker 1588, 1592. 53. Thomas Young 1589.
54. William Burles (I) 1589 - 1609 (6).
55. Ralph Breeder 1592 - 1608 (5).

(c) 1594 - 1661

56. John Brooke 1594, 1598.57. John Martin 1595, 1599*.
58. Thomas Hutt 1596 - 1624 (8) 59. Elisha Garrington 1599, 1603.
60. John Amory 1599, 1606. 61. John Maldon 1602.
62. John Soan 1605 - 34 (8). 63. Thomas Preston 1603.
64. Edward Hastler 1606 - 22 (5). 65. Benjamin King 1607, 1611.
66. Matthew Abraham 1607. 67. Christopher Living 1610, 1614.
68. Robert Snape 1611. 69. John Pratt 1612, 1616.
70. John Luffkin 1613, 1617. 71. William Francis (I) 1615 - 39 (7).
72. George Purkis 1615 - 32 (5). 73. John Clark 1618 - 31 (4).
74. William Burles (II) 1620. 75. John Edwards 1621 - 29 (3).
76. Jeremy Pratt 1624. 77 Thomas Welles 1616, 1630.
78. Thomas Plume 1627 - 49 (6). 79. John Sammes 1628.
80. William Browning (II) 1630. 81. James Maldon 1632.
82. Thomas Ruck, 1633, 1637. 83. Joseph Hills 1634.
84. Samuel Bedell 1635 - 51 (5).
85. William Francis (II) 1636-44 (3).
86. Ruben Robinson (I) 1636 - 48 (4). 87. Thomas Clark 1638.
88. Jeremy Browning 1638, 1642. 89. Edward Everley 1641.
90. Edward Whitefoot 1642 - 61 (6). 91.John Steevens 1643 - 1659 (5).
92. Peter Jarvis 1645. 93. William Walker 1646 - 61 (5).

(d) 1648 - 1688

94. James Starling 1648 and 1660 - 69 (5). 95. Thomas Langdell 1649.
96. Thomas Gillingwater 1652 - 60 (3).
97. William Jarman 1652 - 60 (3). 98. John Jennings 1654 - 65 (3).
99. Thomas Ewyn 1654, 1658. 100. John Purkis 1655, 1659.
101. Samuel Plume 1662 - 1670. 102. John Harrison 1660.
103. Henry Symond 1660 - 70 (3). 104. Ruben Robinson (II) 1663.
105. John Hart 1663. 106. Francis Gournay 1664 - 76 (4).
107. Thomas Horsenail 1665 - 73 (3).
108. Philip Ralling 1667 - 91 (7).
109. Samuel Pond 1667 - 86 (5).
110. Robert Jennings 1670 & 1674 - 86 (5).
111. Anthony Gratiano 1672, 1674. 112. Abel Hawkes 1673, 1677.

113. Sir William Wiseman, baronet, 1676 - 84 (3).
114. Anthony Bramston esquire, 1677, 1681.
115. William Vernon (II) 1678, 1682. 116. John Cockerell 1680, 1684.
117. Christopher Jaggard 1681. 118. John Pond 1683, 1686.
119. Michael Cooper 1685. 120. John Wasse 1685.

## MAYOR

1687: John Pond
1688: Thomas Coe.

# Appendix II

## BURGESSES IN PARLIAMENT FOR MALDON, 1504 - 1688

1. 1504
(a) Sir William Say of Broxbourne, Herts.
He had been M.P. for Plympton, 1472-5 and a Knight of the Shire for Hertfordshire, 1485-95. In 1504 he was also a commissioner for the collection of the lay subsidy in Hertfordshire. His daughter married Henry Bourchier, Earl of Essex, who was the patron of Beeleigh Abbey at Maldon.
(b) Thomas Hintelsham, esquire, of Brentwood, Mount Bures and Earls Colne.

Both men are recorded as being admitted freeburgesses in the Maldon court roll of 1504 (D/B 3/3/63 m.1).

2. 1510
(a) Thomas Hintelsham, esquire.
(b) Sir Richard FitzLewes of Heron (Ingrave), Essex.

At the Epiphany Court at Maldon, 1510, Hintelsham's election and oath as a freeburgess was recorded *eo quod electus est burgensis parliamenti cum Ricardo FitzLewes milite, et juratus est* (D/B 3/1/2 f.66v). There is no record of Sir Richard taking the freeman's oath on this occasion, for a second time, as Hintelsham did in 1511.

3. 1512
(a) Thomas Cressener, esquire, of Bures, Whissonsett and London.
(b) Thomas Hintelsham, esquire.

There is no record of the M.P.s elected for Maldon in this parliament other than the memoranda in the borough's own records. The chamberlains' account for Michaelmas 1511 - Michaelmas 1512 include £7 - 8s - 3d paid 'for the expenses of Master Cressener, one of the burgesses of this town at the parliament this year.' He is not recorded as taking the freeman's oath in 1511 or 1512.

4. 1515
(a) Unstated. Possibly either Hintelsham or FitzLewes.
(b) John Strangman, gentleman, of Rayleigh and Rochford.

5. 1523
(a) John Boosum, gentleman, of Stody and Whissonsett, Norfolk.
(b) Thomas Wyborough or *Wiburgh*, Bailiff of Maldon.

6. 1529
(a) Thomas Tey, esquire, of Layer de la Haye, Essex.
Sworn 29 September 1529. Son and heir of Sir Thomas Tey of Layer de la Haye who is listed in the 1524 lay subsidy and was assessed then on lands to the value of £100.
(b) Edward Payton, esquire, of London and Calais. Born at Wicken, Cambridgeshire. Sworn as a freeburgess of Maldon at his election, 18 October 1529.

7. 1536
(a) William Harris, gentleman, of Mundon, Rochford, Southminster, and Lincoln's Inn. He was father of Vincent Harris, M.P. in 1572.
(b) John Raymond, gentleman, son and heir of George Raymond of Little Dunmow.
Both men were sworn freeburgesses 29 May 1536.

263

8. 1539
(a) John Edmond, gentleman, of Lincoln's Inn and born at Cressing Temple near Witham. In 1542 he was described as of Little Waltham near Chelmsford and Boreham.
(b) William Benham (or Bonham) gentleman, of Stanway near Colchester and Peldon.
Both elections are recorded in D/B 3/1/2 fll5.

9. 1542
(a) Edward Bury of Eastwood and Rayleigh. Born at Runwell. His uncle, John Strangman, had been M.P. for Maldon in 1515.
(b) Henry Dawes of Maldon and of Launde, Leicestershire.

10. 1545
(a) Sir Clement Smith of Middlemead in Little Baddow.
(b) Nicholas Throckmorton. of London.
There is no local information for these two elections.

11. 1547
(a) Sir Clement Smith.
(b) First, Henry Dawes, gentleman (as for 1542) until his death in 1550, after which his seat was taken by …
(c) Second, William Bassett, probably a younger son of John Bassett of Gt Chishall, Cambridgeshire, and a relative of Sir Thomas Tey.
There is no local record of his election to serve for the borough.

12. 1553 (March)
(a) Sir Walter Mildmay of Apethorpe, Northants, son of Thomas Mildmay, mercer, of Chelmsford.
(b) First, Anthony Browne, esquire, of South Weald, Essex, who subsequently accepted election as M.P. for Preston, Lancashire; His place was taken by …
(c) Second, Henry Fortescue, esquire, of Faulkbourne Hall.

13. 1553 (October)
(a) Anthony Browne, esquire, of South Weald, Essex, Reader of the Middle Temple, 1553.
(b) John Raymond, gentleman (as in 1536).

14. 1554 (April)
(a) Thomas Hungate, esquire, of Hungate, Yorkshire (West Riding).
(b) Edmund Tyrell, gentleman, of Beeches in Rawreth.

15. November 1554
(a) Anthony Browne, esquire, of South Weald.
(b) John Wiseman, esquire, of Great Canfield, Auditor to the 16th Earl of Oxford (1542) and one of the Auditors of the Court of Augmentations, 1536-44.

16. 1555
(a) Sir Henry Radcliffe, a younger son of Henry Radcliffe, 2nd Earl of Sussex, of New Hall, Boreham, and Woodham Walter.
(b) Richard Weston, esquire, of Skreens Park, Roxwell, and Hatfield Broad Oak. Reader of the Middle Temple in 1555. He also acted as Counsel for the borough in the 1550s.

264

17. 1558 (January)
(a) Edmund Tyrell of Beeches.
(b) First, Roger Appleton, esquire, of Dartford, Kent and of South Benfleet. He died in 1558 and was replaced by ...
(c) Second, Henry Golding, esquire, of Little Birch, the third son of John Golding, esquire, of Halstead. In 1549 he had been a trusted servant of Edward Seymour, Duke of Somerset (at the Duke's fall from power as Protector) and he had some standing in the 16th Earl of Oxford's household through his half-sister's marriage to the Earl. He was elected in Appleton's place 30 October 1558 (D/B 3/1/6 f.28r).

18. 1559
(a) Sir Henry Radcliffe.
(b) Henry Golding, esquire.

19. 1563 - 1567
(a) John Lathom, gentleman, of Sandon and the Middle Temple, Recorder of Maldon.
(b) Richard Argall, gentleman, of London and East Sutton, Kent.

20. 1571
(a) First, Peter Osborne, esquire, of South Fambridge, of Chicksands, Bedfordshire, and Ivy lane, London, second son of Richard Osborne of Tiled Hall, Latchingdon, by Elizabeth Coke. However, he was also elected one of the M.P.s for Guildford and was replaced by ...
   Second, George Blyth of Cambridge and London, formerly deputy Regius Professor of Greek at Cambridge University (1562) and son of John Blyth, Regius Professor of Physic there. By 1571 he had joined Peter Osborne as a counsellor of Lord Burghley and he was also Osborne's brother-in-law.
(b) Gabriel Croft, esquire, of Claughton, Lancashire, and of London. He had been a servant of Thomas Radcliffe, 3rd Earl of Sussex, and Auditor for Ireland when he (Radcliffe) was Lord Deputy there. The elections of Osborne and Croft are recorded in D/B 3/1/6 f.118r.

21. 1572 - 1583
(a) Thomas Gent, esquire, of Moyns, Steeple Bumstead and the Middle Temple; Recorder of Maldon. In 1567 he had been elected an Alderman and J.P. of the borough. He was also Counsel to Edward de Vere, the 17th Earl of Oxford, and steward of the earl's courts in 1571.
(b) First, Vincent Harris, esquire, of the Friars Mansion, Maldon, J.P. for Essex 1571 and a Captain of Musters of the Essex Militia. He was the fourth son of William Harris of Southminster, M.P. in 1536. He died in April 1574 and was buried in All Saints' Church, Maldon. His seat in the Commons was taken by ...
   Second, Edward Sulyard, esquire, of Flemings, Claydon and Runwell, whose election at Michaelmas is recorded 1575 (D/B 3/1/6 f.73v) and the expenses of the election are given in the borough chamberlains' account for 1575-6.

22. 1584 - 1585
(a) Edward Lewknor, esquire, of Denham, Suffolk and Kingston Buci, Sussex. He had once shared a chamber in the Middle Temple with James Morris, who became Recorder of Maldon.
(b) William Wiseman, esquire, of Maldon and Mundon, and of Lincoln's Inn. He was the 7th son of John Wiseman of Felsted.
   An agent of Sir Robert Rich in Essex, he had been Escheator for Essex and Hertfordshire in 1558 and was a Justice of the Peace and an Alderman of the Corporation of Maldon, 1578-81.

23. 1586 - 1587

(a) John Butler, esquire, of Thoby and Little Birch, and of Sharnbrook, Bedfordshire. He had married the widow of Christopher Harris of Margaretting and of Maldon; his brother-in-law (by his sister's marriage) was Robert Wright, the chaplain of Lord Rich at Rochford Hall; and his son-in-law was the son of Alderman William Vernon of Beeleigh, M.P. 1588-9.

(b) Edward Lewkenor, esquire.

A draft note on the election by the Corporation and freeburgesses (D/B 3/1/8 f.12) shows the names of forty three freemen (which was under half the total number at that time) listed under the names of the candidates for whom they had voted: Master Butler: 13; Master Lewkenor: 22; Master Wiseman: 8.


24. 1588 - 1589

(a) John Butler, esquire.

(b) William Vernon, gentleman, of Little Beeleigh.

25. 1593

(a) Thomas Mildmay, esquire, of Moulsham. Son of the High Recorder of Maldon, Sir Thomas Mildmay of Moulsham.

(b) Edward Lewkenor, esquire.

The elections were made on 29 February 1593 (D/B 3/1/8 ff.105 -106r).


26. 1597 - 1598

(a) Thomas Herrys, esquire, of the Friars Mansion, Maldon, son of Vincent Harris. He married Cordelia, daughter of John Gill of Wyddial, Hertfordshire. He was knighted in 1603 and had been a J.P. for Essex from 1592.

(b) William Wiseman, esquire, styled Deputy Recorder of Maldon.

 (M.P. in 1584, 1601.)


27. 1601

(a) William Wiseman, esquire. (As for 1584 and 1597.)

(b) Richard Weston, esquire, of Roxwell. (Created created Earl of Portland, 1633.)


28. 1604 - 1611

(a) First, Sir Edward Lewkenor. He died in 1605 and was replaced with ...

    Second, Theophilus, Lord Howard de Walden, who became a Baron in 1610 and was replaced by ...

    Third, Sir Robert Rich, who was elected and sworn a freeburgess of Maldon 19 February 1610.

(Subsequently he became the 2nd Earl of Warwick and Lord High Admiral of England.)

(b) First, William Wiseman, esquire, Deputy Recorder of Maldon. He died in 1610 and was replaced by ...

    Second, Sir John Sammes of Langford, who was elected and sworn a freeburgess 25 January 1610.


29. 1614

(a) Sir John Sammes of Langford.

(b) Charles Chibborne, esquire, of Messing, serjeant-at-law and Recorder of Maldon.

The election of both occurred 9 March 1614 (D/B 3/1/19 f.70r).


30. 1621 - 1622

(a) Sir Julius Caesar, Master of the Rolls, High Steward.

(b) Sir Henry Mildmay of Great Waltham, Master of the King's Jewel House.

31. 1624
(a) Sir Arthur Harris of Creeksea and Woodham Mortimer.
(b) Sir William Masham, Baronet, of High Laver.

32. 1625
(a) First, Sir Arthur Harris, who was elected at Maldon 12 April 1625 but was also elected a Knight of the Shire for Essex 3 May 1625, decided to serve for the county and was replaced for Maldon by ... Second, Sir William Masham who was elected and sworn a freeburgess 4 July 1625 (D/B 3/1/19 f.201v).
(b) Sir Henry Mildmay.

33. 1626
(a) Sir William Masham. Sir Francis Barrington, in a letter dated 3 January 1626, recommended the Bailiffs of Maldon to secure Sir William's election.
(b) Sir Thomas Cheeke of Pirgo, Hornchurch.
Both were elected (and Sir Thomas sworn) 11 January 1626 (D/B 3/1/19 f.207r).

34. 1628 - 1629
(a) Sir Henry Mildmay.
(b) Sir Arthur Harris.
Both were elected 28 February 1628 and Sir Arthur Harris was sworn a freeburgess 8 March 1628 (D/B3/1/19f.342v).

35. 1640
(a) Sir Henry Mildmay, High Steward of the Borough.
(b) John Porter, esquire, counsellor-at-law and Recorder of Maldon.
Election date: 16 March 1640 (D/B 3/1/20 f.100r).

36. 1640 - 1653
(a) Sir Henry Mildmay.
(b) Sir John Clotworthy of Holborn, Middlesex.

37. Parliaments of 1653 - 1658
No returns, no local information.

38. 1659
(a) Colonel Sir Henry Mildmay of Graces in Little Baddow.
(b) Colonel Joachim Matthews, Recorder of Maldon. He died in May or June 1659.
There is a memorandum of these two men's election on 4 January 1659: D/B3/1/20 f.239v.

39. 1660
(a) First, Sir Henry Mildmay of Graces. He was declared a traitor in 1660, degraded from his knighthood and sentenced to life imprisonment. His election was consequently declared null and void. He was replaced by ...
    Second, Edward Harris, esquire and barrister, of Great Baddow and Lincoln's Inn.
(b) Tristram Conyers, esquire, of Walthamstow, counsellor- at-law and Recorder of Maldon.
The elections of Mildmay and Conyers on 12 April 1660 are recorded in D/B 3/1/20 f.247v; and the election of Edward Harris, 'none gainsaying', is in the same register, f.250v.

40. 1661 - Janury 1679
(a) First, Sir John Tyrrell. He died in 1677 and was replaced by Second, Sir William Wiseman, Baronet, of Rivenhall, and an Alderman of the Borough of Maldon.
(b) Sir Richard Wiseman, Baronet, of Willingale.
The elections of Sir John Tyrrell and of Sir Richard Wiseman on 10 April 1661 are recorded in E.R.O. D/B 3/1/20 f.266r and of Sir William Wiseman, 26 February 1677, in D/B 3/1/21 f.145r.

41. March - July 1679
(a) Sir William Wiseman, Baronet, of Rivenhall.
(b) Sir John Bramston, Knight of the Bath, of Skreens Park, Roxwell, and High Steward of the Borough.

In the March election John Lamotte Honeywood, who was son-in-law of Sir William Wiseman, was an unsuccessful candidate. He became an M.P. for Essex in the October 1679 election.

42. October 1679 - January 1681
(a) Sir William Wiseman of Rivenhall.
(b) Sir Thomas Darcy, Baronet, of Braxted Lodge.
Elections, 6 October 1679: D/B 3/1/21 f.185r.

43. March 1681
(a) Sir William Wiseman.
(b) Sir Thomas Darcy .
Elections, 7 March 1681: D/B 3/1/21 f.199r.

44. 1685 - 1687
(a) Sir John Bramston.
(b) Sir Thomas Darcy
Elections, 8 April 1685: D/B 3/1/21 f.235v.

# Appendix III

## SOURCES

### MANUSCRIPT SOURCES

Detailed references to the sources on which this study has been based are available in an annotated manuscript of this book in the Essex Record Office. This manuscript also includes an essay on estimates of the population of Maldon. The following notes are intended only as a guide to the range and nature of the source material on the borough of Maldon 1500 - 1700.

### LONDON: THE PUBLIC RECORD OFFICE

State Paper Office
S.P. 12/ 80 Certificate of vagabonds arrested April 1571;
   / 70 Expenses on borough armaments April 1570;
   /119/21 Return of numbers of innholders, taverners and tipplers in five Essex Hundreds and Maldon 1577;
   /178 Depositions against Mark Wiersdale April 1595.

Exchequer
Lay subsidy returns 1524: E.179/108
   /147 (Colchester), /148 (Maldon), /149 (Dunmow Hundred),
   /152 (Barstable and Chelmsford Hundreds),
   /154 (Lexden Hundred, Witham and Winstree Half-Hundreds).
Lay subsidy returns 1525: E.179/108
   /161 (Thaxted), 170 (Maldon), /172 (Hinckford Hundred), /174 (Witham and Great Coggeshall), /176 (Braintree and (Bocking).
Lay subsidy return 1526: E.179/108/206 (Maldon).
Lay subsidy returns 1541-45: E.179/108
   /228 (Dengie Hundred 1541), /244 (Dengie Hundred 1544),
   /267 (Dengie Hundred 1545).
Chantry Commissioners' Certificates: E.301
   /19/31 Certificates of chantries 1547; /20/49 valuation of Maldon religious guilds 1549.
Port Books: E.190/587/9, E.190/589/9 (Port of Maldon 1568); E.190/598/14 (Port of Maldon 1603-1604).

War Office
W.O. 30/48 Survey of beds and stabling 1686.

Prerogative Court of Canterbury
Registers of wills.

## LONDON: BRITISH LIBRARY
Harley MS 595 Report by the Bishop of London on jurisdictions within his diocese, July 1563.
Harley MS 1541 Notes taken 'In Maulden-Church called All Saints' c1638.

## LONDON: COLLEGE OF ARMS
Richard Symonds' notes on Essex churches, volume 3.

## GREATER LONDON RECORD OFFICE
Will of George Gifford, clerk 8 May 1600 (DL/C 359 'Sperrin' ff.210v-211r).

## WESTMINSTER ABBEY MUNIMENTS
From the College of St Martin le Grand, London, the Abbey received the two prebends of Keton's and Cowpe's in Great Maldon and the Peculiar Jurisdiction formerly of the College was from 1509 exercised by the Dean of Westminster in St Mary's parish, Maldon. Among the Westminster Abbey Muniments [WAM] are these survivals of that jurisdiction: WAM 8124 and 38408 (Visitation Charge and expenditure 1566), WAM 8125 (letter from stipendiary curate 1596), WAM 9769, 9770, 9875, 13238 and 9771 (grants of offices of Commissary, Vicar General and Registrar of the peculiar jurisdiction, seventeenth century), WAM 8132, 8133, 8134 and 8136 (surveys of Keton's and Cowpe's prebendal estates in Maldon, seventeenth and eighteenth centuries).

## WESTMINSTER PUBLIC LIBRARY
Wills, inventories, probate acts, administrations of estates, together with stray notes taken at Visitations of St Mary's parish, all formerly part of Westminster Abbey's muniments. There are twenty seven wills and inventories of Maldon inhabitants in seven collections styled *Wykis, Bracy, Maldon, Smith V* and *Act Books I, III and V*.

## OXFORD: BODLEIAN LIBRARY
MS Bodley 73, miscellaneous notes and extracts about the Carmelite Order compiled by Dr John Bale c1525, which include notes on the Friary at Maldon. MS Top.Essex 33771, *The Clark Papers*: twelve volumes of notes on Maldon from the borough archives compiled by Dr Andrew Clark, Rector of Great Leighs, Essex, 1904-1907.

## CHELMSFORD: ESSEX RECORD OFFICE

I. Records other than those of the Borough of Maldon.

The Calendars of Assize and Quarter Sessions Rolls. They include the Hearth Tax returns of 1662-1673, of which those used in this study for Maldon are: Q/RTh 1, 5, 7, 8 (1662, 1671, 1672 and 1673).

Diocesan Records. The majority of the wills of Maldon inhabitants (other than the sources noted above) are preserved in the probate records of the Bishop of London's Consistory Court:

D/ABR (registers of wills 1553-1561, 1564-1570 and 1660-1858), D/ABW (separate wills 1441-1858);

The records of the Archdeaconry of Essex, which included All Saints' and St Peter's parishes, Maldon, are the Act Books for 1560 and 1563-1640 (class D/AEA), records of the Archdeacons' Visitations 1565, 1580-1641 and 1662-1672 (class D/AEV) and depositions in ecclesiastical causes 1576-1592, 1600-1613 and 1626-1642 (class D/AED).

The tithe apportionments and maps of 1834, 1838 and 1848 for the three Maldon parishes are classed D/CT 22, 23 and 27.

The parish registers of baptisms, burials and marriages have been deposited with the Essex Record Office by the clergy and parish councils of All Saints' with St Peter, Maldon, and St Mary, Maldon.

Manorial and other collections include the conveyance of Great and Little Maldon manors 1692 (D/DA T209); a valuation of the estates of Sir Thomas Darcy, 1545 (D/DGe M135); court rolls, rentals and a survey of the manor of Beeleigh Abbey, 1571-1759 (D/DMb M33, M37, M25, P5); and an Extent of the estates in Essex of John de Vere, late Earl of Oxford, made in 1563 during the minority of Edward, 17th Earl of Oxford (D/DU 65/72).

The manorial and other collections also include volumes of pedigrees compiled in 1634, c1650 and 1630-1640 from the official records of the Heralds' Visitations (D/DQs 41, 42 and 44); a memorandum on the discipline of the Corporation of Maldon 1598 (D/DQs 133/1); letters patent for the repair of St Mary's church tower in Maldon 18 July 1628 (D/DQs 134); and the Report of the Town Clerk for the Borough of Maldon to the Charities Commission, 1897 (D/DQs 137/6).

The following transcripts held in the Essex Record Office were also used in the preparation of this study: Essex portions of Bishop Henry Compton's Census 1676 at the William Salt Library, Stafford (T/A 40); the sixteenth century account book of the Holy Trinity Guild, Saffron Walden (T/A 401/2); MS. History of Essex, compiled c1710-30 by William Holman of Halstead (T/P 195/9/1).

II. Maldon Borough Records deposited in the Essex Record Office.

Charters: D/B 3/13/1 - 15, of which /1-/9 and /12/15 are *inspeximi* of previous charters. The two charters by which the borough was incorporated are: D/B 3/13/10 (1554) and /11 (1555). The dates of the other charters are: 1290 (/1 and /2), 1330 (/3), 1377-8 (/4 and /5), 1400 (/6), 1416 (/7), 1454 (/8), 1525 (/9), 1559 (/12), 1592 (/13), 1604 (/14) and 1630 (/15).

Books: D/B 3/1/1 (1384-1449); D/B 3/1/2 *Registrum Goldborne* (1457-c1550) containing Courts of Election, enrolled deeds, memoranda of freemen's admissions, oaths of officers, additional customs or ordinances, fragments of chamberlains' accounts and some early apprenticeship covenants (1547-1553); D/B 3/1/3 *The White Book* which was begun in 1555 as a chartulary, continues as a custumal and also contains copies of oaths, memoranda on cases concerning the borough liberties, leases of borough property, contributions of armour to the town, and other entries were made in it, haphazardly, down to 1760; D/B 3/1/4 *Admiralty Courts* 1574-1639. The following books contain a medley of Corporation business, of Quarter and Petty Sessions, Courts of Election, of Record and (occasionally, down to book /14) of Pie Powder, lists of freemen and decenners, the admission of freemen and elections to parliaments:

| D/B 3/1/ 5 | 1557-1566 |
|---|---|
| / 6 | 1566-1583 |
| / 7 | 1572-1593 |
| / 8 | 1583-1595 |
| / 9 | 1596-1604 |
| /10 | 1605-1623 |
| /11 | 1623-1636 |
| /12 | 1655-1670 |
| /13 | 1675-1681 |
| /14 | 1681-1692 |
| /20 | 1631-1664 |
| /21 | 1666-1690 |
| /22 | 1674-1678 |
| /23 | 1678-1696 |

Specialised registers of the Court of Record: enrollment of apprentices' indentures, D/B 3/1/33 (1565-1651) and /37 (1667-1769); conveyances and other title deeds, D/B 3/1/34 (1574-1660) and /35 (1661-1741).

Chamberlains' Accounts. These are not collected in one class in the borough archives but have been scattered among miscellaneous rolls and were not sorted at the official cataloguing in the 1930s for the National Register of Archives. A handlist of the surviving account rolls for the use of students wishing to locate rolls for particular years is available in the Essex Record Office, which lists all from 1500 to 1689 in chronological order with their catalogue numbers.

Miscellaneous Bundles. These are the remnants of the town clerks' filing system but they no longer preserve any order. They include letters received and drafts of letters sent out, notes of court business and Corporation resolutions, bills and jottings relating to the chamberlains' expenditure, papers preparatory to sessions of courts (including some constables' returns of names of decenners) and drafts of replies to conciliar orders.

Court Rolls. These run (with gaps) from 1402 to 1513 as D/B 3/3/1 -64. They contain similar types of borough business to the later court books, overlapping with the registers D/B 3/1/1 and /2, but exclusively containing pleas in the borough court, especially pleas of debt.

## MALDON: THOMAS PLUME'S LIBRARY

The Library of Dr Thomas Plume, bequeathed to trustees created by his will of 1704, is a museum of sixteenth and seventeenth century European printed scholarship and polemic. It contains few manuscripts other than notebooks and some papers belonging originally to Dr Plume which have no relevance to Maldon itself but it also has transcripts of the baptism, marriage and burial registers of All Saints', St Peter's and St Mary's parishes and deposited deeds relating to 28 High Street, Maldon.

## MALDON: PRIVATE PROPERTIES

Since the 1970s many collections of title deeds, mostly of the eighteenth and nineteenth centuries have been placed on deposit in the Essex Record Office by solicitors' firms. I have also been allowed to see privately held collections of title deeds by courtesy of Mr and Mrs H. Springett and Mr and Mrs G. Wheeler and Mr R. Wheeler, to whom my thanks are here repeated.

## PRINTED SOURCES

Anon. *A Detection of Damnable Driftes Practized by Three Witches Arraigned at Chelmisford in Essex .. executed in Aprill 1579*.
London. No date.
Beckett, R.B. (editor). *John Constable's Correspondence. Part II*. Suffolk Records Society, Volume VI (1964).
Bernard, Richard. *The Shepheard's Practise*. 1609.
Bindoff, S.T. (editor). *The House of Commons 1509-1558*. Part I. (The History of Parliament.) 1982.
Bolton, James L. and Maslen, Majorie M. (editors). *Calendar of the Court Books of the Borough of Witney*. Oxfordshire Record Society, Volume LIV (1985).
Bramston, Sir John. (Ed. P. Braybrooke.) *Autobiography*. Camden Society 1845.
Brigg, W. *Genealogical Abstracts of Wills Proved in the Prerogative Court of Canterbury, Register 'Wootton'*. Volume VI. 1913.
*Calendar of Grants of Probate and Administration of the Commissary Court of the Venerable Dean and Chapter of Westminster*. 1864.

Charity Commission. *Reports*. 1817.

Commisioners of the Public Records. *General Report*. 1837.

Dalton, Michael. *The Country Justice*. The 1682 edition has been used in the preparation of this study.

Davis, H.W.C. (editor). *Regesta Regum Anglo-Normannorum 1066 – 1154*. Volume I. Oxford University Press. 1913.

Deed, S.G. *Catalogue of the Plume Library at Maldon, Essex*. Maldon. 1959.

Emmison, F.G. *Wills at Chelmsford*. Volumes I and II. Record Society Limited, publications 78 and 79. 1958.

Emmison, F.G. (editor). *Wills of the County of Essex, England*. Volume 1, 1558-65. National Genealogical Society, Washingtom D.C. 1982. Volume 2, 1565-71; Volume 3, 1571-77. New England Historic Genealogical Society. 1983 and 1986.

Emmison, F.G. (editor). *Essex Wills:The Archdeaconry Courts 1577-1584* and *Essex Wills: the Archdeaconry Courts 1582-1592*. Essex Record Office and Friends of Historic Essex. 1987 and 1989.

Firth, C.H. and Rait, R.S. (editors). *Acts and Ordinances of the Interregnum, 1642-1660*. 1911.

Fowler, R.C. (editor). *Beeleigh Abbey*. Privately printed, 1924.

Gifford, George. *Fifteene Sermons upon the Song of Salomon*. 1598.

Gifford, George. *A Discourse of the Subtill Practises of Devilles by Witches and Sorcerers*. 1587.

Gifford, George. *A Dialogue Concerning Witches and Witchcraftes*. 1593.

Gifford, George. *Sermons upon the whole Booke of the Revelation, set forth by George Giffard, Preacher of the Word at Mauldin in Essex*. 1599.

Green, M.A.E. (editor). *Calendar of the Proceedings of the Committee for Compounding etc., 1643-1660*. 1889.

Harrison, William. *The Description of England*. [(Ed. G. Edelen). Ithaca, New York. 1968.]

Hasler, P.W. (editor). *The House of Commons 1558-1603*. Part I. (The History of Parliament.) 1981.

Henning, B.D. (editor). *The House of Commons 1660-1690*. Part I. (The History of Parliament.) 1983.

Historical Manuscripts Commission. *House of Lords MSS*. Reports 4-9.

Historical Manuscripts Commission. *Calendar of the Cecil Manuscripts at Hatfield House, Hertfordshire*. 1883.

Hughes, Leonard. *Guide to and History of All Saints' Church, Maldon*. 1909.

*Journals of the House of Lords*. Volume V (for 1642).

King, H.W. 'Inventories of Church Goods, 6th Edward VI'. *Transactions of the Essex Archaeological Society*, old series, Volume V (1873).

Lewis, Samuel. *Topographical Dictionary of England*. 7th edition. 1849.

Lidderdale, W.A. (editor). *Collection of Miscellaneous Grants*. Harleian Society, Volume LXXVI (1925).

Livock, D.M. (editor). *City Chamberlains' Accounts in the Sixteenth and Seventeenth Centuries*. Bristol Record Society, Volume XXIV (1966).

Mabbs, A.W. (editor). *Guild Stewards' Book of the Borough of Calne, 1561-1688*. Wiltshire Archaeological and Natural History Society. Records Branch, Volume VII (1953).

Members of Parliament: Part I. *Parliaments of England, 1213-1702*. (Return in part to an Order of the House of Lords.) 1879.

Metcalfe, W. (editor). *Visitations of Essex*. Harleian Society, 1868.

Newcourt, Richard. *Repertorium Parochiale Londiniense*. 1708.

Norden, John. *Description of Essex*. Camden Society, Old Series, Volume IX. No date.

Ordnance Survey. *Gazetteer of Great Britain*. Southampton, 1969.

Palmer, W.M. *Cambridge Borough Documents*. Volume I. Cambridge. No date.

Peile, John. *Biographical Register of Christ's College, 1448-1905*. Cambridge University Press. 1910.

Tawney, R.H. and Power, Eileen. *Tudor Economic Documents*. 1924.

Reaney, P.H. *Place-Names of Essex*. Place-Name Society. Cambridge University Press. 1935.

Round, J.H. *Register of the Scholars admitted to Colchester School, 1637-1740*. Colchester. 1897.

Rylands, W.H. *Grantees of Arms to the end of the Seventeenth Century*. Harleian Society, Volume LXVI (1915).

Savage, R. and Fripp, E.I. (editors). *Minutes and Accounts of Stratford-upon-Avon*. Volume I. Dugdale Society. 1923.

Squibb, G.D. *Reports of Heraldic Cases in the Court of Chivalry, 1623-1732*. Harleian Society, Volume CVII (1956).

Thirsk, Joan and Cooper, J.P. *17th Century Documents*. Oxford University Press. 1972.

*Valor Ecclesiasticus*. Record Commission. 1825.

Venn, J. *Biographical History of Gonville and Caius College*. Volume I. Cambridge University Press. 1897.

Venn, J. and Venn, J.A. *Alumni Cantabrigienses*. Part I. Cambridge University Press. 1922.

Ward, Samuel. *A Collection of Such Sermons and Treatises as have been written and published [by Samuel Ward]*. 1636.

Wardle, F.D. (editor). *Accounts of the Chamberlains of the City of Bath, 1568-1602*. Somerset Record Society, Volume XXXVIII (1923).

## SECONDARY SOURCES

Anglin, Jay Pascall. 'The Court of the Archdeacon of Essex, 1571-1609: an institutional and social study'. (Unpublished Ph.D. thesis, University of California-Los Angeles, 1965.)

Arkell, Tom. 'Multiplying Factors for Estimating Population Totals From the Hearth Tax'. *Local Population Studies* number 28, Spring 1982.

Benham, W. Gurney. 'Arms of the Essex Boroughs'. *Essex Review* XXIII (1914). Reprinted as: *Essex Borough Arms*. Colchester. 1916.

Beresford, M.W. *New Towns of the Middle Ages*. 1967.

Bond, Shelagh and Evans, Norman. 'The Process of Granting Charters to English Boroughs, 1547-1649'. *English Historical Review*, XCI (1976).

Boynton, Lindsay. *The Elizabethan Militia, 1558-1638*. 1967.

Bridbury, A.R. 'English Provincial Towns in the Later Middle Ages'. *Economic History Review* XXXIV (1981).

Britnell, R.H. *Growth and Decline in Colchester, 1300-1525*. Cambridge University Press. 1986.

Brunton, D. and Pennington, D.H. *Members of the Long Parliament*. 1954.

Burch, Thomas K. 'Some demographic determinants of average household size: an analytic approach'. In Laslett, P., *Household and Family in Past Time* pp.91-102.

Burley, K.H. 'Economic Development of Essex in the later Seventeenth and early Eighteenth Centuries'. (Unpublished Ph.D. thesis, University of London, 1957.)

Burley, K.H. 'Analysis of Bishop Compton's Census of 1676: Ongar Hundred'. *Victoria County History of Essex* IV. 1963.

Calamy, Edward (Editor: Samuel Palmer). *Nonconformists' Memorial*. 1775.

Camden, William. *Britain, or a Chorographical Description of ... England, Scotland and Ireland*. (Translation by Philemon Holland) 1637.

Chambers, J.D. *Population, Economy and Society in Pre-Industrial England*. Oxford. 1972.

Chancellor, Frederick. *Ancient Sepulchral Monuments of Essex*. Chelmsford. No date.

Clark, Andrew. 'Maldon Civil Courts, 1402'. *Essex Review* XVI, 1907.

Clark, Andrew. 'Maldon records and the drama'. *Notes and Queries* 10th Series, VII and VIII, 1907.

Clark, Andrew. 'Essex Woollen Manufacture, 1629'. *Essex Review* XVII, 1908.

Clark, Peter, and Slack, Paul. *Crisis and Order in English Towns 1500-1700*. 1972.

Clark, Peter (editor). *Country towns in pre-industrial England*. Leicester University Press. 1981.

Clark, Peter. *The English Alehouse. A Social History 1200-1830*. 1983.

Clarkson, L.A. 'English Economic Policy in the Sixteenth and Seventeenth Centuries: the Case of the Leather Industry'. *Bulletin of the Institute of Historical Research* XXXVIII, 1965.

Clayton, K.M. *Landforms of Parts of Southern Essex*. Institute of British Geographers, publication 28. 1960.

Coldewey, John Christopher. 'Early Essex Drama: a history of its rise and fall, and a theory concerning the Digby Plays'. (Unpublished Ph.D. thesis, University of Colorado, 1972.)

Collinson, Patrick. *The Elizabethan Puritan Movement*. 1967.

Collinson, Patrick. 'Lectures by Combination: Structures and Characteristics of Church Life in 17th-Century England'. *Bulletin of the Institute of Historical Research*, XLVIII, 1975.

Collinson, Patrick. *The Religion of Protestants: the Church in English Society, 1559-1625*. Oxford University Press. 1982.

Conzen, M.R.G. 'The Use of Town Plans in the Study of Urban History'. in H.J.Dyos (editor), *The Study of Urban History*. 1968.

Cornwall, Julian. 'English Country Towns in the Fifteen Twenties'. *Economic History Review* XV, 1962.

Cornwall, Julian (editor). Lay Subsidy Rolls for the County of Sussex, 1542-1525. *Sussex Record Society* LVI.Lewes. 1956.

Cornwall, Julian. 'Evidence of Population Mobility in the Seventeenth Century'. *Bulletin of the Institute of Historical Research*, XV, 1967.

Credit Communal de Belgique. *Finances et Comptabilité urbaines du XIIIe au XVIe Siècle*. Pro-Civitate, Collection Histoire nr.7. Brussels. 1964.

Crowley, D.A. 'The Later History of Frankpledge'. *Bulletin of the Institute of Historical Research*, XLVIII, 1975.

Cruikshank, C.G. *Elizabeth's Army*. Oxford University Press. 2nd edition, 1966.

Curtis, Mark H. 'The Alienated Intellectuals of Early Stuart England'. *Past and Present* no.23 (1962).

Danes, John. *Paralipomena Orthographiae, Etymologiae, Prosodiae, una cum Scholiis*. 1638.

Danes, John. *A Light to Lillie: being an easie method for the better teaching and learning of the Latine tonge*. First edition 1637; second edition 1643. (Facsimile edition of the first edition, Scolar Press, Menston. 1968.)

Davids, T.W. *Annals of Evangelical Nonconformity*. 1863.

Dickin, E.P. 'Notes on the Coast, Shipping and Sea-borne Trade of Essex from 1565 to 1577'. *Transactions of the Essex Archaeological Society* XVII, 1926.

Dobson, R.B. 'Admissions to the Freedom of the City of York in the Later Middle Ages'. *Economic History Review*, XXVI (1973).

Dyer, Alan D. *The City of Worcester in the sixteenth century*. Leicester University Press. 1973.

Dyer, Christopher. 'The consumer and the market in the later middle ages'. *Economic History Review* XLII (1989).

Elton, G.R. *Reform and Renewal: Thomas Cromwell and the Common Weal*. Cambridge University Press. 1973.

Everitt, Alan. 'Social Mobility in Early Modern England'. *Past and Present* no. 33, 1966.

Everitt, Alan. 'The Marketing of Agricultural Produce'. In Thirsk, Joan (ed.) *The Agrarian History of England and Wales* IV. (Chapter 4).

Everitt, Alan. 'Urban Growth, 1570-1770'. *The Local Historian* VIII, 1968.

Everitt, Alan. 'The English Urban Inn, 1560-1760'. In Everitt, A. (editor), *Perspectives in English Urban History*. 1973.

Fell-Smith, C. 'Schools'. *Victoria County History of Essex* II, 1907.

Fitch, E.A. *Maldon and the River Blackwater*. Privately printed. No date but c1900.

George, R.H. 'Charters Granted to English Parliamentary Corporations in 1688'. *English Historical Review* LV 1940).

Glass, D.V. *Population in History*. 1965.

Goody, Jack, Thirsk, Joan and Thompson E.P. (editors). *Family and Inheritance*. Cambridge University Press. 1976.

Goose, N.R. 'In Search of the Urban Variable: Towns and the English Economy, 1500-1650'. *Economic History Review* XXXIX (1986).

Gramolt, David William. 'Coastal Marshlands of East Essex between the Seventeenth and Mid-Nineteenth Centuries'. (Unpublished M.A. thesis, University of London, 1960.)

Grieve, Hilda. *The Sleepers and the Shadows. Chelmsford: a town, its people and its past.* Volume I, *The Medieval and Tudor Story*. Chelmsford. 1988.

Harris, Jesse W. *John Bale: a study in the minor literature of the Reformation.* Illinois Studies in Language and Literature XXV, 4. Urbana, Illinois. 1940.

Hill, Christopher. *Society and Puritanism*. 1964.

Hoskins, W.G. 'The Rebuilding of Rural England, 1570-1640'. *Past and Present* no. 4. 1953.

Hoskins, W.G. *Provincial England*. 1963.

Hoskins, W.G. 'An Elizabethan Provincial Town: Leicester'. In Plumb, J.H. (editor), *Studies in Social History*. 1955.

Houghton, K.N. 'Theory and Practice in Borough Elections to Parliament during the later Fifteenth Century'. *Bulletin of the Institute of Historical Research* XXXIX (1966).

Howell, Roger. *Newcastle-Upon-Tyne and the Puritan Revolution*. Oxford University Press. 1967.

Hull, Felix. 'Agriculture and Rural Society in Essex, 1560-1640'. (Unpublished Ph.D. thesis, University of London, 1950.)

Hunt, William. *The Puritan Moment. The Coming of Revolution in an English County*. Harvard University Press. 1983.

Keeler, Mary Frear. *The Long Parliament, 1640-1641, a biographical study of its members*. American Philosophical Society Memoirs, volume 36. Philadelphia. 1954.

Laslett, P. 'Size and Structure of the Household in England over Three Centuries'. *Population Studies* XXIII. 1969.

Laslett, Peter (editor). *Household and Family in Past Time*. Cambridge University Press. 1972.

Laslett, Peter. 'Mean household size in England since the sixteenth century'. In *Household and Family*.

Laslett Peter. 'The History of the Family'. In *Household and Family*, pp. 1-89.

Leland, John. *Itinerary*. Editor, Lucy Toulmin Smith. 1909.

Livock, D.M. 'Accounts of the Corporation of Bristol: 1532 to 1835'. *Journal of Accounting Research*, 3. 1965.

Lockridge, K.A. 'The Population of Dedham, Massachusetts, 1636- 1736'. *Economic History Review* XIX, 1966.

MacCaffrey, W.T. *Exeter, 1540-1640*. Harvard University Press. 1958.

Macfarlane, A.J. *Witchcraft in Tudor and Stuart England*. 1970.

Macfarlane, A.J. 'Witchcraft in Tudor and Stuart Essex'. *Association of Social Anthropologists of the Commonwealth*, monograph 9. 1970.

Malden Historical Society. *Malden's Celebration of the Massachusetts Bay Colony Tercentenary, May 1930*. Malden, Massachusetts. 1931.

McClure, Peter. 'Patterns of Migration in the Later Middle Ages: The Evidence of English Place-Name Surnames'. *Economic History Review* XXXII (1979).

McKinley, R.A. *Norfolk Surnames in the Sixteenth Century*. (Leicester University Department of English Local History Occasional Papers, 2nd Series number 2.) Leicester University Press. 1969.

McKinley, R.A. *Norfolk and Suffolk Surnames in the Middle Ages*. English Surnames Series II. Chichester. 1975.

McKinley, R.A. *The Surnames of Lancashire*. English Surnames Series IV. 1981.

Meopham, W.A. 'Municipal Drama at Maldon in the Sixteenth Century'. *Essex Review* LV and LVI, 1946 and 1947.

Morant, Philip. *History of Essex*. 2nd edition, Chelmsford. 1816.

Neale, Sir John. *The Elizabethan House of Commons*. 1949.

Newton, K.C. and McIntosh, M. 'Leet Jurisdiction in Essex Manors Courts during the Elizabethan Period'. *Transactions of the Essex Archaeological Society* XIII (1981).

Nicholls, Laura M. 'The Lay Subsidy of 1523'. *University of Birmingham Historical Journal* IX, 1964.

Oxley, James. *The Reformation in Essex to the death of Mary*. Manchester University Press. 1965.

Palliser, D.M. *The Age of Elizabeth: England under the later Tudors 1547-1603*. 1983.

Patten, John H.C. 'The Hearth Taxes, 1662-1689'. *Local Population Studies* no. 7, Autumn 1971.

Patten, John H.C. 'The Urban Structure of East Anglia in the Sixteenth and Seventeenth Centuries'. (Unpublished Ph.D. thesis, University of Cambridge, 1972.)

Patten, John H.C. *Rural-Urban Migration in Pre-Industrial England*. School of Geography, University of Oxford, Research Papers. No.6. 1973.

Patten, J.H.C. 'Urban Occupations in Pre-Industrial England'. *Transactions of the Institute of British Geographers*, (New Series) II (1977).

Patten, John H.C. *English Towns 1500-1700*. Folkestone. 1978.

Petchey, William John. 'The Borough of Maldon, Essex, 1500 - 1688'. (Unpublished Ph.D. thesis, University of Leicester, 1972.)

Petchey, W.J. *The Intentions of Thomas Plume*. Maldon (Trustees of the Plume Library). 1985.

Pilgrim, J.E. 'The Rise of the 'New Draperies' in Essex'. *University of Birmingham Historical Journal* VII, 1959.

Plumb, J.H. *The Growth of Political Stability*. 1967.

Poos, L.R. 'Population and Resources in Two Fourteenth-Century Essex Communities: Great Waltham and High Easter, 1327-1389'. (Unpublished Ph.D. thesis, University of Cambridge, 1984.)

Poos, L.R. 'The Rural Population of Essex in the Later Middle Ages'. *Economic History Review* XXXVIII (1985).

Pound, J.F. 'The Validity of the Freemen's Lists: Some Norwich Evidence'. *Economic History Review* XXXIV (1981).

Pound, J.F. 'Social and Trade Structure'. In Clark, P. (editor): *The Early Modern Town*, pp.141-145. (The Open University) 1976.

Pound, J.F. 'The Social and Trade Structure of Norwich, 1525-1575'. *Past and Present*, no. 34. 1966.

Prescott, H.F.M. *Mary Tudor*. 1939.

Pringle, R.Hunter. *Maldon and Braintree District*. Report to the Royal Commission on Agriculture. 1898.

Redmonds, George. *Yorkshire West Riding*. English Surnames Series I. Chichester. 1973.

Reed, Michael. 'Economic structure and change in seventeenth -century Ipswich'.In Clark, P. (editor), *Country Towns in pre-industrial England*.

Roker, L.F. 'The Flemish and Dutch Community in Colchester in the Sixteenth and Seventeenth Centuries'. (Unpublished M.A. thesis, University of London, 1963.)

Round, J.H. 'Killegrews alias Shenfields'. *Transactions of the Essex Archaeological Society*, new series XIV, 1918.

Rutledge, Elizabeth. 'Immigration and population growth in early fourteenth-century Norwich: evidence from the tithing roll'. *Urban History Year Book*, 1988, pp.15-30.

Shipps, Kenneth W. 'Lay Patronage of East Anglian Puritan Clerics in Pre-Revolutionary England'. (Unpublished Ph.D. thesis, Yale University, 1971.)

Slack, P.A. *Poverty and Policy in Tudor and Stuart England*. (Themes in British Social History) 1988.

Smith, Harold. *Ecclesiastical History of Essex*. Colchester. No date (but 1937).

Smith, John Raymond. 'The Borough of Maldon, 1688-1768'. (Unpublished M.Phil. thesis, University of Leicester, 1981.)

Spufford, Margaret. *Contrasting Communities*. Cambridge University Press. 1974.

Stephens, W.B. 'The Cloth Exports of the Provincial Ports, 1600-1640'. *Economic History Review* XXII (1969). Subsequent discussions *ibid*. XXIV (1971.)

Stone, Lawrence. 'Social Mobility in England, 1500-1700'. *Past and Present*, no. 33. 1966.

Strype, John. *The Life of John Whitgift*. 1718.

Taylor, E.G.R. 'Robert Hooke and the Cartographical Projects of the late Seventeenth Century (1666-1696)'. *Geographical Journal* XC. 1937.

Thirsk, Joan. 'Industries in the Countryside'. In *Essays in the Economic and Social History of Tudor and Stuart England* (Economic History Society). Cambridge University Press. 1961.

Thirsk, Joan (editor). *The Agrarian History of England and Wales* Volume IV, 1500-1640. Cambridge University Press. 1967.

Thirsk, Joan. *Sources of Information on Population, 1500- 1760*. Canterbury. 1965.

Thrupp, Sylvia L. 'The Problem of Replacement Rates in Late Medieval English Population'. *Economic History Review* XVIII, 1965.

Tittler, Robert. 'The Emergence of Urban Policy, 1536-58'. In Tittler, R. and Loach, J. (editors), *The Mid-Tudor Polity*. 1980.

Tittler, R. 'The Incorporation of Boroughs, 1540-1558'. *History* February 1977.

Tittler, R. 'Incorporation and Politics in Sixteenth Century Thaxted'. *Transactions of the Essex Archaeological Society* VII (1976).

Tyack, N.C.P. 'Migration from East Anglia to New England Before 1660'. (Unpublished Ph.D.thesis, University of London, 1951.)

Tyacke, Nicholas. 'The Rise of Arminianism Reconsidered'. *Past and Present* no. 115 (1987).

Walters, John. 'Grain Riots and Popular Attitudes to the Law: Maldon and the Crisis of 1629'. In Brewer, John and Styles, John (editors) *An Ungovernable People: the English and their Law in the Seventeenth and Eighteenth Centuries*. New Brunswick, N.J. 1980.

Walters, John and Wrightson, Keith. 'Dearth and the Social Order in Early Modern England'. *Past and Present* no. 71 1976.

Weinbaum, Martin. *The Incorporation of Boroughs*. Manchester University Press. 1937.

Weinbaum, Martin. *British Borough Charters, 1307-1660*. Cambridge University Press. 1943.

Willan, T.S. *The English Coasting Trade, 1600-1750*. Manchester University Press, 1938.

Williams, N. 'The Maritime Trade of the East Anglian Ports, 1550-1590'. (D.Phil thesis, University of Oxford, 1952, posthumously published in the series *Oxford Historical Monographs*, Oxford University Press. 1989.)

Williams, Penry. *The Tudor Regime*. Oxford University Press. 1979.

Woodward, D.M. 'Sources for Urban History: 1. Freemen's Rolls'. *The Local Historian* IX, 1970.

Woodward, Donald. "Swords into Ploughshares": Recycling in Pre-Industrial England'. *Economic History Review* XXXVIII (1985).

Wrightson, Keith and Levine, David. *Poverty and Piety in an English Village: Terling, 1525-1700*. New York. 1979.

Wrigley, E.A. *Identifying People in the Past*. 1973.

Abbot, George ( Archbishop), 238, 240

Abingdon (Oxon), 11

Abraham, Matthew, 32; William, 32, 195

Acts of Parliament, 126-7, 167; on aliens, 56; for dissolution of chantries & religious guilds, 92; on excommunication (1552), 170; for dissolution of chantries and religious guilds, 92; for a lay subsidy (1523), 10; on paupers and vagrants, 47; for preservation of clothing trades, 168; for repair of decayed towns (1541-1544), 88-90, 93, 126, 128; to remedy decay of corporate towns (1554), 127; sumptuary laws, 167-8; Statute of Artificers (1563), 45, 127, 168; Act of Uniformity (1559), 168, 196; Act of Uniformity (1662), 252-4; Statute of Usury (1571), 131; Statute of Wills (1540), 83; Statute of Winchester (1293), 168

actions of account (pleas of), 168

actors, visiting the town, 161, 180, 198; noblemen's companies, 173-4; final visit, 174; see also plays, Town Play

Adamthwaite, John, 51, 62

Admiralty, Borough Court of, 46, 57, 113, 143, 150, 168, 181, 272; Bailiffs' jurisdiction, 152, 165-6; Exhortation for, 159; oar, 159, 180; Order for Keeping the Court, 159; seal, 152-4

Admiralty, High Court of, 57, 144-5, 165; Vice-Admiral of England, 165

adultery, 170, 203

affeirors, 226-7

age at death, 202, 241

Agricultural Commissioner's Report, 67

agricultural labour, 45

Alba, Duke of, 131-2

Albert, Robert, 195; Thomas, 52

Alcock, Robert, 104

alderman, 60, 119, 156, 166, 207

aldermen, 161-3, 169, 180, 184, 229; abused, 185-6, 220-1; ejected, 219; as J.P.s, 154, 167; religious attitudes (c1558-60), 151; sequence of offices, 155; social rank of, 71, 162; as trustees, 240

Aldham's, 80, 84, 86(m), 87-88, 120, 139

ale brewing, 115-116

alehousekeeper, 111, 167, 222; alehouses, 54, 169; The Bell, 135 (m); The George, 5(m), 117, 146

aliens, 33, 54-57, 115; oath of obedience, 55; ordinance for, 55, 115; origin of term 'Dutchman', 54

All Saints and St Peter, Vicarage of, 170, 202, 209; bowling alley at, 210; patronage of, 170, 197, 209, 231, 235; stipend of vicars, 231, 235; vicarage house, 90, 202, 229, 233; vicars, 197-8, 202

All Saints' church, 3, 9, 32, 57, 70, 71, 98, 119, 135 (m), 136, 170, Plate 10; styled 'All Hallows', 134; belfry, 214; Charnel House, 191; Cammock monument, 71, 73; Darcy's chantries, 90, 92; exterior, 99; interruption of sermon in, 212; pieta in, 192; Protestant associations, 199; pulpit, 212-3; spire, 179; Bishop Aylmer's Visitation at, 207

All Saints' parish, 7, 78, 80, 99, 170, 191; churchwardens' loans, 179; Overseers of the Poor, 179

Alleyn, Edward (of Hatfield Peverel), 239-40; George, 258

almshouse(s), 5(m) 20

Althorne, Vicarage of, 234, 241

amicus certissimus, 63

Anabaptism, 171, 218

Anderson, Joan (alias Carpenter), 58; William, 58

Andrew Aylewyn's (messuage), 5(m)

Andrews, Benjamin, 102-103

Angel, Joan, 63

Annable, Robert, 54

Antwerp, 196

apothecary, 82

apparitor, 214

Applemarket, 136; applemonger, 113

Appleton, Roger, 119

apprentices, 44-45, 63, 111, 123, 128, 169, 221; ages, 30, 44; and servants, 45; catchment area for, 54, 63, 65(m); Custumal reference to, 44-45; enrolled indentures, 44-45, 61, 63, 64, 70, 107,

122, 124, 162, 168, 170, 272; freedom
(of the borough), 44-45; long-distance
migration of, 63; parental occupations,
45; rampage by, 124, 140; residential
pattern (1570s), 30, 44
arbitration, 166
Archdeacon of Essex, 236; court of, 170,
171, 173, 202, 220; Office against
Wiersdale, 209; Visitation (1585), 208,
212; Archdeaconry of Essex, 170, 201,
271; *see also* Palmer, Robert
Archdeaconry of Colchester, 170, 201
archdeacons' courts, 28, 214
Ardleigh, 81
Arminianism, 236; Arminius, Jacobus,
238
arms and armour, 169
Arthur, William, 228-30
*Articles touching Preachers*, 206, 213
*As You Like It*, 53
Asheldham Hall, 70
Ashpoole, Thomas, 259
Askrigg (Yorks), 61-62
Assembly of the House, 156
assistants, 157
assize rent, 55, 88-89, 93-95, 137, 174;
conversion to Ferm Rents, 88, 94, 174;
assize rental, 88-9, 93-5,
Assizes, 28, 33, 166, 171-2
attorney (for Corporation), 181
Attwood, William, 257-8
audit, 159; auditor, 163
Augmentations, Court of, 126; Auditor,
126
Augure, William, 116
autobiography, 72, 189
Awnger's (tenement), 147
Aylesbury (Bucks), 11; borough charter,
130, 151
Aylett, Dr Robert, 244
Aylewyn, Andrew, 88
Aylmer, John (Bishop of London 1577-
94), 207, 213; Visitation by, 207, 236

Backhouse, Elias, 49
`Baddow', 36; Baddow, Great, 215;
Baddow, Little, 97, 170, 234, 250
Baggeman, John, 88; Baggeman's
(messuage), 4(m)
Bailiffs (of Maldon borough), 41, 60, 125,

150, 203, 212, 215; listed, 260-2; abuse
of, 184-5, 190, 214, 260-2; Admiralty
jurisdiction of, 159; Admiralty lawsuit
against, 144; alien as, 56-7; authority of,
154, 157-60, 165, 168, 250; complaints
about, 214, 222-3, 227; control of
parliamentary elections, 248, 250-2;
demotion of, 166, 216, 251; duties,
responsibilities, 26, 119; election
criticised in sermon, 215; election of
(1592), 227-8; fees of, 178, 180-1;
livery allowance to, 180; origin of
offices (in Maldon), 150; subsidies to
borough, 160, 169; as tenant-occupiers,
82; time on official activity, 169; wealth
of, 161-2
Bailiffs' activities: accusations v. Robt.
Palmer, 213-4; contract, 113; arrest of
suspects for The State, 252;
authorisation of expenditure, 160, 174;
economic policy, 106, 133-6, 142, 180;
entertainment of guests, 139, 180;
establishing prices, 129, 131, 142;
licensing settlement, 49-50; licensing
actors' performances, 173-4, 216;
actions in external courts, 166; pre-
vention of preaching, 244; and Princess
Mary Tudor, 142, 150-151; patronage of
Protestantism, 199-200, 208;
supervision of borough property, 180
Bailiffs and Aldermen as trustees, 21
Baker, Robert, 54
baker, 111, 120
Bale, John, 189-193, 270
Ball, Thomas, 71
ballad-singer, 221
bankruptcy, 132-3
Bantoft, William, 81, 212; daughter's
marriages, 81, 219
baptisms, 16-18, 32, 72, 80, 271
barber-surgeon, 76, 186; barber's shop,
185-6
Barking, 63
Barling, 69
Barn Wick, 70
Barnardiston family, 163; John, 22, 163,
234, 259, and family of, 259; Sir
Nicholas, 234
barrier in river, 144
Barrington family, 234
Barsham (Suff), 238

Bartholomew Fair, 128
Bath: city chamberlains' accounts, 174, 177-8
Battes, [   ] of Braintree, 146
Battle (Sx), 84
Baude's (Bawde's), 4(m), 84, 88, 135(m)
baymaker, 13
Baynard manor, Messing, 25
bays and says, 13, 61; bay-weaving, 123
beadle, 180
Bean Mead, 86(m), 87
Beccles (Suff), 234
Beckingham Hall, B~, Stephen, 97
Bedell, Samuel, 21
Bedfordshire, 116
Beeleigh, 8(m), 57; Beeleigh Abbey, 3, 9, 25, 97, 133, 191, 193; bailiff of estates, 161; buried treasure, 172; corrodian of, 70; Jesus Chapel of, 193; rebuilding at, 97
beer, 111-118, 141, 240
Beerhouse, The, 117
Bekke's (tenement), 5(m)
Bell Inn, 135(m), 137
bell ringer, 46, 161, 180, 213
Benfleet, South, 119
Benham, Richard, 56, 161, 191
benevolences, 175-6
Bentley, John, 259
Bermondsey, 254
Bernard, Richard, 206
Berry, Dorothy, 145
betterment migration, 52-53, 61-62, 70
Bevercoats (Notts), 196
Beza, Theodore, 238
Bible: 101; English translation of, 190, 192; St John's Gospel, 238, Book of the Revelation, 188, 205, 224, 235; Testament with the great Annotations, 238; Tremelin's Bible, 238
Bideford (Devon), 11
bigamy, 58
Billericay, 36, 49, 54
billeting, 14
Bindoff, S.T., 89
Birch, Little, 125
Birch, Thomas, 140
Bishop's Castle Field, 86(m)
Bishop's Hall manor, Chelmsford, 77

Bishops of London, 98, 134, 201, 210, 213, 228, 230, 236, 249; manorial jurisdiction in Maldon, 77, 125, 150, 154; see also Aylmer, Bonner, Fletcher, Ridley, St Roger Niger
Blackmore, 49
blacksmith, 36, 78, 112, 184
Blackwall, 179
Blackwater Estuary, 1-2, 69, 145, 150, 194
Blackwater river, 1, 10, 69, 112, 179; Blackwater and Chelmer Navigation, 146
Blue Boar, 60-61, 87, 94, 120, 135(m), 137-9, 174, 184, 223
Blunt William, 74
Bocking, 11-13, 19, 43, 145
Bolton-by-Bowland (Yorks), 58, 60-61
Bonayre, John, 115
Bonner, Edmund (Bishop of London 1539-49 & 1553-59), 195
Bonner, John, 126
Book of Common Prayer (1549), 193; (1552), 194; (1559), 195-6, 197, 202, 206, 208, 241, 243
Book of Discipline, 211, 244
books, 102, 237-9
Boreham, 72
Borough of Maldon: evolution, 7; medieval burgesses' rights, 77, 125, 150; court business, 46, 163; Liberty of, 165, 169; Lordship of, 24, 90, 125; Secrets of, 164, 183, 184, 223; see also Aldermen, Bailiffs, Court of Election, Court of Record, Custumal, Oaths
Borough English, 77, 82-84, 105
Borough Hills, 145-6
Boston (Lincs), Hussey Tower, 90
Boswell, John, 56-57, 94, 125, 151, 194-5
Bourchier, Henry, Earl of Essex, 142, 249; Bourchier's Quay, 5(m)
bowling alley, 135(m), 210
Bownd, Nicholas, 236, 238
Bradhedd, Adam,184
Bradwell-juxta-Mare, 69, 74
Braintree, 11-13, 74, 112, 124, 145-6, 198; market area of, 65; Classis of, 202
Brakett, Hugh, 54
Bramston, Sir John (Lord Chief Justice), 72, 244, 257; Sir John (baronet), 72,

252, 256; Francis, 258; Sir Moundeford, 76, 258; Roger, 72

brasier, 96

Braxted, Great, 70

breach of covenant, pleas of, 129

bread, 111

Breeder , Ralph, 14, 69, 111, 122, 124, 169, 219, 235, 243; feoffees of, 84, 235

Brentwood, 33, 74, 107, 137, 166, 172, 199-200

*brethelde brawlers*, 167

Brett, Richard, 196; William, 69

Brett, Sir Robert, 71

brewer(s), 55, 111, 114-118; brewer's manager, 110, 129; brewery, 4(m); brewing, 131-2; Brewing House, The, 116

bricks (and tiles), 91, 97-98, 112

bricklayer(s), 98, 111; brickmaker, 68, 130

Brick Building, 98; Brick Cross, 179; Brick Prison, 172

Brightman, Thomas, 238

Bristol, 105

Britnell, R.H., 105

Brockis (Brocas), Benjamin, 123

Bromley, Richard, 52

Brook, [   ], Carmelite Prior, 193

Brooke, John, 217, 219-21, 223, 227-8, 240

Browning, Jeremy, 245; William, 214-5

Brownists, 216, 217, 220-21, 236

Bryant, Robert, 107

Buckingham, 151

building, 114; fashions of local gentry, 97-98; materials, 97-99

Bull, The, 96

Bull Ring, the, 118, 135(m); bull-baiting, 167

'bullimong', 120, 140, 143

Bullock Yard, 86(m), 87

burgage tenure, 80

Burgess, John, 70

Burgess Mead, 86(m)

Burgesses in Parliament *see* Members of Parliament.

Burghley, Lord (William Cecil), 125, 202, 203, 207

burials, 16-18, 49, 70, 80; last rites, 193, 196, 271

Burles, William, 185

Burles, [   ] *the propertie plaier*, 198

Burley, K.H., 13

Burnham on Crouch, 65, 68, 98, 118, 119

Burton, John, 61-62

Bury, Edward (M.P.), 126

Bush, John, 161

butcher(s), 68, 85, 87, 96, 114, 118-119, 167

Butcher Row, 87, 98, 118, 134-6, 135(m), 140

Butcher, Sir Edward (J.P.), 71

butchers, 85, 145; *see also* Butcher Row.

Butler, John (of Thoby), 207-8, 234

Buttermarket, 135(m), 136, 140

Butt Lane, 4(m), 87, 96; butts, 86(m), 87, 180

bye-laws, *see* ordinances

Cade, John, 94-95, 116, 148

Caesar, Sir Julius, 250, 256, 257

Calderdale, 61

Calvin, John, 188, 215, 238-9; Calvinism, 236-238

Cambridge (borough), 11, 174

Cambridge University, 33, 45, 57, 74, 162, 197, 199-201, 231; colleges of: Christ's, 72, 74, 200-1, 230-1; Emmanuel, 81, 203, 233, 241; Gonville Hall (Caius College), 72; Jesus, 72; Magdalene, 209; Pembroke, 236; Trinity, 199; Trinity Hall, 241; St John's, 241

Cambridgeshire, 71, 116

Camden, William, 245

Cammock family, 71; coat of arms, 73; Frances, 72; Thomas, 71-72, 121, 234

Canfield, Great, 126

Canterbury, 57

capital investment, 115, 121

Capstack, Henry, 61-62, 122

Carden, John, widow of, 185

Carmelite Friary (Maldon), 3, 4(m), 85, 95. 189-91, 193, 246, 270; (Colchester), 191

Carpenter, George, 58

Carr, John, 260

carrier, 137

Carter, Ann, 145-6

cash bequests, 81, 122, 169; *see also* coin

Catalogues, *see* decenner, freemen

catchment areas (population), 54, 59, 62-63, 65

Catton, Nicholas, 21
Causeway, The, 10, 85, 117, 172, 178
Cecil, Sir Robert (Secretary of State), 187, 224
Cecil, William, *see* Burghley.
Census (1801), 23
Chadderton, Laurence, 203, 233
Chafford Hundred, 116, 131
chamberlains (borough), 20, 159-60, 164, 180-1, 197
chamberlains' accounts, 106, 159, 173-183, 233, 272; receipts: Assize Rents, 55, 88-89, 93, 137, 174; fines, 31, 60, 128; landcheaps, 77-80, 98, 174; loans, 20; Hythe rents, 146; Water Bailiffs' receipts, 118, 140-41, 147-8, 168, 175-7, *and* Fig. 16, Table 6; expenditure: 248; barrier across river, 144; burning iron, 47; Civil War expenses, 251-2; copy of Act of Parliament, 89; costs of Admiralty lawsuit, 144; dredging, 146; execution, 171; fees of legal counsel, 178; gifts, 145, 150, 174, 200, 201, 235; lawsuit costs and damages, 144; message carrying, 47; Moot Hall maintenance, 181; moving a building, 98. 146; prisoners' maintenance, 47, 171-2; punishment of vagrants, 47; `rewards' to performers, 173, 198; `rewards' to clergy, 234, 236-7; searching female vagrants, 47; selection of vicar, 231; subsidies to clergy stipends, 231-2, 235; tobacco, 181; Town Clerk's gown, 163; Town Play, 190
Chancellor (diocesan), 76
chandler (tallowchandler), 52, 107
Chandler, Alice, 172; John, 103
Channel Islands, 55
chantries in Essex, 92; chantry certificates (for Maldon, 1549), 89, 269; chantry priest, 196
Chantry House, 135(m)
Chapman, Edmund, 180, 199
Chapman and André's Map of Essex, 6, plan of Maldon, 85
charitable trusts, 21
Charles I (King of Gt Britain 1625-49), 57, 120, 183
Charles II (King of Gt Britain 1660-85), 244, 252

charters (Maldon borough), 77, 125, 134, 150-54, 255, 271; contents of charters of incorporation, 25, 89, 127-130, 151-4, 165-6, 174, 177; James II's charters, 14, 252; Admiralty charter, 150
Cheese (Chese), Thomas, 163, 238-9, 259
Chelmer river, 1, 9-10
Chelmsford Hundred, 65
Chelmsford, 10-12, 18, 19, 36, 42, 48, 49, 54, 65, 68, 74, 80-81, 100, 105, 112, 119, 134, 137, 172, 190, 198, 199, 250; survey of tenures, 80; market of, 58, 65, 112; Walker map of, 77, 80
Chequers Lane, 97
Cheyney, John, 191
Chibborne, Charles, 144-5, 257
Christmas, Peter, 231
Church John, 90-91, 93, 125-126, 137, 151, 161-3, 195
churches (Maldon) *see* All Saints', Beeleigh Abbey, St Helen's Chapel, St Peter's, St Mary's, *and* churchwardens, Carmelites, parishes
churches (out of Maldon) *see* Heybridge, Layer Marney, Norwich, Roxwell, Sandon, Woodham Walter
church vestments, 197-8
churchwardens, 169; (All Saints' and St Peter's), 20, 197
Civil War, 251-2
Clark, John, 131, 145, 240; Thomas, 60, 245
Clay, John, 32
clergy, 71, 123, 162, 241; *and see* Arthur; Crackenthorpe; Dawes, Wm; Frith; Gifford, George; Gifford, Samuel; Grey; Hawdon; Hewitt; Horrocks; Johnson, Nich; Marshall, Stephen; Nash, Wm; Palmer; Pratt, Elisha; Robinson family; Rogers, John I; Rogers, Ric.; Simpson, John; Spigurnell, Thos; Tay; Wiersdale; Williams, Robt; Withers, Fabian & George
Clerk of the Market, 113, 151, 177; Court of, 46, 128, 168, 170, 181; Royal Clerk, 151, 165
clockmaker, 76
cloth, borough duty on, 143
clothier, 60, 63, 123, 216, 227
clothing, 122; clothing makers, 62, 114

clothing trades, 114, 123 *and see* Textiles.
co-heiresses, 82-3
coal, 100, 113, 115, 120, 140-3, 146;
    heaps, 86(m); imports (1641-47), 146;
    Newcastle measure, 141
coastal shipping, 69-70, 133
coats of arms, 71, 119, 154, 181
Cobbes-at-the-Corner, 4(m), 96
Cock, The, 5(m)
Coe, John, 259; Matthew, 117
Coggeshall (Great), 11-13, 18, 198
coin, 101; circulation of, 7, 129
Colchester, 10-13, 47, 57, 74, 100, 105,
    112, 119, 137, 165, 180, 187, 190, 191,
    194, 199, 236; beer brewing at, 115;
    Castle, 172; market area, 65; Mid-
    summer Fair, 36; poor of, 19, 21; siege
    of, 251
Cole, Alice, 198; George, 144-5
collarmaker, 111
Collett, John, 103; Richard, 112
Colliers' Reach, 145
Collin's (tenement), 4(m)
Collinson, P. 203, 211, 218
Colne (Lancs), 61
Colne River, 67
Combinations of Clergy, 234
Commission on Corporation accounts, 223
Committee for Plundered Ministers, 233
Common Council (borough), 150, 157,
    167
common informers, 46, 60
common rights, 89
commonland, 87, 89, 222
commonwealth ideas, 125-126, 128
*commorantes*, *see*: foreigners
communal strategy, 125
communicants in 1547, 89
communications, 63, 69
Company, The, 154; *see* Corporation
Constable, John, 1
constables, 46-47, 167, 180-1, 184;
    Frankpledge duties, 27
conveyances, 77, 80-81, 94, 103, 120,
    168-9, 272; to uses, 83
Conyers, Tristram, 258
Cook, Andrew (of Mundon), 238
cook, 76, 103
cooper(s), 63, 115-116, 140
Cooper, Michael, 21

Cope, Sir Anthony, 207-8
Corn Cross (Cornmarket), 134, 135(m),
    136, 140; Corn Hill, 98
Cornish, William I, 51, 62, 148; William
    II, 63, 148
Cornwall, 58
Corporation of Maldon, 13, 18, 48, 93,
    106, 127, 154-64, 203, 223; abuse of,
    170-1, 183-6, 199, 216, 220-21; accused
    of turbulency, 146; ambitions, 125;
    appointments, 126, 155; archives, 46,
    163, 255, 272; chaplain, 180; complaint
    to Privy Council, 221; composition,
    154-164 *passim* , 170; corporate respon-
    sibility, 154; 'counterfeit corporation',
    224; creation of, 70; dissidents in, 215-
    7, 223-4; dissolution of, 46, 255;
    ecclesiastical involvement, 197-200,
    207-9, 231, 235, 252; elections to, 70;
    exclusions from, 215; expulsion of
    headburgesses, 185, 243; frankpledge
    jurisdiction, 25; improvements to
    Hythe; lawsuits, 30, 144, 163; leases of
    oyster fishing, 113, of Portman Marsh,
    117, 222; limitations on action, 171-3;
    membership, 139, 154-5, 220, 227;
    policy on urban decay, 140; popular
    attitude to, 183-6; quarrel with Robt
    Palmer, 211-15, 217, 221, 223; voting,
    227-228, 231; *see also* affeirors,
    Aldermen, assistants, Bailiffs,
    constables, chamberlains' accounts,
    Common Council, communal strategy,
    Courts, Members of Parliament, Quarter
    Sessions
Corpus Christi, Feast of, 93, 195
Cottingham's (tenement), 4(m), 147
cotton, 111
counsellor-at-law, 74, 126, 144-5, 178,
    257-8
Court of Election, 23-4, 31, 42, 150, 155,
    272; of 1594, 217
Court of Record, 46, 77, 83-4, 131-2, 168,
    272; *and see* pleas of debt
courts, 125; *see also* Admiralty, Clerk of
    the Market, Peace (Petty Sessions),
    Quarter Sessions
Coventry, 107, 114
Cowl, The, 170

Cowper, Francis, 172; Cowper's (tenement), 4-5(m)
Cowpe's Land, 86(m)
Crackbone, John, 88; Crackbone's (messuage), 4(m), 84, 99
Crackenthorpe, John, 74; Richard, 74
Cranke's (Great and Little), 4-5(m), 88
credit facilities, 64, 130-1; creditors as plaintiffs, 64
Creek of Maldon, (and Port of), 69, 119
Creeksea (Cricksea, Crixseth), 74, 76, 98, 250
Cressing, 74
Crewe, Thomas, 144-5
Croft, Gabriel (M.P.), 72
Cromwell, Gregory, 74, 125
Cromwell, Thomas (Earl of Essex), 74, 125-126
Crom Well [Cromwell, The], 72, 121, conduit, 4(m); Cromwell Downs, 86(m); Cromwell Hill, 3; Cromwell Stile, 86(m)
Crooked Croft, 86(m). 121
Crosse's Great Tenement, 4(m), 135(m), 136-7
Crouch River, 72
curates: of All Saints, 20, 231; stipendiary (St Mary's), 170, 199, 221, 228, 233,
currier, 113, 121
customary inheritance: see Borough English.
Customer (of Port of Maldon), 163
customs of the borough, 24, 82, 93, 125, 183; Custumal of Maldon, 46, 77, 82-83, 106, 116, 118, 128-129, 141-14, 150, 156-7, 165-167, 184, 272; revision, 46, 83, 134, 154; inmates, 49-50, 97; tolls on freight, 141, 143; waterside trade regulations, 142
cutler, 113
Cutts, John, 249

Da Salvo, Johannes, 54
Danbury, 1, 76, 92, 101, 113, 156, 201, 250
Danes, John, 74-75, 161
Darcy's Chantries, 90, 92; Darcy family, 90, 92, 97, 105, 154, 249; D~, Sir Thomas (Baron D~), 92, 126, 271; D~ (Darcy's) Tower, 90-93, 126-7, 135(m),

161-2, 246; D~'s Wharf, 5(m); see also Moot Hall (new)
Dartford (Kent), 119
Dawes (Dowes), Henry (M.P.), 74, 89, 125-126
Dawes, John, 12, 89, 107, 125, 132-3, 161, 197
Dawes, William, 74, 197
decenner (term), 24; Catalogues of decenners, 22, 26-33, 71, 105, 163; Oaths of, 26, 47, 168, 203; parish listings, 27
Dedham, 12, 45, 231; Dedham Conference, 202, 206-7, 235, 237
Dee, John, 172
Defoe, Daniel, 76
deforciants, 27
Dengie Hundred, 65, 69, 70, 119, 240
Denham (Suff), 207
Dent (Yorks), 61-62; Dentdale, 61-62, 122
Depeis, Mardochaeus, 57
detinue , 168
Devereux, Robert, Earl of Essex, 235-6, 256
Devonshire, 42, 58, 251
Dewes, Paul (of Stowlangtoft), 117; D`Ewes, Sir Symonds, 117
Deyre, John, 115-116
Diglitt, Thomas, 233
Directory, The , 211, 243
Dissenters, 252, 254
distraint of goods, 186
Doctor of Civil Law, 57
Dodderidge, Sir John, 71
Domesday Survey, 7
Doncaster, 187, 189, 225
Donne, John, 61
Dorislaus (Doresley), Isaac; John, 57
Dovehouse Garden, 86(m)
Dowman, William, 196
Downham, George (Bishop of Derry), 238
Dowsett, Edward, 68
draper, 62, 103, 112, 122-123, 136
dress-making, 76
Drumelzier (`Dromelzane') Scotland, 56
drunkenness, 184, 227, 237, 240
Dry Drayton (Cambs), 201
dual occupations, 107-112
dual residence, 68
Dubois (Duboys), Jehan, 142, 150-1

ducking stool, 5(m), 172
Dudley, John (Duke of Northumberland), 92, 150-1
dunghill (midden), 94, 170; *and see* : Town Dunghill
Dunkirk(ers), 133
Dunmow, Great, 12, 198; Little, 195
Dutch influence, 115, 190; Dutch rebellion against Spain, 57, 132, 203
Dutchman, John, 56
`Dutchmen', 54, 115
duties charged at the Hythe, 118, 141, 143
Dyer, A.D., 111
dyer, 123

Earls Maldon, 25
Easterlings, 56
Eastwood, John, 172; Thomas, 186
Edmonds, John, (M.P.), 89
education, 72, 74, 210; *see also* Danes, John; Dawes, Henry; Leach, Henry
Edward VI (King 1547-53) reign, 33, 92, 125, 150, 171, 197
Edward the Elder (W. Saxon king), 7
Edwards, John I, 139; John II, 184
election to grace, 238
Elizabeth I (Queen 1558-1603), religious settlement, 187, 197, 207
Elmstead, Margaret, 88
elopement story, 72, 234
embroiderer, 124
Emenote, Simon, 115
emigration, 16, 34-50, 77, 82, 84, 243; of freemen, 41-43, 60
Emperor (Charles V), 150, 239
employment, seasonal, 36, 54
enclosure, 87; of common pastures, 222
encroachments, 88, 93-94, 96-97
*Encyclopaedia Londiniensis* , 3
England, Robert, 191
enlisted men, 54
enquiry on grain supplies (1608), 111, 117
entrance rates, 35-36
Essex, 50, 58, 97, 117, 120; alien community in, 54, 57; cheese measure of, 141; Forest of, 1, 68; gentlemen, 123, 125; manorial leet courts in, 25, 68; Quarter Sessions, 71; stiles of, 67; traders of at Heybridge, 143; *see also* Archdeaconry, Assizes

Essex, Earls of (Bourchier family), 125, 141-2
essoins, 27
estreats (profits) of courts, 174-7
Eve, Thomas, 162; William, 111
excommunication, 170, 197, 214
executions, 33; of Anne Carter, 145; of impostor, 33; at Maldon, 171, 190; of Maldon witches, 172
exhibitions for scholars, 62
exit rates, 35-6
expulsions (from the town), 47-48

Fairfax, Sir Thomas, 251
Fairs, 31, 106, 121, 125, 127-128, 140, 184
Fairstead, 43
falcon mews, 2
Fambridge, North, 72; and Ferry 54
families, histories of, 42-43
Faulkbourne Hall, 97
Faversham (Kent), 11
Feering, 105, 132
fees, 33, 178, 180-1, Table 7
Felgate, [    ], surveyor, 6
Felsted, 198
felt-making, 123
ferm rents, 150, 154
field names, *see:* Aldham's, Bean Mead, Bishop's Castle Field, Bullock Yard, Burgess Mead, Crooked Croft, Friars' Fields, Gravel Pits Land, Hopyard, Katherine Downs, Lodge Leas, Milkwell, Mill Field, Priest's Croft, St George's Croft, Tenterfield, Town Downs, Wayer Mead, Winton
finance (of the borough): appeals to outsiders, 179-80; balance of accounts, 174; cash supplies, 177; emergencies, 173, 177-8; interest on loans, 179; loans to borough chest, 20, 144, 178-9; nature of receipts, 174-80; property investment policy, 174; requisite expenditure, 181-2; sale of property/rents, 178-9; *see also* chamberlains' accounts
Finch, Ezekiel, 21
fines, 225-6
fish, 112; fishing, 76, 113
Fishmarket, the, 134; Fish Stalls, 134, 135(m), 136
fishmonger, 111, 113

Flanders, 120; Fleming, Peter a, 170;
Flemings, 33, 54, 56; Flemish
influences, 190
fletcher, 31, 76, 172
Fletcher, Richard (Bishop of London
1595-96), 187, 206, 224, 228, 236
floods, 178
food and drink trades, 114 *et seq.*
Ford, Richard, 49
foreigners *(commorantes)* , 31, 71, 106,
112, 177, 179, 183
fornication, 170, 203
Fowle, William, 69
Fox, Peter, 115
Foxe, John, *Book of Martyrs* , 171, 190
Framlingham (Suff), 58, 151
Francis, William, 82, 240
Frank alias Dyrek, Richard, 56-57
Franke, Richard, 202, 208-9, 231, 235;
Thomas, 197, 200
frankpledge, views of, 25-33, 46-47, 84,
167, 216
freemen (freeburgesses), 13, 24, 26, 32,
60, 64, 70, 81, 117, 130-1, 150, 183,
222; admission memoranda, 14-16, 31,
41-42, 49, 52, 64, 252, 272; admission
fees, 15, 32-3, 42, 62, 174-7, 242;
aliens, 55, 56-57; annual numbers, 15,
34, 42, 178; apprentices as, 45, 81;
Catalogues of, 22-24, 32, 41; catchment
area of, 54, 59, 62-65, 65(m); charity
for, 21; disaffected, 126, 223; emigration, 15-16, 60, 81, 242; `forinsec' (non-
resident), 41, 252; lawsuits of, 165-6,
178; loss of freedom, 55, 132, 164, 166;
membership of The Company, 154-6; as
M.P.s, 74, 162, 165, 180; oath of, 24,
164-5, 168, 203; pledges, 48, 106, 131-
2; pledges in witchcraft prosecutions,
173; scot-and-lot obligations, 177;
voting for M.P.s, 206-7, 248-51
Friars' Fields, 56, 85, 86(m); F~ Gate,
135(m); F~ Mansion, 3, 4(m) 85, 86(m),
95, 97; *and see* Carmelites
Frith, John (of Hawkwell), 210-11
Fullbridge, 4(m), 9, 14, 85, 103, 112-113,
121, 143, 172, 177-8; F~ House, 117;
F~ Street, 3, 85, 115; F~, Stephen of, 9
fuller, 68, 123; fulling mill, 117, 123
Furnes, Thomas, 60-62, 70, 81, 107, 137

Gale, [   ], 171
gallows, 151
games, 132, 167
gardens, 87, 119-120, 142
gardener, 120; London Company of
Gardeners, 120
Gardiner, Sir Thomas, 148
Garni(d)ge, Geoffrey, Jeffery, 52
Garrington, Alice, 80; Elisha, 80-81, 216
Garstang (Lancs), 62-63
Gate Street, 3
Gates, Anne, 185
Gaywood, John, 93; Robert, 125, 151, 196
general handymen, 54
Gent, Thomas, 257
gentlemen, gentry, 42, 60, 64, 70-1, 96,
100, 113, 120, 122-3, 148, 161, 184,
220, 227, 247-5
George, The, 5(m), 117
Germans, 54; Germany, wars 1520-1555,
239; wars 1618-1648, 54
gibbet, *see* gallows.
Gifford family, 200-1, 241; Agnes, 229,
239-40, 243; George I: 194, 210, 230,
234-5; as vicar of All Saints', 200, 206-
7; deprivation, 2079; licensed as
preacher, 202, 208-10; pastoral activity,
201-4, 206, 219-20; and Classis organisation, 202, 206-7, 211-12; publications,
173, 199, 211, 218, 235; opinion on
dissension, 224; preaching of, 188, 201,
205, 210-11, 213, 228-9; supporters
(`favourers'), 199, 207-8, 216-7, 219-
20, 226, 236; on witchcraft, 173;
settlement with Robt Palmer, 229; will,
190, 202, 229, 270; death, 230; George
II, 45, 241, 243-4, 251; Jeremiah, 241,
243; Samuel, 241; William, 45, 241,
243
glover(s), 48, 52, 58, 63, 85, 97, 103-104,
107, 111, 113, 114, 120-121, 227
Goddard, Robert, 141; Thomas, 148;
Goddard's Wharf, 5(m)
Goldborne, Philip, 126, 258
Goldhanger, 2
Golding, Henry (M..P.), 125-126
government (borough) *see* Bailiffs,
common council, Corporation, courts,
finance
Gowton, Francis, 191, 196

Graces, Great, 97
Grantham (Lincs), 49
Gratiano ('Graham'), Antonio, 57
Gravel Pits Land, 86(m), 87, 113
Grays Thurrock, 69
Great Maldon, 8(m), 25, 271
Grecian, 57
Greenham, Richard, 201
Greenwich (Kent), 243
Greenwich, East (Kent), manor of, 80
Grenerise, Winken, 57, 190
Grey, Enoch (of Wickham Bishops), 244-5
Grey Friars (Colchester), 191
Grey, Lady Jane, 151
Greyhound, The, 4(m)
Grieve, H., 77, 80
Grindal, Edmund (Archbishop of Canterbury 1576-83), 200-1
grocer, 52, 111, 113
groundage and bulkage, 141
Guelderland, 57
Guernsey, 55
guilds religious, 56, 191, 192, 269; guildhall, 134
guns, 168; gunsmith, 76, 113
Guy, Robert, 69

Haberdasher(s), 42, 45, 81, 94, 107, 122-124, 169
Haddon Hall (Derby), 60
Hadleigh, 1
Hadleigh (Suff), 18,
Hague, The, 57
Halstead, 12, 188
Hammond, Nowell, 163, 259
Hampshire, 74
Hampton Court Conference, 236
Hanningfield, 130
Hanworth, Christopher, 239
Harding, Thomas, 214
Harris (Herris) family, 74, 76, 97-98, 126, 250; Sir Arthur, 257; Christopher, 74; Mrs Mary, 72; Thomas, 117, 226-7; Vincent , 95, 119-120; William (of Mundon), 85, 95, 126
Harrison, Jonas, 112
Harrison, William, 99-103
Harsnett, Samuel, 236

Hart, Edmund, 103-104; Henry, 219; Richard, 115
Hartlepool, 141
Harvey, George, 71; H~, Goodman [ Josias], 47
Harwich, 12-13, 19, 49, 100; corporation of, 165
Hastler family, 148; Edward, 145; Humphrey, 155, 166-7; John, 74, 196
Hatfield Broad Oak, 126, 197, 208
Hatfield Peverel, 239-40
hatter, 122
haven, 'decay' of, 14, 148
Haverhill (Suff), 63
Hawdon (Hawden), Ralph, 202, 219, 230, 240
Hawkes, James, 120
Hawkins, [    ], 242
Hawkwell, 74, 210
Hayes, William, 70
Hazeleigh, 198
headburgesses, 82, 155-8, 184-5, 226
Hearse, Rose, 112
Hearth Tax returns, 12, 18-20, 23, 100, 104, 270
hedgebreakers, 167
Hendrijk, Harman, 195
Henry II (King 1154-89), 125
Henry V , 124
Henry VII (King 1485-1509), 92
Henry VIII (King 1509-47). 92, 119, 125, 188
Henshawe, Michael, 259
heralds, 154, visitations by, 56, 60, 271
heretics in Essex, 171, 190, 195
Hertzz, Richard, 54
Hewitt, Israel, 231-3
Heybridge, the, 14
Heybridge 8(m), 10, 49, 54, 70, 112, 117, 141-6, 172, 177; churchwardens' account book, 192, 196; Play of, 198; trade dispute with Maldon, 143-4, 164
High Commission, Court of, 194, 206, 208, 210-11, 217, 219, 221, 257
High Recorder, 256
High Steward (of the borough), 144, 178, 181, 249, 250, 251, 256-7
High Street, 6, 85, 87, 93-94, 96, 99
High Wycombe (Bucks), 11
Hills, John, 141; Joseph, 63, 242

Hog Field, 86(m)
holidays, 63
Holman, William (antiquary, d.1730), 57, 72, 271
Holy Communion, 195
`hopharlots', 101
hops, 115-117, 120, 131-2; Hopyard, The, 120
Hornchurch, 21
Horndon-on-the-Hill, 199
Horrocks, John, 233, 252, 254
Hosier, Judith, 124
Hoskins, W.G., 43, 78, 105, 107, 113
Houlden, John, 101
House of Commons, petition to, 244-5
House of Correction, 20
House of Lords, petition to, 141, 143-6, 164
household size (average), 88, 94
householders, 80, 89
house names: *see* Andrew Aylewyn's, Baggeman's, Bawde's, Beerhouse, Brewing House, Bull, Cobbes-at-the-Corner, Crackbone's, Cranke's (Great and Little C~), Elmstead's, Middle House, Nether House, Page's, Payne's, Pepper's, Ridler's, Scarlett's, Sergeant's, Smallwares', Spencer's (alias Hardings), Spread Eagle, Star, Three Mariners, Upper House, Wrenche's; *and see* Figure 1
house prices, 78-79, 81, 94, 117; inns, 139
houses (discussed), 55, 81, 94, 96, 101-4; conversions into, 94, 147; extensions, 96-97; fifteenth century, 88; fittings, 96-100; furnishings, 101-3; new, 93-94, 97-98; ownership, 80; rebuilding, 97, 98, 104-105; rented accommodation, 80, 101; rooms, 101-104; standard of (for artificers), 104; subdivision, 49, 54, 84, 97, 105
housing: area, 9-10, 80, 84-95; site of Darcy's mansion, 92-93
Howard, Thomas (Lord Howard de Walden), 250
Hoye, Francis, 101
Huddersfield (Yorks), 60
Huddleston, Edmund (Cambridgeshire), 71
Hull, F., 50

Hundred Lane *see* Rankstile Lane.
Hunne, John and Robert, 101
Hunt, Edmund, 172, 215, 223
Hunt, George (and wife Sarah), 63
hunting, 76
Hunwicke, John (Colchester), 21
husbandman, ~men, 52, 68, 70, 96, 111, 120, 213
Hutt family, 42-43; Hutt, Thomas I, 43, 227-8, 230
Hythe (of Maldon), 6, 7, 9, 69, 86(m), 87, 94, 98, 111, 117-8, 120, 140-4, 146-8, 151, 172; cargoes (foodstuffs, timber, chalk, fulling earth, canvas, dyestuffs), 111, 131-2, 134, 141-5; *see also* : beer, coal, hops

Immigration (Maldon), 16, 32-50, 65(m), 100, 194-6, 250
incest, 170
incorporation, 125, 150-4, 180
infanticide, 115, 172
Ingatestone, 137
inheritance, 82-84, 105; by females, 77, 82-84; impartible, 82; partible, 61-62; in~ of property, 64, 78; *see also* Borough English
inmates, 49-50, 54, 84, 97; definition, 49
innkeeper, 60, 103, 111, 131-2; inn manager, 61
inns, 117, 136-40, 185; games played at: 167; bowls, 210; Privy Council survey (1577), 137, 269; War Office survey (Essex), 137-8, 269; inns (Maldon), *see* Blue Boar, Jolly Sailor, King's Head, New Inn, Rose and Crown, Saracen's Head, Star, Welcome Sailor, White Horse; *and see* alehouses
inventories, 99-103, 122, 270
investment in shipping, 69-70
Ipswich, 11, 21, 141, 194, 243; Staple of, 69; Town Preacher of, 203, 226, 233, 240
Ireland, Army for, 71
Irishmen, 54; soldiers, 14

Jacob's Cross, 3, 5(m), 86(m), 87; Jacob;s (tenement), 5(m)
James I (King 1603-25), 183, 236
James II (King 1685-88), 14, 182, 253 (Plate 14)

Jarman, William, 146
Jenkins, John, 36
*Jethros Justice of Peace* , 203
Job's Hill, 86(m)
Johns alias Rogers, William, 27
Johnson, Widow [    ] (of Heybridge), 146
Johnson, Abraham, 146; Adrian, 56; alias
    Peter, Henry, 56; Nicholas, 197
joiner, 52, 68, 101, 112, 213, 217; joinery,
    100-103
Jolly Sailor Inn, 94
Josua (Joseway), Richard, 96, 98, 155,
    179, 198, 214, 227; widow of, 219
judicature of first instance, 151
juggler, 161
Justices of the Peace, 60, 71, 154, 157,
    215, 242

Katherine Downs, 86(m)
Kedington ( *Ketton* , Suff), 163, 234, 259
Kelvedon, 13, 101, 105, 120, 200, 240
Kent. 67, 117, 120
Kersey cloth, 111, 131
Keton's Land, 86(m); Lane, 3
Kett's Rebellion (1549), 248
Kettle (Ketyll), John, 52
King, Gregory, 6; Thomas, 116; William,
    49
King's Head, 135(m), 137, 165
King's Majesty's Patentees, 80
Kingsman, Jasper, 103
`Kirby' (Yorks), 63
Kirk, Peter, 27
Knight, Stephen, 171

Labourer(s), 48, 50, 64, 89, 111, 120, 147
Lancashire, 51, 60; Lancaster, 63
landcheap, 61, 77-79, 81, 98, 168, 174-7,
    249
landworkers, 54
Langford, 8(m), 54, 116, 202, 230, 234;
    manor of, 25
Latchingdon, Tiled Hall, 126
lattices, 106
Laud, William (Archbishop 1633-41), 244
Launde (Leics), 125
Lavenham (Suff), 11, 18
lawyer(s), 123, 125, 233; law chambers,
    71
Lawling Creek, 69

lawsuits, 30, 144-5, 178, 223
lay subsidy, 10-12, 18-19, 23, 89-90, 269;
    aliens in (poll tax), 55; assessments, 18,
    56, 90, 161; surnames in, 31, 44; seas-
    onal migration, 53-54
lay impropriation, 215
Layer Marney, 54, 71, 92, 97
Leake, Mary, 241
leaseholding, 81
leather searchers, 121, 177; Leather Stalls,
    136; leatherwork, 68, 114, 120-122
Lectures, 233, 234
Lee, Edward, 49
Leech, Benjamin, 74
leet courts, 25, 33, 47; steward of, 163,
    259
Leez Priory, 71-72
Leicester, 107, 114, 177, 187
Leigh (on Sea), 69, 107, 233
Leigham's Court, Streatham (Mddx), 125
Leland, John, 105, 130
letters, 48, 169; to Dean of Westminster,
    228-30
Lewkenor, Sir Edward, 207-8, 234, 249-
    50
Leyden (Holland), 57
Lichfield (borough charter), 151
limeburner, 68, 111; limekiln, 5(m), 142;
    limestone, 140
Lincoln's Inn, 126
Lincolnshire, 61
linendraper, 32, 42, 82, 241
litigants at Maldon, 31, 32, 64, 66(m), 70
Little Maldon, manor of, 7, 8(m), 9, 25,
    60, 126, 142, 148, 271
Living (Liffin), Christopher, 96
Lob Hole, 134, 140, 172
Lock, John, 216, 223-4; Lock's
    (tenement), 5(m)
Lodge Leas. 87
lodgers, 49, 70
Lollards, 188
Lombards, 56
London, 36, 39, 58, 60-61, 63, 69, 71, 76,
    115, 119-120, 123, 131, 140, 148, 186,
    194, 198, 237, 240; All Hallows
    Barkingchurch, 197; Lombard St, 186;
    Middle Temple, 89, 209-10; Newgate
    Gaol, 214; St Katherine's Stairs, 141; St
    Paul's Cathedral, 196; Tower, 164, 208;
    Tower Wharf, 141

Long Market House, 136
Loughborough alias Brewer, John, 116
Lovell, Walter, 216, 220-1
Low Countries, 60, 150; *see also* aliens, Dutch influence, Flemings
Lowther, Widow [    ], 80-81
Luffkin family, 240; Elias, 120
Luther, Martin, 188

Maces, 180, 182 (Plate 9), 252
Machyn, John, 258
Maenere (Maynere), Oliver, 61 *Magna Charta de Maldon* , 153 (Plate 6), 154
Maidstone (Kent), 60
Malden (Massachusetts), 242
Maldon family, 42, 241-2; Aaron, 74; Jacob, 242; John I, 42, 81, 94, 124, 184, 219, 237, 241-2; William (of Chelmsford), 190, 192
Maldon area, 1, 65-69
Maldon, acreages, 7; burgh of, 3, 4(m), 7; as `Camulodunum', 24; Georgian, 3, 6, 95; grammar school, 4(m), 72, 74, 84, 161, 235, 241, 243; manorial jurisdictions in, 25, 80, 90, 125, 150; militia, 13-14; plans of, 6, 141-2; tenures in, 80; urban status, 10-14; Port of Maldon, *see* Creek of M~; *see also* : Camden, William; Constable, John; Leland, John; Earl's M~; Great M~; Hythe, Little M~; Town Play
Maldon Hall, 9, 60
maltster, 116; malt barley, 116, 118, 131, 140-1, 143; maltings, 95
Man, William, 170
Manners, Moses, 47
Manning, John, 96; Margaret (widow), 96
Marchant, Michael, 185
Margaretting, 74, 250
mariner(s), 13, 33, 49, 69, 141
Market Cross, 134, 135(m); market functions, 130; market looker(s), 118, 184
Market Hill, 3
Market Place (Maldon), Plate 1, 7, 81, 87, 96, 121, 134-6, 140; market days, 151; *see also* Brick Building, Brick Cross, Brick Shop, Bull Ring, Butcher Row, Buttermarket, Cornhill, Cornmarket, Fairs, Fish Stalls, Lob Hole, Long Market House, Market Cross, Mercery Row, New Market Place

market gardening, 87, 119-120
market-day sermons, 212
Marlorat, Augustin, 238
Marney, Henry, 2nd Lord M~, 54
marriage, 81, 96; certificate, 58, 271
Marshall, Henry, 58; Stephen and Susanna (Shipton), 240
Martin, John, 219, 230
Mary I (Queen 1553-58), 125, 150-1, 190, 194; as Princesss Mary Tudor, 142, 150
Masham (Yorks), 197
Masham, Sir William, 251
Mason, Hugh, 243
Massachusetts, 242
Master of the King's Jewel House, 251
Master of the Rolls, 144
Master, Principal, Royal Navy, 70
Matthews, Henry, 220; Joachim, 258
Maydenpond, 3
Mayland, 2, 54, 234
Mayor (of Maldon), 180, 262
Meeting, The, 254
Members of Parliament, 10, 15, 89, 119, 125-126, 165, 226, 263-8; elections, 162, 183, 207, 248-51; of Mary I's reign, 151, 195; and Puritans, 202, 206-8
Mendham, John, 78
mercer, 122
Mercery Row, 96, 134, 135(m)
merchant, 61, 94, 107, 148, 162, 196
merchant-stranger, 55, 60-61
merchant tailor, 76, 241; Merchant Tailors' School, 162
*Merchant of Venice* , 132
Messing, 25, 70, 85, 257
Messing, John, 191
metalwork, 68, 114
*Michaelmas Term* (Thos. Middleton), 123
Michaelson, Andrew, 82, 116, 129; Joan (widow), 82
Middleburgh (Zeeland), 133
Middle House, The, 93, 135(m)
migration, 39-50; long-distance migration, 51, 53-63; short-distance, 51, 64-70, 65(m), 68; and title to property, 84; betterment, 52-53, 56, 60, 61; contest mobility, 61-62; distances travelled, 57, 64; rural-urban, 18, 51-53; subsistence, 53-54; and the local community, 74; to America, 242-3

Mildmay family, 76, 97, 234, 250; Henry, 72; Sir Henry, 250-1, 256; Sir Thomas (of Moulsham), 234, 256; properties in Maldon, 134
militia, 13-14, 122, 159
Milkwell, 86(m), 87
milk house, 101
Mill Field, 85, 86(m); Mill Road, 3
Minckes, James, 144
Mirfield (Yorks), 60
mirrors, 100, 102
Momford, Andrew, 219
monumental brass, 119, 196; other monuments, 41, 71
Moore family, 42-43; Nicholas I, 43, 195; Williamine, widow, 96
Moot Hall (to 1576), 52, 134, 135(m), 140
Moot Hall (from 1576), 3, 81, 92-93, 142-3, 180, 248, 252; charterhouse of, 164, 223; dovehouse, 136; gaol of, 172, 254; purchase and conversion, 93, 162-3, 181; renovation, 136; table of tolls, 142
Morris, James, 257; John, 63, 173, 214, 216, 218, 220 1, 224
Mortar, Bearing The, 170
Morville, Giles, 55
Motte, John, 68
Moulsham, 11, 77, 250
Mountnessing, 70
Muffet, Mary, 102, 124, 233; Peter, Thomas, 102
Mundon, 95, 97, 184, 207, 238
murder, 115, 171-2
musician(s), 76, 183
Mystic River (Massachusetts), 242

Nash, John I, 45, 96, 259; John II , 45; William I & II, 241
Nether House, The, 93, 135(m)
Netherlands, 117-118, 132
Nethersall, Robert, 107
New Drapery, 61
New England, 242-3
New Inn, 60, 94, 135(m), 136-7, 210, 215; Lane, 94
New Market Place, 134, 135(m), 142
Newcastle-Upon-Tyne, 141, 187; N~ chaldron, 141; siege of, 146, 148
Newcombe, William, 184
Nicholl(s), Elias, 186

Night Watch, 167, 180, 184
Norden, John, 90-91
Norfolk, 67, 112
Norris, William, 49
Northallerton, 63
Northampton, 105, 107, 114
Northamptonshire, 61, 71
Northey Island, 8(m), 145
Norton, Cold, 241
Norwich, 57, 61, 218, 236
notary, 163
Notley, Black, 67, 74
Nottingham, 11, 60

Oaths of affeirors, 226; aldermen, 158; allegiance (to Crown), 220, 242; Bailiffs, 159; decenners, 157; freemen, 24; headburgesses, 158; (Royal) Supremacy, 242; oaths as charges, 158; copies of, 272
oatmeal, 117, 134; ~ bin, 136; ~ mill, 117; ~maker, 117
occupations, 105, 120; see : alehouse-keeper, apothecary, apparitor, applemonger, auditor, baker, barber-surgeon, baymaker, blacksmith, brasier, brewer, b~'s manager, bricklayer, brickmaker, butcher, carrier, chandler, clergyman, clockmaker, clothier, clothing makers, collarmaker, cook, cooper, coastal shipping, counsellor, currier, Customer, cutler, draper, dress-making, drover, embroiderer, estate management, farmer, fletcher, gardener, general handyman, glover, grocer, gunsmith, haberdasher, hatter, husbandman, innkeeper, inn manager, ironmonger, joiner, landworkers, lawyer, limeburner, linendraper, maltster, manorial bailiff, mariner, Master (Principal), mercer, merchant, merchant tailor, musician, notary, oatmeal-maker, painter, peddler, pewterer, physician, proctor, Reader of the Middle Temple, saddler, salt-refiner, salt-weller, scrivener, sea-waller, seamstress, servant, shearman, shipwright, shoemaker, stocking-knitting, surgeon, tailor, tanner, textile supplier, textile trades, unmarried

craftsmen, vintner, weaver, wheel-wright, wool comber, woollen-draper, wool factor, yeoman
occupations: in the Maldon area, 107, 111-113; diversification, 61-62
*officina(ae)* , 31
Ogilby, John, 6
Ongham, Thomas (of Burnham), 118
opprobrium, 183-4, 214
orchards, 87, 120
ordinances (bye-laws), 93, 143-5, 157, 169, 177
Ordinaries (of ecclesiastical jurisdictions), 170
Orinell, Henry, 194
Orwell river, 133
Osborne family, 126; Nathaniel, 98
Ostend (Belgium), 117, 131
overseers of the poor, 20, 169-70; of St Mary's parish, 20
owner-occupation, 80
Oxford, Earls of (De Vere), 125, 137, 161
oysters, 112-113, 145, 174, 179

Packhorses, 176
Pagett, John, 192; Page's (messuage), 84
Paglesham, 49
painter, 76; pictures, 102-103
Palmer, Robert, 209-21, 224, 226, 229-30; Articles against, 217, 223; as Official, 211-2, 215
papists, 151, 194-5
Parham, John, 47-48
parishes (Maldon), 7; boundaries, 8(m) 6-9, 169; constables, 27, 169; registers, 28, 210; *see also* All Saints', church-wardens, St Peter's, St Mary's, wards
parliament, 88-89, 151; elections for, 89, 248-252; Long P~, 251; Short P~, 183
Parochial Inquisition, 241
Parr, William (Earl of Essex), 126
patrons, 234; patronage, 62-63, 76, 170, 197, 209, 231, 235; *see also* Franke
Patten, J.H.C., 61, 112
Paycocke family, 11
Payne, William, 184; Payne's (messuage), 4(m), 104
Peace, breaches of, 167; Commission of the Peace, 154, 157, 167; Petty Sessions, 46, 168

Peacock family, 148; John, 32
peddler (petty chapman), 48, 221
Peldon, 206
penance, 170
Pepper (Pepir), Henry, and Pepper's (messuage), 4(m), 88
persistence rate, 35
Petchey, Thomas, 116, 131-2
Peterman's alias Drakes, 4(m), 135(m)
Peterson, Cornelius, 93, 115, 190
petitions, 140, 143-4, 203, 206-7, 244-5
Pettit, [   ], widow, 21
Petty Sessions, *see* Peace
Peverel, Isabel (widow), 116
pewterer, 96, 113; pewter ware, 102-103, 113
pharmacy, 43, 76
Philip II (King of Spain 1556-98), 203
physician(s), 43, 49, 57, 67, 76
pie powder court, 128, 168
Pike (Pyke), Edward, 63, 117; Humphrey, 258
pillory, 136, 152
piracy, 133
place-names, 1-2
plague, 13, 16-18, 63, 148, 180, 259
plays, 161, 198; players *see* actors
pleas, 129, 152; in courts outside the borough, 165-7; of *detinue*, 129, 168; of debt, 61, 64, 70, 95, 107, 112, 116, 129-132; debtors, 103, 130-3, 168; of trepass and special trespass, 129, 168
Pledger, Jeremiah (Jeremy), 112, 217
Pleshey College, 196
pledges, 48
Plume family, 148; Samuel, 243; Thomas I, 74, 113, 156, 162-3, 242, 243, 245, 259; Thomas II (1630-1704) 74, 243; Plume Library, 3, 98, 238-9, 243, 273
Plymouth (Devon), 131
Plympton (Devon), 43, 195
Pocklington (Yorks), 196
Poles, Humphrey, 197
Pond, Samuel, 120
Pope, Robert, 80-81, 241
population, 18, 22-23, 67, 88-90, 93-95; male (1569-82), 33-34; mobility, 33-45, 51-54; models of, 38-40; pressure, 61-62
Port of Maldon, *see* Creek of M~

Porter, John, 257; Thomas, 82
Portman (Potman) Marsh, 8(m), 10, 86(m), 117, 172, 222
Poulter, family, 32; Margaret, 32; Richard, 70; William, 69-70, 96, 155
Pound, J.F., 107
Pound, the, 86(m)
Powell, Thomas, 220
Pratt family, 241; Elisha, 81, 241; Elizabeth, 239, 243; Jeremiah (Jeremy), 184, 241; John, 80-81, 122, 124, 213-4, 219; Samuel, 78, 241
preaching, 228, 233-4
precedent cases, 84, 166
Precisians, 216
Presbyterians, 203, 243, 254; reform programme, 207, 211, 218, 236
Prescott, H.F.M., 150-1
Price, John, 36
Priest's Croft, 86(m), 142
prisons, 151, 172; see also Brick Prison, Lob Hole
Prittlewell, 74, 198
Privy Council, 13-14, 151, 169, 171, 187, 203, 208, 211, 221, 223-5; see also inns, survey of
proclamations (royal), 161, 183, 252
proctor, 186
property holders, 65(m), 66
Prophesyings, 193, 198-200, 234
Protestants, 188, 192-5
proverbial sayings, 13, 67, 226
Pulley, William, 165
Purchas, George, 94, 240
Purfoot, Andrew, 54
Puritans, 81, 187, 206-9, 218, 221, 234; and Prayer Book rubrics, 201; black-lists of clergy, 210; changing character, 236-44
Purleigh, 54, 81, 141; manor of, 25
Pynde, Richard, 258
Pynnell, Henry, 81, 93, 126, 136, 195; Pynnell's (tenement), 135(m)

Quarter Sessions (County), 71
Quarter Sessions (Borough), 46, 48-50, 84, 87, 129, 157, 166-8, 170, 184, 203, 222, 226, 233
Quo Warranto , writ of, 165
quays, 143

Radcliffe family, 76; Sir Thomas (3rd Earl of Sussex), 166
Radwinter, 99
ramparts, 251
Ramsden Bellhouse, 74
Rankstile (Runsell) Lane, 3
rape, 171
Raven, William, 69
Rawreth, 54
Ray, John, 13, 67
Rayleigh, 65, 68, 198; vicarage of, 202, 230
Rayne, 72
Rayner, Edward, 96, 133
Reade, Edward I, 103; Edward, II, 103; William, 119
Reader of the Middle Temple, 126
`Rebuilding, The Great', 78, 95
Recorder, 74, 144-5, 166, 171, 178, 181, 249, 257-8
Redesdale (Nbld), 61
regalia, 180, 182 (Plate 9)
regulations for trade, 106, 121
religious guilds: see Guilds
religious observances, 191-3
rent, 80-81
replacement rates, 36-39
Republican theories on sovereignty, 57
residence, units of, 37-38; residential categories, 28-31, 33-39
retail trade, 128-129
retirement, 70
Rettendon, 130
reversions, 78, 139
Reynoldes, John, 257; William, 134
Rich, Frances, 71, 234; Robert, Lord Rich, 71-72, 202, 207, 234; Robert, 2nd Earl of Warwick, 165
Ridler's (messuage), 4(m), 94
Ridley, Nicholas (Bishop of London 1550-53), 171
riots, 145-6
Ripon (Yorks), 187
Rivenhall, 197
rivers see Blackwater, Chelmer, Crouch, Mystic, Orwell, Thames, Tyne
roads, 69; and see transportation
Roberts, Richard, 103
Robinson family, 42-43, 148; Elias and Reuben, 43

Roebuck Street, 3
Rochell, Thomas, 139; William, 70, 78, 219, 230
Rochester, Sir Robert (of Terling), 151
Rochford, 1, 52, 119; Hall, 71-72, 202; Hundred, 48, 65
Rogers, John I (of Dedham), 45, 231, 233; John II, 45; Richard (of Wethersfield), 202, 205; Timothy, 94, 99
Roman Catholic historical writing, 239
Romford, 74, 199, 210, 233, 257
Roo, Cuthbert and Stephen, 30, 31
Rose and Crown Inn, 96
Rotherham, Sir John, 257; John (jnr), 258
Roxwell, 126; church, 41; Newlands, 41; Skreens Park, 72
Royal arms, 181-2, 182, 193, 252; `State Arms', 252; Royal Injunctions, 209; Royal Navy, 70; Supremacy, 192; style and title, 208
Ruck, Thomas, 242
Rudland, John, 124, 140, 145
Runsell Green, 47
Rye, 224

Sabbath Day observance, 203
saddler, 183, 241
Saffron Walden, 10, 12, 19, 52; Holy Trinity Guild of, 174, 271
St Albans (Herts), 63
St George's Croft, 86(m), 142
St Giles' Hospital, 3; and Fair,128
St Helen's Chapel, 4(m), 192; Cross, 3, 4(m); Gate, 135(m); Lane, 3, 72, 85, 135(m); Well, 121
St Lawrence (parish name), 74, 234, 241
St Martin-le-Grand (London), 7
St Mary's church (Maldon), 7, 9, 87, 142, 151, 196, 221, 228; beacon, 14; church-yard, 142; collapse of tower, 13-14, 98, 142, 229-30; inventory (1552), 193; Puritan scheme for, 229-30; rebuilding of tower, 98, 230
St Mary's parish, 20, 48, 95, 142, 170, 202, 241, 252
St Mary's Parsonage, 86(m)
St Osyth's Abbey, 92
St Peter's church (Maldon), 3, 7, 87, 135(m); reconstructed, 98, 243; redundancy of, 14; tabernacle in, 192; see also Maldon, grammar school

St Peter's Lane, 3, 81, 85, 93, 97, 134, 135(m)
St Peter's parish, 7-9, 78, 93, 116, 142, 170, 191; poor of, 227
St Roger Niger (Bishop of London 1228-41), 193
Salisbury, 218
saltbin, 136; s~cotes, 2, 120, 142; s~ refiner/weller, 68, 112, 146
Saltcote (Salcott), 2
Salter, Blaise, 163
Sammes, John, 116; Sir John (of Langford), 234, 250; Thomas 113; Dr [ ], preacher, 236
sanctuary, 133
Sandeford, wife of Robert, 78
Sandon, 97; Play of, 198
Sandwich, 187, 245
Saracen's Head, 135(m), 137, 139, 197
Sayer, John, 78; Sayer Sparrow's (tenement), 4-5(m)
Saykin's, 4(m)
Scarlet's (messuage), 82
schismatics, 217, 220
Schoolmaster's (tenement), 4-5(m)
schools (grammar) 74, 162; see also Maldon, grammar school
scolds, 167
scot and lot, 14, 144, 161, 175, 179
Scots, 54, 56; students, 199-200
Scott, Richard, 220, 236
scrivener, 163, 214, 238
sea-waller, 68, 94
seals of the borough, 152-3
Seaman, George, 49
seamstress, 74, 124, 172
Seares, James, 97
Second Part of a Register, The, 209
Sedbergh (Yorks), 62
Senley (Guelderland),
Separatists, 218-9, 236
Sergeant, Richard, Sergeant's (messuage), 88
serjeants-at-mace, 31, 81, 103, 177, 180-1, 186, 193
sermons, 174, 198-200, 212-3, 231, 233
servant, 48, 56, 58-59, 64, 102, 111, 115, 168-9, 184, 242; of the Duke of Somerset, 125

Seymour, Edward (Duke of Somerset), 125-126
Sharpe, Robert, 72, 259
shearman, 43, 101, 123, 228
Shele, Thomas, 144
Shergate, Thomas, 107 Sherman, John, 72
Ship Money, 14
Ship Inn, 117, 147
ship building, 69, 113, 142; s~ timber, 32
ships, 13, 69-70, 140-3; *The Black George*, 117, 131-2; *The Dorothy*, monger, 69; *The Dragon*, 69; *The Harry*, 118; *The Mary* of Benfleet, 119; *The Mary Grace*, 69; *The William*, crayer, 69; Flemish, 131-2, 145; *see also* Tyneside
Shipton, John, 184, 227, 237-41, 242; Susanna, 240; Thomas, 237
shipwrecks, 132
shipwright, 32, 69, 111, 113
shoemaker(s), 54-56, 58, 103, 105, 107, 111, 114, 120, 195; shoemakers' petition, 14, 106
Shopland Parsonage, 69
shops, 103-104; purchase of, 78
short-distance mobility, 64
Shotley (Suff), 32
Shrill, Dengie, 70
silk-weaving, 123-124; silkwoman, 124
Silver Street, 96, 98
silverware, 102, 196
Simpson, John, 233-4, 238; Mary, 233; Richard, 112, 122, 124
Skarlett, Richard, 68, 112
Skikes *see* Sligges Lane
Skreens, *see* Roxwell
Slack, P., 218
Slater, William (of Heybridge), 146
Sleidanus (Sleydan), Joannes Philippson, 239
Sligges (Skikes) Lane, 3, 87, 135(m)
Smallwares' (messuage), 97
Smith, J.R., 42
Smith, Brice, 30; Ellen, 172; Jasper, 223; Nicholas, 199; William, 69
smuggling, 60-61
Snape, Robert, 148, 170, 178
Snoreham, 82, 241
Soan, John,162-3, 186, 239-40; William, 20, 215-6, 220, 224, 240

Solemn League and Covenant, 243
Somerset, 58; Duke of, *see* Seymour
Songer, Jerome, 259
sorcery, 171-3, 197, 203
Southend on Sea, 1
Southminster, 54, 95
Sparrow, Anthony, 125-126, 151, 163-4, 169-70, 258
Spencer's alias Harding's (messuage), Spencer's Mead, 86(m), 98
Spigurnell, John, 215-7, 224, 228; Thomas, 195, 221-2, 225
Spread Eagle, 96, 123, 135(m), 136-7, 139
Sprignell family, 148; Sir Robert, 120
Spring family (Lavenham), 11
Spuddell (Spodell), John, 31, 103, 193
Spufford, Margaret, 194, 201
Stafford, 11
Stambridge, Great, 233
Stamford (Lincs), 11
Stanhope, Dr (Bishop's Official), 236
Stansgate, 69
Star, The, 135(m), 137, 139-40, 191, 231
Star Chamber (Court of), 222, 235
Starling, James, 251
Steeple Bumpstead, 257
Steven, Henry, 112
stipends, 231, 233
Stock, 56
stocking-knitting, 62, 122
stocks, 136, 140, 184
Stode, Robert, 103
Stoke-by-Clare (Suff), 52
Stokes, William, 195-6
Stourbridge Fair, 128, 201
Stow Maries, 234, 240; Play, 198
Stratford-upon-Avon (accounts of), 174, 177
street names, *see*: Butt Lane, Cromwell Hill, Causeway, Fullbridge Street, High Street, Keton's Lane, Market Hill, Runsell Lane, St Helen's Lane, St Peter's Lane, Sligges (Skikes) Lane, Wantz Road
Stretton, John, 221
strict settlement, 96
Strype, John, 203, 218
student-preacher, 200
Sturgion, Samuel, 213
Sturry, Alexander, Matthew, 52

subsidy see: lay subsidy
Sudbury (Suff), 11, 21, 32, 107, 151, 195
Suffolk, 48, 63, 112, 117, 120
suicide, 103, 115
surgeon, 76, 113, 220
surnames, 41, 44, 51,
Survey of Crown Lands, 78-80
survey of tenures, 78-81
Surveyors of Highways, 167, 169-70
Sussex, Earls of, 76, 166; chaplain of, 200
Swaffham (Norf), 130
Swan, The (alias Wood's Brewhouse), 4(m)
Synod of Dort, 238

Tailor, 45, 62, 81, 111, 122-123, 191, 241
Tanner, John, 233
Tainterhawe, Little, 120; T~ Pasture, 86(m), 123
Tainterfield (Tenterfield), cloth-tenters, 85, 123
Tanner, John, 71
tanner, 68, 82, 121; tan pits, 85, 104; tanneries, 121
Tay, William (of Peldon), 206-7
tenants, 80
Terling, 43, 198
testimonial, 48
textile manufacture, 12-13, 48, 105, 114, 123; supplier, 114; trades, 55, 62
Thames river, 65, 67, 69, 119, 133
Thaxted, 10, 12, 100, 249
Thirsk, J., 61
Three Mariners (tenement), 4(m), 94
Throckmorton, Nicholas (M.P.), 126
Thurrock, 69
Thurstable Hundred, 65, 119
Tilbury Camp, 214
Tillingham, 112
tithes, 191, 198
tithing, 25
Tollesbury, 69, 133, 198
Tolleshunt Darcy, 68; T~ Major, 97
tolls, 143, 145, 148, 175-6, 249
Topley (Topliffe), Anthony, 51, 220
Totham, Great, 68, 112; T~, Little, 43, 68, 250
Totnes (Devon), 58
Town Clerk, 22, 33, 45, 48, 96, 163-4, 177, 238, 255, 258-60; fees, 142, 181;

financial duties, 159, 180; recording bargains, 142; papers of, 169
Town Downs, 86(m), 87, 222; T~ coal, chalk heaps, 5(m); T~ Dunghill (midden), 4(m), 87, 94, 135(m); T~ House, 5(m); T~ Lecturer, 233; T~ Play, 189-90, 197-8, 200, 247; T~ Quay (and Crane), 5(m); T~ Storehouse, 5(m), 98, 146; T~ Well, 117
trades, 107-110; see also: occupations
trading area, 134-6; private trading, 139
transvestism, 197
Trappes, Thomas (Danbury), 78
travel certificate, 63
Tremelin, John Immanuel, 238
Trowers, Thomas, 113, 171, 185
`Trudge Over the World', 194
Truro, 58
tumbril, 151
Twedy family, 56-57; William, 56, 71
Tyne river, 187; colliers, 141; Tynemouth, 148
Tyrell, Edmund, 195

Ultimogeniture, 82
Ulting, Play of, 198
unemployed persons, 47-48
unmarried mother(s), 169, 172; unmarried craftsmen, 168
Upper House, The, 93, 93, 135(m)
urban crisis, 114; decay, 12-14, 88-90, 93, 151
Utopia , 126

Vacant house sites, 20, 89
vagrancy, vagrants, 47, 54, 168-9, 171
Vansior, Dijrek, 133
vegetables, 120, 134
Vere, De, estates, 249, 271; household officials, 125; John, 15th Earl of Oxford, 189: John, 16th Earl of Oxford, 125-126
Vereing's Croft, 86(m), 120
Vernon family of Beeleigh, 41, 57; coat of arms, 60; William (d.1611), 60, 157, 162-3, 166, 207, 216, 223, 228, 231
victuallers' recognizances, 137, 167
Vinas (Vyves, Vince), William, 57
vineyard, 86(m), 120, 142

vintner, 61, 76, 98, 107
voters, 248-9; voting, 206

Wage-earners, 20, 105-106
Wakefield (Yorks), 220
Wakering, Great, 209
Waldegrave, Sir Edward, 151
Walker, G., 62
Walker, John (Archdeacon of Essex 1571-85), 200
Walker, John (surveyor), 77
Walker, Joseph, 47
Walker, Thomas (Alderman), 58, 60, 62, 219
Wall, Agnes, 47
Walley, Robert, 94, 99
Walloons, 54
Walsingham, Sir Francis (Secretary of State 1573-90), 60
Waltham, Great, 209, 215; W~, Little, 196
Wantz Road 3; *and see* Runsell Lane
Ward, Samuel (Town Preacher, Ipswich), 226, 240
wardmen, 24, 150; wards, 169, 197
wardship, 78, 84
Warehouse, The (tenement), 4-5(m)
water supplies, 67, 72, 85, 104, 116, 117, 121
Watson, William, 49
Wate, John, 242
Wayer Mead, 86(m), 87
Weald, South, 208
weaver, 63, 68, 101, 113, 123
Webb, Goodwife [   ], 172
Welcome Sailor Inn, 104
Welles (Mason), Hester, 243
Welles family, 42-43; Christopher, 70, 85; John, 104; Thomas, 43, 104, 227-8; Thomas (of Feering), 104
Welles, Thomas (butcher), 144-5, 243
Wensleydale (Yorks), 61-62
Wentworth, Peter (M.P.), 207-8
Wersoppe, Joan, 12
West Ham, 12, 19
Westminster, 120, 164
Westminster Abbey, 7, 98, 233; Peculiar Jurisdiction, 170, 202, 270
Wethersfield, 202, 240, 242
Weydown, Great, 86(m)
wheelwright, 68, 132

*White Book of Maldon*, 164
White Friars *see* Bale, Brook, Carmelite Friary.
White Hart (Brenchley's), 4(m)
White Horse Inn, 135(m); Yard, 94
White, John, 238
Whitgift, John (Archbishop 1583-1604), 202-4, 204 (Plate 11), 206, 212, 236, 244
Whittington, Dick, 52
Wickham Bishops, 70; rector of, 244-5
wicks, 2, 68
widows, 21, 70, 96, 102
Wiersdale, Mark, 208-9, 269
Wigborough, Great, 70
wild fowling, 76, 168; wildfowl, 150, 174
Williams, Richard, 213, 217, 219; Robert, 197-8, 199
wills as evidence of living standards, 21, 100-103, 120; of religious attitudes, 190-2, 196
windmill, 85, 117
Winterbourne, Daniel, 84, 97; John, 84
Winthrop, John, 242
Winton pasture, 86(m), 87, 120
Wiseman, John (M.P.), 126; Margaret, 173; Sir Robert (of Rivenhall), 71; Sir William, bart, 252, 257; William, 30, 71, 207, 257
witchcraft, 172-3, 203
Witham Hundred, 65
Witham, 10, 12, 13, 54, 56, 68, 100, 112, 145, 259
withdraughts of action, 129, 176
Withers, family, 200; Fabian, 199-202; George (Archdeacon), 200-1
Withers, Thomas, 196
wives of itinerant servants, 60
Wode, Thomas, 115
Wood, Richard, 119
Woodham Ferrers, Play of, 198
Woodham Mortimer, 1, 197, 250
Woodham Walter, 2, 76, 150
woolcomber, 123, 214
woollendraper, 94, 242
wool factor, 61
woolpacks, 143
Worcester, 111
workshops, 101-104
Wratting, Great (Suff), 63

Wrenche, Thomas, 103; Wrenche's
  (tenement), 4(m), 103-104
Wright, Euseby, 257; John, 71, 257;
  Robert, 202
Wyborough, Thomas, 12, 161
Wyrley, John (of Dodford, N'hants), 71

Yarmouth, Great, 61
yeoman, ~men, 68, 69, 107, 112, 120, 141,
  227, 233
York, 58, 63, 242
Yorkshire, 60, 63
Young, Thomas, 41